# NEW DIRECTIONS IN GERMAN STUDIES
## Vol. 12

*Series Editor:*

## Imke Meyer
Director, School of Literatures, Cultural Studies and Linguistics, and Professor of Germanic Studies, University of Illinois at Chicago

*Editorial Board:*

**Katherine Arens**
Professor of German, University of Texas at Austin

**Roswitha Burwick**
Distinguished Chair of Modern Foreign Languages Emerita, Scripps College

**Richard Eldridge**
Charles and Harriett Cox McDowell Professor of Philosophy, Swarthmore College

**Erika Fischer-Lichte**
Professor of Theater Studies, Freie Universität Berlin

**Catriona MacLeod**
Edmund J. and Louise W. Kahn Term Professor in the Humanities and Professor of German, University of Pennsylvania

**Stephan Schindler**
Professor of German and Chair, University of South Florida

**Heidi Schlipphacke**
Associate Professor of Germanic Studies, University of Illinois at Chicago

**Ulrich Schönherr**
Professor of German and Comparative Literature, Haverford College

**James A. Schultz**
Professor of German and Chair, University of California, Los Angeles

**Silke-Maria Weineck**
Professor of German and Chair of Comparative Literature, University of Michigan

**David Wellbery**
LeRoy T. and Margaret Deffenbaugh Carlson University Professor, University of Chicago

**Sabine Wilke**
Professor of German, University of Washington

**John Zilcosky**
Professor of German and Comparative Literature, University of Toronto

Volumes in the series:

Vol. 1. *Improvisation as Art: Conceptual Challenges, Historical Perspectives*
by Edgar Landgraf

Vol. 2. *The German Pícaro and Modernity: Between Underdog and Shape-Shifter*
by Bernhard Malkmus

Vol. 3. *Citation and Precedent: Conjunctions and Disjunctions of German Law and Literature*
by Thomas O. Beebee

Vol. 4. *Beyond Discontent: 'Sublimation' from Goethe to Lacan*
by Eckart Goebel

Vol. 5. *From Kafka to Sebald: Modernism and Narrative Form*
edited by Sabine Wilke

Vol. 6. *Image in Outline: Reading Lou Andreas-Salomé*
by Gisela Brinker-Gabler

Vol. 7. *Out of Place: German Realism, Displacement, and Modernity*
by John B. Lyon

Vol. 8. *Thomas Mann in English: A Study in Literary Translation*
by David Horton

Vol. 9. *The Tragedy of Fatherhood: King Laius and the Politics of Paternity in the West*
by Silke-Maria Weineck

Vol. 10. *The Poet as Phenomenologist: Rilke and the* New Poems
by Luke Fischer

Vol. 11. *The Laughter of the Thracian Woman: A Protohistory of Theory*
by Hans Blumenberg, translated by Spencer Hawkins

Vol. 12. *Roma Voices in the German-Speaking World*
by Lorely French

Vol. 13. *Vienna's Dreams of Europe: Culture and Identity beyond the Nation-State*
by Katherine Arens

Vol. 14. *Thomas Mann and Shakespeare: Something Rich and Strange*
edited by Tobias Döring and Ewan Fernie

Vol. 15. *Goethe's Families of the Heart*
by Susan Gustafson

Vol. 16. *German Aesthetics: Fundamental Concepts from Baumgarten to Adorno*
edited by J.D. Mininger and Jason Michael Peck

# Roma Voices in the German-Speaking World

## Lorely French

Bloomsbury Academic
An imprint of Bloomsbury Publishing Inc

B L O O M S B U R Y
NEW YORK • LONDON • OXFORD • NEW DELHI • SYDNEY

Bloomsbury Academic
An imprint of Bloomsbury Publishing Inc

| | |
|---|---|
| 1385 Broadway | 50 Bedford Square |
| New York | London |
| NY 10018 | WC1B 3DP |
| USA | UK |

www.bloomsbury.com

**BLOOMSBURY and the Diana logo are trademarks of Bloomsbury Publishing Plc**

First published 2015
First published in paperback 2016

© Lorely French, 2015, 2016

All rights reserved. No part of this publication may be reproduced or transmitted in any form or by any means, electronic or mechanical, including photocopying, recording, or any information storage or retrieval system, without prior permission in writing from the publishers.

No responsibility for loss caused to any individual or organization acting on or refraining from action as a result of the material in this publication can be accepted by Bloomsbury or the author.

**Library of Congress Cataloging-in-Publication Data**
French, Lorely, 1957- author.
Roma Voices in the German-Speaking World / Lorely French.
pages cm. -- (New directions in German studies)
Includes bibliographical references and index.
ISBN 978-1-5013-0279-4 (hardback)
1. German literature--Romani authors--History and criticism. 2. Romanies in literature. I. Title.
PT170.R63F75 2015
830.9'891497--dc23
2015000341

ISBN: HB: 978-1-5013-0279-4
PB: 978-1-5013-2649-3
ePub: 978-1-5013-0280-0
ePDF: 978-1-5013-0281-7

Series: New Directions in German Studies

Cover design: Andrea F. Bucsi
Cover image © John Sappington/Hojda Stojka

Typeset by Fakenham Prepress Solutions, Fakenham, Norfolk NR21 8NN

*In memory of my parents, Edward B. French, MD, and
Elsa A. French*

# Contents

|  |  |  |
|---|---|---|
|  | *Illustrations* | ix |
|  | *Preface and Acknowledgments* | xi |
|  | Introduction: "For only together we are strong" | 1 |
| 1 | Justifications, Theories, and Methodologies | 11 |
| 2 | "I am eternally proud to be a Gypsy": Roma Voicing Ethnicity | 41 |
| 3 | "I couldn't talk with anyone else about this": Roma Voicing Gender | 73 |
| 4 | "We were totally uprooted": Romani Perspectives on the *Porrajmos*/Holocaust | 111 |
| 5 | "I live with my deceased": Trauma, Gender, and Ethnicity in Autobiographies by Ceija, Karl, and Mongo Stojka | 133 |
| 6 | "It was, because it wasn't": Gender and Ethnicity in Folk Tales, Fairy Tales, and Wonder Tales | 153 |
| 7 | "The emotions are autobiographical, the story is fictional": Violence in Mariella Mehr's Trilogy | 173 |
| 8 | "It is a kind of life in conflict, between two worlds": Voices of the Post-*Porrajmos*/Holocaust Generation | 201 |
|  | Epilogue: Writing as "the art of survival" | 231 |
|  | *Appendix: Biographies of Romani Writers* | 237 |
|  | *Bibliography* | 245 |
|  | *Index* | 263 |

# Illustrations

Cover image: "Sidi, meine Mama" (Sidi, my Mama) by Ceija Stojka. Photo by John Sappington. Printed with permission from Hojda Stojka.

1. Ceija Stojka in her apartment in Vienna, 2009. She is not ashamed to show her tattooed number "Z 6399" from Auschwitz on her arm. Photo by Kristen Almgren.   2
2. Cover of *Falter* magazine showing Mongo Stojka's role as the family patriarch. Reprinted with permission from the publisher.   16
3. Vienna Collection Camp (possibly Wanko) with Eva Ritter. Photo reprinted with permission from the Bundesarchiv in Berlin.   28
4. School for Sinti and Roma children in northern Berlin in 1913. Children were given a plot of land to develop and become sedentary. Photo reprinted with permission from the Bundesarchiv in Berlin.   59
5. *Stolperstein* (Stumbling Stone) memorial to German Sinti boxer Johann "Rukeli" Trollmann. Photo by Cindy Parsons.   85
6. Berlin-Marzahn Ghetto (?) (1936–45), where Otto Rosenberg and Ewald Hanstein lived. Photo reprinted with permission from the Bundesarchiv in Berlin.   119
7. Dotschy Reinhardt. Copyright by Uwe Hauth.   202
8. Simone Schönett. Copyright by Eva Asaad.   203
9. Stefan Horvath. Photo by Horst Horvath.   203
10. Mahnmal für Roma und Sinti (Memorial for Roma and Sinti), Oberwart, Austria. Photo by Christian Ringbauer.   223

# Preface and Acknowledgments

Writing this book has taught me that all families have their stories. One of our family stories was that our paternal grandmother was a "Gypsy." No one ever researched our genealogy, however. As evidence we relied on stereotypical images of "Gypsies"—our grandmother's dark, wild, curly hair; her exquisite jewelry and flowery dresses; her ability to read tea leaves. She was a teenager when she emigrated in the nineteenth century from Ireland to Massachusetts. In the United States she met my grandfather, also an immigrant from Ireland via Newfoundland. They married and settled in Everett, near Boston, where they raised four children. My grandfather worked as a policeman and must have witnessed the racial tensions riddling Boston's ethnic neighborhoods in the early twentieth century. In this environment, the family probably did not want to draw attention to my grandmother's heritage, if, indeed, she was a "Gypsy." In fact, my grandmother's supposed "Gypsy" background seemed more a dark secret than a source of pride. My father had stories from his childhood of visitors coming surreptitiously to his house where his mother read tea leaves and told fortunes, but he knew little about her background. Later, our oldest sister visited a cousin in Ireland who also stated our grandmother was supposedly one quarter "Gypsy," although no one had more specific information.

In relating this family legend, I am not trying to be a "Gypsy wannabe." Neither do I mean to privilege myself as more capable than anyone else to study Roma because of my supposed heritage. I recognize that I was not raised with any knowledge of Romani traditions, history, or customs, and that I have come to study Roma of my own volition. People often ask what motivated my interest and research, however. In response, I usually do not immediately tell them this family legend for fear they might think I am invoking such an unearned privilege. Instead, I describe my circuitous journey in arriving at the topic, from an initial fascination with learning languages, to a focus on German, to an eventual desire to discover more about a highly misunderstood and rarely researched ethnic group. I tell them about all I have learned from writings and art by Roma and from Roma I have met. I stress that I want to spread that knowledge to others.

Through exploring Roma voices, however, I have learned most from the unfounded family legend about my grandmother, namely to regret my ignorance about her heritage. I regret I am no longer able to ask her or my father more questions. I regret I did not record their stories. Those regrets have made me want to ensure other Roma voices are not silenced, lost, forgotten, or ignored. For this reason, I preface my book with this family legend.

I have had much help and support along the way to completing this book. I began this project in 1997 when I received a Pacific University Summer Faculty Grant to research Afro-Germans and Roma in Germany. Pacific University then awarded me a Faculty Development Award in summer 2004 and two sabbaticals in 2003–4 and 2010–11. I am thankful for these opportunities to research on site in Germany, Austria, and Switzerland. I am grateful to the Fulbright Commission for the semester I spent in spring 2003 as Distinguished Chair in Gender Studies at the University of Klagenfurt in Austria. The faculty I met were supportive and helpful—Doris Moser, Gerda Moser, Karl Stuhlpfarrer, Primus-Heinz Kucher, Irene Bandhauer, Susanne Dermutz, and Hubert Lengauer—and I thank them. I am indebted to students there for their inspiration, and especially Manuela (Granig) Drobesch and Nicole Schickbauer for invaluable assistance and friendship. I also thank Beate Eder-Jordan, who was generous with her time and expertise in meeting me at the University of Innsbruck. I owe thanks to Gernot Haupt, who has continued to supply me with bibliographical references. I am also grateful to Gabriele Fenkart and Margret Kobalter for their friendship with me and my son Leif during our time in Klagenfurt. Carmen and Sepp Granig deserve special thanks for welcoming me into their home whenever I have visited Austria.

Meeting Ceija Stojka, Mongo Stojka, Harri Stojka, Nuna Stojka, Hojda Stojka, Ruzsa Nikolić-Lakatos, Mariella Mehr, Dotschy Reinhardt, and Simone Schönett, albeit briefly, beginning in 2003, has profoundly deepened my understanding of Romani cultures. I am thankful for their time and stories. In 2009 I co-organized, with Michaela Grobbel, the first travelling exhibit of Ceija Stojka's artwork in the United States—shown at Pacific University in Oregon, Sonoma State University in California, and West Branch Gallery in Vermont. Working intensely with Ceija Stojka's art, autobiographies, stories, and diaries afforded me the opportunity to immerse myself in background material on Romani history, language, social conditions, and customs. I am indebted to individuals and organizations, too numerous to list here, who supported the exhibit with time and funding. I feel fortunate to have worked on this significant project with Michaela Grobbel, Karen Brodsky, Amy Rahn, Teri Swenson, Chris Curtis, Andrea Driendl, Katie Reen, Jeremy Hoff, and my brother, Ed French.

At Pacific University, colleagues Cheleen Mahar, Martha Rampton, Roylene Read, and Victor Rodriguez have been supportive and inquisitive about the progress of my manuscript. The three weeks Cheleen, Roylene, and I spent in Germany and Austria, including a visit to Ceija Stojka's Viennese apartment, cemented lasting memories. Pacific University library faculty and staff deserve special thanks for locating many obscure books for me. I am hugely fortunate to have Pauline Beard—English professor and editor *par excellence*—provide helpful commentary on the manuscript. I also thank Pacific University students Britta LaVoie, John Reinert, and Jamison Soupir, for staging an important exhibit on Roma for my seminar; Jacob Arzt, Maria (Walters) Vander Meulen, and Kristen Almgren, for assistance on the Ceija Stojka exhibit; and Amber Anderson, for help in preparing the manuscript for publication. Professors Phil Ruder, Erich Kleinknecht, and JayCee Whitehead have graciously answered questions in their respective research areas of economics, psychology, and sociology.

Outside of Pacific University, I thank Tina Gerhardt at the University of Hawaii, Manoa, for her suggestions on the manuscript's first draft and her wonderful work as my sabbatical replacement. Carol Silverman at the University of Oregon offered excellent comments on the manuscript, as did anonymous readers. Sin E. Ma deserves special thanks and love for continued friendship, musings, and love. I am grateful to Peter Becker, Claas Christophel, Gudrun Doringer, Anna Heggenberger, Conny Loder, Sanja Reiß, Anja Peters, and Rikarda Suciu, for assistance in so many ways—acquiring materials for me in Germany and Austria; hosting me on visits; assisting in teaching classes; lending their friendship. I am also tremendously grateful to the editors and staff at Bloomsbury—especially Imke Meyer, Haaris Naqvi, and Mary Al-Sayed—for answering all my questions promptly and thoroughly.

I would not have accomplished this project without my large family, really, all my brothers and sisters and their spouses and children and grandchildren. Special thanks and love go out to my spouse Jimmy Draznin and son Leif Draznin-French, the former for his patience and fortitude during this long project, the latter for his irreplaceable company while I was researching abroad and for exciting stories about his own "Roma adventures." This book is dedicated to the memory of my parents, Edward B. French and Elsa A. French, whose legacies stay alive in family and community stories.

Versions of Chapters Five and Six have previously appeared, respectively, in *German Studies Review*, 31.1 (February 2008): 65–86; *Pacific Coast Philology*, 49.1 (University Park, PA: Penn State University Press, 2014): 5–24. I thank the editors.

# Introduction: "For only together we are strong"

> Together, jointly and not alone,
> for only together we are strong.[1]

With poignant words—"for only together we are strong"— Ceija Stojka, an Austrian Romani writer, artist, singer, storyteller, and spokesperson for human rights, calls out for solidarity among Roma. In 1988 she published the first widely read autobiography by a Romani citizen in German-speaking countries.[2] In an interview, she stressed the need for Roma to speak up, or else they will "tumble into a hole."[3] Luckily, Romani writers have not disappeared. Ceija Stojka's work has inspired many to follow suit. The numerous autobiographies, novels, tales, and narratives I investigate here offer testimonies to their courage to express themselves publicly. Readers should listen to what they have to tell.

This book has two purposes. The first is to promulgate the voices of many diverse Roma who have published autobiographical and literary works in Germany, Austria, and Switzerland. Reading their stories will counteract centuries of silencing. In using the written word to relay

---

1 "Amenca ketane taj na korkori ke feri ketane sam zurale. Gemeinsam, zusammen und nicht alleine, denn nur zusammen sind wir stark." Ceija Stojka, "Amenca ketane," in *Romane Gila: Lieder und Tänze der Roma in Österreich*, edited by Ursula Hemetek, with Walter Deutsch, et al. (Vienna: Österreichische Dialektautoren and Institut für Volksmusikforschung an der Hochschule für Musik und darstellende Kunst, 1992), 46. All English translations are mine, unless otherwise noted.
2 Ceija Stojka, *Wir leben im Verborgenen: Erinnerungen einer Rom-Zigeunerin*. (1st edn 1988; 4th edn, Vienna: Picus, 2003).
3 "in ein Loch hineinkippen." Ceija Stojka, "'Du darfst keine Andere sein': Ceija Stojka im Gespräch mit Karin Berger," in Ceija Stojka, *Verborgenen*, 154. Ceija is also not afraid or ashamed to show her arm with her number "Z 6399" tattooed on it from Auschwitz as a symbol of her survival. See Illustration 1.

2  Roma Voices in the German-Speaking World

Illustration 1: Ceija Stojka in her apartment in Vienna, 2009. She is not ashamed to show her tattooed number "Z 6399" from Auschwitz on her arm. Photo by Kristen Almgren.

their views, Roma ensure cultural longevity and shared memories. Their publications provide fascinating glimpses into misunderstood and misrepresented worlds. Navigating historical persecutions and perceptions, such texts reveal shared values as well as ambiguous, complex, and multifaceted viewpoints. They demonstrate how the process of identity construction is a constant one involving both self-formation and imposition from the dominant society. In negotiating between many influential worlds, writers exhibit constancy while warding off cultural ossification. They remain both tenacious and adaptable.

The second purpose is to examine Romani writers' perspectives on ethnicity and gender, two topics that have received scant scholarly attention. Their intersection is central to constructing Romani self-identity and collective consciousness. Ceija Stojka, for example, represents an independent, literate, stable, and hard-working writer and artist, thereby challenging stereotypes of illiterate, nomadic, and unindustrious Roma. She also mitigates the patriarchal structure many scholars have discerned in Romani cultures. Finding Romani female and male writers who share Ceija Stojka's qualities is not impossible.

**Outline of Chapters**

Chapter One provides answers to three main questions: Why focus on German-speaking countries? Why investigate published literary and autobiographical texts? What theories and methodologies prove most useful for my study? A survey of studies related to Romani culture, writings by German-speaking Roma, and Romani perspectives on gender and ethnicity will identify lacunae I hope my book will fill. Ideas other marginalized writers espouse, especially African-American feminists, will prove useful for my study, as will theories of intersectionality, hybridity, and post-colonialism.

Chapter Two delves into theories on ethnicity. Ethnic identity construction is a constant process involving internal self-formulation and externally imposed definitions. Those within the ethnic group, and not solely those outside the group, must play a major role in defining their own characteristics. For German-speaking Roma, externally imposed political, historical, social, and cultural factors have included racial profiling, persecution, forced migratory activities, and unavailable educational opportunities, all pervading their history from the fifteenth century to the present. Dominant societies excluded Roma and made them examples of what some sociologists term "racialized ethnicities," whereby characteristics caused largely by social and economic conditions become perceived as innate racial traits.[4] Common images pejoratively and monolithically portray Roma as nomadic, illiterate, uneducated, isolated, and hostile

---

4  Rebecca Jean Emigh, Eva Fodor, and Iván Szelényi, "The Racialization and Feminization of Poverty?" in *Poverty, Ethnicity and Gender in Eastern Europe during Market Transition*, edited by Rebecca Jean Emigh and Ivan Szelényi (Westport, CT and London: Praeger Publishers, 2001), 6.

towards non-Roma. An overabundance of romanticized depictions of Roma as carefree and exotic fails to recognize historical persecution. What do Roma think about these images? In both Chapters Two and Three I examine published autobiographical writings of over 20 Roma who grew up in Germany, Austria, and Switzerland during the 1920s and 1930s to garner their perspectives on ethnicity and gender. All Roma discussed survived Nazi persecution, and confronted not only cultural taboos but also personal inhibitions to tell their stories years later. Their writings allow a trajectory to emerge, revealing how viewpoints on gender and ethnicity developed over time. In Chapter Two, I investigate Roma's attitudes towards integration and assimilation, travelling, the Romany language, literacy, education, and diversity. In Chapter Three, I examine their perspectives on gender roles related to purity and pollution practices; culinary and domestic rituals; birth, illness, and death; courtship, marriage, and family life; work, storytelling, and music making. Both chapters substantiate the argument that gender norms become tightly interwoven with ethnicity. Some customs point to patriarchal, patrilineal social structures with set gender norms sometimes intended to limit women's power and influence. These structures, however, are not always binding. Autobiographies reveal cracks in the patriarchal system and the ways both sexes mitigate restrictive norms.

Chapter Four details Nazi attempts to silence Roma through policies including breaking up families, separating the sexes, and endeavoring to annihilate the entire ethnic population. Still, the *Porrajmos/* Holocaust became a unifying force for Roma. After briefly reviewing Nazi policies, I look at the impact that sterilization, sanitary conditions, shaving of hair, sexual mistreatment, and requests for compensation after the *Porrajmos/*Holocaust have exerted on sentiments regarding assimilation and national identity.

Historical and social contexts for gender norms related to ethnicity pave the way for subsequent close textual analyses of individual writers' works. Chapter Five focuses on autobiographies of siblings Ceija, Karl, and Mongo Stojka, all major Austrian Romani writers, artists, and spokespeople for human rights. My analysis investigates the complex ways in which the three handle the aftermath of horrendous Nazi persecution. Their autobiographies are rich treasures to study the impact of trauma and gender on the narrative process and on individual and collective memories. Concentrating on three stories about shared tragedies, I investigate the "fragile power"[5] of memory

---

5   Daniel L. Schacter, *Searching for Memory: The Brain, the Mind, and the Past* (New York: Basic Books, 1996), 308. I thank Jacqueline Vansant for references to Schacter's studies.

and suggest ways to interpret discrepancies that can arise in trauma victims' narratives.

Chapter Six looks at folk tales, wonder tales, and fairy tales.[6] The texts are mostly originally oral tales passed down through generations. Contemporary storytellers retold the stories to scholars, who recorded, transcribed, translated into German, and then published them in bilingual editions. This multi-layered, complex process reinforces Bhabha's notions of hybridity and mimicry, but also looks beyond these concepts to discern how storytellers create new forms of cultural texts. The texts have the potential to assume lives of their own when audiences must devise meanings for what frequently appear to be nonlinear, noncohesive narratives with rapidly paced events. In creating "disorder to create order,"[7] Romani tales also appear not static or stable and Romani cultures not monolithic. Theories regarding the genre of magical realism also assist in understanding how combining reality with magic engenders the flexibility to transform values and morals, and to pose alternatives to gender norms and ethnic stereotypes.

Nazi persecution is, unfortunately, just one of several historical injustices Roma have faced. Mariella Mehr is a Swiss Jenisch writer, Jenisch being a subgroup of travellers mostly in Switzerland and Austria. Mehr fell victim to the systematic, Swiss government-sanctioned program "Hilfswerk für die Kinder der Landstrasse" (Relief Agency for Children of the Road), organized by the social agency "Pro Juventute." From 1926 to 1973 the foundation removed children from their parents to prevent travelling lifestyles. Mehr was one of over 600 children who suffered abduction. Chapter Seven concentrates on how ethnicity, gender, and violence complexly interconnect in Mehr's writings. The

---

6  Jack Zipes distinguishes "folk tales" from "fairy tales"; the former originated orally; the latter were written consciously as literary works. "Wonder tales" are usually a subset of folk tales, including anecdotes, initiations, animal tales, and legends: *Breaking the Magic Spell: Radical Theories of Folk and Fairy Tales*, revised and expanded edition (Lexington, Kentucky: University of Kentucky Press, 2002), 28. Roma distinguish several categories for their stories, the two most common for Lovara, for example, include *paramiči*—fairytales and other fictitious stories—and *tertenetura*, containing stories about actual occurrences or ones deemed to be true; tales about interactions with mulo, or the death spirit; and legends about the figure of Bagara, from whom most Roma supposedly originate: Petra Cech and Christiane Fennesz-Juhasz, "Märchen, Erzählungen und Lieder der Lovara," in *Fern von uns im Traum... /Te na dikas sunende... : Märchen, Erzählungen und Lieder der Lovara./Lovarenge paramiči, tertenetura taj gjila*, edited by Petra Cech, et al. (Klagenfurt and Celovec: Drava, 2001), 400. I use "folk tales," or simply "tales," or "stories," or a listing of "folk tales, fairy tales, and wonder tales" for all categories.
7  Zipes, *Why Fairy Tales Stick: The Evolution and Relevance of a Genre* (New York/London: Routledge, 2006), 15.

message that violence will only beget more violence underlies her protagonists' traumatic experiences. Mehr's journalistic and reflective essays, as well as her life as a prolific writer and active spokesperson against injustices she has witnessed, offer inspirational, creative models for positive social and political change. Links between the body, language, and power in her works invoke theories by Foucault and Monique Wittig, as well as those on female sadomasochism and violence.

In the past decade, a younger generation of Romani writers and cultural spokespeople has begun to publish. Chapter Eight analyzes works by writers born after the *Porrajmos*/Holocaust. Simone Schönett is an Austrian Jenisch writer; Dotschy Reinhardt is a German Sinti singer and writer; and Stefan Horvath is the first Romani author from Oberwart in Burgenland, Austria, where a large Romani community has resided for at least two centuries. Their works reveal an awareness of topics weaving Romani ethnicity and gender together—family, storytelling, language, work practices, a shared history of persecution, cultural norms and customs, and diversity—and comment on the impact of transformations in ethnic practices and gender norms on their respective Romani cultures.

**Terminology**

The term "Roma" may not be as widespread in English as "Gypsy." While many scholars have articulately described the term already, I still need to explain my choice of words. I employ "Roma" as a self-ascribed word that Roma people use to identify themselves. The male is a "Rom" in singular, "Roma" in plural; the female a "Romni" in singular, "Romnija" in plural. The language is Romany, and I employ "Romani" as the adjective, as in "Romani literature." In contrast, "Gypsy" is a word the Gadže, or non-Roma, founded, one evoking a long history of stereotypical images. The etymology of "Gypsy" derives from the misconception that Roma originally came from Egypt, and not from northwest India, which linguistical data strongly suggest. Although the etymology of the German word "Zigeuner" is not totally clear, linguists surmise it most likely stemmed from Byzantine Greek "athinganoi," referring to a sect of "untouchables" in the Phrygia region in what is today Turkey, another false origin. "Zigeuner" has negative connotations in German, including references to kinds of kebabs called "Zigeunerspieß," literally a "skewered Gypsy." One would not refer to a "Romaspieß."[8] Likewise, English contains the pejorative designations of "academic Gypsies" and "Gypsy blood," and not "academic

---

8   Erich Hackl, "Vorwort," in *Geboren bin ich vor Jahrtausenden ... Bilderwelten in der Literatur der Roma und Sinti* by Beate Eder (Klagenfurt: Drava, 1993), 15–16.

Roma," or "Roma blood." The verb to be "gypped" also derives from the pejorative, widespread, false belief that all "Gypsies" steal. When "Gypsy" appears in quotation marks in my study, I am indicating a designation from outside, as when Nazis used "Zigeuner"/"Gypsy" in a racialized context. Or, an author may refer to a character as a "Zigeuner"/"Gypsy." Some German-speaking Roma also prefer "Zigeuner," or even "Gypsy" in English because those terms evoke their long traditions, and most people are still more familiar with these words than with "Roma." Many members of the Stojka family, for example, do not shy away from using "Zigeuner" at times. Some use "Zigeuner" because they have roots extending back over two centuries in what is now Austria. Seeing themselves belonging to both Austrian and Romani worlds, they do not want to lose recognition in either. When a quote contains "Zigeuner," I translate it as "Gypsy."

In Germany one often refers to "Sinti and Roma" separately, with Sinti the particular Romani subgroup in Germany since the fifteenth century, and Roma all other subgroups, particularly those who have emigrated from Eastern Europe in the past two to three decades. Considering Sinti are Roma, I find this separate classification tautology, ultimately setting up a false dichotomy. Therefore, I include Sinti under the term Roma, although when Sinti identify themselves as such specifically, I use that designation. The male is a "Sinto," and the female, a "Sintiza, Sintizza, Sintitsa, Sinteza, Sintezza," depending on how one wishes to spell the oral rendition.[9] Regarding writers' individual names, I use either first and last names together, or just first names, or just last names, because the writers themselves use all these self-referential options. I also include Jenisch as a Romani subgroup, which I explain in Chapter Seven on Mariella Mehr, a classification that might be controversial because some scholars do not see Jenisch as holding blood ties with other Roma. I see Jenisch as suffering the same ethnic persecution as other Romani subgroups.[10] Consequently, I share Liégeois's dilemma in finding it difficult to come up with: "... a single term for a number of communities that wish to have distinct identities, and equally hard

---

9   Dotschy Reinhardt, *Gypsy: Die Geschichte einer großen Sinti-Familie* (Frankfurt a. M.: Scherz and S. Fischer Verlag, 2008), 37.
10  See Thomas Huonker, *Diagnose: "moralisch defekt". Kastration, Sterilisation und Rassenhygiene im Dienst der Schweizer Sozialpolitik und Psychiatrie 1890–1970* (Zürich: Orell Füssli, 2003); Thomas Huonker, *Fahrendes Volk—verfolgt und verfemt: Jenische Lebensläufe* (Zürich: Limmat Verlag, 1987); Thomas Dominik Meier and Rolf Wolfensberger,*"Eine Heimat und doch keine". Heimatlose und Nicht-Sesshafte in der Schweiz (16. – 19. Jahrhundert)* (Zürich: Chronos Verlag, 1998); *Radgenossenschaft der Landstrasse: Dachorganisation der Jenischen der Schweiz,* http://www.radgenossenschaft.ch/

to make a book title out of a list of names."¹¹ Identifying all subgroups as Roma poses the best solution.

"*Porrajmos*/Holocaust" refers to persecution of Roma during Nazi times. "Porrajmos," or "porajmos,"¹² or "porraimos"¹³ means "the devouring" in Romany, and Roma have used this term to identify their experiences, but not without controversy, because it can also mean "violation" or "rape," a connotation that some Roma find offensive.¹⁴ An alternate term is "Samudaripen," "mass killing,"¹⁵ but I still opt for *Porrajmos* because of its more widespread usage.

Another term needing explanation is "minority." Publicly and privately, Ceija Stojka spoke vehemently against using "Minderheit" in German. Officially, the word means "a minority population" in English, but in German, "minder" means "lesser." Ceija insisted she does not want herself or Roma to be known as "lesser." I respect her feelings and thus have avoided using "minority" in this context. I employ "minority" only when talking about public policies using the expression "minority rights," and even so, I place the word in quotation marks. Ceija has cleverly devised an alternative term, "Wenigerheit," literally meaning groups of people who are fewer in numbers. Unable to find an equally elegant English expression, I use "marginalized" or other adjectives reflecting Roman's oppressed status rather than "minority."

My study cannot be, and does not intend to be, exhaustive. Unfortunately, I have had to omit many Romani voices.¹⁶ First, I focus largely on published prose—autobiographies, novels, short stories, tales, and narratives. Hence, major omissions include dramas, song lyrics, and performance pieces. Also, my concentration on written texts excludes other significant media—music, art, films, performances,

---

11  Jean-Pierre Liégeois, *Roma in Europe* (Strasbourg: Council of Europe Publishers, 2007), 11.
12  Raul Hilberg, "Gypsies," in *The Holocaust Encyclopedia*, edited by Walter Laqueur (New Haven: Yale University Press), 274.
13  Isabel Fonseca, *Bury Me Standing: The Gypsies and Their Journey* (New York: Vintage, 1995), 253.
14  Ian Hancock, "On the Interpretation of a Word: Porrajmos as Holocaust," 2006. The Romani Archives and Documentation Center, http://www.radoc.net/radoc.php?doc=art_e_holocaust_interpretation&lang=ry&articles=true
15  *Samudaripen-Porrajmos: Roma Holocaust.* https://groups.yahoo.com/neo/groups/Roma_Holocaust/info
16  Two major authors I do not investigate are Jovan Nikolić, because his works are originally in Serbian and Serbo-Croatian and largely about his experiences growing up in Serbia in previous Yugoslavia, and poet Ilija Jovanović, because I concentrate on prose. Toninato includes extensive analysis of poetry by Roma in several countries, and does look specifically at Nikolić's and Jovanović's poetry, among others: Paola Toninato, *Romani Writing: Literacy, Literature and Identity Politics* (New York/London: Routledge, 2014), 77–8, 92–136.

Introduction: "For only together we are strong"  9

social media—although Roma are actively producing such.[17] The richness of the writings I analyze warrants its own space, and other forms of expression will have to wait for further opportunities. I hope my study inspires others to carry on what I have begun here—highlighting Roma voices—in the same way the voices of Lily van Angeren-Franz, Philomena Franz, Ewald Hanstein, Stefan Horvath, Elisabeth Kreutz, Friedrich Kreutz, Hildegard Lagrenne, Mariella Mehr, Anna Mettbach, Joseph Muscha Müller, Mišo Nikolić, Dotschy Reinhardt, Lolo Reinhard, Otto Rosenberg, Simone Schönett, Bernhard Steinbach, Ceija Stojka, Karl Stojka, Mongo Stojka, Latscho Tschawo, Walter Winter, and so many others have inspired me.

---

17  For analyses of art, see *Ceija Stojka (1933–2013): "Sogar der Tod hat Angst vor Auschwitz." "Even Death is Terrified of Auschwitz." "Vi o Merimo Daral Katar o Auschwitz,"* edited by Lith Bahlmann and Mathias Reichelt (Nuremberg: Verlag für Moderne Kunst, 2014); Lorely French, "LIVE-DANCE-PAINT-WRITE: A Multi-Media Project on Romani ("Gypsy") Artist, Writer, Singer, and Educator Ceija Stojka," *Interface: The Journal of Education, Community, and Values* 10.3 (April 2010), http://commons.pacificu.edu/cgi/viewcontent.cgi?article=1015&conte xt=inter10; Moritz Pankok, ed., *Ort des Sehens. Kai Dikas. Place to See 2*, foreword by Ceija Stojka and introduction by André J. Raatzsch (Berlin: Kai Dikas, 2012); *Ceija Stojka: Auschwitz ist mein Mantel: Bilder und Texte*, Christa Stippinger, ed. (Vienna: Edition Exil, 2008); Susan Tebbutt, "Disproportional Representation: Romanies and European Art," in *The Role of the Romanies: Images and Counter-Images of "Gypsies"/Romanies in European Cultures*, edited by Nicholas Saul and Susan Tebbutt (Liverpool: Liverpool University Press, 2004), 159–77; Susan Tebbutt, "'My Name in the Third Reich was Z:5742': The Political Art of the Austrian Rom, Karl Stojka," in *Scholarship and the Gypsy Struggle: Commitment in Romani Studies*, edited by Thomas Acton (Hatfield, Hertfordshire: University of Hertfordshire Press, 2000): 69–80. For Romani theater see: Michaela Grobbel, "Crossing Borders of Different Kinds: Roma Theater in Vienna," *Journal of Austrian Studies*, forthcoming 48.1 (Spring 2015). For multimedia, one need only search for "Roma," "Sinti," "Kalderash," "Vlax," "Lovara" on Facebook to find numerous sites—Open Society Roma Initiatives, Romani Language-Romani Chib, and Romano Centro—with active participants using social media for self-expression. Within the scope of my study, which focuses on Roma writers in the German-speaking world, I do not have space for an exhaustive comparative analysis of Romani texts and of scholarship on those texts in other countries. For a recent, albeit also not exhaustive, account of the state of research on Romani literature from a European comparative standpoint, see Julia Blandfort, *Die Literatur der Roma Frankreichs*, Memesis: Romanische Literaturen der Welt, ed. Ottmar Ette, 60 (Berlin, Munich, Boston: de Gruyter, 2015), 8–13.

## *One* Justifications, Theories, and Methodologies

**Why Focus on the German-Speaking Countries?**
Roma have had a long, intricate history in the German-speaking countries. The first records in what is today Germany registered the arrival of so-called "Tartars" in Hildesheim in Lower Saxony in 1407.[1] In 1414, chroniclers documented the "Heiden" (heathen) in Basel, Switzerland, who most likely were early wandering Roma. Most Roma have been settled in what were the Austro-Hungarian territories since the fourteenth and fifteenth centuries.[2] A major wave of Roma then arrived in Germany and Austria between 100 and 200 years ago, mostly from Hungary and Eastern Europe. At the beginning of the 1970s, Germany saw an influx of Eastern European Roma searching for employment. Austria's and Germany's geographical positionings in central Europe and their longstanding social, political, economic, and cultural connections with Eastern European countries have made these two German-speaking nations major migration destinations for Roma after the collapse of the Eastern Bloc in the early 1990s.[3]

Today, Roma whose writings I investigate belong to one of six main subgroups residing in Germany, Austria, and Switzerland. The Sinti live mostly in Germany, although also in Austria and Switzerland. Burgenland-Roma, Lovara, Gurbet, Kalderash, and Arlije are mainly in Austria, although these subgroups also are in Germany

---

1 Joachim H. Hohmann, *Geschichte der Zigeunerverfolgung in Deutschland*, rev. edn (Frankfurt a. M.: Campus, 1988), 17–18.
2 Cf. Will Guy, *Between Past and Future: The Roma of Central and Eastern Europe* (Hatfield, Hertfordshire: University of Hertfordshire Press, 2001); and Angus Fraser, *The Gypsies* (Oxford and Cambridge, MA: Blackwell, 1995), 60–83.
3 Susan Tebbutt, ed., *Sinti and Roma: Gypsies in German-Speaking Society and Literature* (New York and Oxford: Berghahn, 1998), xv.

and Switzerland.⁴ My study also includes Jenisch, who reside mostly in Switzerland but also in Austria and Germany. Many of the authors use the German term "Stamm," meaning "tribe," "clan," to signify their particular subgroup. All have had permanent residences in one of these countries for most of their lives. If they have travelled, their journeys have been usually just seasonal. Thus, I am looking at families who have resided in the countries for decades, even centuries, and not at post-communism immigrants arriving in the past two-and-a-half decades. According to recent estimates, 120,000 Roma and Sinti live in Germany today.⁵ In Austria, estimates place the number at 25,000.⁶ In Switzerland, the Roma Foundation estimates that 50,000–60,000 reside there.⁷

Historically many German-speaking Roma have followed customs that ethnographers have observed in other Romani subgroups at various times, albeit with numerous variations and exceptions, including American Roma living in California;⁸ Travellers in England;⁹ and Vlach Roma in Hungary.¹⁰ More complete investigations of customs appear throughout my study, but a basic, brief description of some shared characteristics proves useful here for

---

4  Dieter Halwachs distinguishes five subgroups: "Romani in Österreich," in *Die Sprache der Roma: Perspektiven der Romani-Forschung in Österreich im interdisziplinären und internationalen Kontext*, eds Dieter W. Halwachs and Florian Menz (Klagenfurt: Drava, 1999); *Rombase* adds a sixth, Gurbet, http://rombase.uni-graz.at/. For German Roma see: Katrin Reemtsma, *Sinti und Roma. Geschichte, Kultur, Gegenwart* (Munich: Beck, 1996).
5  *Nevipe—Rundbrief des Rom e.V.* 42 (January 2010), 7–8. http://www.romev.de/wp-content/uploads/2013/PDF/Rundbrief_42.pdf. Of those 120,000, some 70,000 have German citizenship, and some 50,000 are refugees from the former Yugoslavia. Since the expansion of the European Union into Eastern Europe, more Roma have immigrated to Germany; those numbers remain undocumented. See also "Emils Ring," by Journalists of the Henri-Nannen-Schule, 21 August 2014, http://www.zeit.de/zeit-magazin/leben/2014-07/sinti-hamburg-emil-weiss. I thank Anke Biendarra for this reference.
6  Renata M. Erich, "Roma in Österreich," in Halwachs and Menz, *Sprache der Roma*, 13.
7  Emily Wright, "To be Roma means to be a traveler and thief." Swissinfo.ch., 7 September 2010, http://www.swissinfo.ch/eng/-to-be-roma-means-to-be-a-traveller-and-thief-/28286556
8  Anne Sutherland, *Gypsies: The Hidden Americans* (Prospect Heights, IL: Waveland Press, Inc., 1975; reissued 1986).
9  Judith Okely, "Gypsy Women: Models in Conflict," in *Perceiving Women*, ed. Shirley Ardener, (London: Malaby, 1975), 55–86; Judith Okely, *Own or Other Culture* (London/New York: Routledge, 1996); Judith Okely, *The Traveller-Gypsies* (Cambridge: Oxford University Press, 1983; 1998).
10  Michael Stewart, *The Time of the Gypsies* (Boulder, CO and Oxford: Westview Press, 1997).

formulating a sense of a comparative, collective ethnic identity. Autobiographers born between 1920 and 1940 talk in particular about groups following certain purity and pollution customs, called *mahrime*. *Rombase* identifies *mahrime* categories related to the female body, hygiene, food, illness, death, and the relationship with non-Roma. At moments those customs created separations between men and women, such as when a woman was menstruating or giving birth, and thus considered unclean. Besides specific *mahrime* customs, several talk about arranged marriages accompanied by dowries and bride prices, with virginity at marriage highly valued. Many couples received no legal marriage certificate; they either eloped or lived in civil unions. If the parents or the whole group blessed the union, then the couple was considered married. Families have usually been patrilocal, meaning that upon marriage the bride goes to live with the groom's family. Within the home, women have usually been responsible for childcare, cooking, and cleaning. Outside of the home, men and women have also shown a division of labor by gender. Women were largely the fortune tellers and door-to-door salespeople while men traded horses and performed metalwork and physical labor.

Scholars researching various Romani groups have often seen these customs and practices as entailing a male authority figure and a separation of the sexes whereby women are lesser valued than men, and Romani cultures are viewed as largely patriarchal, albeit with nuances and exceptions.[11] Silverman cogently surmises that Romani

---

11   For women's separate roles among English Roma see: Okely, "Gypsy Women" in *The Traveller-Gypsies*, 201–14. Among Hungarian Roma Stewart observes a "radical, gendered division of social affairs" (*Gypsies*, 54). He admits, however, that as a man, his observations of women's interactions were limited. *Rombase* states that pollution and purity laws are based on a "patriarchal order of society," http://ling.kfunigraz.ac.at/~rombase/. Eder supplies literary images of submissive women and patriarchal norms, especially in Maximoff's stories, in *"Geboren bin ich,"* 217. Leonardo Piasere suggests that the male-dominated ideology of various Romani subgroups can tend towards sacrificing its weakest members—as when women and children beg or sell wares door-to-door—in times of persecution and economic hardship in order to save the entire group: "Quanto può esere plurietnico uno stato?" in *Un mondo di mondi: Antropologia delle Culture Rom* (Naples: l'ancora, 1999), 17. Elisabeth Tauber states women do not sing or dance at public festivals or rituals among Southern Tirolean Sinti and asks whether women play little or no role in Romani representations of cultural identities in *Du wirst keinen Ehemann nehmen! Respekt, Bedeutung der Toten und Fluchtheirat bei den Sinti Estraixaria*, Forum Europäische Ethnologie, ed. Dorle Dracklé et al., 8. (Berlin: Lit Verlag, 2006), 103–21.

cultures are "(ideally) patrilineal and patrilocal,"[12] meaning some customs may originally have supported a patriarchal system, but both sexes have devised strategies to rupture that system when it impinges on individual and collective desires. Silverman qualifies her use of "patriarchal": "Romani culture is patriarchal, but the various forms of gendered power need to be dissected," and factors such as women's participation in education, rituals, and celebrations "may mitigate gendered power."[13] Likewise, Okely refers to the "crevices of ... verbalized activities" that demonstrate women's recognition of their oppression and attempts to break away from restrictive roles.[14] German-speaking Romani women and men, however, through engaging in storytelling and publishing, have been carving out more than just "crevices of verbalized activities." Rather, they have been amassing vast mountains of texts and a legacy of voices to collect shared stories and memories, which still need investigation. An "(ideally) patriarchal structure" also stands behind many customs and ideologies in Romani writings, whereby female and male writers have mitigated patriarchal structures.[15]

The above-mentioned customs appear largely in the autobiographies of older Roma, and with many variances that depend on the individual

---

12   Carol Silverman, *Romani Routes: Cultural Politics & Balkan Music in Diaspora* (Oxford: Oxford University Press, 2012): 62.
13   Ibid., 77.
14   Okely, *Own or Other Culture*, 85.
15   The few studies on gender and ethnicity among German-speaking Roma writers, specifically Ceija Stojka and Mariella Mehr, include: Michaela Grobbel, "Contemporary Romany Autobiography as Performance," *German Quarterly*, 76.2 (2003): 140–54; Roxane Riegler, *Das Verborgene sichtbar machen: Ethnische Minderheiten in der österreichischen Literatur der neunziger Jahre*, Austrian Culture 43, Margarete Lamb-Faffelberger, General Editor (New York, Washington, D.C., Baltimore, Bern, Frankfurt, Berlin, Brussels, Vienna and Oxford: Peter Lang, 2010), 81–101; Susan Tebbutt, "Disproportional Representation"; Susan Tebbutt, "Marginalization and Memories: Ceija Stojka's Autobiographical Writing," in *'Other' Austrians: Post-1945 Austrian Women's Writing*, ed. Allyson Fiddler (Bern: Peter Lang, 1998), 141–52; and Susan Tebbutt, "Stolen Childhood: Austrian Romany Ceija Stojka and her Past," *Holocaust Studies: A Journal of Culture and History*, Children of the Holocaust, special issue, ed. Andrea Reiter, II.2 (Autumn 2005): 37–61; Michele Ricci Bell, "Lyrical Redefinitions of Heimat in Mariella Mehr's *Nachrichten aus dem Exil* and *Widerwelten*," *German Quarterly*, 83.2 (Spring 2010): 189–211; Carmel Finnan, "From Survival to Subversion: Strategies of Self-Representation in Selected Works by Mariella Mehr," in Saul and Tebbutt, *Role of the Romanies* 145–55; Kim Fordham, "Fear of Difference and its Consequences in Selected Works of Mariella Mehr," in *Crossing Over: Redefining the Scope of Border Studies*, eds Antonio Medina-Rivera and Diana Orendi (Newcastle: Cambridge Scholars Publishing, 2007), 75–86.

and the subgroup. Much has changed since these writers were growing up. German-speaking Roma in general do not adhere to purity and pollution customs much anymore; or, if they do, they are less strict in practicing them. Some customs and values, however, have persisted in many groups. The naked body has been a site for shame, meaning that public nudity, particularly when both sexes are present, is taboo. Talk about the body, especially between men and women in connection with sexuality and with sexual acts, is forbidden. Many subgroups also discourage public displays of affection between couples. Women have often controlled the family's finances. All the writers are polyglots, with some Romani dialects being a first language for many. Many have rituals for the dead because of strong beliefs in afterlife spirits, called *mulo*. Although they have permanent residences and are not nomadic, members often stress their love of travel; they take pride in their ease to adapt to new places based on their polyglotism and their history of forced movement due to political, social, and economic circumstances. Both sexes engage in one or many of the visual, performing, and fine arts—music making, writing, painting—professionally, privately, or both. Respect for the elders, desire to have children, and marital fidelity create strong family bonds. Kinship—the sense of belonging to a large, extended family—emerges in references to well-known families, including Reinhardt, Weiß, Rosenberg, and Rose in Germany; Stojka, Lakatos-Nikolić, and Horvath in Austria.[16]

The writers' main unifier has been the history of persecution, especially the *Porrajmos*. Although Roma throughout the world have witnessed torment, treatment in German-speaking countries has been especially notorious. Details appear throughout my study, but a brief account here introduces low points. Initial reactions of people's curiosity in German, Austrian, and Swiss territories in the fifteenth century rapidly turned into hostility, discrimination, and banishment. Soon after the arrival of the travelling groups, officials in many German states proclaimed Roma "vogelfrei" (outlaws) who could be killed without penalty and even with bounty. In the eighteenth century, Maria Theresia enacted restrictive policies, including laws prohibiting travelling and speaking Romany. Under the Nazis, over 80 per cent of Roma in German-speaking areas were murdered. State-sanctioned agencies continued to discriminate against Roma into the 1970s, especially the Pro-Juventute "Hilfswerk für die Kinder der

---

16   For media coverage on the Weiß family, see "Emils Ring," http://www.zeit.de/zeit-magazin/leben/2014-07/sinti-hamburg-emil-weiss. For the Stojkas, see Wolfgang Paterno, "Die Stojkas: Eine spezielle Wiener Familie. Ihr Patriarch Mongo Stojka im Porträt," *Falter* 20/04 (14–20 May 2004): 72–3. See Illustration 2.

Illustration 2: Cover of *Falter* magazine showing Mongo Stojka's role as the family patriarch. Reprinted with permission from the publisher.

Landstrasse" program in Switzerland.[17] In Austria in the 1950s and 1960s the state removed children from their families, placing them in institutions where they were brutally mistreated.[18] In Germany and Austria after World War II, many Roma never received full compensation for torture and material losses under the Nazis, or if they

---

17 *Radgenossenschaft der Landstraße*, www.radgenossenschaft.ch/
18 *Jenischer Kulturverband Österreich*. http://members.aon.at/jenisch.at/

finally did, the legal process for requesting restitution was gruelling and humiliating. In the twenty-first century, Roma have encountered renewed targeted discrimination and violence in reaction to migrations from Eastern European countries.[19] Non-Roma fascination with Romani language, music, and customs has accompanied ostracization. Some of the most important linguistical findings on the origins of Romany stemmed from German-speaking researchers during the eighteenth and nineteenth centuries, including proving Romany to be an Indic language with roots in Sanskrit, tracing its dialects throughout Europe, compiling written linguistic records and lexica, recording oral stories as archival material for further studies.[20] Eighteenth-century influential treatises, such as Grellmann's, also ushered in derogatory traits characterizing Roma as lazy, thieving, murderous, and incendiary, and Romani women as overly sensual.[21]

19  Incidents of discrimination and assaults against Roma are too numerous to list here. For recent discriminatory attitudes towards Roma in Germany, see the 2014 survey by the Federal Anti-Discrimination Office, in which one in three Germans answered that they do not want to live next to Roma; more Germans preferred to live next to asylum seekers and Muslims than to Roma: *Zwischen Gleichgültigkeit und Ablehnung: Bevölkerungseinstellungen gegenüber Sinti und Roma* (Berlin: Zentrum für Antisemitismusforschung and Institut für Vorurteils- und Konfliktforschung, e.V., 2014), 155–7. http://www.antidiskriminierungsstelle.de/SharedDocs/Downloads/DE/publikationen/Expertisen/Bevoelkerungseinstellungen_Sinti_und_Roma_20140829.pdf?__blob=publicationFile. In Austria, recent laws against beggars are rooted in discrimination against Roma: Stefan Benedik, Barbara Tiefenbacher, and Heidrun Zettelbauer, *Die imaginierte "Bettlerflut": Temporäre Migrationen von Roma/Romnija—Konstrukte und Positionen* (Klagenfurt: Drava, 2013).

20  The first explication of Romany as Indic was in Johann Rudiger, *Von der Sprache und Herkunft der Zigeuner aus Indien* (Hamburg: Buske, 1790). The first connection between Romany and Sanskrit occurred in Augustus F. Pott, *Die Zigeuner in Europa und Asien. Ethnographischlinguistische Untersuchungen, vornehmlich ihrer Herkunft und Sprache nach gedruckten und ungedruckten Quellen* (Halle: E. Heynemann, 1845). One of the earliest trackings of Romani dialects through Europe was in Franz Miklosich, *Ueber die Mundarten und die Wanderungen der Zigeuner Europas*. Denkschriften der kaiserlichen Akademie der Wissenschaften, Philosophisch-historische Klassen, vols 21–31 (Vienna: n.p., 1872–80). Alaina Lemon provides bibliographical references on these linguistic developments in "Telling Gypsy Exile: Pushkin, India, and Romani Diaspora," in *Realms of Exile: Nomadism, Diasporas, and Eastern European Voices*, ed. Domnica Radulescu (Lanham, Boulder, New York and Oxford: Lexington Books, 2002), 29–48.

21  Heinrich Moritz Gottlieb Grellmann, *Die Zigeuner. Ein historischer Versuch über die Lebensart und Verfassung, Sitten und Schicksahle dieses Volks in Europa, nebst ihrem Ursprunge* (Dessau/Leipzig: n.p., 1783). For a critique of Grellmann, see Wim Willems, *In Search of the True Gypsy. Gypsies as Object of Study during the Enlightenment, Romanticism and Nazism* (London: Frank Cass, 1997). 22–92;

## 18 Roma Voices in the German-Speaking World

Still, early German linguistical studies proved to be stepping stones in tracking origins of Romani European migrations back to Northwest India. Today, the University of Graz in Austria houses the "[romani] Projekt" conducting ongoing linguistical research.[22] Besides linguistical studies, scholarship on Roma in the German-speaking countries during the past 30 years has largely focused on Nazi persecution and its aftermath, with most studies concentrating on the perpetrators' viewpoints.[23] While documenting Nazi perse-

---

and David Mayall, *Gypsy Identities 1500–2000: From Egipcyans and Moon-men to the Ethnic Romany* (London and New York: Routledge, 2004), 32–3; 152–3.

22  *[romani] Projekt*, http://romaniprojekt.uni-graz.at/index.en.html. See also Halwachs, "Romani in Österreich;" and Mozes Heinschink, "E Romani Čhib— Die Sprache der Roma," in *Roma: Das unbekannte Volk: Schicksal und Kultur*, eds. Mozes F. Heinschink and Ursula Hemetek (Vienna: Böhlau Verlag, 1994), 110–28.

23  At the risk of excluding some key studies on Nazi persecution of Roma in German-speaking countries, the following include the major ones I used in my study: Florian Freund, Gerhard Baumgartner, and Harald Greifeneder, *Vermögensentzug, Restitution und Entschädigung der Roma und Sinti. Veröffentlichungen der Österreichischen Historikerkommission. Vermögensentzug während der NS-Zeit sowie Rückstellungen und Entschädigungen seit 1945 in Österreich*, 23.2 (Vienna/Munich: Oldenbourg, 2004); Ian Hancock, "Gypsy History in Germany and Neighbouring Lands: A Chronology Leading to the Holocaust and Beyond," in *The Gypsies of Eastern Europe*, eds David Crowe and John Kolsti (Armonk, N.Y. and London: M. E. Sharpe, Inc., 1991), 11–30; Ian Hancock, "'Uniqueness' of the Victims: Gypsies, Jews and the Holocaust," in *Without Prejudice: The EAFORD International Review of Racial Discrimination* 1.2 (1988): 45–67; Gernot Haupt, *Antiziganismus und Religion: Elemente einer Theologie der Roma-Befreiung* (Vienna/Berlin: LIT Verlag, 2009); Gernot Haupt, *Antiziganismus und Sozialarbeit: Elemente einer wissenschaftlichen Grundlegung, gezeigt an Beispielen aus Europa mit dem Schwerpunkt Rumänien* (Berlin: Frank & Timme, 2006); Ulrich Herbert, *National Socialist Extermination Policies: Contemporary German Perspectives and Controversies* (New York: Berghahn Books, 2000); Donald Kenrick and Grattan Puxon, *The Destiny of Europe's Gypsies* (London: Chatto-Heinemann for Sussex University Press, 1972); Julia von dem Knesebeck, *The Roma Struggle for Compensation in Post-War Germany* (Hatfield, Hertfordshire: University of Hertfordshire Press, 2011); Ulrich König, *Sinti und Roma unter dem Nationalsozialismus: Verfolgung und Widerstand* (Bochum: Studienverlag Dr. N. Brockmeyer, 1989); Michail Krausnick, *Wo sind sie hingekommen? Der unterschlagene Völkermord an den Sinti und Roma* (Gerlingen: Bleicher Verlag, 1995); Guenter Lewy, *The Nazi Persecution of the Gypsies* (Oxford/ New York: Oxford University Press, 2000); Gilad Margalit, *Germany and its Gypsies: A Post-Auschwitz Ordeal* (Madison: University of Wisconsin Press, 2002); Benno Müller-Hill, *Murderous Science: Elimination by Scientific Selection of Jews, Gypsies, and Others, Germany 1933–1945*, translated by George R. Fraser (Oxford: Oxford University Press, 1988); Reemtsma, *Sinti und Roma*; ed. Romani Rose, *"Den Rauch hatten wir täglich vor Augen": Der nationalsozialistische Völkermord an den Sinti und Roma* (Heidelberg: Wunderhorn and

Justifications, Theories, and Methodologies 19

cution is important, sole focus on historical annihilation of Roma ultimately undermines active, progressive strides by Roma to ensure that their culture, stories, artwork, and language not only survive, but also thrive. Through shared memories and strategies to adapt to transitioning social, political, and economic circumstances, Roma have displayed the "constancy and flux" that are necessary for ethnicities to endure.[24] While not ignoring the past's devastation, Roma have actively been interpreting their histories and defining their identities. Romani voices from these countries need to be heard.

Ceija Stojka's push for Roma to go out into the world and make their voices heard correlated with ongoing laments about missing Romani perspectives in primary and secondary texts. Regarding historical inquiries, in 1981 Krausnick observed limitations in finding original sources by Roma. Instead, the historian has to rely on "the accounts of those who misunderstand, despise, persecute, and murder."[25] Other historians have remarked on the absence in court records of testimonies by Romani victims of Nazi persecution, largely due to the courts' belief that Roma lacked credibility as witnesses.[26] Accessible records on Roma history have mainly been documents compiled by the police directly before and during Nazi times, and only sought to demonstrate the "Gypsies'" so-deemed criminal and asocial propensity.

Concerning literary studies, some researchers believe that Romani literary narratives are largely oral and best garnered by eavesdropping.[27] Literary works by non-Roma have promulgated, on the one hand, perpetually negative stereotypes of wandering marauders, beggars, and swindlers, or, on the other hand, romanticized clichés of travelling

---

Dokumentations- und Kulturzentrum Deutscher Sinti und Roma, 1999); Erika Thurner, *National Socialism and Gypsies of Austria* (Tuscaloosa: University of Alabama Press, 1998); Michael Zimmermann, *Rassenutopie und Genozid: Die nationalsozialistische "Lösung der Zigeunerfrage,"* Hamburger Beiträge zur Sozial- und Zeitgeschichte, 33, ed. Michael Wildt (Hamburg: Hans Christians Verlag, 1996); and Michael Zimmermann, *Verfolgt, vertrieben, vernichtet: die nationalsozialistische Vernichtungspolitik gegen Sinti und Roma* (Essen: Klartext, 1989).

24 Anthony D. Smith, *National Identity* (Reno and Las Vegas: University of Nevada Press, 1991), 25.
25 "die Aufzeichnungen der Verkenner, Verächter, Verfolger und Mörder angewiesen," Michail Krausnick, *Die Zigeuner sind da. Roma und Sinti zwischen Gestern und Heute* (Würzburg: Arena, 1981), 10.
26 Margalit, *Germany*, 136–8; Thurner, *National Socialism*, 2.
27 Eder (*Geboren*, 78) cites Block's statement about Romani literature being largely oral and best discovered through eavesdropping, a statement that is still included in the 2001 edition of *Kindlers Neues Literatur Lexikon*: Martin Block, "Die Literatur der Zigeuner (Sinti und Roma)," *Kindlers Neues Literatur Lexikon*, 20 (Munich: Kindler Verlag, 2001): 569.

musicians, caravans, fortune telling, and cooking over open campfires. Breger shows how works by Grimmelshausen, Goethe, Eichendorff, Achim von Arnim, and Kleist developed coded discourses about Roma—on the one hand espousing freedom, desire, and exoticism; on the other hand wildness, demonic powers, and chaos—that persist into present times.[28] Other scholarship has appeared since the 1980s investigating the image of Roma in German literary works by non-Roma.[29] Such literary textual analyses, of course, are crucial for understanding complex interactions between Roma and non-Roma and the ways in which Roma have felt compelled to adapt to the dominant culture. But such studies outnumber those looking at Roma's writings, thus fostering an image of Roma as objects of others' narratives and not subjects of their own.

In the past couple of decades some studies looking at Romani culture through Roma's words have appeared. Unfortunately, such studies have been few and far between.[30] Until the early 1990s, the

---

28 Breger, Claudia, *Ortlosigkeit des Fremden: "Zigeunerinnen" und "Zigeuner" in der deutschsprachigen Literatur um 1800* (Cologne: Böhlau, 1998).
29 Klaus-Michael Bogdal, *Europa erfindet die Zigeuner: Eine Geschichte von Faszination und Verachtung*, 4th edn (Berlin: Suhrkamp, 2013); Petro-Gabriele Briel,*"Lumpenkind und Traumprinzessin": zur Sozialgestalt der Zigeuner in der Kinder- und Jugendliteratur seit dem 19. Jahrhundert* (Gießen: Focus, 1989); Rajko Djurić, *Roma und Sinti im Spiegel der deutschen Literatur: ein Essay. Mit einem Vorwort und Einleitungskapitel von Joachim S. Hohmann*. Studien zur Tsiganologie und Folkloristik 13 (Frankfurt a. M.: Lang, 1995); Nicholas Saul, *Gypsies and Orientalism in German Literature from Realism to Modernism* (London: Legenda, 2007); Nicholas Saul and Susan Tebbutt, *The Role of the Romanies: Images and Counter-Images of "Gypsies"/Romanies in European Cultures* (Liverpool: Liverpool University Press, 2004); Wilhelm Solms and Daniel Strauß, eds, *"Zigeunerbilder" in der deutschsprachigen Literatur*. Schriftenreihe des Dokumentations- und Kulturzentrums Deutscher Sinti und Roma (Heidelberg: Dokumentations- und Kulturzentrum Deutscher Sinti und Roma, 1995); and Tebbutt, *Sinti and Roma*.
30 For comparative studies of Romani literature in German-speaking countries see Djurić, *Roma und Sinti*; Eder, *Geboren*; Beate Eder-Jordan, "Ausbruch aus der Anonymität: Roma-Literatur im historischen und kulturellen Kontext," in *Meine Wahl zu schreiben—ich kann es nicht. Gedichte (Romanes, deutsch) und Bilder*, by Ceija Stojka (Landeck: EYE: Literatur der Wenigerheiten, 2003), 65–75; Erika Giorgianni, "Der Mut des Wortes: Zeitgenössische Zigeunerliteratur in Österreich," Tesi die Laurea, Universita' ca' Foscari di Venezia. 2002; *Liebchen, sag/Vitamia, dimmi: 60 Jahre Mariella Mehr/A Mariella Mehr per I suoi 60 anni*, Fondazione Franco Beltrametti (Lugano: Arti Grafiche Veladini, 2007); Herbert Uerlings, "Fremde Blicke. Zur Repräsentation von 'Zigeunern' in der Schweiz seit dem 19. Jahrhundert (Gottfried Keller, Carl Durheim, Mariella Mehr)," in *Fremde Arme—arme Fremde: "Zigeuner" in Literaturen Mittel- und Osteuropas*, eds Iulia-Karin Patrut, George Guţu, and Herbert Uerlings, Inklusion/Exklusion: Studien zu Fremdheit und Armut von der Antike bis zur Gegenwart 3 (Frankfurt a. M.: Peter Lang, 2007),

Justifications, Theories, and Methodologies 21

paucity of published works by Roma has been the main reason for scholarly lacuna. Fortunately, much has changed in that time. The increasing number of published writings by German-speaking Roma has assured that their voices are not completely silent. In 2001, 13 years after her path-breaking autobiography appeared, Ceija Stojka asserted that Roma have developed enough trust to write about themselves publicly.[31] My Appendix includes biographies of 20 writers whose works I analyze. Throughout the book I rely on at least 59 autobiographical, fictional, and narrative texts by Romani writers, many of which have appeared since Ceija's autobiography.

Besides publishing, Roma in German-speaking countries have been forming organizations to understand their cultures and languages. Too many exist to list here, but I will mention only a couple of the most well-known ones whose endeavors I reference at various points. In Germany, there are over 35 organizations and social agencies at the state level whose main focus is Roma.[32] The Dokumentations- und Kulturzentrum der Sinti und Roma (Documentation and Cultural Centre of Sinti and Roma) in Heidelberg, also the seat of the Zentralrat deutscher Sinti und Roma (Central Council of German Sinti and Roma), and the Sinti Allianz in Deutschland are the two main national organizations.[33] The Romano Centro in Vienna represents all Romani subgroups in Austria.[34] The Amerlinghaus in Vienna promotes multicultural groups in Austria, including Roma.[35] The Jenischer Kulturverband Österreich provides information on the history, art, and music of Jenisch in Austria.[36] In Switzerland, the Rroma Foundation/Rromani Fundacija in Zürich funds projects developed by and for Roma.[37] The Radgenossenschaft der Landstrasse and the Genossenschaft fahrendes Zigeuner-Kultur-Zentrum concentrate on "Fahrende" (Travellers), many of whom are

---

143–202; and Marianne C. Zwicker, "Journeys into Memory: Romani Identity and the Holocaust in Autobiographical Writings by German and Austrian Romanies" (PhD Dissertation, University of Edinburgh, 2009). https://www.era.lib.ed.ac.uk/bitstream/1842/6201/1/Zwicker2010.pdf. See also footnote 15 above (page 14) for studies related specifically to gender.

31  Ceija Stojka, "Unsere Seele war krank/Amari odjori sas nasvali," *Fern von uns im Traum*, 317.
32  *Roma und der Arbeitsmarkt: Berufs-und Bildungsförderung für Sinti und Roma in Deutschland*, Berliner Institut für Vergleichende Sozialforschung (Berlin: Edition Parabolis, 2007).
33  *Dokumentations- und Kulturzentrum deutscher Sinti und Roma*, http://www.sintiundroma.de; *Sinti Allianz Deutschland*, http://sintiallianz-deutschland.de
34  *Romano Centro*, http://www.romano-centro.org
35  *Amerlinghaus*, http://www.amerlinghaus.at/
36  *Jenischer Kulturverband Österreich.* http://members.aon.at/jenisch.at/
37  *Rroma Foundation/Rromani Fundacija.* http://foundation.rroma.org/

Jenisch.[38] Collectively, these organizations sponsor readings, newsletters, concerts, art exhibitions, and political activities, ensuring the visibility of Romani cultures. Their existence—along with the complex long history of Roma in Germany, Austria, and Switzerland; the three countries' central European locations allowing migratory accessibility; scholarship historically displaying strong interest in Romani languages, cultures, and histories; and opportunities that German-speaking Roma have seized to publish and organize—further substantiates reasons for focusing on Roma writings in these countries.

## Why Investigate Published Texts, and Especially Literature and Autobiographies?

In looking at Roma's voices, I aim to avoid "the filter of the scholarly abstracted language of the experts" that can alter speakers' commentary and overshadow fine nuances and complexities of first-person perspectives.[39] Historians and sociologists have often consciously excluded literary works in their analyses. Certain historians distinctly state that they do not want to consider literary texts in their investigations because they find the material lacking in objectivity.[40] But literary studies can offer much to historical inquiry.[41] Knesebeck's recent extensive study on the Romani struggle for compensation in post-war Germany supplies examples of the rich dimensions victims' stories add to historical inquiry. She views Roma's post-war personal testimonies as reflective of a collectively remembered past that added a much-needed perspective to "historical truth."[42] Insightful findings emerge in the differing values Romani victims and non-Romani legal officials and politicians show when referring to concentration camp internment, forced labor, and sterilization. For over three decades after the war, courts often categorically denied Roma compensation because official policy had not classified persecution of Roma in general as racially motivated. When deciding on individual Roma cases, courts based their decisions not only on doubts about this racial motivation, but also on the extent of persecution-related physical injury, pain, and earnings capacity. Percentage calculations quantified the persecution's impact on earnings capacity. Contrastingly, autobiographical accounts show Roma gauging their losses more in terms of humiliation, psychological

---

38    *Radgenossenschaft der Landstrasse: Dachorganisation der Jenischen der Schweiz*, http://www.radgenossenschaft.ch/
39    "den Filter der wissenschaftlich abstrahierten Sprache der ExpertInnen." Haupt, *Antiziganismus und Religion*, 45.
40    Cf. Meier and Wolfensberger, *"Eine Heimat."*
41    Uerlings, "Fremde Blicke," 143n. 1.
42    Knesebeck, *Roma Struggle*, 51.

turmoil, family deaths, community dissolution, and cultural losses than physical disabilities or percentage calculations. Damage to the quality of their lives was more devastating than that to their earnings capacity. These differing values often hindered Roma in formulating arguments to satisfy courts' demands, thus often leading to courts denying or reducing the compensation amount. In demonstrating these differing values, Kneseback occasionally cites from published autobiographies, but she mostly works with video testimonials from the United States Holocaust Memorial Museum and from the Fortunoff Video Archive and the SHOAH video Testimony Collection at Yale University, plus documents in legal files.[43] Thus, one still needs to ask what and how exactly do published autobiographies and literary texts contribute to a better understanding of Romani cultures?

One answer lies in Gayatri Spivak's introduction to three stories by Bengali writer Mahasweta Devi, in which she addresses the interconnection between "the literary text and the textile of activism."[44] In talking about the necessity to translate Devi's literary works into English, Spivak employs terms that have become her trademarks—apropos of discussions on Rom—including the subaltern, ethical singularity, responsibility, and accountability. Spivak cautions against using the word "subaltern" too loosely; it is not "just a classy word for oppressed, for Other, for somebody who's not getting a piece of the pie."[45] Subaltern peoples have had their voices written out of the dominant narrative; they do not achieve a dialogic level of utterance. They might speak, but no one in the dominant group listens. Subaltern peoples are forced to listen to the dominant group, but are not allowed to speak with them. The lack of Romani voices in the publishing market and in scholarship evinces their subaltern status.

Spivak defines "ethical singularity" as an intimate and individual relationship between the speaker and the listener involving "responsibility and accountability."[46] Having been denied this dialogic reciprocity, the subaltern must speak and be listened to in order to earn respect.[47] Spivak expounds on effective means to facilitate ethical singularity. She finds them in Devi's literary works in which figures break the usual cataloguing of "same-and-othering" by engaging in dialogic reciprocity. Consequently, Spivak raises concerns about the ability of methods

---

43  Ibid., 52n. 1.
44  Gayatri Chakravorty Spivak, "Translator's Preface," in *Imaginary Maps: Three Stories by Mahasweta Devi* (New York and London: Routledge, 1995), xxvi.
45  Leon De Kock, "Interview with Gayatri Chakravorty Spivak: New Nation Writers Conference in South Africa." *Ariel: A Review of International English Literature* 23.3 (July 1992): 29–47, 45.
46  Spivak, "Translator's Preface," xxv.
47  Ibid., xxvi.

and texts other than literary ones to enact ideal situations in which "responses come from both sides" and there is "responsibility and accountability."[48] Fieldwork accounts and technical papers fall short of capturing the subaltern's knowledge and perspectives. In contrast, the literary text is able to connect the written word and social engagement.[49] Spivak admires Devi's literary work for the "love" that manifests itself in the individual and intimate relationship between speaker and listener, the call for collective solidarity, and the ultimate activism arising from the writing act, key concepts for Romani literary writing as well.

From another perspective, Anthony Smith offers political, historical, and economical justifications for literary texts in ethnic communities, or what he calls "*ethnies*."[50] In investigating the role *ethnies* play in forming national identities, he emphasizes the indispensable part a literary tradition takes in nation building. Regarding *ethnies* that have been unsuccessful in forming an ethno-political nation, the pressures of integration have "eroded the cultures of many smaller ethnic categories that lacked literary traditions."[51] In contrast, successful *ethnies* have had a literary history. Literature assisted groups in formulating "a sense of their common history and destiny."[52] Literary images helped them to "invent" and "reinvent" themselves "through the uses of landscape and history and the resuscitation of dying customs, rituals, and languages."[53] By composing what Smith calls "ethnohistories," ethnic communities have fashioned heroes, symbols, rites, and ceremonies that restored collective dignity and offered a "promise of immortality."[54] Although the Roma have no geographical national territory in the sense that Smith defines a nation, the Romani rights movement does include advocates for forming a Romani nation. In response, Romani rights activists have created symbols to unify Roma and to legitimize their place in European politics and the world.[55] While none of the writers I discuss call for a specific Romani nation as a self-governing, territorially separate nation-state, they all strive for an ethnically communal voice. As German, Austrian, and Swiss

---

48  Gayatri Chakravorty Spivak, "Afterword," in *Imaginary Maps: Three Stories by Mahasweta Devi* (New York/London: Routledge, 1995), 200.
49  Ibid., 201.
50  Smith, *National Identity*, 21.
51  Ibid., 136.
52  Ibid., 137.
53  Ibid., 140.
54  Ibid., 161.
55  Silverman lists attributes of the Romani nation as "a unifying label (Roma), a singular narrative of Indian origin, the Holocaust as a symbol of oppression, a flag, a literary language, and an anthem," and rightly sees these symbols as common European national tropes (*Romani Routes*, 48).

citizens, they have lived in nations whose most significant features are literacy, a strong literary history, and universal education. They feel strong allegiances to the countries in which they live and do not want to be perceived as "Ausländer" ("foreigners"), a term with derogatory connotations. Instead, they want to weave their life stories and literature into the dominant discourse.

Writing and publishing, however, have not come easy for Romani writers, not because of insufficient skills or desires, but rather historical, political, and social suppression. Centuries of silencing have wrought much harm. Many writers needed encouragement even to begin to tell their stories, and then required help writing, editing, and publishing. Narrations by Ceija, Karl, and Mongo Stojka, for example, all had the assistance of editors who listened to narrated stories and helped write them down.[56] Mišo Nikolić's two books resulted from workshops at the Amerlinghaus in Vienna.[57] Stories in the collections *Fern von uns im Traum* and *Der Rom und der Teufel* comprised part of Mozes Heinschink's oral history project, whereby he and co-workers taped and transcribed tales.[58] Lily van Angeren-Franz received help from Henny Clemens, Dick Berts, and Hans-Dieter Schmid in publishing her orally recounted memoir.[59] Ulrich Enzensberger assisted Otto Rosenberg in writing *Das Brennglas*.[60] Karin Guth used conversations with Walter Winter to render his biography and publish it with his permission.[61]

---

56  Ceija Stojka, *Verborgenen*; Ceija Stojka, *Reisende auf dieser Welt: Aus dem Leben einer Rom-Zigeunerin* (Vienna: Picus, 1992); Karl Stojka, *Nach der Kindheit im KZ kamen die Bilder*, ed. Gerald Grassl (Vienna: VIDO—Verein zur Information der Öffentlichkeit zu Kunst, Wissenschaft und Kulturpolitik, 1992); Karl Stojka and Reinhard Pohanka, *Auf der ganzen Welt zu Hause: Das Leben und Wandern des Zigeuners Karl Stojka* (Vienna: Picus, 1994); and Mongo Stojka, *Papierene Kinder: Glück, Zerstörung und Neubeginn einer Roma-Familie in Österreich* (Vienna: Molden, 2000).
57  Mišo Nikolić, *Landfahrer: Auf den Wegen eines Rom* (Klagenfurt: Drava, 2000); Mišo Nikolić, *... und dann zogen wir weiter: Lebenslinien einer Romafamilie*, mit einem Vorwort von Mariella Mehr (Klagenfurt: Drava Verlag, 1997).
58  *Fern von uns im Traum ... /Te na dikas sunende ... : Märchen, Erzählungen und Lieder der Lovara./Lovarenge paramiči, tertenetura taj gjila*, eds Petra Cech et al. (Klagenfurt: Drava, 2001).
59  Lily van Angeren-Franz, *Lily: Das Leben der Sintizza Lily van Angeren-Franz von ihr selbst erzählt aufgezeichnet von Henny Clemens und Dick Berts."Polizeilich zwangsentführt,"* ed. Hans-Dieter Schmid, Quellen und Dokumentationen zur Stadtgeschichte Hildesheims, ed. Herbert Reyer, Stadtarchiv Hildesheim, Bd. 15, trans. Martina den Hertog-Vogt (Hildesheim: Verlag Gebrüder Gerstenberg, 2004).
60  Otto Rosenberg, *Das Brennglas*. Aufgezeichnet von Ulrich Enzensberger mit einem Vorwort von Klaus Schütz (Munich: Knaur, 1998; 2002).
61  Walter Winter, *Z 3105: Der Sinto Walter Winter überlebt den Holocaust*, ed. Karin Guth (Hamburg: VSA-Verlag, 2009).

Given this assistance, some might ask whether the term "writers" applies to these Roma. Their own assertions about the writing, editing, and publishing processes, however, prove they are self-determined, self-directed, and self-aware about their roles as writers. The increase in Roma's published works has not happened by chance. Writers have reflected on and then realized that shared cultural memories would dissolve if not captured quickly, and concerted dedication to preserving their voices in written form was imperative. A continuing thread in their writings has been propagation of cultural artifacts—recipes, legends, memories of happy and sad times, oral tales, descriptions of nature, songs, melodies, autobiographical accounts, fictional stories—to pass from one generation to the next.

In light of Roma's complicated oral history, publication of such artifacts makes messages more powerful and the writing process more deliberate. While Romany is historically considered an oral language, and thus non-Roma have often considered Roma illiterate, recent research indicates some Roma in earlier centuries did write in German. Breger points out the increasing number of historical, regional studies documenting written records in the German principalities in the eighteenth and nineteenth centuries.[62] Although such documents are spurious, they demonstrate ways in which Roma expressed themselves and learned the written German language. Other evidence demonstrates that the largely oral culture of Roma may not have been an ahistorical phenomenon, but rather a product of a socialization process and of a politics of persecution that aristocratic governments carried out in the late seventeenth and early eighteenth centuries.[63] Documents from this time show how Roma attempted through written letters and petitions to struggle against their ostracism. They explicitly ask to be included in important aspects of the dominant culture, and especially to participate in the military.[64]

---

62  Cited in Barbara Danckwortt, "Franz Mettbach—Die Konsequenzen der preußischen 'Zigeunerpolitik' für die Sinti von Friedrichslohra," in *Historische Rassismusforschung. Ideologen—Täter—Opfer. Mit einer Einleitung von Wolfgang Wippermann*, ed. Barbara Danckwortt, Thorsten Querg, und Claudia Schöningh (Hamburg: Argument, 1995), 273. Toninato shows how Roma were aware of the existence and power of writing from their earliest appearances in Europe, as evidenced by their use of "letters of protection" (*Romani Writing*, 7–24). Toninato also explores Romani non-alphabetic writing, such as trail signs and graphic codes, and their mixture of oral and written modes of communication (*Romani Writing*, 42–68).

63  Thomas Fricke, *Zigeuner im Zeitalter des Absolutismus. Bilanz einer einseitigen Überlieferung. Eine sozialgeschichtliche Untersuchung anhand südwestdeutscher Quellen* (Pfaffenweiler: Centaurus, 1996); and Ulrich F. Opfermann, *"Dass sie den Zigeuner-Habit ablegen." Die Geschichte der "Zigeuner-Kolonien" zwischen Wittgenstein und Westerwald* (Frankfurt a. M.: Peter Lang, 1996).

64  Breger, *Ortlosigkeit*, 7 n. 18.

Justifications, Theories, and Methodologies 27

Such documentation of attempted communication, however, represents an anomaly in the long history of Roma in German-speaking areas, with horrific Nazi persecution immeasurably magnifying fears, resentment, and humiliation, thereby hampering expression. Ceija Stojka admits the mistrust that biased studies such as those by Eva Justin—assistant to racial scientist Robert Ritter in examining Romani children for the Nazis—have bred among Roma.[65] The overwhelming anxiety of Roma to tell their stories compels one to ask less about why German-speaking Roma did not publish much before the 1990s, and more about what motivated them to begin writing at all. Multiple instigators have prevailed. Hübschmannová, writing in 1991, suggests two reasons for the increase in Romani writers in general in Europe at that time.[66] The first points to developing educational opportunities, and the second to a burgeoning desire to overcome the sudden political and social isolation that many Roma were experiencing, especially related to the Eastern Bloc's collapse. Margita Reiznerová, born in 1945, at the time Chair of the Association of Romani writers, states: "I feel so lonely, imprisoned in the modern town quarter, with no Roms to talk with, that I have to write to avoid becoming mad."[67] Reiznerová claimed to be writing to reach out to other Roma, but her actions also educated non-Roma. Otto Rosenberg attributed his willingness to tell his story to the lapse of time since his internment in Auschwitz, which created a necessary emotional distance. Rosenberg felt he was telling his story as part of a larger one about the persecution of his family and Roma as "his people" ("seine Menschen").[68] His motivations thus echoed Ceija Stojka's adage that "together we are strong" and Reiznerová's desire to unite with other Roma. Walter Winter presented another perspective: Roma had not chosen silence; rather, they had been unable to talk about their experiences due to mistrust, fear, anguish, and humiliation. Even more significantly, no one ever asked or seemed interested in Roma's stories.[69] Winter also feared that survivors of the Nazi era were dying out, and with them their witness accounts. Ceija Stojka, when talking about why she published her stories about Auschwitz, stressed the need to counter beliefs that Auschwitz did not exist. She also wanted to pass down stories to her own children and to their children's children, continually educating them about their history.[70]

---

65  Ceija Stojka, "Unsere Seele," 315–16. See Illustration 3 for a picture of Eva Ritter at a Viennese camp, possibly Wanko-G'stätten, where the Stojkas often camped.
66  Milena Hübschmannová, "Birth of Romani Literature in Czechoslovakia. Social and Political Background," *Cahiers de Littérature Orale*, 30 (1991): 95.
67  Reiznerová, 95; cited in Hübschmannová, 95.
68  Otto Rosenberg, *Brennglas*, 108.
69  Winter, *Z 3105*, 85.
70  Ceija Stojka, "Unsere Seele," 309.

Illustration 3: Vienna Collection Camp (possibly Wanko) with Eva Ritter. Photo reprinted with permission from the Bundesarchiv in Berlin.

Roma choosing to publish thus coincides with social action, a theory that Carolyn R. Miller advocates. The autobiographical genre becomes important as a life story and a significant medium to "encode or reinforce particular values in ways that may shape culture and history."[71] Further, personal narratives and literary writings become part of what Anthony Smith calls "ethno-histories," having the primary function "to provide a satisfying answer to the problem of personal oblivion."[72] Literature—like other forms of art, ceremonies, and symbols—creates an arena "in which individual identity is most closely bound up with collective identity."[73] Autobiographies and literary writings invoke memories and collective stories while promising immortality. Thus, at the same time as I wish to promulgate Roma writings for political and social reasons, I also stress their aesthetic value in lending insights into how, why, and what we read. Autobiographical and fictional literature such as Gajarawala's book on Indian Dalit—"untouchable caste," a subaltern group not unlike Roma in their equally marginalized positions—also provides a theoretical model with which to view intersections of

---

71  Carolyn R. Miller, "Genre as Social Action," *Genre and the New Rhetoric*, eds Aviva Freedman and Peter Medway (London: Taylor and Francis, 1984), 29–30.
72  Smith, *National Identity*, 160.
73  Ibid., 162.

politics, history, and aesthetics occurring in Roma's writing. In Dalit literature, Gajarawala sees "a movement that claims to represent in its protagonists a collectivity, while insisting at the same time on their own radical individualism, as well as a movement that derives legitimacy from historical specificity while asserting a kind of posthistorical consciousness."[74] Dalit life-writing exists "at the intersection of the individual and communitarian" and complexly articulates a "'Dalit personhood,' one that overlaps with the testimonials, political participation, and the demand for human rights."[75] Analysis of Roma's writings will reveal differences between the two groups' narratives, the main one being Dalits' conception of narrative time as "non-national, nonhistorical, event-driven, and most importantly, *nonhistoricist.*"[76] In contrast, Roma adamantly conceptualize nation and history—and their exclusion from and desired inclusion in such—to present new paradigms for their individual and collective identities. Still, Gajarawala's emphasis on Dalit literature as introducing new questions, new vocabulary, new ways to look at the "quotidian," and new types of realism in the realms of "the folk, the vernacular, and the oral"[77] finds echo in Roma literature.

Using personal narratives and literature as political, social, and aesthetic means to interpret cultures does not come without complications, however. Throughout my analysis I rely not only on published personal and fictitious works, but also on personal interviews and e-mail correspondences, especially with Ceija Stojka, Dotschy Reinhardt, and Mariella Mehr. Therefore, I am working both within and outside of Romani discourse, at once analyzing cultures from outside while presenting voices via personal assertions. The movement between these two spaces can be tricky, entailing a potential gap between personal statements and truth. All narratives—whether written or oral—can stand as examples of self-fashioning. Contradictions may surface in writers' observations, either in their own autobiographies, or between autobiographies by different writers, or between published statements and those asserted in private interviews. Readers encounter elements found in many autobiographies, including inadequate information, contradictions, fluidity of identity, selective memory, multiple discourses, and experiences mediated through language and memory.[78] For Roma—having faced not only a history of suppression but also

---

74   Toral Jatin Gajarawala, *Untouchable Fictions: Literary Realism and the Crisis of Caste* (New York: Fordham University Press, 2013), 171.
75   Ibid., 178.
76   Ibid., 173.
77   Ibid., 200.
78   Sidonie Smith and Julia Watson, *Reading Autobiography: A Guide for Interpreting Life Narratives*, 2nd edn (Minneapolis and London: University of Minnesota Press, 2001; 2010).

continued threats of silencing—literature might, indeed, provide a shield for such battles. Writing about trauma can cause varying renditions of the same story, as evident in the three Stojka siblings' autobiographies. In fairy tales and folk tales, reality and magic often stand side by side as indicators of how literature can mask fantasies. Mariella Mehr recognizes the slippery slope between autobiography and fiction when she describes her works in an interview: "The emotions are autobiographical, the story is fictional."[79] Such assertions warn literary scholars to exercise caution when interpreting any statement as truth or fact.

Ambiguities and discrepancies signal cultural negotiations and demand "situated knowledge" and subjective positioning that contrasts with positivist epistemology.[80] Distant, "objective" knowledge is virtually impossible due to our subjective positioning. Researchers, no matter the field, are always "in the belly of the monster."[81] Consequently, I read personal narratives and literature not necessarily to find truth or facts, but rather to afford insights into Roma's lives from their perspectives, telling readers "as much about the Roma's own hierarchy of values and what mattered most to them."[82] Such readings show an "acknowledgement of multiple views" that postmodernism has incited.[83] Fieldwork and ethnographies remain viable tools for garnering Romani perspectives, but analysis of all kinds of texts becomes key to accessing necessary multiple views and cultural diversity, which all these writers emphasize. As a literary scholar who has learned much from historians, anthropologists, sociologists, and political scientists, I wish to respect what I read and hear as a researcher, interpret within the space of my own "situated knowledge," and then, in turn, write a story of which I am then part.[84]

## What Theoretical Background Helps Contextualize the Interconnection Between Ethnicity and Gender?

The first purpose of my book—to promulgate the voices of many diverse Roma who have published autobiographical and literary

---

79 Katharina Döbler, "Nachwort," in Mariella Mehr, *Daskind* (Zürich and Frauenfeld: Nagel & Kimche, 1995; Berlin: Ullstein, 1997), 232.
80 Donna Jeanne Haraway, *Simians, Cyborgs, and Women: The Reinvention of Nature* (London: Free Association Books, 1991), 188.
81 Ibid.
82 Knesebeck, *Roma Struggle*, 52.
83 Silverman, *Romani Routes*, 15.
84 I am indebted to Angela Kóczé for her reflections on "situated knowledge": "Gender, Ethnicity and Class: Romani Women's Political Activism and Social Struggles" (PhD Dissertation, Central European University, Budapest, Hungary, 2011): 13. www.etd.ceu.hu/2012/sphkoc01.pdf

works in the German-speaking world—stems largely from Western feminist debates of the past 40 years concerning the intersection of ethnicity and gender. Feminist activists of color have been moving forces behind a "coming to voice," with the notion of "voice" serving as "a metaphor for speaking the formerly unspeakable, a thematics of speech and silence."[85] Originally, feminists' "coming to voice" meant expressing a nascent subjectivity previously repressed by unequal gender relationships. Talking about lived experiences and offering socially unsanctioned critique eventually motivated marginalized groups to publicize incidents of injustice, oppression, and human rights violations through life writings. While "coming to voice" may seem empowering, however, inherent risks also exist, including possible public condemnation, ostracism, or threats to family members.[86] Writers might also face retraumatization, shame of public exposure, and disappointment at finding apathetic readership. Conflicting sentiments of empowerment and risk are apparent in Roma voices.

Audre Lorde and bell hooks, two African-American writers and scholars, were pioneers in encouraging women of diverse ethnicities and cultural heritages to speak out against oppression. Both women have inspired countless international "women of color" to "voice" their observations and critiques, thereby creating an array of literary texts too numerous to list here. Both women lived through the early stages of the American feminist movement in the 1970s and observed how Caucasian, middle-class, heterosexual, educated women spoke in wide-sweeping generalizations on behalf of "all women" with little regard for historical and social contexts dividing women by race, ethnicity, and class.[87] Lorde and hooks have sought positive, constructive solutions to these divisions and stressed that feminism needs to include more writings by "women of color" in scholarship and the classroom. Both have emphasized the necessity for Caucasian women and men in particular to study and teach literature by women of color and thereby engage everybody as allies in the struggle against oppression.[88] They have believed that feminist theorists who insist on rights also have the responsibility to provide the conditions for

---

85   Smith and Watson, *Reading Autobiography*, 84.
86   Ibid., 85.
87   Audre Lorde, "The Master's Tools Will Never Dismantle the Master's House," in *Sister Outsider: Essays and Speeches* (Freedom, CA: The Crossing Press, 1984), 110–13.
88   Audre Lorde, "Age, Race, Class, and Sex: Women Redefining Difference," in *Sister Outsider: Essays and Speeches* (Freedom, CA: The Crossing Press, 1984), 114–23.

those rights.⁸⁹ Practice has to accompany theory when advocating for visibility of oppressed voices. Welcoming, and not solely "advocating the mere tolerance of difference between women," was key for Lorde, as she entreated activists to focus on women's many differences.⁹⁰ Likewise, hooks has argued for equal yet different voices in the feminist movement. She has focused more on building up what feminists had already accomplished and less on stressing the work that remained.⁹¹

Lauding the accomplishments of women of color, Lorde highly influenced the Afro-German women's movement in the early 1980s, provoking a larger discussion on the relationship between ethnicity and gender in German-speaking countries.⁹² In Spring 1984, Lorde led a seminar at the Free University in Berlin, inspiring the first collection of essays, poems, scholarly treatises, interviews, and autobiographical stories by Afro-German women, *Farbe bekennen*.⁹³ The authors identified numerous discriminatory practices, prejudices, and stereotypes in workplace and everyday interactions, including situations when Caucasian Germans met Afro-Germans for the first time and, basing their opinions of Afro-Germans purely on skin color, expressed surprise that the Afro-German were really Germans and could speak German. While many male Afro-Germans shared these problems, Afro-German women identified other concerns, placing them in "multiple jeopardy."⁹⁴ Many witnessed firsthand the difficulty of breaking down stereotypical portrayals of them solely as erotic and exotic creatures, thereby ignoring their intellectual capacities. As with Afro-Americans, Afro-Germans also felt somewhat betrayed by Caucasian feminists who often spoke on behalf of all women with little regard for the specific concerns of women of color. Given Nazi doctrine—whereby biology became destiny—Afro-German women wanted to focus on individual histories and not risk essentializing women under one rubrik. While many Black feminists' efforts in

---

89    Rosemarie Putnam Tong, *Feminist Thought: A More Comprehensive Introduction*, 3rd edn (Boulder: Westview Press, 2009), 231.
90    Lorde, "The Master's Tools," 111.
91    hooks, bell. *Feminism is for Everybody: Passionate Politics* (Cambridge, MA: South End Press, 2000), 59–60.
92    Jennifer Michaels, "The Impact of Audre Lorde's Politics and Poetics on Afro-German Women Writers," *German Studies Review*, 29.1 (February 2006): 22–40. Dagmar Schultz, *Audre Lorde: The Berlin Years 1984–1992* (New York: Third World Newsreel, 2012), DVD.
93    *Farbe bekennen: Afro-deutsche Frauen auf den Spuren ihrer Geschichte*, eds Audre Lorde et al. (Berlin: Orlando Verlag, 1986).
94    Deborah King, "Multiple Jeopardy: The Context of a Black Feminist Ideology," *Feminist Frameworks*, 3rd edn, eds Alison M. Jaggar and Paula S. Rothenberg (New York: McGraw-Hill, 1993).

the US and Germany emphasized legal equality, most struggled to combat sameness and value difference. Margaret Wright expressed this sentiment cogently: "In black women's liberation we don't want to be equal with men, just like in black liberation we're not fighting to be equal with the white man. We're fighting for the right to be different and not be punished for it."[95] Equality did not mean homogeneity. Acknowledging that racism and violence affected women and men, however, many Afro-American feminists welcomed men into the movement and considered their perspectives on equality.[96] Likewise, I have consciously included male Roma voices for their valuable views on gender roles. As will continually resurface in autobiographies, neither males nor females have wanted their voices standing as sole representatives of Romani culture.

Romani writers in my study have never referred to Afro-American or Afro-German texts, theories, or political actions, and yet these marginalized groups share many historical and theoretical concerns.[97] The designation "women of color" for Romani women also seems appropriate. In what are historically predominantly Caucasian cultures, Roma have often been singled out as people with darker hair, eyes, and complexions. Searching for identities, exploring histories, and forming communities have become main theoretical concerns for Roma and other people of color, between whom Lorde wished for a worldwide connection.[98]

Jews comprise another major group whose history—at least in Europe—mirrors that of Roma; at times I compare the two groups when talking about confrontations with racism, colonialism, class oppression, fascism, and anti-Semitism in German-speaking countries.

---

95   Margaret Wright, "I Want the Right to Be Black and Me," in *Black Women in White America*, ed. Gerda Lerner (New York: Pantheon Books, 1972), 608.
96   hooks, for example, praises what she sees as advanced feminist thinking that was not "anti-male," but rather "anti-sexist" and developed forms of "alternative masculinity" (*Feminism is for Everybody*, 67).
97   Tebbutt finds parallels between the treatment of Blacks by Whites and that of Roma by non-Roma (*Sinti and Roma*, 129). Roma involved in the project "Decade of the Roma 2005–2015" display interest in connecting European Roma's challenges with the struggle of African-Americans, although not focusing on gender: Adna Karamehic-Oates, "European Roma Learn from African American Rights Struggle," *Open Society Foundation* http://blog.soros.org/2010/06/european-roma-learn-from-african-american-rights-struggle/. Kóczé expresses her indebtedness to Black feminist criticism and literature for her research on Hungarian Romani women's political activism and social struggles ("Gender," 121–2). Silverman points to Romani musicians infusing African-American rap styles into their music (*Romani Routes*, 26).
98   Audre Lorde, "Apartheid U.S.A.," in *A Burst of Light: Essays by Audre Lorde* (Ithaca, NY: Firebrand Books, 1988), 30.

Roma often refer to interactions with Jews when discussing assimilation, integration, racism, genocide, ethnic identity, compensation for wrongdoings, and restitution for losses. As with Roma, Jews have had to live with the uncanny myth of being perpetually nomadic—with the image of "the Wandering Jew"—since 70 AD when Romans destroyed the Second Temple in Jerusalem. The Jewish diaspora scattered them all over the world, but the majority have been sedentary for centuries. Despite the "homes" that some Jewish people eventually found throughout Europe, they have never been considered "at home" there, just as Roma have been everywhere and nowhere. Jewish identity, like that of Roma, has been both self-constructed and imposed. Centuries of persecution and the devastating effects of the Nazi's racial oppression have forced identity constructions. Roma and Jews in German-speaking countries have shared questions and concerns related to assimilation and integration into their "host" countries.

Differences between the two groups, however, exist. First, Jews as a people aspired to returning to a specific geographic homeland, namely Jerusalem, whereas Roma have never aspired to return to India. Jews in diaspora perpetuated an image of Jerusalem based on the time before Roman destruction, and, "throughout the Exile, it was this image that kept the nation from disappearing."[99] As controversial as Israel has been as a "homeland" for Jews, Israel is nevertheless now a reality. Whereas the Jews have a geographical territory as a nation-state, Roma do not. Second, unlike Roma, Jews had strong, influential spokespeople and lobbying groups attempting to lead people towards specific goals. Through the Zionist movement in the late nineteenth century, the idea of a nation swelled into reality after Nazi persecution. Strong organizations for Jews, or lack thereof for Roma, influenced battles over post-war compensation. Romani struggles to prove their persecution was racially motivated have been at times very different from Jewish experiences. A third, and perhaps most significant, difference for my study concerns the presence of the written word in both cultures. Although Jewish early history is largely oral, Jews immortalized cultural practices and versions of their history in writing through the Talmud and the Torah. Stories form a large part of both groups' collective identities, but the written textual aspect of Jewish heritage engendered a significant difference by connecting the peoples, no matter where they were. As Cohen states: "… the Jews became a meta-people. They lived not in the world, but in their stories about the world. They lived in a text."[100] The Talmud and the Torah have been

---

99  Rich Cohen, *Israel is Real: An Obsessive Quest to Understand the Jewish Nation and its History* (New York: Farrar, Straus and Giroux, 2009), 85.
100  Ibid., 74.

bonding tools in travel and exile, telling stories of exiles, battles, persecutions, and travels; and enumerating purity laws around food and the body. Having these written documents has standardized histories and practices. In contrast, Romani writers' texts are new phenomena.

Developing an aesthetic answer to systematic discrimination, as Romani writers, women of color, and Jews have been doing, involves addressing questions about identity representation and politics. Marginalized groups have discovered they must specify common characteristics to unify them and create solidarity. Concurrently, they must emphasize diversity among themselves to combat stereotypes. In this balancing act they walk the fine line between essentializing and dispersing their collective identity. While critiquing essentialism, hooks writes about this necessity to develop a consistent core identity.[101] Thus, writers of marginalized groups—Roma included—must often employ "*strategic* use of positivist essentialism" to maintain some traits they see imperative to their survival.[102] Some Roma prefer to use the term "Zigeuner" or "Gypsy," for example, despite these words' pejorative and historically false connotations, because these terms and the images many non-Roma associate with them often carry more marketable weight for publication. Images of carefree, wandering bands of musicians emerge at times in Roma's writings, only to be counteracted by discriminatory and persecuting situations, creating constant paradoxes and ambiguities. Those same writings, however, as well as theories about marginalized writers, remind readers never to ignore the material conditions and history influencing aesthetic representation.

The pathbreaking theories on racism and sexism in the 1970s and 1980s paved the way for theories of intersectionality—a term Kimberlé Crenshaw coined in 1991—that also apply to Roma.[103] In trying to comprehend the nature of violence against women, Crenshaw questioned the narrow studies focusing only on gender. Instead, she believed race, class, and gender all affected women's status. Scholars advocating intersectional methodologies—mostly sociologists—began investigating how social problems, knowledge, and power intertwined with sexism and racism. Co-constituted factors also included ethnicity, physical ability, age, and sexuality. Comprehending the relationship

---

101 bell hooks, *Yearning: Race, Gender, and Cultural Politics* (Boston: South End, 1990), 130.
102 Gayatri Chakravorty Spivak, "Subaltern Studies: Deconstructing Historiography," in *Selected Subaltern Studies*, eds Ranajit Guha and Gayatri Chakravorty Spivak (Oxford: Oxford University Press, 1988), 13.
103 Kimberlé Crenshaw, "Mapping the Margins: Intersectionality, Identity Politics, and Violence against Women of Color," *Stanford Law Review*, 43.6 (1991): 1241–99.

between these entities moves the discussion beyond mere analysis to engagement with projects fostering social justice.[104] Intersectionality theories developed into critical social practice that set out to "create a holistic approach to the eradication of disparities."[105] That approach involved working with schools, prisons, and crisis centers to place into praxis the theories pointing to the roots of social injustices.

In exploring Roma voices, the argument that racism and sexism are co-constituted into social problems that in turn become catalyzed by knowledge and power relations demands investigation into both gender and ethnicity. Two main goals that scholars outline for intersectionality relate to my project: "1) Placing the lived experiences and struggles of people of color and other marginalized groups as a starting point for the development of theory; and 2) Exploring the complexities not only of individual identities but also group identity, recognizing that variations within groups are often ignored and essentialized."[106] Writings bring to life lived experiences and struggles. Through publishing, Roma foreground individuals, whether autobiographical or fictional, who collectively depict diversity.

Researchers of intersectionality are now working in the fields of sociology, legal studies, political science, geography, psychology, economics, and post-colonial studies. Unfortunately, not all scholars of intersectionality deem personal narratives and literature as worthy of examination or as effective means to eradicate social inequalities. Wing—a proponent of investigating intersectionality between race, class, and gender in academic legal studies—recognizes the importance of using narratives as a methodological approach, and yet also points out the possible controversy surrounding such. She cites detractors who find personal narratives "nonlegal, lacking intellectual rigor, overly emotional, and subjective."[107] Instead, she states, legal documents, governmental policies, court reports—basically objective data written from a second party—can lend more insight into oppressive measures. Likewise, some intertextuality scholars have recently criticized what they see as a turn inward, or a shift "to the level of personal identity narratives," whereby emphasis on analysis of personal narratives reflects the shift "away from social structural analyses of social problems"

---

104 Patricia Hill Collins, *Black Feminist Thought: Knowledge, Consciousness, and the Politics of Empowerment* (New York: Routledge, 2000), ix.
105 Bonnie Thornton Dill and Ruth Enid Zambrana, "Critical Thinking about Inequality: An Emerging Lens," in *Emerging Intersections: Race, Class, and Gender in Theory, Policy, and Practice* (New Brunswick, NJ and London: Rutgers University Press, 2009), 5.
106 Ibid.
107 Adrien Katherine Wing, "Introduction," in *Critical Race Feminism: A Reader*, 2nd edn (New York and London: New York University Press, 2003), 6.

and away from discerning "how governmental social policies might address this intractable social problem."[108] Here, Patricia Hill Collins doubts that personal narratives and theories behind their significance as performances and texts have been harbingers of changes. She contrasts narrative formulations of self-identity with documentation of court proceedings, statistical analysis, and governmental reports, and thereby establishes a dichotomy between, on the one side, the writing and analysis of personal narratives and literature and, on the other side, social engagement.

This dichotomy is false. Roma in the German-speaking countries who have written about their own lives, the lives of families and friends, and shared cultural practices, historical events, and stories confront, and not reproduce, racism and sexism. Intersectionality calls for considering numerous diverse factors when investigating individuals' and groups' fluctuating identities. Therefore, examining the multifarious means to express those identities—autobiographical writing, oral storytelling, singing, performing, cooking, creating art—is necessary for a more complete image of an ethnic group with which to break the bonds that foment racism and sexism. The hesitations of Roma writers against even beginning to tell their personal stories exemplify the kind of social engagement that intersectionality promotes.

In fact, personal narratives and literary narratives have been the main ways that women in marginalized groups internationally have developed empowerment strategies similar to those "giving voice" to African-American women. Women in colonized countries or cultures have crafted some of the most constructive and powerful writings. Equally, some scholars have also applied the terms "colonialism" and "post-colonialism" to Roma's past and present situations.[109] With "colonialism" understood in a broader sense, not just in reference to a specific powerful nation or peoples acquiring domination over others, the term connotes continual exertion of economic, political, social, military, cultural, and linguistic power over those viewed as weaker and insignificant. The "colony" in such instances includes subaltern peoples whom the colonizers feel require suppression. "Colonialism" becomes "a way of maintaining asymmetrical relations of economic and political power."[110] To these powers I would add cultural, literary, and linguistic. In comparing Roma with colonized peoples, I rely on post-colonial theory to analyze Roma's writings. Regarding intersections of ethnicity and gender, Spivak's urgings to give voice to the subaltern again prove useful as post-colonial theoretical backdrops. In

---

108   Collins, *Black Feminist Thought*, ix.
109   Kóczé, "Gender," 34.
110   Ibid.

"Can the Subaltern Speak?" Spivak undertakes a Derridean reading of the colonial discourses enveloping the practice of suttee—widow sacrifice in India.[111] While Spivak states that she does not advocate the killing of widows, she sees the need to examine the act in its social, historical, and economic context to understand the sacrifice as grounded in superstition and not in crime. Created in a context without a space for the sexed subaltern to speak and at a site of enforced public silence, such acts can serve as possible gestures of free will and freedom. Spivak's call for contextualizing cultural practices proves significant for examining Roma's perceptions about gender. Unlike Spivak's grim example of the suttee's self-immolation as one way the subaltern might speak, however, Roma voices present more constructive, positive methods of expression.

Bhabha refers to those who do not fit into any set national mold as "colonials, post-colonials, migrants, minorities—wandering peoples who will not be contained with the *Heim* of the national culture and its unisonant discourses but are themselves the marks of a shifting boundary that alienated the frontiers of the modern nation."[112] These identity fluctuations create a cultural hybridity allowing many cultures to mix and flow into each other. In response to systems of power, Roma defy categorization by nationhood and thereby develop strategies to move easily between cultures and nations. One must not, however, be too quick in applying Bhabha's hybridity concept to Roma. Silverman presents a cogently nuanced discussion of hybridity theories in relation to Romani music. In general, scholars have positively espoused hybridity as challenging "Eurocentric master narrative, homogenization of ethnic identities, and the assumption that nations are composed of singular nationalities."[113] Citing various scholars, Silverman raises three major critiques against this celebratory concept of hybridity. First, she states: "Hybridity is now so fashionable and applied to so many situations that it has begun to lose its specificity."[114] The second questions the concept's abstractness and potential for "losing sight of precisely the material realities that inform the imaginary."[115] The third is that the theory of hybridity "takes on a life of its own in identity discourse and loses political mooring."[116] In marketing Romani music, hybridity becomes a catchword to sell concerts and albums, a "Disney version of

---

111 Gayatri Chakravorty Spivak, "Can the Subaltern Speak?" in *Marxism and the Interpretation of Culture*, eds Cary Nelson and Lawrence Grossberg (Urbana and Chicago: University of Illinois Press, 1988).
112 Homi Bhabha, *Nation and Narration* (London: Routledge, 1994), 15.
113 Silverman, *Romani Routes*, 42.
114 Ibid.
115 Ibid., 43.
116 Ibid.

multiculturalism: watered down, safe, distant."¹¹⁷ In many ways, critics of hybridity echo intersectional theorists' critiques against personal narratives' potential to implement social change. Given complexities on both sides of the argument, Silverman chooses not to adopt an "either-or" stance on whether hybridity should be extolled or not. Instead, she advocates for "a focus on representation, performance, and aesthetics while still maintaining a solid connection to material conditions and history."¹¹⁸ In other words, the aesthetic hybridity that Romani musical performances display has not come without blood, sweat, and tears in historical, political, economic, or cultural realms.

The same is true for literature. Unlike Romani musical performances, however, which have grown in popularity, and which many musicians and producers hope will sustain them financially, the writings I analyze are not bestsellers, nor did the writers intend them to be. While Roma's writings connect historical, economic, social, and literary factors, marketing the texts does not have as high stakes as with musical performances. With writing being more divorced from economic sustainability, writers might be able to take more risks. Therefore, valorizing hybridity as an aesthetic strategy possessing radical potential to reject stereotypes and classifications by colonizing powers seems appropriate for Romani writings. At the same time, hybridity as a theoretical model for understanding historical and social backgrounds might at times be misleading. Reacting to the state of "culture's in-between" that Bhabha sets up with his essay by that name,¹¹⁹ Adelson questions notions of hybridity for portraying cultures as possibly somehow eternally stuck in the middle, flanked by two static cultures with immutable characteristics.¹²⁰ Roma do not stand merely "between" cultures. Just as threads of solidarity and continuity are thick in Roma writings, so, too, are those of cultural transistions, fluctuations, and flexibility. Thus, an approach employing theoretical models related to feminism, women of color, intersectionality, postcolonialism, and hybridity as they apply to each individual writer's topics seem most appropriate. Ultimately, however, letting the writers speak for themselves becomes imperative.

---

117 Ibid., 45.
118 Ibid., 46–7.
119 Homi K. Bhabha, "Culture's In-Between," in *Questions of Cultural Identity*, eds Stuart Hall and Paul Du Gay (London, Thousand Oaks and New Delhi: Sage Publications, 1996), 53–60.
120 Leslie Adelson, "Against Between: A Manifesto," in *Unpacking Europe: Towards a Critical Reading*, eds Iftikar Dadi and Salah Hassan (Rotterdam: NAi Publishers, 2002), 244–55.

## Two "I am eternally proud to be a Gypsy": Roma Voicing Ethnicity

Ethnic identity is a dynamic process of formation and reformation, where, in the words of historian Robin D. G. Kelley, "the identities that you cling to are within the context of other people making identities and imposing them on you."[1] A historical outline will demonstrate how dominant groups in Germany, Austria, and Switzerland forced and manipulated Romani identity through discriminatory practices from the fifteenth century to the rise of Nazi power in the 1930s. In the absence of Romani voices, I have to base my account until the early twentieth century on chronicles by non-Roma.[2] Beginning with the generation born in the 1920s, autobiographers provide perceptions on their ethnicity in relationship to non-Roma. Writers reference discriminatory laws that ultimately led to ethnic construction. Policies and doctrines forced migration, forged language barriers, enforced illiteracy, produced segregation, fostered marginalization,

---

1  Robin D. G. Kelley, "Interview with Robin D.G. Kelley. Edited Transcript," California Newsreel, 2003. http://www.pbs.org/race/000_About/002_04-background-02-05.htm
2  My overview of the history of Roma before 1933 relies on detailed accounts by Fraser (*Gypsies*); Reimar Gilsenbach, *Weltchronik der Zigeuner. 2500 Ereignisse aus der Geschichte der Roma und Sinti, der Luri, Zott und Boza, der Athinganer, Tattern, Heiden und Sarazenen, der Bohémiens, Gypsies und Gitanos und aller Minderheiten, die "Zigeuner" genannt werden*, vol. I: Von den Anfängen bis 1599. Studien zur Tsiganologie und Folkloristik 10 (Frankfurt a.M.: Peter Lang, 1994); Reimer Gronemeyer, ed., *Zigeuner im Spiegel früher Chroniken und Abhandlungen. Quellen vom 15. bis zum 18. Jahrhundert* (Gießen: Focus, 1987); Joachim Hohmann, *Zigeuner und Zigeunerwissenschaft: Ein Beitrag zur Grundlagenforschung und Dokumentation des Völkermords im "Dritten Reich"* (Marburg/Lahn: Guttandin & Hoppe), 1980; Margalit, *Gypsies*; Claudia Mayerhofer, *Dorfzigeuner: Kultur und Geschichte der Burgenland-Roma von der ersten Republik bis zur Gegenwart* (Vienna: Picus, 1987); Reemtsma, *Sinti und Roma*; and Tebbutt, *Sinti and Roma*.

and thereby imposed identities on Roma. Roma reformulate those impositions in constructing an ethnic identity that is at once constant to maintain internal solidarity and fluctuating to meet external demands.

My analysis relies on autobiographies by Lily van Angeren-Franz, Philomena Franz, Ewald Hanstein, Anna Mettbach, Mišo Nikolić, Otto Rosenberg, Ceija Stojka, Karl Stojka, and Mongo Stojka.[3] When necessary, I draw on narratives of Elisabeth Kreutz, Bernhard Steinbach, Hildegard Lagrenne, and Friedrich Kreutz;[4] Josef Muscha Müller's autobiography;[5] and Walter Winter's story.[6] While numerous other autobiographical accounts are now available in published form, I base my choice on similarities allowing for collective and comparative studies.[7] With a few exceptions, all autobiographers were born between

---

3  Angeren-Franz, *Leben*; Philomena Franz, *Zwischen Liebe und Haß: Ein Zigeunerleben* (Freiburg, Basel and Vienna: Herder, 1992); Ewald Hanstein, *Meine hundert Leben: Erinnerungen eines deutschen Sinto*, aufgezeichnet von Ralf Lorenzen, mit einem Geleitwort von Henning Scherf (Bremen: Donat Verlag, 2005); Anna Mettbach and Josef Behringer,*"Wer wird die nächste sein?" Die Leidensgeschichte einer Sintezza, die Auschwitz überlebte* (Frankfurt a.M.: Brandes & Apsel, 1999); Nikolić, *Landfahrer*; Nikolić, ... . *und dann zogen wir weiter: Lebenslinien einer Romafamilie*; Rosenberg, *Brennglas*; Ceija Stojka, *Verborgenen*; Karl Stojka, *Kindheit*; Stojka and Pohanka, *Auf der ganzen Welt*.

4  *"Da wollten wir frei sein!": Eine Sinti-Familie erzählt*, ed. Michail Krausnick. Mit Fotos aus dem Familienalbum, aus dem Bundesarchiv Koblenz und von Klaus Fark (Weinheim and Basel: Beltz Verlag, 1983).

5  Josef Muscha Müller, *"Und weinen darf ich auch nicht..." Ausgrenzung, Sterilisation, Deportation—Eine Kindheit in Deutschland* (Berlin: Parabolis, 2002).

6  Winter, *Z 3105*, 9.

7  When appropriate, I cite from other testimonies, including Krimhilde Malinowski, *Das Schweigen wird gebrochen: Erinnerungen einer Sintezza an den Nationalsozialismus*, ed. Norbert Aas (Bayreuth: Bumerang-Verlag, 2003); Lolo Reinhardt, *Überwintern: Jugenderinnerungen eines schwäbischen Zigeuners. Ergänzt von seiner Schwester Märza Winter. Mit einer Erzählung von Richard Scherer*, Monika Döppert, ed. (Gerlingen: Bleicher Verlag, 1999); Franz Rosenbach,*"Der Tod war mein ständiger Begleiter": Das Leben, das Überleben und das Weiterleben des Sinto Franz Rosenbach. Von ihm selbst erzählt und dokumentiert von Norbert Aas* (Munich: Bayerische Landeszentrale für politische Bildungsarbeit, 2005); Erich Renner, ed.,*"Und wir waren auch Naturmenschen": Der autobiographische Bericht des Sinti-Musikers und Geigenbauers Adolf Boko Winterstein und andere persönliche Dokumente von und über Sinti und Roma*, Studien zur Tsiganologie und Folkloristik, ed. Joachim S. Hohmann, 22 (Frankfurt a. M., Berlin, Bern, New York, Paris and Vienna: Peter Lang, 1997); and Anja Tuckermann,*"Denk nicht, wir bleiben hier!": Das Lebensgeschichte des Sinto Hugo Höllenreiner* (Munich and Vienna: Carl Hanser Verlag, 2005). Latscho Tschawo's autobiography is interesting for the period after World War II. He purposely chose not to talk about the two years he was in concentration camps as a boy, however: *Die Befreiung des Latscho Tschawo: Ein*

"I am eternally proud to be a Gypsy": Roma Voicing Ethnicity 43

1920 and 1940, and thus their works cover the oldest time periods about which German-speaking Roma have written. All published their autobiographies decades after World War II. All works appeared originally in German, with the exception of Angeren-Franz's autobiography, originally published in Dutch because she resided in Holland after the war. My selection encompasses as equal an amount of males (eight) and females (six) as possible.

Autobiographers display a desire to relate stories about cultural values to demonstrate they survived Nazi persecution and can resist global homogeneity. After years of disgrace, many Roma have begun to see that they can openly express pride in their traditions, as Karl Stojka proclaims: "God made me a Gypsy in this world, and I thank God for that and will be eternally proud to be a Gypsy."[8] Bernhard Steinbach echoes these sentiments: "I am proud that I am a Sinto. That we have to deny our identity as Sinti and assimilate—that cannot be the right way. I am what I am. I am not allowed to deny that. I do not need to hide myself."[9] This pride inspires Roma to tell their stories and me to interpret them.

### Ethnicity: Theories and Definitions

In his study on the contemporary central European Romani movement, Vermeersch identifies three main scholarly conceptualizations of Romani ethnic identity.[10] While his readings of scholarly works are simplified, he outlines well the pitfalls awaiting researchers in developing a working definition of ethnicity and offers material to formulate a saleable description of Romani ethnicity. The first conceptualization sees Roma as one primarily diasporic group having common historical roots and migratory patterns. Proponents use mostly linguistical data to trace a direct linear route from the Punjab region of northwestern

---

*Sinto-Leben in Deutschland* (Bornheim-Merten: Lamuv Verlag, 1984), 10. These works, however, seem more ethnographical and biographical than autobiographical, and thus I use them mostly to corroborate the autobiographical writings I use. My selection, of course, is not meant to undermine the value of these works.

8   "Gott hat mich zu einem Zigeuner auf dieser Welt gemacht, und ich danke Gott dafür und werde ewig stolz sein, ein Zigeuner zu sein." Karl Stojka, *Kindheit*, 52.

9   "Ich bin so stolz darauf, daß ich Sinto bin. Daß wir unsere Indentität als Sinti verleugnen und uns anpassen—das kann nicht der richtige Weg sein. Was ich bin, das bin ich. Das darf ich doch nicht verleugnen. Ich brauch mich nicht zu verstecken." *"Da wollten wir frei sein,"* 70.

10  Peter Vermeersch, *The Romani Movement: Minority Politics and Ethnic Mobilization in Contemporary Central Europe* (New York and Oxford: Berghahn Books, 2006), 13–20.

India to Roma's arrival in Europe at the end of the thirteenth century.[11] Critics of this theory find the focus on diaspora neglects variances among Romani groups, exoticizes Roma by separating them from European history and culture, and overlooks the subgroups' own criteria for membership.[12]

Vermeersch's second conceptualization concentrates on shared characteristics in Romani lifestyles and behaviors. As examples, Hancock and Fraser refer to common cultural practices and interpretations of the world. Fraser cites criteria the Court of Appeal in England used in 1988, which determined "Travellers" were not a race, but an ethnic group with two major common characteristics: first, "a long shared history of which the group is conscious as distinguishing it from other groups, and the memory of which it keeps alive;" and second, "a cultural tradition of its own, including family and social customs and manners, often but not necessarily associated with religious observance."[13] Other characteristics helping to define an ethnic group include: "a common geographical origin, or descent from a number of common ancestors; a common language; a common literature peculiar to the group; a common religion different from that of the neighbouring groups or the general community; and being a minority or being an oppressed group within a larger community."[14] Not all these traits must exist in any one group. Fraser's definition corresponds to a "constructivism" theory of ethnicity, whereby exclusion can exert a large influence on establishing ethnicity as one group often defines itself by marginalizing another.[15] This second conceptualization's efforts to valorize the "Romani lifestyle" can potentially bring respect and understanding to Roma. Still, Vermeersch points to the risk of oversimplifying historical, political, and social conditions contributing to the "Romani lifestyle," and of perpetuating stereotypes of Roma as inherently nomadic, marginal, socially deviant, exotic, and primitive.

---

11  As examples, Vermeersch cites Ian Hancock, "The Eastern European Roots of Romani Nationalism," in Crowe and Kolsti, *The Gypsies of Eastern Europe*, 133–50; Fraser, *Gypsies*; and Donald Kenrick, "Romanies without a Road," *Contemporary Review*, 232 (1978): 153–6.
12  See Okely, *Traveller-Gypsies*, and Willems, *In Search*.
13  Fraser, *Gypsies*, 6; quoted from *Commission for Racial Equality v Dutton*, Court of Appeal, 1988.
14  Ibid.
15  See Fredrik Barth, ed., *Ethnic Groups and Boundaries. The Social Organisation of Culture Difference* (Boston: Little, Brown, 1969). For an overview of scholarship related to theoretical categories concerning "ethnicity" and "ethnic groups," see Wilfried Heller, "Zur Bedeutung von Ethnizität in Transformationsländern unter dem Einfluss von Globalisierung," in *Ethnizität in der Transformation*, eds Wilfried Heller et al. (Vienna and Berlin: LIT Verlag, 2006), 9–25.

"I am eternally proud to be a Gypsy": Roma Voicing Ethnicity 45

As with the diasporic conceptualization, "lifestyle" theories usually ignore Romani voices as self-identities. The third conceptualization stresses "biological kinship" and addresses genetic relationships among Roma. While this conceptualization is now decades old and not accepted among scholars, Vermeersch cites Hancock's 1992 essay describing "genetically related people."[16] Proponents imply Roma made their journey from India to Europe "intact," and thus with a preserved genetic make-up. Critics say the biological kinship model harkens back to theories of "primordialism," seeing ethnicity as a set of objective, essentialist, inborn characteristics such as blood relations, geographic territory, and values. Primordialism could lead to racial theories subscribing to the "one-drop rule," or the "hypo-descent rule" that Melvin Harris outlines, meaning that anyone with any known Roma "blood" type corresponding with Indian origins is Roma.[17] Determining genealogical "purity of blood" comes dangerously close to Third Reich methods of devising policies based on the degree of presumed biological ancestry.

Vermeersch proposes a fourth conceptualization, which he shares with Okely, Stewart, Guy, and Willems, and which is useful for my study. Romani identity is not "a matter of biology, lifestyle, descent, or any other group characteristic; but rather ... the product of classification struggles involving both classifiers and those classified as Roma."[18] As an example of how both non-Roma and Roma have constructed Romani identity, Vermeersch cites the process of arriving at the self-proscribed term "Roma." Roma, being dissatisfied with other group labels encompassing pejorative, romanitic, or exotic images—Gypsy, Zigeuner, Tsigane, cigán, cikán, cigány, and so forth—sought to create a more positive, even neutral connotation and to connect all groups culturally, socially, and politically. They defined their ethnicity in reaction to external labelling, a process building on Geertz's theory of "relative constructivism," where ethnicity is understood as largely constructed and not solely primordial.[19]

None the less, humans do frequently assign value to primordial characteristics vis-à-vis ethnicity because those characteristics form part of historical and social experiences. Again, at times those inside

---

16 Hancock, "Eastern European Roots," 134–5.
17 Melvin Harris, *Patterns of Race in the Americas* (New York: W.W. Norton, 1964). See Fraser for a description of blood types and gene frequencies and patterns researchers have discerned for Roma (*Gypsies*, 24).
18 Vermeersch, *Romani Movement*, 13.
19 Clifford Geertz, ed., *Old Societies and New States: The Quest for Modernity in Africa and Asia* (New York: The Free Press, 1967). I use Heller's term here, in German "relativierte konstruktivistische Ansätze" ("Bedeutung von Ethnizität," 18).

the group depend on what Spivak calls "*strategic* use of positivist essentialism" in order to reinforce solidarity and reach certain political or social gains; or they use characteristics with which others have defined the group.[20] Hence, people inside and outside the ethnic group remain in constant negotiation and renegotiation over self-defined and externally assigned characteristics. The boundaries that differentiate the ethnic group from the dominant group are continually in flux, and individual members of the ethnic group can carry multiple identities.

Geertz's attempt to reach a balanced view of ethnicity, however, makes it easy at times to conflate the terms "race" and "ethnicity." Kelley, for example, talks about race in the same way relative constructionists talk about ethnicity. His quote at the beginning of this chapter focuses on race fluidity and the constant negotiations occurring between one's selves and outside contexts. In the context of Roma, however, "ethnicity" could replace "race" in his quote. Several Romani autobiographers use words like "race" to identify Roma, frequently concording with the terms "tribe" and "clan," to connote a bonded group. The term "ethnicity," however, purposely avoids connections that the German word "Rasse" (race) has with the Nazi eugenics program. One can talk of Roma being racialized and suffering under racism, but scholars today do not talk of Roma solely as a "race." Kelley's definition of racism appropriately describes how an ethnicity can become racialized: "[Racisim] is not about how you look, it is about how people assign meaning to how you look."[21] The process of racialization occurs when one group defines what it sees are innate characteristics in another group without considering how that group would define itself.

Péter provides a case study showing the process of racialization as it affects Roma.[22] In conducting an empirical investigation of a small Romanian industrial town, he discovered how marginalization of workers there created an ethnicity from those living in extreme poverty with little chance of escape due to economical restructuring. Because their poverty caused them to be isolated from the "outside world," they assumed the undesirable label of being "Gypsies" and were thereby "racialized." Marginalization and racism continued to legitimize their poverty and blocked their way to scarce resources. Péter showed ethnic group formation did not result from a primordial, original cultural

---

20   Spivak, "Subaltern Studies," 13.
21   Kelley, "Interview," http://www.pbs.org/race/000_About/002_04-background-02-05.htm
22   László Péter, "How Extreme Marginalization Generates Ethnicity," ed. Wilfried Heller et al., *Ethnizität in der Transformation. Zur Situation nationaler Minderheiten in Rumänien*, Wiener Osteuropa Studien, 21 (Vienna and Berlin: LIT, 2006), 99–118.

"I am eternally proud to be a Gypsy": Roma Voicing Ethnicity 47

kinship traceable back to a shared past. Instead, social circumstances and interactions between the marginalized group and the "outside world" contributed to a dynamic process ultimately building the group's identity and any classification and labels attached to the group. Ultimately, ethnic construction became a result of what Péter referred to as a "classificatory struggle" between "*classifiers*—those who hold different kinds of power, especially economic—and the *classified*—those who lack any form of power."[23] Ethnic idenification comes to rely on the existence and recognition of group and nongroup identities. Sennett defines ethnic identity in a similar circuitous manner based on an "awareness of difference" and a "history of displacement."[24] Within this perpetual cycle, traits that social, economic, or political circumstances might have originally caused evolve into characteristics deemed "innate" racial ones.

The racialization of Roma occurred in tandem with developing national identities as *ethnies*, to rely again on Anthony Smith's term, coalescing around concepts of nation and belonging. Smith describes a dynamic process similar to those Kelley and Péter observe, whereby an *ethnie* contributes to defining itself at the same time that *ethnie* works within the confines of historical, political, and social factors involved in nation building. An ethnic group becomes "a type of cultural collectivity, one that emphasizes the role of myths of descent and historical memories, and that is recognized by one or more cultural difference like religion, customs, language or institutions."[25] He points out the common confusion between race and *ethnie*, with the latter "constituted, not by lines of physical descent, but by the sense of continuity, shared memory and collective destiny, i.e. by lines of cultural affinity embodied in distinctive myths, memories, symbols and values retained by a given cultural unit of population."[26] In contrast to nations, ethnic communities "need not be resident in 'their' territorial homeland. Their culture may not be public or common to all the members. They need not, and often do not, exhibit a common division of labor or economic unity. Nor need they have common legal codes with common rights and duties for all."[27] Indeed, German-speaking Roma possess neither a territorial homeland nor a nation state with governing legal codes, but their subgroups have lived in nations since their inception. Possessing

---

23   Ibid., 102.
24   Richard Sennett, "The Rhetoric of Ethnic Identity," in *The Ends of Rhetoric: History, Theory, Practice*, eds John Bender und David Wellbery (Stanford: Stanford University Press, 1990), 198.
25   Smith, *National Identity*, 20.
26   Ibid., 29.
27   Ibid., 40.

cultures without a nation, Roma have had to find other strong identifying ethnic characteristics besides geographical territory. This task has been daunting because modern identity has often become inextricably linked to nationality. In fact, so many negative images against Roma—travelling bands of illiterate beggars and stealers—arose during times of nation building and nationalism. This is not surprising when one considers, as Gellner concludes, that key traits of nationalism are "homogeneity, literacy, anonymity."[28] As nations congealed around these values, Roma, who have not appeared to fit within them, have fallen out.

The main collective memory that Roma in German-speaking countries share does not concern homogeneity, literacy, or anonymity, but rather historical persecution. Yet many Roma insist on their citizen status in their respective countries. In writing they attempt to retain distinctive memories, symbols, and values from individual and group histories often intersecting with national histories. In publishing, Roma want past, present, and future generations to remember those intersections that the dominant discourse of national histories has not always depicted. Instead, national histories often portray Roma as constructing barriers between Roma and non-Roma, living in extreme self-inflicted isolation, resisting assimilation, speaking different languages, and adhering to strange customs. Thus, Roma become perceived as nomadic, illiterate, uneducated, noncommunicative, nonassimilated, and nonintegrated outsiders.

### History, Marginalization, Assimilation, and Integration

Karl Stojka expresses the main historical and social reasons for the barriers that have hindered relations between Roma and non-Roma and for the solidarity Roma have found among themselves. Roma are humans just like everyone else, Stojka proclaims, only they have lacked a stable place and a home and thus are in constant danger of losing themselves and their identities. Centuries of living in fear, mistrust, and danger have created boundaries and bonds: "For this reason the Gypsies have always banded together, have nurtured their customs, traditions and their language and were always mistrustful when some stranger, a Gadže, came and wanted to know something about them."[29] Roma have lived for centuries with state-sanctioned laws, policies, and social

---

28 Ernest Gellner, *Nations and Nationalism*, intro. by John Breuilly, 2nd edn (Ithaca: Cornell University Press, 1983; 2008), 132.
29 "Daher haben die Zigeuner immer fest zusammengehalten, haben ihre Bräuche, Traditionen und ihre Sprache gepflegt und waren stets mißtrauisch, wenn jemand Fremder, ein Gadsche, kam und etwas über sie wissen wollte." Stojka and Pohanka, *Auf der ganzen Welt*, 7.

images designating them as different. Historical documents by non-Roma observers have characterized Roma as distinct from other people in those countries. The racism and sexism one sees in chroniclers' records echoes the Eurocentric process of historicization that scholars of post-colonialism have analyzed in other cultures and historical time periods.[30] The earliest extant descriptions of Roma in the German-speaking countries focus on physical appearance, clothing, livelihood, social roles, and customs. The first records in the fifteenth century announcing the arrival of so-called "Tartars" in Hildesheim in Lower Saxony in 1407, or "Heiden" (heathens) in Basel, Switzerland in 1414, or groups observed passing through northern German territories of Holstein, Mecklenburg, and Pomerania, refer to them as "wandering horde[s]" of men, women, and children who "were very ugly in appearance and black as Tartars," camped out, had chieftains, were pagans, and "were however great thieves, especially their women."[31] Scholars often trace the beginnings of the connection between nation building and racism in Germany only back to the early nineteenth century.[32] Already in the fifteenth century, however, exclusionary racial profiling surfaces in pejorative characterizations of Roma as "dark skinned" and "dark haired." Numerous persecutory measures initiated in the fifteenth century coincided with the birth of the nation state, which attempted to eliminate difference to strengthen national unity.[33] In

---

30   Said's *Orientalism*, for example, speaks of colonialist Western powers forming images of the Orient through highly politicized and suspect scholarship: Edward Said, *Orientalism* (New York: Vintage Books, 1979). Susan Zantop points out Said's oversight of issues of gender and sexuality in her *Colonial Fantasies: Conquest, Family, and Nation in Precolonial Germany, 1770–1870* (Durham, NC and London: Duke University Press, 1997), 5; 212–13 n. 16. Still, Said's perceptions on Eurocentric identity formulations in colonized countries are now classic.
31   Translated from Latin in Hermann Cornerus, *Chronica novella usque ad annum 1435*, in J. G. Eccard, *Corpus historicum medii aevi* (Leipzig, 1723), vol. 2, col. 1225. Quoted in Fraser, *Gypsies*, 67.
32   El-Tayeb cites references in the nineteenth century to keeping the "black blood" of colonized African countries out of the German nation: Fatima El-Tayeb, "Foreigners, German, and German Foreigners: Constructions of National Identity in Early 20th Century Germany," ed. Salah Hassan and Iftikhar Dadi, *Unpacking Europe: Towards a Critical Reading* (Rotterdam: Museum Boijmans Van Beuningen and NAi Publishers, 2001), 72–81. Zantop refers to the "invention of the German race" as formulated by Meiners in his series of articles on racial features that appeared in the 1790s (Zantop, *Colonial Fantasies*, 81–97). Sollors talks about technological inventions in the eighteenth and nineteenth centures that contributed to the rise of nationalisms and ethnicities: Werner Sollors, ed., *The Invention of Ethnicity* (Oxford: Oxford University Press, 1989), xi–xii.
33   Mirella Karpati, "Geschichtliches," in Anno Wilms, ed., *Zigeuner* (Zürich and Freiburg im Breisgau: Atlantis Verlag, 1972), 9–11.

the eighteenth century, skin and hair color would become physical markers connecting "one physical property to all others—physical, moral, aesthetic, and intellectual alike" and "create an avalanche of determinacy or inevitability. Even on the rhetorical plane, anatomy becomes destiny."[34] In Christoph Meiners's influential late eighteenth-century treatises, in which skin color predominantly determined one's position in a so-deemed natural hierarchy, "Gypsies," whom Meiners concluded were not of "German blood," came out at the bottom.[35] Bhabha observes how "skin, as the key signifier of cultural and racial difference in the stereotype, is the most visible of fetishes, recognized as 'common knowledge' in a range of cultural, political and historical discourses."[36] In the building of stereotypes, skin becomes the sign of "national 'identity'."[37] Within the largely Caucasian populations of German-speaking countries, Roma have become "the other" based largely on skin color.

Just as prevalent as observations on darkness of skin and hair are remarks about Roma's "deceptive nature."[38] Definitions of deception evolved for each sex. Chroniclers most often coupled Romani women's fortune-telling skills and desires with a so-deemed propensity for "deceit" and thievery.[39] This legendary connection became the main

---

34  Zantop, *Colonial Fantasies*, 85.
35  See Christoph Meiners, "Über die Farben, und Schattierungen verschiedener Völker," *Neues Göttingisches historisches Magazin* I (1792): 611–72, http://www.ub.uni-bielefeld.de/diglib/aufkl/neugoemag/neugoemag.htm; Christoph Meiners, "Über die Verschiedenheit der cörperlichen Grösse verschiedener Völker," *Neues Göttingisches historisches Magazin*, I (1792): 697–726, http://www.ub.uni-bielefeld.de/diglib/aufkl/neugoemag/neugoemag.htm. Meiners places "Zigeuner" in groups of people whom he claims do not meet European standards of strength, morality, and industriousness ("Ueber die Farben," 667; translated into English by Zantop, *Colonial Fantasies*, 88–9).
36  Homi K. Bhabha, ed., *The Location of Culture* (London and New York: Routledge, 1994), 78.
37  Ibid., 80.
38  Hall observes some Early Modern England glossaries suggest that "gypsy" denotes "Egyptian" in abbreviated form, but "it typically carries connotations of darkness as well as associations with lechery and deceit," pointing out that Sir Thomas Brown calls "gypsies" "Counterfeit Negroes" in the section "Of Gypsies" in his *Pseudoxia Epidemica*. Kim F. Hall, *Things of Darkness: Economies of Race and Gender in Early Modern England* (Ithaca and London: Cornell UP, 1995), 154, n. 27.
39  In 1550, chronicler Sebastian Münster published his influential, popular *Cosmographia*, which ultimately went through 35 editions in five languages over 84 years. One hundred and thirty four years after the arrival of the first documented Roma in Germany, Münster characterizes the "Züginer" as a "ongeschaffen, schwartz, wüst und onfletig volck, das sunderlich gern stilt, doch allermeist die weiber, die also iren mannen zu tragen." ("unformed,

rationale for expelling groups, as when the Bishop of Paris ordered all Roma to leave the city in 1427.[40] Some clergymen believed letting Roma read one's fortune was a sin.[41] Consequently, officials and clerics frequently equated fortune telling with magic, leading to expulsion or even death in areas with laws against its practice. Such was the case in 1556 when Kurfürst August I. von Sachsen threw "several Gypsies" ("etliche Zigeuner") from the Dresden bridge into the Elbe River because they were practicing "evil arts" ("böse Künste"), or "magic" ("Zauberei").[42]

Male Roma gained a reputation for the groups' deceitful leaders who assumed aristocratic titles and carried letters explaining reasons why Romani groups might be travelling. Such was the case with the so-called "Duke Michael of Egypt" who arrived in Basel in 1422, and whose letter allowed him to enter the city.[43] As time went on, however, officials received those letters with increasing skepticism, thus contributing to the stereotype of the deceptive Romani male leader. Whether Roma fabricated such letters or not remains unknown, lacking historical documents with their viewpoints to interpret their intentions. Both sexes were accused of stealing food and begging, leading to eighteenth-century decrees to condemn Roma to death, as in Austria's Burgenland province.[44]

Establishing well-demarcated categories connecting race, skin color, and gender roles allowed non-Roma to define what they perceived as

---

    black, desolate and scurrile people, who especially like to steal, and above all the women, in order to support their husbands.") Sebastian Münster, *Cosmographia* (Basel: Henrichum Petri, 1550), ccc–ccci. Subsequently, he also describes the old women who engage in fortune telling and are able to tell how many children someone will have, and whether the babies will be boys or girls.

40  Fraser, *Gypsies*, 77.
41  Gilsenbach, *Weltchronik*, 186–7.
42  Ibid., 170. Owen Davies devotes space in his book on witchcraft, magic, and culture from 1736 to 1951 in England to Roma as fortune tellers: *Witchcraft, Magic and Culture 1736–1951* (Manchester and New York: Manchester University Press, 1999), 258–65; and to the Vagrancy Act and the Witchcraft Act, which allowed for the prosecution of fortune tellers (55–6; 72–4); and to cases of accusations of witchcraft against "gypsies" (35–7; 134; 188; 196). Records from witch trials in German-speaking countries, however, apparently do not list any Roma as magicians or witches: Jonathan B. Durrant, *Witchcraft, Gender and Society in Early Modern Germany* (Leiden and Boston: Brill, 2007), xvi. Gilsenbach provides a reason for that lack of accusations: a person could be convicted of witchcraft only if she or he had cavorted with the devil and thus given up Christian beliefs. Roma were considered "heathens;" thus, this stipulation did not apply (*Weltchronik*, 141).
43  Fraser, *Gypsies*, 71.
44  Mayerhofer, *Dorfzigeuner*, 12–23.

the groups' innate traits and to marginalize—or, according to Barth and Péter, to racialize—the excluded groups' members. The traits non-Roma assigned to Roma in these early settlement years were in many ways total opposites of traits many in the German territories wished to see in themselves. Margalit writes: "Settled Christian society regarded itself as white not only in complexion but also metaphorically, as an expression of moral purity. The negative stereotype of the Gypsy 'other' crystallized into a cultural memory over the generations and helped Germans form their own sense of belonging."[45] Views of moral purity played themselves out in judgments of Roma as deceitful. The image of Roma as "black" eventually infiltrated European folklore and became equated with the devil and evil.[46]

In reference to this ideology of settled, Christian, Caucasian society, the parallel between the status of Roma and Jews again becomes apparent. Prejudices against nomadism, dark complexions, and exoticism affected both Roma and Jews. The Middle Ages saw the beginnings of the mysterious myth of the "Wandering Jew" whom everyone began to claim to have seen everywhere in the world. In Germanic lands, people asserted spotting a "Wandering Jew" in Hamburg in 1547, in Lübeck in 1603, in Bavaria in 1604, in Leipzig in 1642, in Frankfurt in 1676, in Munich in 1721.[47] As Jews became more prevalent, "blackness" became associated with "Jewishness" as well. Black was not only a different pigmentation to Caucasians, but also a symbol for the sexuality, disease, and madness in the other.[48] Still, differences between Jews and Roma exist. The Jews and their spiritual beliefs were not unknowns. Roma, in contrast, represented a totally new unknown, making them at once exotic, mysterious, feared, and threatening. The Middle Ages did not stop the Jews from continuing to write—especially so-called "souvenir books"—ensuring that communities would live on perpetually, at least through their words and memories.[49] Roma have not left such souvenirs.

As "dark, deceptive, heathen, outsider" travelling Romani groups became more common, cities began denying them access, as in Frankfurt am Main, which drove Roma violently out of the city and closed its walls to them in 1449 and 1454. Alternatively, cities expelled them by giving them money to leave, as in Bamberg in 1463.[50] Whereas in earlier

---

45  Margalit, *Germany*, 10.
46  Ibid., 9.
47  Cohen, *Israel*, 73.
48  Sander L. Gilman, *Difference and Pathology: Stereotypes of Sexuality, Race, and Madness* (Ithaca/London: Cornell University Press, 1985), 35.
49  Pierre Vidal-Naquet, *The Jews: History, Memory, and the Present*, trans. and ed. David Ames Curtis (New York: Columbia University Press, 1996), 59–60.
50  *Rombase*, http://ling.kfunigraz.ac.at/~rombase/

years people had felt they were fulfilling the Christian duty of donating alms to the poor by giving money to Romani groups, subsequent residents banned Roma outright to avert what were seen as potential problems. Two documents represent the first officially sanctioned, widespread legal measures against Roma: first, an edict from Elector Albrecht Achilles of Brandenburg in 1482 prohibiting Roma from remaining in his territory and threatening a penalty against resisters; and second, the declaration from the Parliament session in Lindau in 1497 proclaiming Roma "outlaws" (*vogelfrei*). Thus came permission to kill and capture Roma without suffering legal ramifications. In 1591, Kaiser Rudolf II in Austria renewed the law his father, Kaiser Maximilian II, had ordered in 1560 and had then updated in 1572 and 1578, which called for expulsion and extermination of all Roma found in Austrian territory.[51] In Switzerland, too, laws prohibiting Roma from staying in various parts of the country were enacted in 1471 and 1571. Many of these earliest perceived differences and resulting conflicts between Roma—who were travelling from the East into Western countries—and the populations residing in the West—as portrayed, for example, by the chronicler Hermann Cornerus in 1435—persist into postmodern times.[52] Roma have constantly experienced problems with documentation, legitimacy, and misperceptions of culturally moral differences. Writing in the twentieth century, autobiographers continue to point to incidents when they are singled out for being dark skinned and thereby excluded from the dominant Caucasian group.[53]

While early pejorative stereotypes persisted, other images evolved portraying Roma as exotic without differentiating between subgroups and delving into historical particulars. Women in the first century of migration were depicted as wearing just shifts covered by garments looking like blankets, but slowly images portrayed them with more opulent accessories of silver earrings and jewelry.[54] Thus evolved the stereotype of the "exotic Gypsy," entailing sexualized images of female

---

51  Gilsenbach, *Weltchronik*, 203.
52  Reimer Gronemeyer, and Georgia A. Rakelmann, "Rom Zigeuner auf dem Weg in die Postmoderne," *Roma: Das unbekannte Volk: Schicksal und Kultur*, eds Mozes F. Heinschink and Ursula Hemetek (Vienna, Cologne and Weimar: Böhlau Verlag, 1994), 14–18.
53  Ewald Hanstein states that people called him "Schwarzer" when he was growing up: Hanstein, *hundert Leben*, 13; that name stuck with him even later in life (ibid., 132). Joseph Muscha Müller had a rude awakening as a child when a "Weihnachtsmann," or the German equivalent to a Santa Claus, refused to give him a gift at a public ceremony because of Müller's darker skin: Müller,"*Und* weinen," 40. His classmates began calling him a "Mulatte" (ibid., 64). Others mistook him for a Jew (ibid., 77).
54  Fraser, *Gypsies*, 77.

Roma continuing into contemporary times. Silverman observes "the marketing of Romani dance and the trafficking of Romani images have always capitalized on the sexuality of females."[55] Although in the fifteenth and sixteenth centuries exoticism still related mostly to outer appearances, early depictions planted seeds for later sexualized and exoticized portrayals on physical and moral levels. Whether characterized negatively—as marauding, begging, swindling vagrants—or romanticized—as carefree, caravanning, dancing, exotic musicians—Roma have evoked a "dream of historylessness," "beyond the reach of the authorities."[56] In literature and folklore Roma appear as "a kind of 'time capsule' storing both national forms (music, traditions) and simpler social past."[57] The stereotype of timelessness couples with that of homelessness, or a certain "Placelessness" ("Ortlosigkeit").[58]

Legends about origins also began to change during the century after Roma arrived in Europe. First references in Europe to a specific place called "Little Egypt" as the wanderers' origin occurred in 1418 in Frankfurt am Main.[59] Later that century, German and Swiss pilgrims to Greece found travellers similar to those in the German-speaking lands in a specific place called "Little Egypt"—the name for a hill, also called "Gype," near Modon (or Methoni, a Venetian colony on the south-western coast of the Peloponnese).[60] Hence, the name "Gypsy" may have originated in English. Over time, however, accounts of a particular place of origin evolved into myths claiming Roma came from an unspecified "very strange and distant" country from which they had been expelled for refusing to relinquish the Christian faith.[61] Unfounded historical accounts ultimately homogenized diverse subgroups into a simultaneously evil and exotic one. Early chronicles showed no interest in understanding individual characteristics that might have identified a subgroup. For example, chronicles related nothing about the language of early groups until well into the sixteenth century. None mentioned communication difficulties.[62] This lacuna implies those residing in the countries made little effort to interact with the arriving groups. Likewise, Roma's reputation as musicians did not gain momentum until a century later.[63] Dominant cultural groups

---

55   Silverman, *Romani Routes*, 121.
56   Katie Trumpener, "The Time of the Gypsies: A 'People without History' in the Narratives of the West," *Critical Inquiry*, 18 (1992): 853.
57   Lemon, "Telling Gypsy Exile," 34.
58   Breger, *Ortlosigkeit*.
59   Fraser, *Gypsies*, 68.
60   Ibid., 51–3.
61   Ibid., 77.
62   Ibid., 79.
63   Ibid., 109.

never showed interest in examining the relationship between groups' origin, appearances, languages, arts, and customs. Policies, decrees, and laws aimed at separating, excluding, or annihilating Roma and their customs continued to escalate from the sixteenth century onwards. Individual laws are too numerous to list here, but between 1497 and 1774, at least 146 decrees were implemented against Roma, most calling for deportation from the German areas.[64] Fraser summarizes: "something like three-quarters of such anti-Gypsy measures identified for 1551–1774 fall within the 100 years following on the Thirty Years War."[65] In the chaotic aftermath of war, legislation tightened against any group officials considered a threat to recovery. All impoverished subjects appearing vagrant and uprooted encountered suppression (1553–4), the most targeted being Roma.[66]

The laws Empress Maria Theresia and, subsequently, her son, Joseph II, enacted between 1740 and 1780 in what is present-day Austria and was then the Habsburg Empire were particularly harsh. These laws' intent was to abolish Roma segregation deemed to be the root of perceived vagrant ways. Policies were thus thought to aid assimilation, but enactment denied cultural values and differences. Decrees required Roma to settle, forbidding owning horses and wagons, speaking their language, wearing any distinctive clothes, and marrying other Roma. Officials removed their children to have farming families raise them.[67] Difference was no longer just observed and tolerated; it became forbidden. The 1773 decree forbidding marriage between two Roma represented an effort "to bring their racial identity to an end."[68] Not only was endogymous marriage illegal, but female and male Roma also had to meet certain requirements in order to marry even a non-Roma. A Romni had to prove her industrious household skills and familiarity

---

64  Margalit, *Germany*, 26.
65  Fraser, *Gypsies*, 153.
66  Karin Bott-Bodenhausen observes that 20–25 per cent of the population in Lippe's rural areas in the seventeenth and eighteenth centuries suffered from poverty: "Kultursplitter," in *Sinti in der Grafschaft Lippe: Studien zur Geschichte der "Zigeuner" im 18. Jahrhundert* (Munich: Minerva-Publikationen, 1988), 130. German Sinti in the eighteenth century never appeared in official records alone, but rather always with groups such as "Landstreicher, Bettel- und Packjuden, Hausierer, fremde Bettler und Kollektanten." ("vagrants, begging and travelling Jews, door-to-door salespeople, foreign beggers and collectives.") Michael Frank, "'... dass hochdero Lande und Unterthanen davon rein und unbeschwert bleiben sollen'—Lippische Obrigkeit und Sinti in der frühen Neuzeit," in Bott-Bodenhausen. *Sinti*, 47–8.
67  "Maria Theresia and Joseph III: Policies of Assimilation in the Age of Enlightened Absolutism," *Rombase*. http://ling.kfunigraz.ac.at/~rombase/cgi-bin/art.cgi?src=data/hist/modern/maria.en.xml; Mayerhofer, *Dorfzigeuner*, 23–33.
68  Fraser, *Gypsies*, 157.

with Catholic doctrine. A Rom had to show his abilities to support a spouse and children. Interestingly, assimilation laws most likely harbingered more restrictive gender roles, considering that Romani women had for centuries earned a livelihood outside the home as fortunetellers and sellers, and Romani men had most likely relied on women for familial financial support. The man now became the sole breadwinner, the woman the housekeeper and purveyor of Christian morals. Anyone engaged in fortune telling—by all accounts an exclusively female occupation—posed an affront to morals and had to relinquish that livelihood.[69]

The Habsburg monarchy had its veneer of multiculturalism and interculturalism. Rulers were famous and infamous for marriages crossing national boundaries to expand their empire. "Bella gerant alii, tu felix Austria nube" ("Let others wage war, thou, happy Austria, marry"): so reads the ironic saying characterizing Austria's empire-building tactics. But only select groups of nations and empires in power could partake of peaceful tolerance. Roma, standing on the ladder's lowest economic, political, and social rungs, remained subjugated. Constructing powerful groups meant excluding the oppressed, or, again, those not conforming to standards of "homogeneity, literacy, and anonymity."[70] Although nationalism in Germany would not come into full force until the late nineteenth century, tides were already churning in earlier centuries. Gellner stresses the false consciousness that arises with nationalism—with homogeneity at its center—to defend continuity, folk culture, and cultural diversity "while in fact it is forging a high culture ... while in fact helping to build up an anonymous mass society."[71] By the end of the eighteenth century, fairer-skinned Caucasians in the Germanic areas were coalescing around national identity politics placing them dominant over those perceived "darker-skinned," and thus morally lacking. As Kelley asserts for the African-American slave trade, in the sixteenth, seventeenth, and eighteenth centuries, the "creation of a color line" and the "invention of a dominant group" congealed into a "racist system of supremacy."[72] So the situation was for Roma.

Deemed vagrant, illiterate, and exotic, Roma could have few hopes to fight restrictive laws. Scant historical documents by Roma during the eighteenth century, however, prove they were not sitting passively on society's margins. Indeed, they were attempting to interact with

---

69   Karin Bott-Bodenhausen, "Prosoziales Verhalten: Formen der Hilfe für Sinti," in Bott-Bodenhausen, *Sinti*, 156.
70   Gellner, *Nations*, 132.
71   Ibid., 119.
72   Kelley, "Interview," http://www.pbs.org/race/000_About/002_04-background-02-05.htm

a variety of other populations—dominant and not—and questioning forced assimilation measures. Bott-Bodenhausen's account of Sinti in Lippe in northern Germany in the eighteenth century describes contact between Roma and shepherds, farmers, potters, Jews, civil servants, and aristocrats, although the frequency of such contact is indeterminable.[73] Court records reveal Sinti writing letters in German to officials, claiming the innocence of fellow Sinti accused of disobeying laws specifically against Sinti and requesting to be freed. These letters—some of the first extant documents by Roma besides earlier "letters of protection" and non-alphabetic writing that Toninato examines—demonstrate a clear declaration of Sinti identity and a conscious decision to speak and act on behalf of others in their group. Other evidence proves attempts to help Sinti comrades escape from jail and to procure justice. Some Roma were thus fighting what they perceived to be unjust treatment and communicating with the dominant population, not just remaining bystanders to unjust social processes.

Two distinct attitudes towards Roma had developed by the nineteenth century.[74] On one side stood those hostile towards Roma and supporting laws aimed at extinguishing them and their customs. By the mid-nineteenth century, an active slave trade of Roma existed whereby Romani families in Eastern European cities such as Bucharest were being sold off for their skills as locksmiths, metal workers, shoemakers, musicians, and farm workers to people in German territories. Selling of Romani workers was thus proceeding full steam even before the American colonial slave trade reached its zenith. On August 7, 1845 a law was issued in Germany banning slave trade, stopping the buying and selling of Roma and others without rights. On the other side stood those wanting meaningful Romani integration into dominant society, including scholars showing interest in Romani languages and cultures, whom I discuss in Chapter One. Likewise, Christian church missionaries began in 1828 to convert Roma through schools and settlements. Among dominant populations were also advocates who favored marriage laws allowing Roma to marry non-Roma.

The relatively short period of freedom and assimilation tactics in the second half of the nineteenth century met its end around 1900, when the police and justice system categorically proclaimed all travelling groups "vagrants" and "criminals." The Bavarian minister of the interior began to establish a card catalogue of all Roma, including fingerprints, photos, police records, and family trees. This racial profiling became

---

73   Karin Bott-Bodenhausen, "Kultursplitter," 179–201.
74   Joachim H. Hohmann, *Verfolgte ohne Heimat: Geschichte der Zigeuner in Deutschland*, Studien zur Tsiganologie und Folkloristik 1 (Frankfurt a. M., Bern, New York and Paris: Peter Lang, 1990), 72–6.

the forerunner for the "Zigeunerzentralstelle" ("Gypsy Central Office") the Nazis established in Berlin. Fear of being arrested for travelling and economical hardship hampering traditional travelling occupations pressured most Roma to take up residence. Scholars, judges, and journalists also began publishing articles from the mid-1920s onwards that openly condemned "Zigeuner" as criminals.[75] Hence evolves the tension Roma felt between standing distinct from non-Roma while confronting pressures to integrate. Many non-Roma perceive Roma as wanting to live on the margins of acceptable behavioral norms, as having an inherent disposition towards isolationism, and as harboring hostilities against those outside their groups. Such was the reasoning behind attempts to force assimilation, such as the school for Sinti and Roma children in northern Berlin in 1913, as pictured in Illustration 4. Autobiographies shed a different light on Roma integration and assimilation. Despite long-standing prejudices and discriminatory measures, Roma autobiographers in the interwar period often made concerted efforts to integrate into society through work and social interactions. Historical sources support their assertions.[76] The success of such efforts varied.

### Integration and Assimilation in the Interwar Era

Ewald Hanstein describes living in Masselwitz, on the outskirts of Breslau, in the late 1920s, when his father found a job as a gardener there. Hanstein's memoirs depict an area where "We lived modestly, but the people were friendly to us."[77] Some Sinti had good positions with the railway or the post office, but in general they led simple lives. Hanstein talks about having meaningful relationships with Jews who lived there, claiming this friendly integration disappeared when the Nazis acquired power: "Before that we had—exceptions aside—not found our heritage to be a problem. In the Bärenstraße there were a few children who yelled 'Gypsies, Gypsies' at us, but didn't we also do that when our relatives came with their wagons?"[78] His specific reference to the Sinti posing "no problem" for others implicitly counters the

---

75  For copies of articles and laws and an analysis of prejudicial "scholarship" and "research" see Hohmann, *Zigeuner und Zigeunerwissenschaft*, 136–262.
76  The Landesverband der Sinti und Roma in Baden-Württemberg reports that in Heidelberg in the 1920s Roma and Sinti were for the most part economically integrated and independent: *Roma und der Arbeitsmarkt*, 17.
77  "Wir lebten bescheiden, aber die Menschen waren freundlich zu uns." Hanstein, *hundert Leben*, 22.
78  "Vorher hatten wir—von Ausnahmen abgesehen—unsere Herkunft nie als Problem empfunden. In der Bärenstraße riefen zwar einige Kinder 'Zigeuner, Zigeuner' hinter uns her, aber taten wir das nicht auch, wenn unsere Verwandten mit ihren Wagen kamen?" (ibid., 23).

"I am eternally proud to be a Gypsy": Roma Voicing Ethnicity  59

Illustration 4: School for Sinti and Roma children in northern Berlin in 1913. Children were given a plot of land to develop and become sedentary. Photo reprinted with permission from the Bundesarchiv in Berlin.

Nazi term "Zigeunerproblem" (Gypsy problem) used to justify racially motivated decrees. In using the designation of "Zigeuner," Hanstein's family takes possession of the ethnic identity attached to the word and depicts family members using the concept of the "travelling Gypsy" playfully among themselves.

Lily van Angeren-Franz describes the many people who let her family use their land to station the wagons. To her, these hosts accepted Romani families and did not perceive Roma as causing any problems. One property owner even offered to take care of Lily's younger siblings to relieve Lily as the babysitter so that she could attend school while her parents were on the road for days at a time. While the police sometimes insisted that the Franz family keep moving, Lily writes, the "normal" population did not discriminate.[79] Before World War II, she remarks, her family really did not experience any poverty.[80] As National Socialists gained power, she notices those who previously had been generous became "discontented" (*unzufrieden*) with Roma.[81] Philomena Franz also sees hostilities that did not exist in the 1920s

---

79  Angeren-Franz, *Leben*, 19.
80  Ibid., 14.
81  Ibid., 31.

developing quickly after the Nazis' ascent to power. The freedoms she saw Roma enjoying during the interwar period disappeared overnight: "We were totally uprooted, totally unhinged."[82] Her use of the forceful verb "herausgerissen" (uprooted; literally "torn up") indicates the family's strong sense of belonging during pre-Nazi times.

Differences among Sinti and other subgroups did exist during the interwar period, but still conviviality between Sinti and other Romani groups, and between Sinti, Jews, and Caucasian farmers and livestock handlers continued. Franz emphasizes: "We were a large family."[83] Using the word "family" indicates a significant feeling of solidarity among people who might not be related by blood or share customs. Cooperation between various Romani subgroups and other outsider groups, especially Jews, is a common theme in autobiographies. Walter Winter is proud of the high reputation his father received as a horse trader and refers positively to interactions between Roma and Jews in the small town of Wittmund in East Friesland.[84] He writes about good feelings his family enjoyed living in the neighborhood, where his father earned respect, the neighbors gathered, and the children played together.[85] Outside his hometown, however, when families travelled, Roma and locals stayed separate, which occurred of their own accord.[86] As with Hanstein and Franz, Winter documents good working and business relationships with non-Romani groups. Outside of business connections, group members gravitated towards each other creating natural affinities, he claims, implying Roma were not consciously or maliciously hindering contact with non-Roma.

Franz Rosenbach claims his family had convivial connections with townspeople in Döllersheim, Austria, where they lived in a two-room apartment in a farmhouse in the early 1930s. His neighbor invited him to cook with her, and he interacted well with his school peers.[87] Rosenbach's picture with his mother, Cäcilie Rosenbach, from 1936 or 1937 depicts how well they integrated into the community.[88] The son's and mother's clothes appear indistinguishable from other

---

82  "Wir wurden herausgerissen, total aus den Angeln gehoben." Franz, *Liebe und Haß*, 43.
83  "Wir waren alle eine große Familie" (ibid., 16).
84  Winter, *Z 3105*, 14.
85  Ibid., 20.
86  Ibid., 22.
87  Franz Rosenbach, *"Der Tod war mein ständiger Begleiter": Das Leben, das Überleben und das Weiterleben des Sinto Franz Rosenbach. Von ihm selbst erzählt und dokumentiert von Norbert Aas* (Munich: Bayerische Landeszentrale für politische Bildungsarbeit, 2005), 16.
88  The picture is on page 32 of Rosenbach, *Der Tod*; observations on the integration that photo depicts come from Norbert Aas, editor of Rosenbach's *Der Tod*, 33.

townspeople's dress. Franz also wore two pins from the winter relief organization in his lapel, showing his support for this Nazi effort. Still, integration did not help them: incrementally the family experienced ostracism and persecution leading to their deportation to Auschwitz.

Stories of integration defy images of Roma constructing barriers to keep Gadže away. Autobiographers' perceptions unveil the discrepancy between intentions behind the official policies and people's everyday lives. Empress Maria Theresia enacted measures to prevent vagrancy among groups of people deemed innately idle and lacking in self-discipline, but autobiographers show no self-inflicted vagrancy or laziness. Instead, they portray the push and pull of integration and ostracization. The fine line between these two developments reached a pinnacle by the end of World War I. Many autobiographers stress how their ancestors fought in World War I alongside non-Roma soldiers, and thus had made concerted integration efforts. Yet, German officials often regarded Roma during World War I as possible spies. Still, Roma's movement during World War I was not yet as restricted as it became in the 1920s. In 1926 the state of Bavaria implemented a law to "combat Gypsies, vagrants, and 'work-shys'" (*Gesetz zur Bekämpfung von Zigeunern, Landfahrern und Arbeistscheuenunwesens*).[89] In 1927, the Prussian Ministry ordered fingerprinting of all Roma and non-Romani vagrants over six years old. In 1929, the state of Hessen enforced a similar law concentrating only on Roma. By the mid-1930s, the Munich agency had files on about 19,000 Roma, representing the majority of those living in Germany at that time. In contrast to these discriminatory efforts, autobiographers prove agile at developing survival tactics endearing them to many non-Romani neighbors, especially in rural areas. Inhabitants in the countryside needed and desired the goods and services—as well as the diversion from mundane country life—that Roma offered. Mayerhofer observes Roma making themselves indispensable by peddling wares, telling fortunes, and repairing tools and equipment. Thus, farmers and tradespeople in Austrian villages often welcomed them as the designated, regular "village Gypsies" (*Dorfzigeuner*).[90]

One does, however, also have to account for the somewhat nostalgic tone the autobiographers use to describe life during the interwar period. Autobiographies written a long time after the events they

---

89   Margalit, *Gypsies*, 32. Michael Burleigh and Wolfgang Wippermann provide a translation of this law in *The Racial State: Germany 1933–1945* (Cambridge: Cambridge University Press, 1991), 114–15.

90   Mayerhofer, *Dorfzigeuner*, 62–3. The attitude towards Roma in urban areas could be much different. Burleigh and Wippermann include the English translation of a citizen initiative from Frankfurt residents in August 1930, objecting to what they perceived as the "Gypsy nuisance" within the city: *The Racial State*, 116–17.

discuss can give a "processed" view of the past.[91] In retrospect, writers could feel nostalgic for pre-Nazi times because of the extreme torture ahead. Compared to Nazi persecution, the interwar period might in hindsight appear as good times. Still, historical evidence supports autobiographers' portrayals of the abrupt arrival of anti-Roma sentiments. Although nation-building had been progressing for centuries, the *Kaiserreich* period from 1871 to 1918 developed a heightened sense of connection between nationhood and ethnicity for those in Germanic territories.[92] Effects of unity building through homogeneity and education did not come into full force until after the First World War. Germany's political weakness from war defeat and loss of colonies and territories sparked widespread nationalism. When the Nuremberg Race Laws went into effect, Roma naturally felt surprised at the differentiation made between Germans and Roma. Knesebeck cites a Sinto who stated that before National Socialist racial policies he had felt like a Sinto and a German at the same time; after racial policies he felt like a Sinto, rather than a German.[93] The stark contrast between feeling part of national unity before the Nazis and then suddenly becoming an outcast after the Nazis' ascent supports other Roma's observations on integration in the interwar period. From the long history of prejudices based on skin colors, customs, work practices, values, and lifestyles arise characteristics continually marking Roma as distinctly different from non-Roma, including nomadism, illiteracy, and unwillingness to integrate or assimilate.[94] Voices of Roma who grew up in the interwar years unveil their perspectives on these images and lend insights into

---

91   Knesebeck, *Roma Struggle*, 175.
92   Dieter Gosewinkel, "Die Nationalisierung der Staatsangehörigkeit im Deutschen Kaiserreich," in *Das Deutsche Kaiserreich in der Kontroverse*, eds Sven Oliver Müller and Cornelius Torp (Göttingen: Vandenhoeck & Ruprecht, 2009), 392–405.
93   Knesebeck, *Roma Struggle*, 162.
94   I am using definitions in the report on Roma in Central and Eastern Europe by the United Nations Development Programme (UNDP): "Integration: The opportunity to participate in socioeconomic life on an equal basis without losing one's own distinct identity (linguistic, cultural), while simultaneously contributing one's individual distinctiveness to the cultural richness of society" and "Assimiliation: Social inclusion at the expense of losing distinct group identity. Assimilation of minorities (usually ethnic) generally requires the sacrifice of their ethno-cultural distinctiveness in order to receive 'entry opportunities.' Assimilation is rarely successful, at least in the short and medium term. Minorities can easily lose elements of their distinctiveness without receiving commensurate 'entry opportunities'" (*Avoiding the Dependency Trap: A Regional Human Development Report* (Bratislava: United Nations Development Programme and the Regional Bureau for Europe and the Commonwealth of Independent States, 2002), 11.)

"I am eternally proud to be a Gypsy": Roma Voicing Ethnicity 63

the process of internal identity self-fashioning while facing external political, economic, legal, and social restrictions.

## Roma as Travellers

The age-old stereotype of Roma having a "natural" predilection for travel surfaces continually. As recently as 11 June 2011, the then Pope Benedict addressed Roma as "a beloved part of the pilgrimaging People of God," and quoted from the Bible, Hebrews 13, 14, stating that "Roma have no city and thus they are always looking for a future one."[95] Although some scholars might support a diasporic conceptualization of Romani ethnicity, no scholar today claims Roma have an innate desire for travel or that they are purely nomadic. First, scholars surmise that "only a tiny fraction" of the world's 12 million or so Roma are truly nomadic.[96] Second, although autobiographers often talk about travelling, they are not referring to perpetual nomadism. Instead, travel often occurred in spring and summer; settled activities took place in winter. Some also travelled on organized pilgrimages (*Zigeunerwallfahrten*), a practice continuing today. Some families also owned travelling wagons, but most usually remained stationed in one place year round by living in a house or converting their wagons into sedentary structures.

Roma in German-speaking countries clearly lived out a history of being pushed out and around, and thus mostly did not have a free choice to travel. For over four and a half centuries, from the time Roma initially began settling in German territories until Germany became a nation in 1871, German territories comprised at least 300 political entities. Close territorial proximity enabled Roma to move across borders away from harsher decrees of one territory into a possibly less strict neighboring area. Some larger German kingdoms enacted restrictive policies against Roma whereas some smaller lands tolerated them.[97] Roma often lived in the woods or in natural areas to hide and have a quick getaway from officials, thus building a special connection with nature and nonurban spaces. Journeying in numbers also brought safety and a sense of security.

Autobiographers stress how travelling belonged to their livelihoods as they sold goods and provided services not otherwise accessible

---

95 "un'amata porzione del Popolo di Dio pellegrinante." "Udienza al rappresentanti di diverse etnie di Zingari e Rom," 11 June 2011. http://www.vatican.va/holy_father/benedict_xvi/speeches/2011/june/documents/hf_ben-xvi_spe_20110611_rom_it.html. I thank Gernot Haupt for this reference.
96 Hancock, "'Uniqueness,'" 50.
97 Margalit, *Germany*, 27.

in the remote places where they did business.⁹⁸ Ewald Hanstein's description of his mixed settled and travelling existence as a youngster seems quite usual. He emphasizes living "almost my entire life in fixed apartments,"⁹⁹ except for when he was in the camp; his family travelled mostly in the summer, not in any year-long nomadic way: "I was actually born while travelling. Before the Nazi era, my family travelled in the summer months by horse and wagon through Silesia."¹⁰⁰ Travelling resulted from an economic adaptation, subsequently symbolically associated with identity. An outside idyllic, romanticized view of such a life conjured up a false image of nomadic freedom.

Certainly, the autobiographers recognize the beautiful side of the carefree, independent life of seasonal travel. But they also emphasize hardships of being constantly on the move and dependent on the elements, local legal codes, and people's attitudes in the places where they set up camp. Lily van Angeren-Franz remembers times when she longed to live in the houses of the people who allowed her family to stay on their land when the family was travelling. After the war, she married a non-Roma, and she and her husband lived in a house in the Netherlands. When she visited her father in Germany, she found his life in a wagon—with so many people around, some sleeping in tents—intriguing, yet strenuous. She had conflicting feelings about the attraction and repulsion of living in a wagon. Faced with having the options of a life of forced, seasonal travelling or a permanent residence, she chose the latter for what she believed to be better for her children.¹⁰¹ Walter Winter praises the travelling his family undertook in summertime when his father decided to sell their house after living there for 15 years and to follow a travelling lifestyle. The winters, however, were especially difficult, when the camper was never warm.¹⁰²

Karl Stojka describes the beautiful natural settings where his family camped, always with a fresh stream and trees, protected from the wind: "Everywhere where there were trees, we were at home because the trees are our brothers. Yes, we grew up with the trees."¹⁰³ But later in

---

98  Krausnick, writing in 1983, states that at most a fifth of Roma in Germany travelled extensively in the summer months to pursue business related to selling and buying antiques and carpets ("*Da wollten wir frei sein,*" 164n. 1).
99  "fast mein ganzes Leben lang in festen Wohnungen." Hanstein, *hundert Leben*, 11.
100 "Geboren bin ich aber tatsächlich auf einer Reise. Vor der NS-Zeit ist meine Familie in den Sommermonaten mit Pferd und Wagen durch Schlesien gezogen" (ibid.).
101 Angeren-Franz, *Leben*, 122.
102 Winter, *Z 3105*, 22.
103 "Überall wo Bäume waren, waren wir zu Hause, denn die Bäume sind unsere Brüder. Wir sind ja mit den Bäumen aufgewachsen." Karl Stojka, *Kindheit*, 10–11.

his narrative, he recognizes the nostalgia he may have for such a life, which taints his view of reality: "Today, all the memories of that seem very romantic to me, but for my parents it was probably not an easy life."[104] When asked whether he longed for a permanent shop after the war to sell his rugs, no longer having to travel around to markets, he immediately answered "Yes." He pointed out that his grandfather and father had both led settled lives.[105] When faced with choosing between a life of compulsory travelling or settled habitation, Stojka, like Angeren-Franz, opted for the latter. Essential is the freedom to choose.

Labelling Roma as nomadic reinforces black-and-white dichotomous situations that do not tell the whole story. The salient issue here involves providing options not restrictions. At no time in the histories of the German-speaking countries, and especially in the 1920s, 1930s, and 1940s, did Roma have the option to travel freely. Anna Mettbach employs the term "Schub" (shove) for the forced Romani migrations, especially during the 1930s.[106] In trying to sell their baskets, her parents would travel to a place, be forced to register, and be allowed to stay for seven to eight days. Often, however, police would order them to leave, frequently accompanying them to the town's or state's border to make sure they left. As Karl Stojka asserts: "We had no place any more because we were robbed of it; for that reason we had to acquire a new home in the harshest of conditions."[107] His lamentations about being "placeless" echo his assertion that those not having a stable place to call home always run the risk of losing themselves.[108]

Travelling with others offered protection against growing mass persecution. Mongo Stojka refers to the tendency of the wagons to journey *en masse* out of individual fears of being a solo traveller: "For we needed one another, the world was such, that they [we] could look after one another."[109] Feelings of togetherness surface in Otto Rosenberg's account of moving to Altglienicke-Bonsdorf near Berlin, where his family rented an apartment and a piece of land to park their wagon. In referring to the "we" who lived there, he clarifies that he includes his grandmother, brothers, sister, uncle and his family,

---

104  "Für mich erscheint das alles heute in der Erinnerung sehr romantisch, aber für meine Eltern war es sicher kein einfaches Leben" (ibid., 25).
105  Ibid., 36.
106  Mettbach/Behringer, "Wer wird," 23.
107  "Wir hatten ja keinen Platz mehr, weil er uns geraubt wurde, daher mußten wir uns dieses Zuhaus unter schwersten Bedingungen neu erarbeiten." Karl Stojka, *Kindheit*, 36.
108  Stojka and Pohanka, *Auf der ganzen Welt*, 7.
109  "Denn man brauchte sich, die Welt war so, daß sie [sic] auf sich aufpassen mußten." Mongo Stojka, "Unsere alte Welt," in *Fern von uns*, 249.

another aunt and her husband, and another family with children.¹¹⁰ Accumulation of an extended family as kinship proved necessary to care for each other and lend moral support in hard times. With closeness of family came community solidarity and proximity. Angeren-Franz describes how impressed her non-Romani husband was by the sense of community he perceived when they visited Lily's father living in a wagon in Germany. Her husband was enthused by the campfires, music, travelling, and comfort.¹¹¹ Winter talks about the travelling lifestyle his father re-assumed after other Sinti accused him of forgetting his origins as a traveller. This accusation prompted his father to travel, at least in summer, with his family in the camper. In summer 1927, he asked a neighbor to build a wagon for him in exchange for his house, and the family took off. Winter refers to the communal feelings that formed around the travelling life when his family surrounded him. As with Rosenberg, by "family," Winter refers to extended kinship including cousins, aunts, and uncles: "Because there were not very many Sinti at that time in Germany we were all relatives and in-laws."¹¹² Autobiographers' feelings of solidarity counter officials' constant demands to move on. Social circumstance of the dominant culture—in defining Roma as nomads and forcing movement from place to place—established a marginalized and segregated Romani ethnicity. Under such conditions, Romani developed unifying ethnic identifiers, one of which was language.

## Language

All the autobiographers spoke Romany with family and friends when growing up. Conservative estimates calculate more than 3.5 million people worldwide speak Romany today.¹¹³ Romany is primarily an oral language with several dialectical subgroups, although interdialectical contact situations, mixed communities, and movements of peripatetic populations have caused overlaps, borrowings, and multidialectical mixings.¹¹⁴ No single dialect is particularly prestigious or powerful, and language usage is dispersed among different countries with different national languages.¹¹⁵ Consequently, autobiographers often portray the language as a unifying force among Roma. As Hildegard Lagrenne asserts: "our language keeps us together. We would be

---

110   Rosenberg, *Brennglas*, 15.
111   Angeren-Franz, *Leben*, 123.
112   "Weil es so viele Sinti damals in Deutschland nicht gab, waren wir fast alle verwandt und verschwägert." Winter, *Z 3105*, 21.
113   Yaron Matras, *Romani: A Linguistic Introduction* (Cambridge: Cambridge University Press, 2002), 238.
114   Ibid., 238–50.
115   Ibid., 251.

destroyed if we did not speak Romany anymore."[116] Winter reveals the feelings of belonging to two worlds through his bilingualism. At 12, he considered himself, on the one hand, German, but on the other hand, a Sinto, a group that had its own ways of living "and above everything else that besides German we could speak another language that other people did not understand."[117] Romany was essential for both developing group identity and promoting individual self-worth.

Autobiographers expressed enthusiasm and relief whenever they encountered another Romany speaker, especially after traumatic incidents such as concentration camp internment or migration to a new country. Sometimes speaking the language could literally be a lifesaver. Karl Stojka relates trying to get back to Vienna after being liberated from Flossenbürg. He had documents in English from Americans, but when he entered the Russian sector around Linz, Russians stopped and questioned him because they did not understand English. Karl began to swear in Romany. Suddenly, another Russian officer told Karl in Romany not to be scared, because the Russian was a Rom, too, and understood Romany. The Russian Rom took Karl to Vienna and gave him a food package when they arrived, where Karl was reunited with his mother and siblings.[118] Likewise, when Ewald Hanstein decided to immigrate from the German Democratic Republic to the Federal Republic of Germany, he felt alone as a refugee in Bremen. He was ecstatic to discover other Roma who spoke Romany: "There were people who understood me without lots of words and who lived with traditions that I recognized from earlier."[119] Language and traditions go hand-in-hand; the loss of one could mean the loss of the other.

Some Roma continue even today to perceive their language as a secret one deserving protection from non-Roma. Hanstein reflects on this notion, recounting the scorn many Sinti have to teach others the language: "'Whoever has a command of our language has a command of us!' The respective people in power use the knowledge of our language and culture to spy on us and to harm us."[120] Knowing the

---

116 "unsere Sprache, die hält uns doch zusammen. Da gehn wir doch kaputt, wenn wir kein Romanes mehr sprechen." Krausnick, *"Da wollten wir frei sein,"* 48–9.
117 "und vor allem außer Deutsch noch eine Sprache sprechen können, die die anderen Leute nicht verstehen." Winter, *Z 3105*, 28.
118 Karl Stojka, *Kindheit*, 34.
119 "Da waren Menschen, die mich ohne große Worte verstanden und in den Traditionen lebten, die ich von früh auf kannte." Hanstein, *hundert Leben*, 127.
120 "Wer unsere Sprache beherrscht, beherrscht uns!" Die jeweiligen Machthaber nutzen die Kenntnisse unserer Sprache und Kultur, um uns auszuspionieren und zu schädigen" (ibid., 30–1). Hanstein's comment references cases such as that of Nazi "researcher" Eva Justin, who learned Romany only to retrieve information that would lead to Roma's persecution.

language can mean power. In hard times, language can protect, as when the Russian Roma saved Karl Stojka, but for those in power, language can also serve as a destroyer, as in Nazi times when Eva Justin learned Romany to betray Roma. Therefore, many Roma have not always perceived Romany as protective, but rather as dangerous when in the wrong hands. When non-Roma do not understand historical reasoning behind Romany's protectorate role, they view its usage as isolationist, and make speaking it a barrier against upward social mobility. In reaction, some Roma have developed a stigma against using Romany and teaching it to younger generations; and some have seen relinquishing the language as an unavoidable consequence of integration.[121] Still others have found possibilities to maintain an ethnic diversity even without using language as a main identifier.[122]

Autobiographies prove language—whether shared with non-Roma or not—has connected Roma together. As with Karl Stojka and Ewald Hanstein, Mišo Nikolić was relieved whenever he found Romany speakers.[123] The self-esteem he and others sensed in knowing another language extended to pride in polyglotism in general. Matras avers: "all adult speakers of Romani are fully bilingual or even multilingual."[124] Language also proves Roma's resourcefulness because "Romani always stands in a diglossic relation to the majority language, and in many cases also to other surrounding minority languages."[125] Nikolić boasted his father knew many languages, and Mišo was happy to know Romanian, French, and German as windows into social opportunities. Winter stresses polyglotism among Roma in his community where Plattdeutsch, Hochdeutsch, and Romany all found a home.[126] Even though the groups spoke various Romany dialects, individual subgroups could understand each other. Winter emphasizes how language bonded concentration camps inmates, including Roma from Poland, Ukraine, France, Belgium, White Russia, Hungary, and Austria.[127] Just as travelling has become an ethnic identifier determined from both inside and outside—although autobiographers reveal not

---

121 Halwachs, "Romani in Österreich," 128–9.
122 Matras, *Romani*, 242.
123 Nikolić, *Landfahrer*, 41.
124 Matras, *Romani*, 238. Polyglotism is a long recognized talent in Roma, which led Archduke Joseph von Habsburg to assert in his 1888 grammar of Romany: "Die Zigeuner sind keine Linguisten, doch sie sind polyglott." ("The Gypsies are no linguists, but they are polyglot.") Cited in Mayerhofer, *Dorfzigeuner*, 56, from: Josef Archiduc Austriae: *Fundamentum linguae Zingaricae*, edited together with Thewrewk E. P. bei Koritschyak J. M. (Budapest, 1888), 7.
125 Matras, *Romani*, 238.
126 Winter, *Z 3105*, 17.
127 Ibid., 82.

having a year-long travelling lifestyle, they do profess a love of travel—so, too, has Romany often marked identity from outside and inside. Even though autobiographers disclose a lack of linguistic unity and universal usage, they still perceive Romany as an ethnic trait.

## Literacy and Education

Along with nomadism and language, non-Roma have often identified illiteracy as a distinguishing feature of Romani ethnicity. Sway, in her account of American Romani subgroups in the late 1980s, for example, concludes that two main reasons—illiteracy and nomadism—have prevented Roma from assimilating completely, despite repeated governmental pressures placed on them to become more mainstream.[128] Sway makes these features appear highly desirable among Roma because without them, she declares, Roma would lose their ethnicity. Trumpener criticizes such stereotypes: "Nomadic and illiterate, they [Roma] wander down an endless road, without a social contract or country to bind them, carrying their home with them, crossing borders at will."[129] Significantly, autobiographers have shown nomadism and illiteracy as neither sole defining aspects of cultural identity nor innate qualities. Rather, nomadism and illiteracy have often resulted from forced discriminatory policies aimed at keeping them socially downtrodden. In contrast to Sway, Roma do not view losing these traits as threats to their ethnic identity. Resistance to forced nomadism and alphabetism has helped maintain cultural bonds. Speaking Romany has been a self-generated communicative tool. Writing and publishing to voice perspectives on Romani cultures, history, and customs have aided Roma in their survival.

Resident Roma in German-speaking countries today are literate. In reaction to assumptions about illiteracy, many autobiographers show pride in family members and friends who could read and write. If they point to literate Roma as exceptions, they stress that illiteracy has been by circumstance and not choice. Hildegard Lagrenne admires her father's abilities to read and write as exceptions to the analphabetism of other Roma in their immediate circles.[130] Hanstein proudly states that his father's literacy could help others to fill out forms and letters. His father instilled in him and his sister the necessity to read and write, and Hanstein emphasizes his own literacy several times.[131] Angeren-Franz

---

128 Marlene Sway, *Familiar Strangers: Gypsy Life in America* (Urbana and Chicago: University of Illinois Press, 1988), 124.
129 Trumpener, "The Time," 853. See also Toninato's *Romani Writing* for positive perspectives on Roma's literacy.
130 Krausnick, "Da wollten wir frei sein," 37.
131 Hanstein, *hundert Leben*, 20, 25, 28, 30.

speaks highly of her mother, who learned to read and write from her parents, a skill no one in their Romani community possessed, not even Lily's father. Lily's mother also taught Lily and her sister Waltraud to read, which helped save them from perishing in Auschwitz. Because the sisters were literate, they both received service jobs in the concentration camps; Lily worked in the records office, where she had to document information on the dead, and Waltraud worked in the clinic. Their chances of survival in such jobs—where they were spared hard physical labor and granted access to possible extra food rations, better clothing, and more sanitary conditions—were higher than those of other inmates.

Others justify their lack of education by pointing to laws restricting access to public schooling. Ceija Stojka talks about her embarrassment at entering second grade as a 12-year-old after World War II because she had not been allowed to go to school earlier, and she really wanted to learn to read.[132] Karl Stojka asserts that no Roma he knew when he was younger had any formal education. For him and his siblings, Nazi prohibition against Roma attending school prevented elementary school education completion. Karl hired a private tutor when he began his rug business in 1948. Good manners were especially important, he emphasizes, to combat non-Roma's stereotypes against Roma.[133] Philomena Franz, too, emphasizes how much others expected Romani children to behave better than they expected other children to behave. Part of that pressure, however, resulted from the reputation her family had as a musical and theatrical group playing for the aristocracy. She distinguishes her family as an "artist family" (*Künstlerfamilie*) who placed high value on outward appearances and the ability to read and write.[134] Even if the Franz family's higher status required them to read and write, autobiographers still stress the necessity for all Roma to combat stereotypes of the analphabet; the older generation always encouraged schooling for the next generation.

Winter attributes his father's inability to read and write to his family's continuous travel when he was younger. Instability made schooling difficulty, and parents needed children to help. Parents were not resisting education, but rather, were faced with conditions preventing formal schooling. Winter's father, because of his own analphabetism, decided to buy a house and live a settled life explicitly for his children to go to school.[135] Hildegard Lagrenne also points to barriers—Nazi laws against education for Roma and internment

---

132 Ceija Stojka, *Verborgenen*, 76.
133 Karl Stojka, *Kindheit*, 14–16, 36.
134 Franz, *Liebe und Haß*, 29–31.
135 Winter, *Z 3105*, 20.

in concentration camps—setting Roma back even further. She, like Winter's father, travelled a lot and later also recognized the travelling lifestyle hindered schooling. Post-World War II, she states, few of the older generation survived to encourage schooling. She attributes her own educational opportunities to the luck she had with teachers.[136] Despite lack of educational opportunities afflicting some Roma, many are proud of the knowledge they acquired from their travelling. Franz attributes her geographical and biological knowledge, which superseded that of her peers, to travelling experiences and wisdom she gleaned from her grandfather, parents, and relatives while on the road.[137] Winter is proud of the special attention his teacher gave him because of his ability to speak two languages and the geographical knowledge he had acquired through travelling.[138] Analphabetism is clearly not a desired state for these Roma. Systematically denied education, however, they see analphabetism as a handicap induced from outside and not as a lack in innate capabilities.

## Diversity

Individual accounts of living arrangements, education, and Romany usage make apparent the diversity among Romani subgroups and their perceptions of their identities. Nikolić refers to other subgroups and the contrasting tension and ensuing friendships between them. His friends included a Muslim Rom, a Sinto, and a Serbian Roma, and sometimes the strained relationships between them lasted almost a week, but they eventually reconciled and were friends again.[139] Recognizing safety in numbers, they resisted homogenization that often lay at the roots of persecution. Nikolić provides further examples of incidents when his family had trouble interacting with other subgroups. His sister Elmija participated in a Romani theater piece, and Miśo comments that, had his father been alive, he would not have allowed her to do so because those running the theater were from a different Romani subgroup than Elmija and her family.[140] Mišo also talks about the disappointment family members of his future wife Ruzsa expressed when they found out she expected a child from him, a Jugoslavian Roma, and not from a Hungarian Lovara.[141] He mentions other subgroups' customs diverging from those of his own Kalderash, sometimes causing misunderstandings. One time his brother became angry when a Hungarian

---

136 Krausnick, *"Da wollten wir frei sein,"* 51.
137 Franz, *Liebe und Haß*, 25.
138 Winter, *Z 3105*, 24.
139 Nikolić, *Landfahrer*, 37.
140 Mišo Nikolić, *... und dann*, 101.
141 Nikolić, *Landfahrer*, 127.

Roma placed a holy candle lit for health and long life under the table. Kalderash did not follow this custom, and Mišo's brother feared burning candles this way was unsafe.[142] Mišo also explains how Kalderash did not fear spirits, whereas other subgroups did.[143] He did not believe in singing at a wake, and it offended him when members of another subgroup sang because he believed a wake should be sad, not joyous.[144] A concluding passage in Mišo's book debunks the stereotype of Roma always sticking together. Everything people say about Roma is not always true, he states. Yes, Roma often stick together when they are in danger, but economics can create cultural divides: "Let's say that when one is richer he looks down upon the others. In turn, the poorer ones envy the richer ones and talk poorly about them behind their backs. A good person is regarded as stupid, one who is brasher and stronger is accepted."[145] Mišo alludes here to cases when ostracism forms ethnic identity and when economic and social factors work against Roma bonding in tough times. Not until decades after debilitating Nazi destruction would some Roma, such as Mišo, be able to rely on literacy and settled conditions to voice opposition to monolithic portrayals of their cultures.

---

142  Ibid., 124.
143  Ibid., 115.
144  Ibid., 128.
145  "Sagen wir einmal, wenn einer reicher ist, der schaut auf die anderen herab. Die Ärmeren wiederum beneiden den Reicheren und schimpfen hinterrücks über ihn. Ein guter Mensch wird für blöd angesehen, ein frecher und starker wird akzeptiert" (ibid., 135–6).

## Three  "I couldn't talk with anyone else about this": Roma Voicing Gender

### Gender and Sexuality

As an increasing number of Roma publish their life stories, previous culturally taboo topics emerge. The intersection of gender roles with ethnicity represents one of the most fascinating and complex of these topics. Kóczé observes that "the centrality of gender activism as a progressive force" is a significant trait that the Romani social movement shares with other social movements.[1] Gender—entailing sexual morality, sexual practices, and perceived bodily differences between the sexes—is fundamental to personal and ethnic groups' identities. What gender norms do Roma depict? For Roma in general, talking about gender norms, especially when involving sexuality, has been and continues to be a sensitive, if not forbidden subject. Angeren-Franz hesitates to talk publicly about her pregnancies and births: "My upbringing as a Sinti woman was deeply ingrained, for I could not talk with anyone else about this. You simply did not do that among us."[2] Even to mention Nazi medical experiments and sterilizations was "taboo" (*tabu*).[3] If women needed to discuss issues about sexuality and the body, then such conversations should have occurred only among female relatives.[4] Angeren-Franz was even reluctant to talk with her male doctor when he asked for details of an operation on her ruptured appendix in Auschwitz.[5] Not wanting to share such information limited

---

1   Kóczé, "Gender," 38.
2   "Meine Erziehung als Sintizza steckte noch tief, denn ich konnte mit niemand anderem darüber reden. Das tat man bei uns einfach nicht." Angeren-Franz, *Leben*, 115.
3   Ibid., 114.
4   Ibid., 115.
5   Ibid., 117.

Roma in their requests for retribution after the war. Hence, when Romani autobiographers have brought up gender-related topics, they display courage in revealing controversial themes in an unprecedented manner. Especially for women, openness contrasts with portrayals of submissive, passive females and dominant, active males. The patriarchal structure weakens as Roma publish stories; consequently, their narratives unveil "realms of female power and influence,"[6] particularly in activities of work, storytelling, and music-making.

At times women autobiographers question barriers against publicly expressing themselves. Angeren-Franz asks: "Should the Gypsy law also prohibit us from speaking about things that were done to us under force?"[7] She believes she is allowed to break cultural taboos to relate stories of her own personal life, just not those of other Roma. She alludes to possible Nazi medical experiments or operations on her childless friend Liesbeth and sister Waltraud, but allows herself only to talk openly about her own life: "I can break my taboos, be it only so that the half million Gypsies who were gassed under Hitler are not allowed to be forgotten, but I cannot break the taboos of others. That would be immoral."[8] Interpreting cultural taboos so personally supports the autobiographical genre's worth in lending insights into Romani customs and values. In interwar accounts, gender norms and values become particularly visible in practices related to purity and pollution customs; birth, illness, and death rituals; courtship, marriage, and everyday life; work; storytelling and music-making. Romani writers' comments further assist in exploring attitudes towards changes in gender relations for older and younger generations.

## Purity and Pollution Customs

Mary Douglas demonstrates how purity and impurity rituals bring order and unity to an experience, representing a way to process and publicly display symbolic patterns.[9] Impurity is not a phenomenon by itself but must exist in relation to purity. This juxtaposition establishes certain dualities—one part of the body opposing another, or men contrasting with women, or one group contrasting with another. Scholars have attempted to analyze the exact nature of the separations occurring in

---

6   Silverman, *Romani Routes*, 109.
7   "Durfte das Zigeunergesetz uns auch verbieten über Dinge zu sprechen, die uns unter Zwang angetan worden waren?" Angeren-Franz, *Leben*, 132.
8   "Ich kann zwar meine Tabus brechen, und sei es nur, um die halbe Million Zigeuner, die unter Hitler vergast wurden, nicht in Vergessenheit geraten zu lassen, aber ich kann nicht die Tabus der anderen brechen. Das wäre unmoralisch" (ibid., 156–7).
9   Mary Douglas, *Purity and Danger: An Analysis of Concept of Pollution and Taboo* (New York: Routledge, 1966; 2002).

purity and pollution customs of various Romani groups. Carol Miller demonstrates how the "ideology of defilement" among American Machvaia Roma creates at least four distinct lines "between the Gypsy and the non-Gypsy, the clean and the unclean, health and disease, the good and the bad."[10] Okely views purity and pollution customs as symbolic of the relationship between English Roma Travellers and non-Roma. Travellers' rituals about women's bodies demonstrate demarcations between the upper/lower and inside/outside of the body in the same way in which Travellers develop inside/outside boundaries with non-Roma.[11] Nyman points out in her studies on aging women in a Polish Roma community two functions of purity and pollution rituals: to maintain an ethnic culture separate from the dominant culture and to preserve social boundaries dividing Roma internally, especially related to gender.[12] Rombase divides purity and pollution customs into four specific categories: 1) the female body; 2) hygiene and food; 3) illness and death; and 4) the relationship with non-Roma.[13]

Not all Romani groups have purity and pollution customs, but German-speaking autobiographers cite several instances of having certain practices before Nazi times. Romany dialects often contain a version of "pollution" and "purity." For many Vlachs, *mahrime* means "ritually unclean" and opposes *uzo*, *zuzo*, or *suso*, meaning "ritually clean." Sinti use palećido (neglected, isolated) and prast(l)o (infamy, outlawed) to describe ritual uncleanliness.[14] Autobiographies reveal most practices as rooted in one or both of two possible separations: the first being an ethnic separation between the Romani subgroup and any group outside that subgroup, but most often non-Roma; the second happens between men and women. These separations may overlap, but the gendered one ultimately prevails. As previous chapters have shown, non-Roma in German-speaking countries have frequently exaggerated or misunderstood ethnic separations between Roma and non-Roma and historically pushed Roma into separation on society's edge. Roma in the 1920s depicted their lives as largely integrated into their communities. In writings by younger generations, as I show later, purity and pollution

---

10   Carol Miller, "American Rom and the Ideology of Defilement," *Gypsies, Tinkers, and Other Travellers*, ed. Farnham Rehfisch (New York: Academic Press, 1975), 41.
11   Okely, *Own or Other Culture*, 63–93.
12   Lynette Marie Nyman, "A Complex Relationship: Menopause, Widowhood, and the Distribution of Power Among Older Rom Women," *Journal of the Gypsy Lore Society*, Series 5, 7.2 (August 1997): 97–117.
13   "Taboo and Shame (Ladž) in traditional Roma communities," *Rombase*, http://ling.kfunigraz.ac.at/~rombase/cgi-bin/art.cgi?src=data/ethn/belief/ladz.en.xml
14   "*mahrime* (ritually unclean)," *Rombase*, http://ling.kfunigraz.ac.at/~rombase/

customs rarely arise, signalling increasing integration. Additionally, in recent times in some geographical areas, non-Roma have forced Roma into the most squalid parts of town through economic and social marginalization and restrictions. Roma are thus left with few options than to live segregated lives and adapt their customs to living conditions. *Rombase* describes one situation: "Thousands of eastern Austrian Roma live at the fringes of the waste disposal sites of the non-Roma and live on the sale of the recyclable waste items."[15] Here class and race intersect, causing multiple levels of discrimination.[16] Forcing Roma to live in filth leaves them no choice but to relinquish rituals. Ostracism inevitably produces prejudices of Roma as squalid and dirty. Roma then write defensively about purity rituals as an intrinsic part of ethnicity. Again, ethnic identity construction involves both formulation within the marginalized group and impositions from the dominant society.

## Culinary and Domestic Rituals

Customs surrounding food preparation and ingestion surface often in the context of Roma and non-Roma interactions. Mongo Stojka describes his family giving strangers food, but then purity laws required them to dispose of the plate and silverware afterwards. "Even if it had been made of gold we would have thrown it away."[17] He specifically identifies strangers with the words "travelling nomads" (*Wanderer*) and their impurity with the Vlach word *mahrime* and Sinti word *praslo* to differentiate perspectives and customs. Latscho Tschawo recounts an incident when a policeman came to a settlement where Tschawo and his wife were living in a camper.[18] Tschawo's wife had just put some soup on the stove. The policeman surged into the wagon, intending to force the Sinti to move on and to accuse them, stereotypically, of stealing chickens. The policeman asked what was in the pot and immediately demanded to look into it. Tschawo explains the customs related to purity with cooking. As Mongo Stojka, too, related, anyone who does not follow Roma customs and then touches food defies pollution dictums. Tschawo claims he did not know the policeman or his background. Perhaps the policeman's wife was a midwife, or maybe he ate horsemeat, two violations of purity laws. Then Tschawo

---

15   *Rombase*, http://ling.kfunigraz.ac.at/~rombase/
16   For multiple discrimination, especial in Eastern Europe, see Kóczé, "Gender," 83–8. A survey of Eastern European Roma shows class, rather than ethnicity, as a major determinate of interactions between Roma and non-Roma, with poor participants having the best interactions, regardless of ethnicity: *Avoiding the Dependency Trap*, 4–5.
17   "Auch wenn er aus Gold gewesen wäre, hätte man ihn weggeworfen." Mongo Stojka, "Unsere alte Welt," 253–5.
18   Tschawo, *Befreiung*, 109–10.

would have had to throw away all his dishes and everything the policeman had touched. This could have costly economic implications, for they would have to buy new dishes. Therefore, he defended his dishes. The policeman finally looked into the pot without permission and saw a chicken. He immediately assumed the chicken had been stolen, and took Latscho into custody. Latscho's final observation about the incident and relationships between Roma and non-Roma presents a vantage point differing from that of the policeman. If the policeman had only asked to look in the pot, Latscho claims, his wife would have opened the pot and shown him the contents, sparing unnecessary commotion. Instead, non-Roma "do not even ask why they are not allowed near the pots."[19] As unsettling as the violation of purity customs might be, Latscho is just as upset about the policeman's disrespectful, prejudicial attitude and his unwillingness to learn from the experience.

Roma prevented food from becoming polluted by throwing silverware away if it fell on the floor and avoiding culinary establishments that prepared horsemeat, even if indirectly, as in zoos, where zookeepers might feed animals with horsemeat. Many anti-pollution measures, however, related to women's bodies, showing that menstruation, sexual, and birthing fluids were considered especially impure when coming in contact with food. A woman's skirt and underwear, for example, were not allowed to touch any food or cooking fire. If they did, the food, skirt, and underwear had to be thrown away. Some accounts stress how food, washing receptacles, and utensils had to remain completely separate from the perceived impure forces. Hildegard Lagrenne states a woman was not allowed to sit on the table. If utensils fell on the ground women were not allowed to walk over them. If a woman sat on top of a beer keg, no one could drink the beer. "Women were held more strictly to the laws, that is the custom," Lagrenne stresses.[20] Young girls were not impure if they were not yet menstruating.

Viewing women's bodies as sources of pollution, and female fluids as less clean than those of males, especially at the onset of menstruation, did not happen just in relation to food and cooking. Angeren-Franz provides a list of some of the rituals her Sinti family followed, including washing women's clothes separately from men's clothes, and undergarments separately from outer garments; concealing women's underwear in a pillowcase before hanging it out to dry; throwing away silverware that had touched the ground; discarding a woman's

---

19   "Die fragen nicht einmal, warum sie nicht an den Topf dürfen" (ibid, 110).
20   "Frauen werden da strenger gehalten, das ist so Sitte." Krausnick, *"Da wollten wir frei sein!"* 46.

skirt when it touched coals where food was being cooked, as well as getting rid of the coals; and never eating anything in a restaurant in a zoo because of the possible connection with horsemeat.[21] She does not give exact reasoning behind such laws, yet these laws imply the uncleanliness of women's sexual organs and bodily fluids.[22] Along these lines, some groups believed men should not walk behind women. Mongo Stojka remarks how his mother and the girls always had to go behind the boys.[23] Mišo Nikolić mentions a Polish Kalderash group that did not allow women to be above men in a house or bed. If a woman threw a shoe at a man, he would be ostracized; or the object the shoe hit, a car, for example, would be unusable thereafter.[24] Mišo points out, however, these customs did not belong to his Kalderash group. Karl Stojka claims a man would be considered impure if a woman walked over his feet while he was sitting down. Others in the subgroup would then avoid him for days afterwards.[25] Female impurity thus had the power to extend beyond the bearer and affect anyone who had contact with the source.

In possessing the potential to ostracize anyone with her skirt, a Romani woman held a power that could fissure the patriarchal system. Carol Miller talks about "skirt tossing pollution" in the context of impurity, morality, empowerment, sexuality, and solidarity among female American Machvaia. "Skirt-tossing" created a scandal and could also demonstrate "a power for penalty by pollution afforded to women."[26] Miller cites from Yoors's *The Gypsies*, recounting the many years he spent as a youth with European Lovara. Yoors writes that women's uncleanliness "assured Gypsy women an absolute sense both of privacy and of protection among their own kind anywhere at large."[27] Nirenberg claims American Machvaia no longer follow the skirt-tossing system exactly because of the immense power it gave women.[28] No German-speaking female autobiographers talk about

---

21   Angeren-Franz, *Leben*, 20.
22   To compare, Carol Miller writes about western American Machvaia in her "Respect and Rank Among the Machvaia Roma," *Journal of the Gypsy Lore Society*, Series 5, 4.2 (August 1994): 75–94; Jerzy Ficowski writes about Polish Roma also observing protective measures: "Supplementary Notes on the Mageripen Code Among Polish Gypsies," *Journal of the Gypsy Lore Society*. Series 3, 30 (1951): 123–32.
23   Mongo Stojka, "Unsere alte Welt," 253.
24   Nikolić, *Landfahrer*, 85.
25   Stojka and Pohanka, *Auf der ganzen Welt*, 26.
26   Miller, "American Rom," 51.
27   Jan Yoors, *The Gypsies* (Prospect Heights, IL: Waveland Press, 1967; 1987), 150.
28   Jud Nirenberg, ed., *Gypsy Sexuality: Romani and Outsider Perspectives on Intimacy* (Mesa, AZ: Clambake Press, 2011), 164.

impurity empowering, but that is not to say that the idea could not underlie such practices and thereby, however unwittingly, mitigate patriarchal structures.

Lily van Angeren-Franz explains that policies related to purity and pollution have been difficult for outsiders to understand. Customs have not existed to punish people, but rather to enforce sanitary measures for the subgroup. In emphasizing cleanliness, Roma counter stereotypes and images non-Roma often have of "dirty" Roma. Autobiographers have frequently shown pride in cleanliness and orderliness within the family home. Anna Mettbach recites a saying her mother repeated in times of extreme poverty: "Poverty doesn't bring dishonor as long as one has water and soap, for cleanliness is half of life."[29] Otto Rosenberg stresses the cleanliness his grandmother kept, thereby dispelling myths of the "dirty Gypsy."[30] Ceija Stojka emphasizes how families always cleaned up after themselves after staying in a site in their wagons.[31] Geography scholar Tim Cresswell observes the strict geographical and spatial order and cleanliness of Romani camps, displaying "family groups, inside/outside divisions, physical proximity, and segmented, hierarchical space within caravans."[32] Concern for the domestic environment, Cresswell argues, might allow Romani groups to defecate in the hedges instead of inside the home and close to the kitchen. Unfortunately, Romani conceptions of order and cleanliness might have appeared disorderly and unclean to non-Roma, just as purity customs might have seemed abnormal.

Clothing choices also adhere to values of cleanliness and orderliness. Philomena Franz elaborates on the beautiful clothes her mother wore when driving the wagon: "She wore long skirts, a satin apron, a beautiful blouse with a small stand-up collar, and along with that, coral jewelry."[33] Her father "went with the fashion. Beautiful hat, manicured beard."[34] Fashionable elegance, she clarifies, was mostly due to her family's livelihood as musicians, but she also wants to emphasize they did not run around in "tatters and rags,"[35] as was the usual depiction of Romani garb. For women, "Gypsy traditional attire" (*Zigeunertracht*),

---

29 "Armut schändet nicht, solange man Wasser und Seife hat, denn Sauberkeit ist das halbe Leben." Mettbach/Behringer, *"Wer wird ..."* 23.
30 Rosenberg, *Brennglas*, 18.
31 Ceija Stojka, "Sie waren Rom vom Stamm der Lowara," in Stippinger, *Ceija Stojka*, 13.
32 Tim Cresswell, *In Place/Out of Place: Geography, Ideology, and Transgression* (Minneapolis and London: University of Minnesota Press, 1996).
33 "Sie trägt lange Röcke, eine Satinschürze, eine schöne Bluse mit einem Stehkrägelchen. Dazu Korallenschmuck." Franz, *Liebe und Haß*, 31.
34 "ging mit der Mode. Schöner Hut, gepflegter Bart" (ibid., 31).
35 "Lumpen und Fetzen" (ibid., 16).

as Mongo Stojka describes his mother's outfit, always embraced "long, broad skirts that reach down to her ankles, earrings, colorful shirts. Overall her clothes create a colorful, happy impression."[36] Instead of viewing skirts as restrictive and adhering to patriarchal norms, women have taken pride in their dress and have honored the solidarity integral to shared customs. As Hildegard Lagrenne asserts, these traditions and purity laws have been handed down through many generations. She also points out when a girl turned 16, she was not allowed to wear pants, a practice that some still follow today.[37] Dotschy Reinhardt states she always wears a skirt or dress in public and in front of her elders. As I discuss in Chapter Eight, Reinhardt cites aesthetics and respect for the older generation—and not restrictive, sexist guidelines—as reasons for her own choice of clothing. Given the potential "skirt-tossing" power, one also has to ask whether Romani women might find added strength and power in wearing skirts and dresses.

Purity categories help reinforce Romani pride and self-respect. As a low status group with a history of unequal relationships with non-Roma, such customs may be a "defence against the inroads of the larger and politically more powerful society."[38] Maintaining confidence in belief systems through reinforcing the importance of rituals avoids directly challenging dominant groups and solidifies subgroups. Viewing Roma's purity customs also causes non-Roma to reexamine their own values. For many Roma, non-Roma have lost a crucial sense of purity. Some habits of non-Roma particularly offensive to Roma are "forgetting to wash in public bathrooms: eating with the fork that they rescued from the floor of the restaurant: washing face towels and tablecloths with underwear at the local self-service laundry: relaxing with their feet resting upon the top surface of the table."[39] Such instances, according to Roma beliefs, invite and spread contagious disease. To return to Latscho Tschawo's suggestion, meaningful dialogue and genuine desire to learn about each other's customs might bring about mutual understanding.

### Birth, Illness, and Death

Various Romani subgroups have considered birthing unclean for the mother and child, a viewpoint coinciding with the general belief in women's unclean bodily fluids. In times when families were still

---

36    "lange, bis zu den Knöcheln reichende Röcke, Ohrringe, bunte Hemden. Insgesamt machte ihre Kleidung einen bunten, fröhlichen Eindruck." Mongo Stojka, *Papiere Kinder*, 45.
37    Krausnick, *"Da wollten wir frei sein,"* 46.
38    Miller, "American Rom," 46.
39    Ibid., 45.

travelling, birthing had to occur in a place away from the wagon. As Angeren-Franz describes, having a child in the wagon would be considered *palischido*, Sinti for "impure" and "outrageous."[40] Childbirth occurred preferably in the hospital rather than at home, or in a tent or other structure separate from the main dwelling place. Winter explains how he and his three older siblings were born in a horse stall, because birthing in the wagon was considered impure, and rural hospitals were not always equipped for childbirth. Mother and child were isolated from everyone else after birth; the duration of the confinement varied. Often the mother had to eat with separate utensils and refrain from cooking for a specified amount of time after birth.[41] The length of time until the woman was allowed to touch cooking utensils after birthing varied among subgroups. Mišo Nikolić states that female Kalderash had to wait six weeks before cooking or touching any dishes.[42] Maria "Märza" Winter claims her father had to wait six months to see the newborn.[43]

Mongo Stojka's recollections contrast with descriptions of women going to the hospital for birthing. He tells of the vehement avoidance of doctors and the belief that doctors were impure. Several reasons could have caused such a reaction, including encountering "impure" personnel and conditions. In Mongo Stojka's case, three women attended the mother, and no man could go near the birthing place for two to three days during and after birthing. Births occurred outside, alongside the wagon, under a tree, as with the births of all his siblings, he claims.[44] No women involved in the birth were allowed back in the wagon. After three days the mother was able to get up and begin work again. If a woman went to the doctor, and the doctor touched her, then she would be considered *mahrime*. Mongo cites an incident with an aunt brought to the hospital screaming all the way. She would not let anyone in the hospital touch her and wanted to jump out of the window and kill herself.

Deemed unclean, death—like birth—represented a transition. Most Romani subgroups have believed in the presence of *mulo*, or spirits of the dead, and have shown profound respect for the dead. Hildegard

---

40   Angeren-Franz, *Leben*, 13.
41   Winter, *Z 3105*, 13.
42   Nikolić, *Landfahrer*, 101–2.
43   Lolo Reinhardt, "Überwintern," 19.
44   Mongo Stojka, "Unsere alte Welt," 255. Ceija has a slightly different story about her birth, namely that she was born in an inn in Kraubath in Steiermark ("Sie waren Rom vom Stamm der Lowara," 11). Karl states that he was born in a wagon on the edge of a stream, without the help of a doctor, in Wampersdorf, near Baden and Vienna (Stojka and Pohanka, *Auf der ganzen Welt*, 20).

Lagrenne says the belief in *mulo* caused a fear of ghosts, and no Sinti would live in a house where someone—Roma or non-Roma—had died.[45] Angeren-Franz states that a wagon in which someone had died had to be burned,[46] although subgroups living in German-speaking countries rarely still follow this practice.[47] Members of the Romani community have shown their honor and respect for the dead through elaborate funerals. Angeren-Franz describes the funeral of her father as a massive procession to which every Roma in the area came, whether they knew the deceased or not. People placed money in the deceased's pockets to pay for crossing the river between life on earth and the realm of the dead. A person with no money would be damned to wander around a kind of no-man's land between the two.[48] Walter Winter states that no music could be played or heard for weeks after the death of a family member.[49]

Death thus could create both frightening and protective spirits. As Philomena Franz remarks, the death of a close relative is a sign of one's own mortality, which introduced an intensified love of life: "From this attitude we create a wisdom about life that every day is beautiful, every advancing day with a little good will can be more beautiful."[50] In school she was proud to know more than her peers about birth and death based on her upbringing. The Sinti belief in reincarnation, she states, instilled in them an important trust in the meaning of life and a different relationship with the dead, who remained omnipresent.[51]

Profound respect for the dead took on heightened significance for Roma, not only in the concentration camps, as the next chapter on Nazi persecution will show, but also in the aftermath of that devastation. Hanstein tells about the horror of discovering that Riespott in northern Germany, where a refugee camp in which he was staying after fleeing the German Democratic Republic was located during the 1960s, was a previous concentration camp. Residents discovered this when they found a skull there, and then, according to beliefs in spirits and

---

45 Krausnick, *"Da wollten wir frei sein,"* 45.
46 Angeren-Franz, *Leben*, 134.
47 *Rombase*, http://ling.kfunigraz.ac.at/~rombase/. Marianne Rosenberg, Otto Rosenberg's daughter, confirms Sinti followed this practice, as her family burned her grandmother's possessions after her death: *Kokolores: Autobiographie* (Berlin: Ullstein. 2006), 50.
48 Angeren-Franz, *Leben*, 134.
49 Winter, *Z 3105*, 19.
50 "Aus dieser Einstellung schöpfen wir die Lebensweisheit, daß jeder Tag schön ist, jeder kommende Tag mit ein bißchen gutem Willen schöner werden kann." Franz, *Liebe und Haß*, 13.
51 Ibid., 26–7.

respect for the dead, no one wanted to live there anymore.[52] Of course, any person—Roma or non-Roma—would be reluctant to live where a concentration camp had once stood. Still, Hanstein's story suggests that officials might have been more sensitive to potential future residents if those residents had been non-Roma.

Angeren-Franz saw the faces of her father, mother, and siblings in dreams after the war. At that time, she did not know if they were dead or alive. The dreams were a bad omen that might indicate their death. Also, because the living should not have apparitions of the dead, her dreams signified her disrespect for them.[53] One was also forbidden to speak the names of the dead to prevent harmfully conjuring them up. When Hanstein was visiting Auschwitz his wife began to read the names of the dead in his family from Tadeusz Joachimowski's "Memory Book" (*Gedenkbuch*). Although he had visited the memorial site before and told his memories to many already, he became overwhelmed at hearing their names out loud: "We honor our dead, their names are sacred. It is so difficult to pronounce and hear them. I have to leave."[54] The taboo against talking about the dead publicly and reciting their names might have prevented Roma from openly telling stories about their family fatalities. For reasons of respect, many Sinti have also been against installing so-called "Stolpersteine" (stumbling stones), embedded in sidewalks thoughout Germany to commemorate victims of the Nazis. Besides respecting the taboo against naming the dead, opponents have feared that pedestrians will disrespectfully be walking over the dead.[55] Respectful interactions with the dead, however, inspire positive emotions. After the visit to Auschwitz, Hanstein felt relieved, attributing his emotions and memories to his inspirational interactions with the dead: "Maybe it is the dead who give me strength. I see them in front of me and know that they are in God's hand. On the way back

---

52   Hanstein, *hundert Leben*, 128.
53   Angeren-Frazn, *Leben*, 113.
54   "Wir verehren unsere Tote, ihre Namen sind uns heilig. Es fällt so schwer, sie auszusprechen und zu hören. Ich muß raus." Hanstein, *hundert Leben*, 45.
55   *Stolpersteine* are gold plaques by artist Gunter Demnig to commemorate extermination and persecution of Jews, Roma, politically persecuted, homosexuals, Jehovah's Witnesses, and euthanasia victims of Nazis: *Stolpersteine*, http://www.stolpersteine.com. On 2 July 2011, I witnessed Demnig installing a Stolperstein in Berlin for Sinto boxer Johann "Rukeli" Trollmann. (See Illustration 5). In his commemoration speech, Dr. Jan Stöß, then Councillor for Education and Culture, described the fears of some Sinti that passersby will be walking over the dead when passing over *Stolpersteine*. See: Lorely French, Louise Stoehr, Gudrun Sherman, "Berlin als interkultureller Text," DVD (Philadelphia: American Association of Teachers of German, 2012), 00:24:40–00:29:27.

to the car the sun comes out. I begin to remember."⁵⁶ Autobiographers repeatedly stress the need to remember the dead or to live with their dead, especially in overcoming grief.

Customs and beliefs related to death have not been gender specific: men and women have received equal respect and treatment after death. In fact, after death, gender seems to have lost its significance: *mulo* have not been specifically male or female, unless the spirits have appeared in the form of the real-life people, in which case they maintain the gender they had in life. Honoring the dead is gender neutral, while birthing rituals are related to women's fluids and impurities in the outside world. As they age, women usually receive more respect as they lose what are perceived as their sexuality and sexual powers. Men, however, also receive that respect as part of a system that honors elders. Rituals and beliefs can thus run the full spectrum—from gender restrictive to gender neutral—and can vary from one subgroup or family to the next.

## Courtship, Marriage, and Family Life

Diverse stories describe the engagement process for a Romani couple. On the one hand, Mongo Stojka refers to the custom of arranged marriages from the time when the children were 10 or 12 years old, when parents sought suitable partners for their children. Mongo alludes to a possible dowry from the girl's family to the boy's family and, less commonly, to a brideprice from the boy's family to the girl's family. The conditions for each were not always totally transparent. Sometimes, Mongo writes, one offered some money or two horses or some other material goods, implying that the dowry or brideprice was not high.⁵⁷ Usually following the patrilineal system the girl joined the boy's family, but when the girl's father had no sons, then he could ask the son-in-law to join their family. Whether that action required a brideprice or a dowry or nothing in exchange is unclear.

On the other hand, Hildegard Lagrenne counters the belief of arranged marriages among the German Sinti, stating that a young boy was allowed to find his wife himself and that the boy and girl had to like each other. The courtship did not last long.⁵⁸ Often the two people who loved each other simply eloped on their own without telling their parents. Sometimes the parents did not want the union to happen. The couple went away for a few nights and came back to announce the consummation of their marriage. Mongo Stojka confirms this custom

---

56   "Vielleicht sind es die Toten, die mir jetzt die Kraft geben. Ich sehe sie vor mir und weiß, daß sie in Gottes Hand sind. Auf dem Rückweg zum Auto bricht die Sonne durch. Ich beginne mich zu erinnern." Hanstein, *hundert Leben*, 46.
57   Mongo Stojka, "Unsere alte Welt," 259.
58   Krausnick, *"Da wollten wir frei sein!"* 48.

"I couldn't talk with anyone else about this" 85

Illustration 5: *Stolperstein* (Stumbling Stone) memorial to German Sinti boxer Johann "Rukeli" Trollmann. Photo by Cindy Parsons.

of elopement, thus drawing attention to the diversity of marriage practices. For him, the couple had to be left alone, and everyone knew they had eloped because they would disappear for a couple of days. Afterwards, however, "the boy could not leave the girl, he would bring shame to the girl. So he had to take her. That was the one concern, the one thing."[59] Implicit here is the importance of the woman's virginity, both for the marriage and for her reputation in the subgroup, a factor that will surface in other accounts.

In cases of elopement the decision seems to have been a mutual one for the man and woman. Lily van Angeren-Franz, too, talks about this custom, emphasizing how unnecessary an official marriage license was to the couple and to Sinti in general. What counted instead was being "considered married in the eyes of the Gypsy community."[60] She repeats this internal Romani understanding when she talks about marrying her first husband Leo, a Dutch non-Roma. She realized

---

59  "jetzt konnte der Bursche das Mädchen nicht verlassen, er hätte Schande über das Mädchen gebracht. Also mußte er sie dann nehmen. Das war die eine Angelegenheit, die eine Sache." Mongo Stojka, "Unsere alte Welt," 259.
60  "in den Augen der Zigeunergemeinschaft verheiratet." Angeren-Franz, *Leben*, 18.

that her Sinti community did not require an official document, even though she had procured one from the Justice of the Peace. Karl Stojka confirms this required internal family and group consent: "With Roma it is so: When an older person says: 'Go and be together', that counts as a marriage, and everyone accepts both as a pair."[61]

In cases not involving elopement, the future bridegroom's family often must ask the prospective bride's family for her hand in marriage, or the future bride must receive her family's approval somehow before marrying. Even Lily van Angeren-Franz, when she was 49, insisted on asking her stepmother, her sister, and her brother-in-law for permission to marry her second husband after her first husband had died. She explains: "That is an old Gypsy custom that I would like to honor. Ultimately, so little is left of our Gypsy culture."[62] Philomena Franz claims that a man, after dating a woman secretly for a while, was supposed to ask her father for her hand in marriage. She states that elopement happened only after the man had asked the women's parents for her hand, but the parents had refused. The couple would then disappear for a few weeks and come back as husband and wife. The family might then have been in a great uproar until the parents realized the marriage could not be changed. Franz, as with Mongo Stojka, implies that the bride's parents had to accept the union when they realized the woman had lost her virginity and thus might not have been able to find another husband.[63]

Lily van Angeren-Franz also alludes to the importance of the woman's virginity before marriage. She describes marrying her first husband and needing to confirm her "feelings of honor as a Sintiza not to share a bed with a man before marriage."[64] Hildegard Lagrenne stresses the importance of virginity among Sinti: "A girl who marries must be untouched. That is still the ideal today."[65] Mišo Nikolić describes a custom at the Kalderash marriage ceremony whereby the bride went to all wedding guests individually, sat down beside them at the table, and kissed their hands. She thereby said goodbye to her previous life and publicly stated that from this night forward

---

61 "Bei den Rom ist es so: Wenn eine ältere Person sagt: 'Geht und seid zusammen', so gilt das wie eine Heirat, und jeder akzeptiert die beiden als Paar." Stojka and Pohanka, *Auf der ganzen Welt*, 97.
62 "Das ist ein alter Zigeunerbrauch, den ich gerne in Ehren halten wollte. Schließlich ist nur so wenig von unserer Zigeunerkultur erhalten geblieben." Angeren-Franz, *Leben*, 154.
63 Franz, *Liebe und Haß*, 32.
64 "Mein Ehrgefühl als Sintiza, nicht vor der Ehe das Bett mit einem Mann geteilt zu haben, musste sichergestellt werden." Angeren-Franz, *Leben*, 112.
65 "Ein Mädchen, das heiratet, das muß unberührt sein. Das ist heute noch das Ideal." Krausnick, *"Da wollten wir frei sein!"* 48.

she would no longer be a virgin. She would wear a headscarf for the rest of her life to show she was married.[66] Mišo also relates an incident between his future wife, Ruzsa Nikolić-Lakatos, and her family. When her father found out that she was illegitimately pregnant, he threw hot soup over her head. He was motivated in part by the fact that Mišo, the father of the unborn child, belonged to the Kalderash, and not to the Lakatos's Lovara subgroup, but also by her loss of virginity. Because the latter caused her family shame, she had to conceal her pregnancy. The family was incensed that a man from another group could take advantage of their daughter and bring them such shame.[67]

Scholarly and autobiographical sources point to Romani requirements of endogamous relationships, where both man and woman were Roma, or, even stricter, from the same subgroup. Many changes have occurred regarding this tradition, however, as economic impoverishment might have influenced the choice to marry exogamously. Marrying a non-Roma might have become less controversial as financial stability and social status override genealogical concerns for "purity of blood." Integrating into the dominant society through intermarriage might have become more important for survival.[68] Whether endogamous marriages remain the norm or not, gender inequities in such have surfaced. For many Romani subgroups "relationships between men and non-Romani women are allowed whereas relationships between women and non-Roma are severely prohibited."[69] Hildegard Lagrenne claims Sinti girls—at least in Germany in the 1980s—rarely married non-Romani men, whereas the attitudes towards Sinti men marrying non-Romani women were much looser. Her brother, for example, married a non-Romani Polish woman.[70] Several reasons for this inequity have emerged, the strongest being that the female holds "the burden of responsibility for the purity of the race."[71] Additionally, the patrilocal/patrilineal nature of Romani culture required that the female join the male's family upon marriage; still, when the couple belonged to the same group, the group did not lose a member. When a male Rom married a non-Romani woman, she most often would join his family and his group. When a Romani woman married a non-Roma, however, she was not obligated to stay within her group. For the survival of the group, gaining a member was better than losing one. Within this patrilocal/patrilineal system, Mayerhofer concludes that a

---

66   Nikolić, *Landfahrer*, 110–11.
67   Ibid., 75–6.
68   Haupt, *Antiziganismus und Religion*, 87–8.
69   *Rombase*, http://ling.kfunigraz.ac.at/~rombase/
70   Krausnick, *"Da wollten wir frei sein!"* 48.
71   Miller, "American Rom," 45.

union between a Romani man and a non-Romani woman could bring advantages to the groom's family that marriage between a Romani woman and non-Romani man could not. Usually, the non-Romani woman—who would go to live with the Roma man's family—would have a better education and might be more knowledgeable in dealing with officials in the area.[72] Still, no pattern of endogamous relationships emerges in the autobiographies. Each describes family members who have married and had children with non-Roma. Although some autobiographers and members of their family have shown preference to marry endogamously, exogamous marriages have not been unusual.[73]

Frequently, life during marriage has displayed a clear division of household labor based upon sex. Women were mostly responsible for acquiring, preparing, and cooking food and for childrearing, whereas men tended the fire and the horses, as with Lovara. Mongo Stojka describes seeing young, beautiful Romani girls wearing necklaces and dresses ritually fetching milk every morning as part of their chores. When they returned, mothers made coffee and eggs for the boys. Mongo thus also references certain gender-related food restrictions, namely, the females did not eat eggs.[74] Whether this restriction was due to economic or cultural reasons is not clear. No other autobiographer mentions this practice.

Exceptions to the division of household labor based on sex also surface. Hanstein talks about an uncle who cooked, cleaned the house, and crocheted bedspreads while his wife went selling door-to-door.[75] Angeren-Franz claims her father helped out when needed, but she admits his assistance was more an exception to the rule than the norm among Sinti.[76] Separate duties could also engender separate household spaces. In Mongo Stojka's stories, men often sat around the campfire and told stories at night while women stayed with young children in the wagon.[77] While in their own space, however, men cooked potatoes and *Kukuruz* (corn on the cob), demonstrating that not only the women

---

72  Mayerhofer, *Dorfzigeuner*, 73.
73  Marital histories of Lily van Angeren-Franz and her friend Rosa epitomize various attitudes Roma take towards mixed marriages. Lily's first husband was Dutch and non-Sinti. Rosa also married a non-Sinti, but they had marital problems, resulting in a child custody battle. Lily decided not to take sides, angering Rosa. To Rosa, Lily's decision to remain neutral represented the betrayal of a fellow Sinteza, and implicit allegiance to a non-Sinti. Rosa deemed exogamous marriages impossible, whereas Lily argued that she was happy in her marriage with a non-Sinto (Angeren-Franz, *Leben*, 126).
74  Mongo Stojka, "Unsere alte Welt," 249.
75  Hanstein, *hundert Leben*, 13.
76  Angeren-Franz, *Leben*, 14.
77  Mongo Stojka, "Unsere alte Welt," 247.

did the cooking. Whether women and children ate the food the men prepared, or whether only the men consumed these special dishes, is unknown. Sharing food would point towards gender equity whereby both sexes engaged in household duties for the entire family. The high value placed on children as part of the large, extended family has precluded abortion, which could ostracize a woman and her family from the group forever. Elisabeth Kreutz points to only one incident in her life where a woman had an abortion. The woman died an "impure person" (*Unreine*) and even her grandchildren suffered.[78] When Angeren-Franz's friend Rosa wanted to abort her child whom she had conceived with a married man, Lily tried to dissuade her. Lily did not argue all Romani were against abortion; rather, she expressed her own individual innocence at the time. "What did one know about abortion then?" she asks. She weighs both sides, realizing that the child was an unborn life, but at the same time, the unborn child did not ask to be conceived under such dire circumstances: "In the end, the child had not asked to be conceived from the meeting of two irresponsible people."[79] Rosa tried to abort the child herself by taking hot salt baths and running up and down the stairs frequently, but she was unsuccessful, and did bear a son. In Lily's comments on abortion, however, signs of individual questioning of beliefs emerge.

A prevalent accusation against Romani men within the perceived patriarchal system has been that they have engaged in culturally sanctioned wife-beating. Ilona Lacková, a Slovakian Romni, relates how beatings belonged to a larger system of male-dominated norms and expectations insisting men should always be in control of women. Other norms for men included going out and drinking with friends, because "A guy who didn't drink wasn't considered a real man."[80] By using their families' money for drinking, men assumed unlimited control of financial means, even when such an action harmed the entire family's situation. Autobiographers do not talk about these pressures, and no written incidents of men beating women emerge.

Males were, however, often under pressure to be their families' main financial supporters, even at a young age. At 14, Hanstein found himself "the man in the family, the breadwinner."[81] Winter stresses that his older brother Erich cooked for the family while their parents sold

---

78 Krausnick, "*Da wollten wir frei sein*," 22.
79 "Was wusste man damals schon über Abtreibung ... . Das Kind hatte schließlich nicht darum gebeten, bei der Begegnung zweier verantwortungsloser Menschen gezeugt zu werden." Angeren-Franz, *Leben*, 139.
80 Ilona Lacková, *A False Dawn: My Life as a Gypsy Woman in Slovakia* (Hatfield, Hertfordshire: University of Hertfordshire Press, 1999), 193.
81 "der Mann in der Familie, der Ernährer." Hanstein, *hundert Leben*, 37.

door-to-door. As the oldest, however, Erich also commanded obedience from younger siblings.[82] As the next section will demonstrate, however, women frequently remained the families' main breadwinners.

Just as the wife should have been loyal to her husband, men, too, were responsible for being true to their wives and the mothers of their children. Mišo Nikolić relates one incident concerning his brother-in-law, Žiko, who had abandoned Mišo's sister and their two children in Yugoslavia without officially divorcing her and then come to Germany. When Žiko was discovered kissing a Romni named Zuna, Zuna's family became upset because even though Žiko was separated from his wife, he was still married. Zuna's mother, "die alte Matrona" (the old matron), came to Hamburg in her huge black Opel, scolded and cursed her daughter, and took Zuna along with Žiko back to Mannheim, implying the two would now have to marry to save Zuna from disgrace. Mišo is disappointed Žiko had an extramarital affair and contemplated beating him up. Because Žiko had abandoned his family, no one would have blamed Mišo for the beating. But Mišo also understands that separation and divorce might be the best options when a man and woman cannot get along. Roma do not condone separation or divorce, Mišo clarifies, but in Žiko's case, divorce would have been better than infidelity and abandonment.[83]

Romani men growing up during war times had to serve their country in the military. Actually, both men and women performed governmental service under the Nazis, but men could receive combat orders.[84] Mettbach talks about her grandfather and other relatives serving in the German army during World War I. Then her father served in the German army at the front in France in World War II after his schooling and before his deportation to a concentration camp. These men "felt like good Germans."[85] Several autobiographers stress this service as proof of familial patriotism.[86] The discriminatory

---

82  Winter, *Z 3105*, 14.
83  Nikolić, *Landfahrer*, 60–1.
84  On June 26, 1935, the National Socialist "Gesetz für den Reicharbeitsdienst" (Law for Service Work for the Reich) required male and female youth between 18 and 25 years old to perform a half-year's service work. After 1939 women could participate on a voluntary basis. Sinti, too, had to fulfill this "Ehrendienst am deutschen Volke" (honorable service of the German people). In 1938–9, Winter dug ditches and drainage (*Z 3105*, 44–6). Tasks included repairing roads, working in the forest, building trails, and helping construct highways. During wartime, service workers erected structures for military action (*Z 3105*, 197n. 2).
85  "fühlten sich als gute Deutsche." Mettbach/Behringer, *"Wer wird ..."* 32.
86  Elisabeth Kreutz's husband, Hildegard Lagrenne's father, served in World War I (Krausnick, *"Da wollten wir frei sein!"* 20). Friedrich Kreutz obtained a driver's license without stating he was Roma. He then enlisted in the army and was a soldier in Berlin, Bromberg, Russia, and Estonia. But when he

racial treatment against Roma before, during, and after World War II therefore became in Roma eyes hypocritical and humiliating. Some customs have transcended gender, however, including those demanding respect for the elders. Mongo Stojka states a 20-year-old could accompany older men into the pub, but those 17 and younger had to stay outside and mind the horses. Age requirements seem less related to standard drinking ages than to respect for elders. Mongo also describes young boys and older men sitting on opposite sides of the room during parties and festivals.[87] Men and women always had to show respect for male and female elders. Language has also reflected such customs, as when Hildegard Lagrenne asserts that no word exists in Romany for "nursing home" (*Altersheim*).[88] In the community, male elders could attain more elevated social status than females by serving as judges and mediators, the highest positions within the internal governance systems. Angeren-Franz talks about her father's role as mediator in community conflicts. She stresses her father's skills in this work, implying the respect he commanded had less to do with his age or his sex than with his abilities.[89] Mongo Stojka observes a community leader was not necessarily the oldest member of the subgroup, but definitely was the wisest.[90] His father, for example, from a very young age often had to settle group and familial disputes.[91] Mongo insists his father's abilities, and not his sex or age, qualified him to be a judge. Still no autobiographer mentions a woman—even an older woman who might have reached a respectable age—as judge or mediator.

Yet all autobiographers cite older female figures they have honored. Otto Rosenberg speaks glowingly about his grandmother who raised

---

was wounded and in the infirmary, his Romani heritage surfaced. Still, he survived and went back to duty. Officials eventually found out he was Roma, and he was then deported to a camp in Kattowitz (ibid., 59–65). Bernhard Steinbach also enlisted in the army and had two uncles and cousins in the army. He was sent to Posen. His father encouraged him to leave the army, believing officials would eventually find out he was Roma. Steinbach told his commandant he was Roma, and 14 days later the army released him. He returned home and was eventually deported to Auschwitz (ibid., 73–4). Hanstein's uncle was called into the army because he was good with horses (*hundert Leben*, 15). Philomena Franz's father and some of his brothers served in World War I, and Philomena's brother was in the army for two years during World War II (*Liebe und Haß*, 43–4). Sinti in Germany were serving in the military for Prussia and other principalities in the eighteenth century: Karin Bott-Bodenhausen, "Prosoziales Verhalten," 153.

87  Mongo Stojka, "Unsere alte Welt," 251.
88  Krausnick, "*Da wollten wir frei sein!*" 49.
89  Angeren-Franz, *Leben*, 14.
90  Mongo Stojka, "Unsere alte Welt," 261.
91  Mongo Stojka, *Papierene Kinder*, 14.

him. As a child he lived with her in the German settlement camp in Berlin-Marzahn; he praises her good nature, her ability to get along with anyone, and her concern for their wellbeing.[92] Rosenberg describes how the women felt responsible to help each other out. Romani women formed tight bonds and took care of children when mothers were away. They made him feel cared for and protected, despite harsh conditions.[93] Hanstein, too, was brought up by his grandmother because his mother was only 17 and too young to raise him. He has only positive remembrances of his grandmother's fortitude. Winter praises his maternal grandmother as a totally modern woman who joined the all-male fishing club and smoked a pipe. Pipe-smoking, however, was no anomaly for women, he claims; many older Sinti women smoked pipes because cigarettes were not fashionable.[94] Mongo Stojka refers to his aunt—*Puri Lina* (old Lina)—as a pipe smoker too.[95] For Winter, pipe-smoking women showed their power in the family. From an outside perspective, he states, one would think the man ruled the household, but women were by no means powerless, especially older women.[96] His paternal grandmother was also strong: she lived on their land, but had her own wagon and hired her own horse tender.[97] Besides displays of independence and strength within the home, women also worked outside the home—a subject to which the next section turns.

## Work

Scholars have shown how Romani women in many countries and for many centuries have engaged in paid labor and have often controlled family finances.[98] Autobiographies portray women and men working outside the home to earn money for the entire family. In many

---

92    Rosenberg, *Brennglas*, 18.
93    Ibid., 13. Historical sources state the water in Berlin-Marzahn was so bad the residents often had to go to the next area to fetch water, which might have been a main reason why women regularly passed in and out of the settlement (Ulrich Enzensberger, "Anmerkungen," in Rosenberg, *Brennglas*, 2, 146). See Illustration 6 (page 119) showing the dismal conditions of the camp.
94    Winter, *Z 3105*, 17.
95    Mongo Stojka, *Papierene Kinder*, 36.
96    Winter, *Z 3105*, 17.
97    Ibid., 18.
98    Beate Eder-Jordan "'Traditionen wurden weitergegeben wie die Märchen': Eine Sintiza gewährt Einblick in ihr Leben," *L'Homme: Zeitschrift für feministische Geschichtswissenschaft* 7.1 (1996): 170–83; Kóczé, "Gender," Carol Silverman, "Music and Power: Gender and Performance among Roma (Gypsies) of Skopje, Macedonia," *Music, Language and Literature of the Roma and Sinti*, ed. Max Peter Baumann, Intercultural Music Studies 11 (Berlin: Verlag für Wissenschaft und Bildung, 2000), 247–62; Sutherland, *Gypsies*; and Tauber, *Du wirst*.

accounts, a clear division of labor by sex appears. The work of men and women, however, varied according to the subgroup's specialty. Lovara and Sinti men handled the horses, and women told fortunes and sold door-to-door. Karl Stojka describes the interwar period, when his family would settle down in late fall and winter and take up travelling to earn money in spring and summer. Men traded horses and women sold lace or cooking spoons.[99] Mongo Stojka's recollections, too, show women working, but he adds fortune telling to their livelihoods as he reminisces about seeing women asking passersby in cars if they wanted their palms read.[100] The age-old, gender-specific livelihood of fortune telling thrived—often supported by non-Roma—despite mistrust and laws forbidding the practice.

Mišo Nikolić states fortune telling was women's work in every Romani subgroup. His mother and grandmother were both fortune tellers, and brothers of his grandmother were horse thieves.[101] Otto Rosenberg, too, describes his mother's fortune-telling enterprises along with selling goods door-to-door, while his father was a horse trader. Boys were trained from their youngest years how to care for and sell the horses. Men held other jobs, too, including making and decorating baskets and furniture.[102] Hanstein's mother, too, went *hausieren*—selling goods door-to-door—and his father traded horses and played music. Hanstein mentions only his mother's daily wages of 10 Marks, implying she provided the family's main financial support. When she came home with the groceries she had bought with her earnings, however, Ewald stresses how his father called all the children in to help her unload.[103] His story depicts how mother, father, and children all contributed to the family's household wellbeing and survival. Rosenberg recounts how Nazis forbade these livelihoods and how outside pressures and discriminatory practices transformed economic and social conditions.

Karl Stojka confirms that women's earning often went towards goods sustaining the family's daily existence, while men's earnings went mostly towards their own businesses and needs. As with Hanstein, Stojka is proud of his mother's good reputation as a seller of quality fabrics and lace.[104] Women showed excellent skills and took pride in their abilities. Angeren-Franz also emphasizes how women were the family's most important breadwinners, and their employment was the

---

99 Karl Stojka, *Kindheit*, 14.
100 Mongo Stojka, "Unsere alte Welt," 251.
101 Nikolić, ... *und dann*, 10, 14.
102 Rosenberg, *Brennglas*, 9, 11.
103 Hanstein, *hundert Leben*, 17.
104 Stojka and Pohanka, *Auf der ganzen Welt*, 23–4.

norm. Her own mother went *hausieren* and sometimes told fortunes. Men, Angeren-Franz states, did a little horse trading and went to the market where they repaired some chairs or played music. Frequently men's days at the market ended early in the pub, as they spent their earnings on alcohol and returned home later without money. She states that her father was an exception because he earned money for the family household through his musical talents. He also helped often with cooking and household chores.[105]

Men's and women's choice of work appears to have depended on mutual agreement. Each sex performed what he or she knew best. Autobiographers praise hard-working and resourceful parents. Regarding fortune telling, autobiographers proudly recount times when women predicted actual occurrences. Elisabeth Kreutz describes the fortune-telling wagon she set up in an amusement park after the war, complete with a sign offering *"Phrenology and Chiromanty"* (*Phrenologie und Chiromantie*). She proudly asserts many customers returned numerous times because everything she predicted came true. She hints at her special powers, lending credence to her spiritual calling as a fortune teller.[106] Her daughter, Hildegard Lagrenne, confirms her mother's special connections with *mulo*, death spirits, a clairvoyance Hildegard feels the younger generation lacks. Her mother had premonitions Hildegard does not have, such as finding food bitter just before someone died or feeling pressure in her chest when something bad was going to happen.[107] By stressing Elisabeth's effective clairvoyant aptitude, Hildegard dispels the image of deceit so often connected with female Romani fortune tellers.

Rather than pointing to special powers, other autobiographers are often more matter-of-fact, even nonchalant in talking about family fortune tellers. Karl Stojka observes fortune telling was a usual livelihood in most families.[108] Some women even admitted their fortune-telling sessions involved more psychological acumen than true mystical connections with a supernatural world. Lily Angeren-Franz relates how her mother was primarily a saleswoman, but she turned to fortune telling when sales were bad. Lily then honestly admits her mother's predictions were only "sometimes" successful. Instead, Lily praises her mother for keenly reading facial expressions and body language, discerning family circumstances so as to orient her predictions towards what clients might have wanted to hear. If she predicted a woman was going to have a baby and then saw the woman was not

---

105 Angeren-Franz, *Leben*, 14–15.
106 Krausnick, *"Da wollten wir frei sein,"* 22.
107 Ibid., 46.
108 Stojka and Pohanka, *Auf der ganzen Welt*, 23.

happy with this premonition, Lily's mother quickly took another look at her hand and changed her prediction. She savvily recognized the economic gain of telling a positive, welcome fortune: "A happy face pays more, my mother always said."[109] Predicting a woman would bear a son was usually good enough for some bacon and vegetables. Stories about women's abilities to tell fortunes—whether due to special intuitions or psychological skills —demonstrate Roma respected this work as much as other livelihoods—selling wares, repairing tools, trading horses, weaving baskets—regardless of whether men or women were performing the work.

Who actually controlled the money, however, varied by household. Tauber, on the one hand, points out the paradox of Southern Tirolean Sinti women going *manghél*, or selling door-to-door, and men at home controlling money women have earned. After women go *manghél*, they divide the money up equally among themselves, with total regard to equal shares and work. They then come home with their earnings, and men administer the finances and decide how to spend the money. Women notice this paradox between financial earnings and power, and they talk openly about the system's inequity.[110] Karl Stojka, on the other hand, describes the household in which he grew up differently—women ruled the finances; in his case, it was his grandmother. She carried all money in a little purse bundled up under her many skirts, never using the bank.[111] Winter's comments about his paternal grandmother's powers in the family, Hanstein's depiction of his mother buying goods for the household from the money she had earned, and Angeren-Franz's description of women as the family's main breadwinners corroborate Karl's story of the women's vital role in managing household finances.

Both sexes frequently performed shared livelihoods; for example, men and women often peddled wares together. Total success involved cooperative efforts. Anna Mettbach talks about both parents being on the road from early spring until fall with the family as they made and sold baskets her father fashioned from willow branches. Although Mettbach does not specify who did the selling, she refers to both parents registering business activities together with the officials as required after 1933.[112] Winter describes how both his parents sold textiles from town to town on bicycles. His mother appeared to have been more well known, as he comments on how grateful the village

---

109 "Ein frohes Gesicht bezahlt mehr, sagte Mama immer." Angeren-Franz, *Leben*, 21–2.
110 Tauber, *Du wirst*, 114–15.
111 Stojka and Pohanka, *Auf der ganzen Welt*, 17.
112 Mettbach/Behringer, *"Wer wird …"* 23.

people were when she came selling goods. His description of the welcome his mother received supports the notion of the "Dorfzigeuner" (village Gypsies) whose accessible services rural residents appreciated. Winter's father also traded horses and occasionally cows on the side.[113] When the family decided to establish a shooting booth at local festivities, everyone in the family—males and females—worked there. His three sisters, brother, and he dressed up in white shirts and blouses and black pants and skirts to make a good impression. Economic success required a collaborative family, Winter stresses.[114]

At times, women had to beg for food for the family, but men also begged when in need. Mišo Nikolić was not humiliated to beg. At one point in France he had four francs left and decided to spend two on a new haircut. He took off his dirty sweater and began begging on the street. By noon he had almost 50 francs.[115] Of course, he was responsible for only his own wellbeing and at that time did not have immediate family to support or help him. Other young boys in his circle of friends stole for an organized crime ring. Mišo did not condone this activity and, instead, reprimanded the ringleader for promoting stealing. If the ringleader had really wanted to help Roma, Mišo contends, he would have instead procured proper documentation to help boys stay legally in the country. Begging would have been more respectable than stealing. Mišo sees a major difference between needing to steal for one's existence and relying on a ringleader who exploited others for his own greed.[116] He also writes about driving with his male friend Tschorkrta, who sold carpets door-to-door while Mišo sold watches on the street.[117] Or Mišo went *hausieren* by himself every day.[118] Men were proud of their work as sellers, such as Karl Stojka when he praises his and his brother's business selling rugs, claiming they were the first in Austria to sell oriental rugs.[119] They never debased such livelihoods as "merely women's work."

One should not glamorize the work many Roma performed, and, at the same time, one should not underestimate its value either. Autobiographies reveal disadvantages and advantages of livelihoods that from the outside might appear unstable. Lily van Angeren-Franz stresses the hardship of pursuing the kinds of piecemeal work Roma traditionally undertook. Acquiring enough money to feed the

---

113    Winter, *Z 3105*, 13.
114    Ibid., 38.
115    Nikolić, *Landfahrer*, 20.
116    Ibid., 29.
117    Ibid., 66.
118    Ibid., 71.
119    Stojka and Pohanka, *Auf der ganzen Welt*, 37.

family was not always easy. To the outside observer, such work might seem haphazard and worthless, yet Lily witnessed the pride her parents took in pursuing independent and self-sufficient livelihoods, for they had a freedom they would not have had by working for someone else.[120] Instead of undervaluing the Roma's work, one should emphasize Roma's adaptability and resourcefulness, desirable qualities even today in a globalized, financially insecure world. Paradoxically, late capitalism requires flexibility, diverse outlooks, and geographical mobility, exact skills Roma have shown in work habits for centuries.[121] In the work Roma perform, "one finds a remarkable degree of cultural energy and creativity as people discover and invent new and surprising ways to manage their existence."[122] Autobiographers assert pride in their work, thereby making a plea for understanding the complexities, diversity, and value of all livelihoods.

## Music-Making and Storytelling

Autobiographers stress the importance of performances in Roma's daily lives. Roma writings abound with dialogues, songs, and stories by the autobiographers, family members, or friends. These activities have occurred everywhere in daily life: at home, in the pub, at the market, and around the campfire at night. For Philomena Franz, performing music was her family's professional livelihood, and all family members—males and females alike—participated. Lily van Angeren-Franz's father was very musical, playing violin, guitar, harmonica, accordion, and many other instruments at family festivities and gatherings. Whenever her family set up camp with other wagons, they played music, sang, and danced.[123] Ewald Hanstein relates how for his father, playing music evolved from a hobby into political engagement. His father started playing guitar, violin, and accordion with Ewald's uncle Karl. Later, when his father joined the Communist Party of Germany (KPD), he played drums in a marching band for the Party. This combination of political involvement and music was unusual.[124] After the war, Ewald founded his own band in Bremen, playing at weddings and other celebrations. For Mišo Nikolić, a passion for music-making evolved into a profession. He always discovered occasions to play music and

---

120 Angeren-Franz, *Leben*, 24.
121 Judith Okely, "Kontinuität und Wandel in den Lebensverhältnissen und der Kultur der Roma, Sinti und Kalé," in *Europäische Roma—Roma in Europa*, eds Reetta Toivanen and Michi Knecht (Berlin: Berliner Blätter: Ethnographische und ethnologische Beiträge 39, 2006), 26.
122 Michael Stewart, "Conclusions: Spectres of the Underclass," eds Emigh and Szelényi, *Poverty*, 194.
123 Angeren-Franz, *Leben*, 17.
124 Hanstein, *hundert Leben*, 18, 20.

later founded a family musical group. After his sad, sudden death in 2008, his wife, Ruzsa Nikolić-Lakatos, assumed leadership of the band. She is still a well-known Austrian singer and performs at international Romani festivals.

Performances in all venues, professionally and privately, have happened when the sexes have been apart and together. In fact, any separate social spheres between the sexes in daily life have often broken down when a performance begins. Thus, the dichotomy between private and public spheres as gendered spaces—whereby the private space women have usually occupied is considered less important and powerful than the public sphere that the men have usually controlled—might be a false one. Silverman poses an alternative to this dichotomy in relation to Romani performance and gender in Macedonia.[125] She shows many forms of public sphere exist: first is the public sphere of the macro society—dominated by non-Roma—but in which Roma often work and try to make political and social changes; second is the larger Romani public sphere, or "Rom community;" third is the extended family within the Romani community; and fourth is the residential, immediate Romani family sphere. The latter two may not be readily accessible to the Gadže public, and yet they have public aspects within Romani communities. Ritual politics—dance and music during celebrations for weddings, circumcisions, housewarmings, births, and so forth—belong to the Romani community's public realm, for they involve power, economics, and performance. The non-Romani macro-political world subsequently has been traditionally male, whereas ritual politics of the Romani world have often been female. Spheres in the Romani world are much more complicated than the simple split between private and public, and women's and men's roles in each are more varied.[126] Silverman's point is that women have a great deal of power in the family and in Roma's "domestic" and "public" community spheres, but perhaps not as much in the macro public sphere.

Winter describes separate social spheres for men and women in campsites, where music and dance then fused together. Men usually went first to a social gathering, and women followed later after putting the children to bed. Adult men and women sat separately and talked until dancing began. Women did not need permission to dance; he recalls his mother kicking off her shoes and dancing first with his father and then by herself.[127] Song and dance became catalysts for the sexes to

---

125 Silverman, "Music and Power," 248.
126 Cf. Cathy N. Davidson and Jessamyn Hatcher, eds, *No More Separate Spheres!* (Durham, NC/London: Duke University Press, 2002).
127 Winter, Z 3105, 22.

come together, but also for women to dance alone, at least for rituals in the public Romani community and families.

In contrast, Mongo Stojka describes how the woman had to wait for the man to invite her to sing or dance. At first females stood at a distance behind males. When dancing began, the woman was allowed to put her hand on the man's elbow, and the man could ask her to sing for him. Singing for him would show her honor for him, which in turn would make the man feel honored. But if he did not ask her to sing, then she was not allowed to sing. "She was allowed to sing when he said so, and the woman was proud and sang him the song."[128] Mongo then relates how sometimes public performances by females in front of entire communities or families could be forays into future marriage proposals; a boy's father who saw the girl sing and dance to her father's music might later have asked the girl's family if their daughter could marry his son. One might see Mongo's description of women dancing solely for men's pleasure as reinforcing age-old stereotypes of deceitful seductresses, as in the operatic figure Carmen. Performances like the ones Winter and Mongo describe, however, were frequently springboards to larger professional careers for many women. The professional singing careers of Philomena Franz, Rusza Nikolić-Lakatos, Dotschy Reinhardt, and Ceija Stojka began in similar "public" Romani community and family performances.

Walter Winters's and Mongo Stojka's contrasting renditions of women's possible roles prove diversity of customs and caution against generalizations. Stewart concludes that Hungarian Vlach "sisters" do not create a gender-specific cultural identity as "brothers" do. Women are missing in public performances, but, paradoxically, mothers, sisters, wives, and daughters of men celebrating their identities as "brothers in song" earn most of the family's money, which, in turn, goes towards the men continuing to make music together.[129] Kertész Wilkinson, however, finds this generalization false. She singles out many instances where women sing as leaders accompanied by men and thus asserts that Stewart's observations might be valid only in some instances or contexts.[130]

---

128  "Sie durfte singen, wenn er es sagte, und die Frau war dann stolz und sang ihm das Lied." Mongo Stojka, "Unsere alte Welt," 257.
129  Michael Stewart, "Brothers in Song: The Persistence of (Vlach) Gypsy Community and Identity in Socialist Hungary," (PhD dissertation, London School of Economic and Political Science, 1987): 239–40.
130  Irén Kertész Wilkinson, *Vásár van előttem : egyéni alkotások és társadalmi kontextusok egy dél-magyarországi oláhcigány lassú dalban/The Fair is ahead of me. Individual creativity and social contexts in the performances of a south-east Hungarian Vlach Gypsy slow song* (Budapest: Institute of Musicology of the Hungarian Academy of Sciences, 1997), 117.

Kertész Wilkinson also confirms women's significance as storytellers, a vital public performatory role. Indeed, both sexes have the freedom to tell stories within the group. Male and female autobiographers extol the storytelling capabilities of men and women in their lives. Mišo Nikolić describes becoming known among fellow travellers for his storytelling abilities. When evening came, and someone asked who could tell a good story, everyone pointed to him and said he should perform, which he did.[131] Ceija Stojka relates how at night while travelling, mothers lay their children down to sleep, and then both parents gathered without children and talked about their ancestors. The children did not want to sleep and often followed parents to eavesdrop secretly. Or at least the children thought they were being secretive. In reality, parents knew the children were listening, and consequently would sometimes tell some "juicy lies" and fictional tales to shock the children. For Ceija, her grandmother told the most wonderful stories. Later, however, Ceija realized that her grandmother's stories were not always true, but rather embellished in order to hold the listeners' attention.[132] Stories of the Stojkas' grandmother and mother continued on, even in the hardest of times. In Ceija's accounts, storytelling was a female occupation. She describes how after her father was deported and then when the family was in concentration camps, her mother used storytelling as a diversion, relating "stories about the good, old, peaceful times."[133] Storytelling became a necessary means to pass down memories and thereby insure immortality.

Otto Rosenberg also recounts how the old women in Berlin-Marzahn were the storytellers around the fire at night. Their vast repertoires included family anecdotes, memories, fairy tales, scary tales, and fictional narratives.[134] Likewise, Philomena Franz praises the storytelling abilities of grandmothers in general.[135] In the opening lines to her own folk tale collection, Franz introduces herself confidently and intimately to her young audience in her storyteller role: "Dear child! I am a Gypsy and my name is Philomena, and I would like to tell you about the Gypsies."[136]

Autobiographers make clear not all the stories told around the fire at night were for children. Yet children and adults made a game of

---

131 Nikolić, *Landfahrer*, 113–14.
132 Ceija Stojka, "Du darfst," 113.
133 "Geschichten von den guten, alten, friedlichen Zeiten." Ceija Stojka, *Verborgenen*, 64.
134 Otto Rosenberg, *Brennglas*, 14.
135 Philomena Franz, *Zigeunermärchen* (Bonn: Europa Union Verlag GmbH, 1989), 39.
136 "Liebes Kind! Ich bin eine Zigeunerin und heiße Philomena, und ich möchte Dir etwas von den Zigeunern erzählen" (ibid., 7).

storytelling. As with Ceija Stojka, who snuck out of her bed to eavesdrop on the stories or cajoled her parents into letting her stay up, Lily van Angeren-Franz recounts how as a curious child she surreptitiously listened to stories intended only for adults. Through stalling around by asking for drinks of water and food, she and her siblings could hear these forbidden stories. Her eavesdropping had consequences, however, as she often could not sleep after scary stories with *mulo* ghostly spirits.[137] Such tales belong to their own category straddling truth and fiction; their truth was rarely questioned. Storytelling did have some restrictions, however. As Lily reveals, matters of sexuality remained between females, if women even talked about them at all. Mongo Stojka describes topics men talked about when they were alone together— business, families, relatives, mutual acquaintances, and sometimes their industrious wives' culinary skills.[138] Some stories may thus never have made their way outside the Romani private sphere. As already noted, Roma also could scorn telling stories about horrific experiences during the *Porrajmos*/Holocaust, too. Luckily, the power of storytelling among Roma has been strong enough to break the silence and suppression.

## Mitigations and Transformations of Patriarchal Norms

A study prepared for the Roma Participation Program for the Open Society proves useful for defining what "patriarchal" means in the context of Roma's values and customs investigated here.[139] Although the study looked at Roma in a time and place—namely, Romania in 2006—differing from those in which the autobiographers have lived and written, comparative standards are still valuable. The study defined its "patriarchal model" as one where the man was the family's leader. Assessment of family life included questions about the age of marriage, responsibility for household chores, leadership in the family, value placed on virginity at marriage, and responsibility for childrearing and the educational progress of the children. Other questions included ones on health and reproductive rights, labor, and housing situations. The study:

> clearly and convincingly shows that Romani women constitute the most deprived category of the Romanian population due to the discrimination and social exclusion they experience as a result of the intersection of race, gender, and class. Within Romania,

---

137 Angeren-Franz, *Leben*, 18.
138 Mongo Stojka, *Papierene Kinder*, 26.
139 *Broadening the Agenda: The Status of Romani Women in Romania. A Research Report Prepared for the Roma Participation Program*, eds Laura Surdu and Mihai Surdu (New York: Open Society, 2006), http://www.opensocietyfoundations.org/reports/broadening-agenda-status-romani-women-romania

Romani women are the ones who are most likely to suffer from inadequate health care and housing conditions, poor quality of education, and lack of job opportunities.[140]

The study's findings corroborate the significance of customs related to courtship, marriage, and family life as indicators of women's status. Autobiographers point to patriarchal norms similar to those in this study. Karl Stojka remarks about the man's dominant role in the family: "The man always wore the pants and had the say in the family."[141] As Ceija Stojka writes, fathers usually wanted boys: "With the Romani man that is such a big honor."[142] No special festivities occurred for the births of girls, but when boys came, everyone celebrated. Mongo Stojka confirms his father's celebratory emotion after his first son's birth in contrast to his disappointment after his daughters' births. When a boy arrived, the father went right to the birthing place, whereas for a girl, the father stayed away:

> When I came into the world my father took me and wrapped me in his shirt because I was his boy, not the boy of his mother, I was his son, his! That is really wonderful when you know what your father has done because of you, and when you get old and hear that you love your father even more, when he has done that with you when you were small.[143]

Mongo's story here contradicts his former assertion that men could not enter the birthing place for two or three days due to purity laws. His father's eagerness points to special occasions that could break traditions. Exceptions to customs are not unusual, but in this case, the deviation reinforces the higher value placed on male children. Mongo's positive reaction to his father's joy demonstrates the self-confidence and pride such attention inspired throughout the male's life. Likewise, Hanstein talks about the undivided attention his grandmother and

---

140  Ibid., 5.
141  "Der Mann hat immer die Hosen angehabt und hatte das Sagen in der Familie." Stojka and Pohanka, *Auf der ganzen Welt*, 26.
142  "Bei den Rom ist das halt eine besonders große Ehre." Ceija Stojka, "Du darfst," 124–5.
143  "Als ich auf die Welt kam, nahm mich mein Vater und wickelte mich in sein Hemd, denn ich war der Seine, nicht der meiner Mutter, ich war sein Sohn, seiner! Das ist wirklich wunderbar, wenn du weißt, was dein Vater deinetwegen gemacht hat, und wenn du alt geworden bist und das hörst, liebst du deinen Vater noch mehr, wenn er es mit dir so gemacht hat, als du noch klein warst." Mongo Stojka, "Unsere alte Welt," 256–7.

female cousin gave him as the household's only boy as the women clearly preferred Ewald as the family's sole male.[144] Many customs, too, placed a higher value on males, but customs also had their anomalies and complications. Regarding pollution and purity beliefs, *Rombase* describes the laws' patriarchal foundations while emphasizing that such laws must be evaluated within individual cultural contexts.[145] While restrictions placed on washing clothes, cooking, and touching might stem from beliefs in the female body's uncleanliness, these laws might also empower and protect women: "In contrast to the religious praxis of the non–Roma, the belief in the mystic abilities of women is much stronger. This 'mystic power' assigns to the woman a certain power and protects her private life."[146] Regarding *mahrime*—impurity and purity—for Romni, Sutherland states "The pollution dangers which a woman presents are a protection for her."[147] If a man mistreated a woman she could threaten to ostracize him with *mahrime* by touching him with her skirt—"skirt-tossing"—or another similar violation. Women's fertility could also empower, as women symbolically become key to the group's survival. Unfortunately, Nazi policies targeting Roma and Pro-Juventute measures against Jenisch demonstrate both the power of women's crucial childbearing roles and the grave consequences of such power.

By stressing woman's sexuality during her reproductive years, Romani customs then allow for heightened respect and loosening of restrictions for post-menopausal women because their sexuality is no longer threatening.[148] Belief in an increase in women's status with age, however, does not apply to all cases, because social constraints of age in Western society at large can also influence status. As Nyman observes for Romani women in southern Poland, "old age and purity in no way compensate for the lack of financial stability, the poor health, the diminished youthful beauty, and the loneliness of the widow's lot."[149] Likewise, when Ceija Stojka wanted to begin painting at 56—an age at which women usually garner respect and not face limitations—her husband was against her artistic endeavors because he believed they would conflict with her household duties.[150] He also did not want her to write down her memories and emotions at first.[151] Older women may

---

144  Hanstein, *hundert Leben*, 12.
145  *mahrime*, http://rombase.uni-graz.at/
146  Ibid.
147  Sutherland, *Gypsies*, 257.
148  *mahrime*, http://rombase.uni-graz.at/
149  Nyman, "Complex Relationship," 97.
150  Heidelinde Prüger, *Zigeuner Sein* (Klagenfurt: Hermagoras/Mohorjeva, 2001), 105; Ceija Stojka, personal interview with Lorely French, January 9, 2009.
151  Ceija Stojka, "Du darfst," 97.

have freedoms related to sexuality, but perhaps few related to social mobility or their perceived familial and community roles. The idea that an older woman commanded respect did not always play out in reality. A comment by Mišo Nikolić reveals this split between the respect older women could garner in their families and the lingering image of older women who had lost a valuable beauty. At one point, he admired a certain older "Matrona" who dominated the decisions in her family;[152] at another point, he described a woman over 40 in derogatory terms for her lack of beauty.[153] For each example of an older woman receiving respect there exists a contrary example.

Women's virginity as a pre-condition for marriage also unveils a patriarchal double standard: men in autobiographies did not have to abstain from sexual relationships before marriage. Still, not all women were rejected if they were not virgins upon marriage. Although Ruzsa Nikolić-Lakatos's father punished her for carrying a child out of wedlock, Mišo, the father of the child, still loved and married her. The practice of the future groom asking for permission from the future bride's father to marry his daughter also corroborates patriarchal norms, but specifics regarding brideprices or the dowry arrangements are not clear. Research has shown brideprices and dowries might either limit or protect women in marriage contracts, depending on historical and social contexts, and on the complex ways in which women's worth became valued or devalued, as the case might have been.[154] Without specifics, one cannot draw concrete conclusions about their ultimate effects.

Gender roles have also often required women to cook and perform all housework while concurrently working outside the home, thereby creating a "double burden" that men did not always have. Exceptions happened, however, such as with Ewald Hanstein, who was the oldest male in the family and responsible for cooking and taking care of his younger siblings. Men also had to cook when women were not allowed to do so, as after birthing. Of course, that exception belonged to an entire belief system that saw women's bodily fluids as both impure and mystic, which, as already argued, could be either derogatory or empowering for the woman.

Such examples prove that for almost every incident with gender inequity there exists a justification or an exception. For Mišo Nicolić,

---

152  Nikolić, *Landfahrer*, 54.
153  Ibid., 109.
154  Siwn Anderson, "The Economics of Dowry and Brideprice," *Journal of Economic Perspectives*, 21.4 (Fall 2007): 151–74; and Laura W. R. Appell, "Menstruation among the Rungus of Borneo: An Unmarked Category," in *Blood Magic: The Anthropology of Menstruation*, eds Thomas Buckley and Alma Gottlieb (Berkeley: University of California Press, 1988), 94–112.

women were always doing the cooking,[155] often while men sat around and talked among themselves.[156] But Nikolić also points out how women's cooking skills could endear them to people and open doors in times of hardship.[157] His wife Ruzsa, who was known for her good cooking, often found them a place to stay in exchange for her services as a cook. Her reputation as a good cook proved advantageous for the entire family and did not limit her talents; she is an accomplished, professional singer with a successful career while also taking care of the home. Mišo showed sensitivity as a man by recognizing the difficulty in juggling all these roles; he also states he tried to help as much as possible.[158]

Walter Winter recounts how after his grandmother's death he and his brother played the radio they had just bought for their grandmother even though Sinti were forbidden to play or listen to music immediately after the death of a near relative or friend. Customs and traditions were not always adhered to, he claims; sometimes exceptions occurred.[159] Hildegard Lagrenne relates how her family did not eat meat after someone had died, a custom she admits may not have existed in all Sinti families. Some might eat meat, but drink no water; some might not wash themselves as long as the dead person remains unburied. Each Sinti family may have had its own personal traditions.[160]

Irregularities may also arise due to the complex nature of autobiography. Trauma, nostalgia, time lapses, social changes, audience, and cultural taboos can all influence a story's content. This is not to question the autobiographies' veracity and moral integrity. The purpose of pointing out varying sides to cultural practices is to direct analysis towards cultural relativism, and not moral relativism. The former pleads for understanding practices within the context of the specific culture from which they derive.[161] The latter recognizes that profound disagreements percolate up among groups of people on a variety of ideas and actions; still "the truth or justification of moral judgments is not absolute, but relative to some group of persons."[162] Thus, moral relativism—in contrast to cultural relativism—does not concentrate as much on cultural context, but rather attempts to displace

---

155 Nikolić, *Landfahrer*, 85, 107–8, 112.
156 Ibid., 85.
157 Ibid., 103.
158 Ibid., 123.
159 Winter, *Z 3105*, 19.
160 Krausnick, *"Da wollten wir frei sein!"* 45.
161 "Relativism," *Stanford Encyclopedia of Philosophy*. http://plato.stanford.edu/entries/relativism/
162 "Moral Relativism," *Stanford Encyclopedia of Philosophy*. http://plato.stanford.edu/entries/moral-relativism/

responsibility for moral wrongdoings by tolerating all actions. In delineating different angles on understanding patriarchy, I am not asking for tolerance of such actions, but rather for understanding cultural contexts and nuances. Despite Romani customs that outsiders may perceive as limiting to women at home, one should not falsely assume those customs have been uniform and universal among all groups and families. One cannot automatically conclude Romani women have all been weak, submissive, and passive in all spheres of their lives and all Romani men have controlled and dominated women. Autobiographies unveil strong women and norms promoting that strength. Roma voices also reveal customs resisting immediate judgment.

Autobiographies prove that women have always worked outside the home, and, in some cases, have been the family's main breadwinners, usually by selling wares door-to-door and at markets. Selling could mean stress, pressure, insecurity, and troubles—with long hours, extensive travelling, and dangerous situations—but also independence, adventure, quality time with female family members, and opportunities to experience the non-Roma world on women's own terms. Autobiographical stories are replete with police encounters, dangerous journeys up and over steep mountains, broken-down cars, dialogues with customers, meetings with other Roma, and gatherings after finishing the long day. Indeed, selling often represents a division of labor by sex, but for women it has guaranteed and justified their existence within the Romani world. Without selling, men and families would not have been able to eat, drink, and play.[163] Without peddling wares, social rejuvenation would cease. Romnija have also been the children's main educators in the home. They have taught songs, recipes, naturopathic medicinal remedies, ancestral stories, and frequently reading and writing.[164] Women are significant storytellers and transmitters of cultural traditions—preparing culinary delicacies, preserving centuries-old healing arts, promoting family and community gatherings and festivals, and transmitting stories publicly so as to ensure the survival of Romani history and culture.

Autobiographers frequently mention that many gendered customs and traditions may not have continued in all or any families since the time the writers were growing up. Regarding courtship, Elisabeth Kreutz—belonging to the oldest generation of Roma writers represented here—describes going to the movies on a first date with her future husband, an unprecedented outing for girls at that time,

---

163 Tauber, *Du wirst*, 118.
164 Hanstein states his mother taught him to read and write (*hundert Leben*, 25). Angeren-Franz recounts how her mother ensured that Lily went to school, and how both parents made her do her schoolwork (*Leben*, 28–9).

because parents forbade girls from going out at all. But Kreutz also recognizes how time has eased such restrictions.[165] Walter Winter, speaking about his grandmother—the pipe-smoking member of the all-male fishing club—says some males had trouble accepting this transformative image. He explains how unconventional gender roles were not always welcome and implies today's generation might be more accepting.[166]

For customs an outside observer might deem restrictive, hearing Roma's own perceptions is important. For example, the "double burden" women face in working inside and outside the home coincides with the high value Roma place on the family. As Dotschy Reinhardt explains, "family" often connotes the concept of the larger extended Romani ethnic group. Everyone older is referred to as one's father or mother or aunt or uncle, and everyone still older as one's grandmother or grandfather; everyone younger is one's brother or sister. To Reinhardt, such designations are simpler than more complex, yet limited ones she sees in her German surroundings.[167] The connection every person holds to a larger familial and communal network has caused women to emphasize the value of their caretaking roles. Reinhardt's concept of family expands beyond the limited scholarly conceptualization of "biological kinship" Vermeersch describes. Instead, kinship is a unit whose members Roma themselves determine. Romani women proudly link their caretaking skills to flourishing cultural communities. For Ceija Stojka, Romani women want to learn to cook, sew, crochet, and knit; if these tasks went undone, she claims, children, families, and ultimately an entire people would perish.[168] Some customs mesh with the high value and respect given to group and familial elders. Reinhardt's belief that women should wear skirts in front of the older generation displays respect. If her grandfather requests this of her, then she has no qualms about honoring his request.[169] In the larger scheme of maintaining cultural values, this request seems minuscule. She is still able to sing and write, which, for the larger goal of transmitting cultural practices, is enormously important.[170]

---

165  Krausnick, *"Da wollten wir frei sein,"* 20.
166  Winter, *Z 3105*, 18.
167  Reinhardt, *Gypsy*, 189–90.
168  Ceija Stojka, "Sie waren Rom," 15.
169  Dotschy Reinhardt, personal interview with Lorely French, Berlin, July 6, 2010.
170  Kristov and WuDunn, in looking at women's global oppression, report on Muslim women who offer a relevant perspective on Westerners' preoccupation with clothing as a sign of oppression. Female Saudi doctors and nurses in Riyadh whom Kristof and WuDunn interviewed found that in concentrating on smaller issues such as clothing, Westerners were patronizing Muslim women and feeling sorry for them. Instead, Westerners should listen

When women face diminished roles and options, however, then change must help solidify and not divide the group. Such is the case when Ceija talks about the limitations that her husband tried to place on her writing and painting. She understands if her husband had ended up curtailing her artistic and written work, then Romani culture stood to lose by excluding a voice from its collective narrative. If women have more freedom and options, then both men and women benefit equally from both sexes' contributions to private and public life. Focusing on "fissures" to crack patriarchal bonds—writing, educating youth, and storytelling—ensures historical and social perpetuity. Silverman refers to "female realms of power and influence" that contradict the patriarchal ideology. For the Balkan women Silverman examines, the "female role in income-producing activities, budget decisions, marriage decisions, information networks, and ritual all mitigate her subordination."[171] For Romani women in the German-speaking countries, the female role in these activities has held true, with the caveat that marriage decisions seem to have only evolved in the younger generation. To this list I would add storytelling and publishing. Female Romani writers extend activities to all spheres—from the immediate residential Romani family circle, to the extended family within the Romani community, to the larger Romani public community, and out to the public sphere of the macro, non-Romani world. Storytelling belongs to women's roles as performers and educators within these private and public spheres. Such roles thereby blur social boundaries, extend the realms of performance into the written word, and concentrate efforts on transformative "fissures."

When Mongo Stojka asks whether old or new ways are better, he turns to family and storytelling as the main factors cementing the culture together. He takes a diplomatic approach, weighing old and new ways carefully. First, finding advantages in both entails respecting elders. His father's own sense of purpose and direction, work ethic, and respect that he instilled in his children inevitably led to their desire to forge new ways to create a better life. When Mongo sees all that today's youth possesses—education and big urban businesses—then he understands the advantages and necessity of new ways, but stresses how the new is built on elders' respect for learning and financial success.[172] Considering elders' values leads Mongo to long for some

---

to concerns about larger issues and try to understand how Muslim women are handling oppression themselves. Nicholas D. Kristov and Sheryle WuDunn, *Half the Sky: Turning Oppression into Opportunity for Women Worldwide* (New York: Vintage, 2009), 154.

171 Silverman, *Romani Routes*, 109.
172 Mongo Stojka, "Unsere alte Welt," 263.

old ways, too. He likes certain customs and images from bygone years, such as eating the food the women prepared and being allowed to sit around the campfire with elders.[173] Those evenings inevitably led to the men telling stories about army life, travel, and homecomings. As the evening continued, other Romani men joined the circle, the most memorable guests being the bear trainers with their bears. Storytelling thus forms his most impressionable images in both the old and the new ways. Ultimately, Mongo states, a Rom or Romni may have to decide between old and new, but the right way will be one the whole family determines together.[174]

Storytelling and family comprise two main elements autobiographers portray as keys to survival. Mišo Nikolić found refuge with family and friends in France, Germany, and Austria as he escaped the turmoil of Yugoslavia. He met extended family—nephews, an ex-brother-in-law, a sister's boyfriend, an ex-girlfriend's cousin—who helped Mišo survive.[175] Otto Rosenberg emphasizes familial closeness before and after Roma were forced to live together in Berlin-Marzahn. Ewald Hanstein, in looking for the rest of his family after the war, states that home for a Sinto is where the family is.[176] Philomena Franz asserts that children represent Roma's highest wealth.[177] High estimation of family, children, and future generations adds value to women's significance in maintaining connections. Extended Romani families and storytelling form two major sites for intersections of gender and ethnicity and will thereby ensure survival of vital cultural traditions. When the Nazis attempted to destroy families and storytelling, little did they know these voices would come back strongly after persecution.

---

173    Ibid., 265.
174    Ibid., 267.
175    Nikolić, *Landfahrer*, 28–9.
176    Hanstein, *hundert Leben*, 78.
177    Franz, *Liebe und Haß*, 26.

# *Four* "We were totally uprooted": Romani Perspectives on the *Porrajmos*/Holocaust

## Ethnic Persecution under National Socialism

Stereotypical perceptions of Roma—nomadism, use of Romany as a "secret" language, illiteracy, and inability and unwillingness to assimilate and integrate—and gender-related customs underlaid Nazi racial policies. Attempts to break up families and to exterminate European Roma mark the depths of centuries-long isolation, discrimination, and persecution.[1] The devastating *Porrajmos*/Holocaust stands as one of the major symbols unifying Roma.[2] Autobiographers comment on how maltreatment violated ethnic identities and gender norms and aimed to destroy individualism and collectivism. They stress individualism among subgroups, but view their stories about the *Porrajmos* as belonging to a shared history. They want to make that history part of the national ones of the countries where they reside.

When Hitler was elected to power in 1933, "a genocidal policy directed specifically at 'a-socials'—a category into which Gypsies fell at that time—was drawn up. From 1934 on, they [Roma] were being sent to camps at Dachau, Dieselstrasse, Marzahn and Vennhausen for

---

1   Margalit calls the discrimination of German Roma beginning in 1933 "unprecedented" (*Germany*, 32). Such treatment had been occurring for centuries, however. Margalit is most likely attempting to counteract a main postwar argument against giving Roma restitution for the Nazis' murderous treatment, namely, that there was no substantial difference between past persecution of Roma before and during Nazi times (*Germany*, 84).
2   For other symbols, see footnote 55, Chapter One above (page 24), from Silverman, *Romani Routes*, 48. Smith observes "genocide and genocidal actions, at least in modern times ... rarely extinguish *ethnies* or ethnic categories. In fact they may do the opposite, reviving ethnic cohesion and consciousness, or helping to crystallize it, as they did with the Aborigines' movement or Romany Gypsy nationalism" (*National*, 31).

sterilization."[3] The Nazi regime immediately issued other new laws and penal codes affecting ethnic communities.[4] Restrictions occurred nationally in all Nazi-occupied territories; countless regional policies also banned Roma from travelling, attending school, marrying, bearing children, and working.[5] In total, estimates of Roma killed during Nazi times have ranged from 500,000 to 1.5 million, with most victims from Eastern Europe. For Germany, estimates of Roma murdered during Nazi times range from 15,000 to 25,000. In Austria, the most accurate estimates place the number at around 11,000.[6]

3   Hancock, "'Uniqueness'," 53.
4   The main national laws and measures affecting Roma included the following: "Nürnberger Rassengesetze" (Nuremberg Race Laws) in 1935, with subsequent commentary adding Roma to those possessing "artfremdes Blut" (blood of a foreign type) and prohibiting them from marrying other non-Roma Germans (Zimmermann, *Rassenutopie*, 89–90); the "Asozialenerlaß" (Asocial Decree) in 1936; the instatement of Dr. Robert Ritter as head of the "Rassenhygienischen und Bevölkerungsbiologischen Forschungsstelle" (Research Unit for Racial Hygiene and Population Biology) in 1936; the expansion of the July 1933 sterilization law, or "Gesetz für Verhütung erbkranken Nachwuchses" (Law for Prevention of Offspring from People Suffering with Hereditary Illnesses), to include Roma; the "Zigeuner-Grunderlaß" (Circular on the Fight Against the Gypsy Nuisance) issued by Himmler on December 8, 1938, the first decree directed solely against Roma (Thurner, *National Socialism*, 11; the entire decree is reprinted in: Hans-Joachim Döring, *Die Zigeuner im nationalsozialistischen Staat*, Kriminologische schriftenreihe aus der Deutschen Kriminologischen Gesellschaft, 12 (Hamburg: Kriminalistik Verlag 1964), 197–207; Burleigh and Wippermann provide an English translation of this law in their *Racial State*, 120–1); the "Festsetzungserlaß" (Arrest Decree) of 1939 outlining measures demanding all Roma register with the "Reich Criminal Police Office–Reich Central Office for the Fight against the Gypsy Nuisance"; decrees in 1939 forbidding Roma from leaving the places where they were staying, outlawing vagrancy in certain strategic areas, and prohibiting fortune telling (Thurner, *National Socialism*, 13); the "Erlaß zur Errichtung von Sammellagern" (Policy for the Construction of Camp Depots) calling for the erection of concentration camps for Roma, although before this decree Roma were already detained in certain "collection camps" in Lackenbach in Burgenland and in Salzburg (Thurner, *National Socialism*, 42); the beginning of deportation in 1940 and 1941 of Roma from Austria and Czechoslovakia into Lodz in Poland—"Ostdeportation" (East Deportation); barring of Roma from serving in the military and loss of citizen rights in 1942; the Auschwitz-Erlaß (Auschwitz-Decree) in 1942 ordering all Roma—regardless of whether their heritage was one-half, or one-fourth, or one-eighth Roma—to be transported to concentration camps, with Auschwitz being the final destination.
5   Thurner, *National Socialism*, 11.
6   Hancock relates difficulties with documenting actual numbers of Roma victims of the *Porrajmos*/Holocaust, including lack of accurate records and scholarly interest ("'Uniqueness'," 54–7). A commonly stated estimate of Roma killed by the Nazi regime in Europe was 250,000. Hancock has stated the figure

"We were totally uprooted" 113

Nazi policies against Roma were racially and ethnically motivated, intended to eradicate the entire Romani population through systematically executed racial profiling and ethnic cleansing. To reach that goal, a main tactic was to isolate Roma from the dominant society as well as from other persecuted groups.[7] Another strategy was to tear Romani families apart, as Otto Rosenberg describes happening in the camps.[8] Intersections between ethnicity and gender pervade emotional reactions of male and female autobiographers to Nazi persecution. Terror affected both sexes, and one sex was not "more persecuted" than the other. Regardless of sex, sterilization, dismal sanitary conditions, starvation, hard physical labor, and eventual death were intended to annihilate all Roma. Roma voices, however, indicate some actions affected one sex more than the other, and they discuss resulting ramifications and reactions. Measures destroying families relied, on the one hand, on discriminatory practices affecting both sexes equally, and, on the other hand, on actions having differing outcomes for women and men. Quantitatively, statistics show that of the 19,180 Roma murdered in Auschwitz, 10,786, or more than half, were women; or almost a third more women were killed than men.[9] Qualitatively, Roma write about specific discriminatory actions affecting women especially physically and emotionally, included shaving of hair, molestation, rape, and violent treatment during pregnancy. For men, autobiographers write especially about isolation from the family, destruction of solidarity,

---

    may be as high as 1.5 million ("Gypsy History," 20). Zimmermann estimates lower, claiming 50,000 as the total Romani victims of Nazi Germany, with 15,000 German Roma and over 35,000 Roma killed in fascist regimes in Croatia and Romania. In all Europe, Zimmer estimates a possible 90,000 victims, but suggests that the total number might exceed these figures (*Rassenutopie*, 284–92; Lewy, *Nazi Persecution*, 221–2). German Roma organizations currently support a figure of 500,000 (Rose, *Den Rauch*, 16). More significant than actual numbers is the percentage killed, ranging from 50 to 70 per cent of the estimated pre-war Romani population, depending on what regions one includes (Hancock, "'Uniqueness'," 55.)

7  Thurner remarks on the total isolation of Roma within the entire concentration camp community as the Nazis strategically tried to pit one inmate category against another (*National Socialism*, 3). Bogdal analyzes stereotypes of Roma in Auschwitz's "Zigeunerlager" (Gypsy Camp) in the autobiography of Lucie Adelsberger, a Jewish doctor working in the infirmary there: *Europa*, 448–50; Lucie Adelsberger, *Auschwitz: Ein Tatsachenbericht. Das Vermächtnis der Opfer für uns Juden und für alle Menschen* (Berlin: Lettner Verlag, 1956), 44–57.

8  Rosenberg, *Brennglas*, 24.

9  Jerzy Ficowski, "Die Vernichtung," in *In Auschwitz vergast, bis heute verfolgt: Zur Situation der Roma (Zigeuner) in Deutschland und Europa*, ed. T. Zülch (Reinbek: Rowohlt, 1979), 135.

and increased feelings of responsibility for family members' survival creating strong psychological pressures.

## Sterilization

Forced sterilization was a main and devastating Nazi measure profoundly disturbing to men and women.[10] However, statistics and autobiographers suggest men and women were affected differently. Bock has conducted the most extensive study of the relationship between gender and forced sterilization policies in Germany, presenting convincing reasons for examining how gender and racism interrelate in sterilization policies and procedures.[11] Bock theorizes that the ideology behind sterilization of so-called "less worthy" (*Minderwertige*) was both "anti-natal" and "pro-conception." In talking about these two concepts, Bock maintains that both compulsory sterilization and forced motherhood show the interrelation between sexism and racism. She defines "racist sexism," which urged procreation among white, upper-middle-class women not just because they were women, but because they belonged to a specific class and race of women. In contrast, Bock sees "sexist racism" as dissuading procreation among poorer women of color not just because they were women, but because they belonged to an "inferior" class and race.[12] Within this dual form of prejudice under Nazis, men may have been sterilized in equal numbers to women, but scant, available data are inconclusive.[13] Although both sexes were

---

10 Accumulative steps leading to forced sterilizations of Roma are complex and include many decrees issued since 1933 and then amended at different times and places. See: Yehuda Bauer, "Gypsies," *Encyclopedia of the Holocaust*, ed. Israel Gutman (New York: Macmillan, 1990), 2: 635–6; Gisela Bock, *Zwangssterilisation im Nationalsozialismus: Studien zur Rassenpolitk und Frauenpolitik* (Opladen: Westdeutscher Verlag, 1986); Kenrick and Puxon, *Destiny*, 65, 68, 75, 80, 90, 96–7, 125, 153, 162, 166, 174, 176–8, 180; Margalit, *Germany*, 32–55; Sybille Milton, "Context of the Holocaust," *German Studies Review*, 13.2 (May 1990): 271–3; Sybille Milton, "Sinti and Roma in Twentieth-Century Austria and Germany," *German Studies Review*, 23.2 (May 2000): 317–31; and Müller-Hill, *Murderous Science*, 39–65. In 1941, the national sterilization law was expanded to include Roma as "asocials." Sterilization of Roma over the age of 12 continued until the end of the war. Zimmermann claims almost 2,000 German Roma not deported to Auschwitz were sterilized between 1943 and 1944 (*Verfolgt*, 57). Even in contemporary times coercive sterilizations of Romni reportedly continue: "UN Presses Czech Republic on Coercive Sterilization of Romani Women." *European Roma Rights Center (ERRC)*. September 4, 2006. http://www.errc.org/cikk.php?cikk=2626See.
11 Bock, *Zwangssterilisation*.
12 Ibid., 420.
13 From extant records, the percentage of women sterilized from the total number sterilized swings between 45 per cent and 55 per cent, depending on the year and the place. Bock surmises in the six years preceding World War II approximately 320,000 men and women were sterilized in equal numbers. These

sterilized in equal numbers, the procedure affected both sexes differently. Sterilization procedures were physically harsher for women, Bock points out, and women's mortality rate appears to have been higher for years with reasonably reliable records. From 1934 onwards, women comprise half of the total people sterilized, but 90 per cent of those dead from sterilization.[14] Women's higher mortality rate caused the Nazis to begin sterilizing more men than women in the regime's later years for fear of becoming too suspect. Male homosexuals may also have been sterilized in higher numbers in later years, adding to sterilized men's increasing numbers as well, but that did not mean women's numbers abated.

Although the total number of Roma sterilized during the Nazi regime is unknown, local records show Roma's sterilization rate to be far higher than that in the average population.[15] Together with Poles and Jews, Roma were the main victims of recorded sterilization experiments after 1941.[16] Bock sees Roma as targets of two types of persecution: one attacked their biological race as "minderwertig" (of lesser value), and one marked their ethnicity as "asozial" (asocial). In comparing Roma to Jews, Bock explains: "If Jews were the object *par excellence* of anthropological racism, then "Asocials" (Community Misfits, Community Incapables) were the object *par excellence* of hygienic racism; Gypsies stood at the crossroads of both."[17] This double burden contributed to higher incidence of sterilization in comparison with other marginalized groups.

Some male Roma report on their own sterilization. Behringer describes the duplicitous struggle of "Bernhard Reinhardt" (a pseudonym to protect his identity) to receive postwar restitution in Germany for the psychological trauma he experienced from his sterilization. Reinhardt was forcibly conscripted into the Nazi military unit, SS-Kompanie Dirlewanger, in 1945 while in a concentration camp.[18] Postwar courts interpreted his conscription as "volunteer"

---

included so-called "asocials"—prostitutes, gays, criminals, mentally challenged, and poor—and "racially inept," such as Jews and Roma. In 1934, the percentage of women sterilized seems to be about 50 per cent. From 1934–7, the percentage is about 48 per cent. Sketchy statistics are available for later years (ibid., 372).
14  Ibid., 12.
15  Ibid., 362.
16  Ibid., 383.
17  "Waren Juden das Objekt *par excellence* des anthropologischen Rassismus, so 'Asoziale' ('Gemeinschaftsfremde', 'Gemeinschaftsunfähige') das Objekt *par excellence* des hygienischen Rassismus; Zigeuner standen im Schnittpunkt beider" (ibid., 363).
18  "Strafkolonie Dirlewanger" was a military unit within the army—commanded, beginning in 1942, by SS-Führer Dr. Dirlewanger—in which many Roma

and "protective" for him against danger. The justice system thus used Nazi language to rule against compensation. His story substantiates the discrimination that subjugated men in particular. The courts first questioned whether Reinhardt's sterilization had reduced his "earning powers" (*Erwerbsminderung/Erwerbsfähigkeit*).[19] According to the *Bundesentschädigungsgesetz* (Federal Law of Restitution) in effect from 1953 to 1965, candidates for restitution had to meet a requirement of at least a 25 per cent reduction in their earning powers to receive restitution.[20] Second, the courts questioned whether his forced sterilization had really been on racial grounds.[21] The courts concluded the Nazi records had cited the reasons for his sterilization as "erbbiologisch" (genetic) and "medizinisch" (medical), with no direct reference to his race, and thus he did not deserve restitution. Arguing further, the court presented a demeaning comparison between a Rom and an alcoholic person. The court stated Nazis would have also claimed they had sterilized an alcoholic person for "genetic" or "medical" reasons, just as they would have claimed for the Rom. If the courts offered the alcoholic person restitution, just as they would the Rom, officials overseeing proceedings believed they would undermine trauma suffered by those who really had been sterilized on racial grounds. Roma faced this negative backward logic in reaction to many restitution requests.

In another case, Josef Muscha Müller's account reveals the violence and horror inflicted on a 12-year-old Romani boy and the traumatic aftermath of World War II. Müller was born in Bitterfeld in 1932 as the son of Sinti parents, but was immediately brought to an orphanage. He found a home with foster parents, the Hinzes, who tried to shield him from harm as violence against Roma escalated. Nevertheless, in

---

concentration camps inmates were forced to serve. The SS euphemistically called such units "Bewährungseinheiten" (protective units), because they contained so-deemed political prisoners, criminals, and concentration-camp inmates "enlisting" under the pretense of needing "protection." See Udo Engbring-Romang, "Glossar," in Mettbach/Behringer, *"Wer wird ..."* 124–5). Otto Rosenberg talks about inmates of Wolfleben being "enlisted" to join Dirlewanger's battalion after being offered freedom, a uniform, food, and training. At first, the idea enticed Rosenberg. He then witnessed the tragic irony when his mother's cousin joined, but then the Russians captured him and sent him to a prisoner-of-war camp, that is, from one camp to another (*Brennglas*, 111). Friedrich Kreutz was also in Dirlewanger's company and reports that Sinti were always put on the front lines (Krausnick, *"Da wollten wir frei sein,"* 79).

19 Mettbach/Behringer, *"Wer wird ..."* 103–4.
20 Walter von Baeyer, "Über die Auswirkungen rassischer Verfolgung von Konzentrationslagerhaft vom Standpunkt des Psychiaters," *Emuna. Horizonte*, 5.1 (1970): 67.
21 Mettbach/Behringer, *"Wer wird ..."* 107.

1944, when he was 12, he was taken away from school to a hospital and sterilized. Müller talks about struggling, crying, and beating on the door as he tried to escape the clutches of those who had brought him to the hospital.[22] His story shows strong attempts to resist the sterilization. Nine days after his sterilization, his parents and members of a resistance group helped him escape from the hospital, aiding him in evading likely deportation to a concentration camp. They hid him in a garden shed and made sure he was never left alone. He was away from home for more than 18 weeks total, 16 of which were spent in hiding. The end of the war brought him out of hiding, but he was afflicted later in life with shame and sorrow at not being able to father children, emotions that also inhibited his long-term relationships with women.

Women write about witnessing sterilizations of female friends and family members while in the camps. Ceija Stojka describes seeing a mound of dead young women and girls in Auschwitz, including her friend Resi, who had been sterilized. Subsequently, Ceija relates how she, her mother, and her sister Kathi were led into the camp hospital, most likely to be sterilized, but then the electricity went out, preventing the procedure.[23] No female autobiographer I look at here talks about her own sterilization.[24] As I observed in Chapter One, women may have been sterilized and were not willing to admit it due to cultural taboos. Women also could have been sterilized without their knowledge. Lily van Angeren-Franz's father admitted he and his second wife, Zwana, had thought Zwana had been sterilized unbeknownst to her in the concentration camp. Luckily, Zwana bore two boys, which dispelled that belief.[25]

## Sanitation

While sterilization could have wiped out all Roma within a generation, other conditions threatened immediate lives and cultures of the living. Lack of sanitary conditions in ghettos—Marzahn in Berlin— and in concentration camps, affected men and women. First, disease resulting from such conditions could extinguish entire families. Second, such conditions defied Romani purity customs. Hanstein describes horrendous conditions under which he and other Roma lived in Marzahn. Huge fields with ditches into which refuse was pumped caused a constant horrible stench. Squalor and proximity to a cemetery defied customs respecting cleanliness and the dead: "The

---

22 Müller, "Und weinen," 87.
23 Ceija Stojka, *Verborgenen*, 52.
24 The one exception I have found is Krimhilde Malinowski who talks about the forced sterilization of her and her sister: *Das Schweigen*, 59–62.
25 Angeren-Franz, *Leben*, 127.

place not only disgusted us, it also totally went against our customs and purity commandments."[26] Hanstein remarks how the same violations occurred in Auschwitz and is repulsed at how men, women, and children had to sit side-by-side at the latrine in public view: "There was no shame, which for us was especially humiliating. Especially for Sinti and Roma the man's respect for the woman is so important."[27] He suggests the man is more disgraced at the inability to show respect for the woman than he is shamed at exposing his body to a woman. Walter Winter, too, laments the loss of dignity resulting from lack of sanitary measures. As with Hanstein, he talks about the open latrines with everyone relieving themselves alongside each other: "One had to do all that in public, in front of everyone, that was totally horrifying for everyone, particularly for the women … . Especially the women, the old women were so ashamed that they were forced to relieve themselves in public."[28] In Winter's account, the respect Hanstein had seen denied to men turns into women's shame.

Other unsanitary conditions, such as living so close to garbage, also went against Romani purity customs. Philomena Franz describes how other groups in the camps went to garbage heaps outside the kitchen to find scraps of food, although they usually found rats there. Roma, she claims, would never think of searching for food in garbage: "But we stayed away from that. We would have rather died".[29] Preference of death over survival in the face of uncleanliness and humiliation proves the high value Roma placed on clean living conditions according with purity customs.

### Shaving of Hair

After arriving at the camps, all Roma faced having their hair shaved. Romani women in particular experienced dishonor from the shearing act, due to the cultural value placed on women's hair. That disgrace receives repeated attention in narratives. Otto Rosenberg tells about a scene in Marzahn when Ritter and Justin were examining Roma as part of their "research." An 80-year-old woman would not answer

---

26 "Der Ort entsetzte uns nicht nur, er widersprach auch vollständig unseren Sitten und Reinheitsgeboten." Hanstein, *hundert Leben*, 27. See Illustration 6 for a picture of the dismal situation in Marzahn.
27 "Es gab keine Scham, für uns eine besondere Erniedrigung. Gerade bei uns Sinti und Roma ist der Respekt des Mannes vor der Frau so wichtig" (ibid.).
28 "Dass man alles öffentlich, vor allen anderen machen musste, war für alle ganz schrecklich, besonders für die Frauen … .Vor allem die Frauen, die alten Frauen haben sich so geschämt, dass man sie zwang, ihre Notdurft öffentlich zu verrichten." Winter, *Z 3105*, 75.
29 "Aber wir hielten uns fern. Lieber wären wir gestorben." Franz, *Liebe und Haß*, 74.

Illustration 6: Berlin-Marzahn Ghetto (?) (1936–45), where Otto Rosenberg and Ewald Hanstein lived. Photo reprinted with permission from the Bundesarchiv in Berlin.

every question immediately. She ran away and tried to hide from maltreatment. Ritter, Justin, and the police found her and cut off her hair as punishment. Rosenberg cannot get over this humiliation: "Horrible, when one thinks about it … . Just imagine, such an old woman! … They did such things!"[30] Ewald Hanstein, who was also in Marzahn, corroborates Rosenberg's story here, also emphasizing women's disgrace in particular at losing their hair.[31]

Lily van Angeren-Franz describes the shaving of women, including pubic hair, before "delousing" in the Auschwitz "Sauna." Her observations about women's shame are especially poignant as she stresses the pleasure the guards obviously took in watching. Her story also reveals the cultural taboo against women talking about their genitalia, making the pubic hair exposure even more shameful: "Especially for older Gypsy women, this was a barely tolerable humiliation. Most of them had never talked about their genitals. Now they had to stand in the presence of many other men and women, relatives and strangers,

---

30 "Furchtbar, wenn man sich das überlegt … . Stellen Sie sich das einmal vor, so einer alten Frau! … . Solche Sachen haben die gemacht!" Rosenberg, *Brennglas*, 26.
31 Hanstein, *hundert Leben*, 31–2.

and let themselves be shaved down under the surveillance of young German brats."³² The humiliation is so strong that Angeren-Franz claims she slowly lost her belief in God, unable to understand how an almighty being could let this happen.

Philomena Franz perceived the choice between having the hair on her head shaved or letting it remain long, and thereby qualifying her for service in the bordello. She refused to join the bordello and asked to be killed on the spot. Instead, the guard pushed her into the chair and began cutting off her hair, leading to another emotional scene when she cried and screamed so that it took three guards to settle her down. As with Angeren-Franz, she equates shaving her hair with testing religious beliefs, stating: "I see Jesus in front of me, the entire scene of suffering. And then the hair-cutting machine goes over my head, from one ear to the other. They cut a cross on me."³³ She describes her relatives' reactions to her unusual hair cut: "'Oh, dear God,' they cry out, 'dear child, what did they do with you—Here we are in hell.'"³⁴ As with Franz, Angeren-Franz uses a religious metaphor to stress the experience's physical and spiritual intensity.

Walter Winter observes how women were especially humiliated in having their "wonderfully beautiful long black hair, some corkscrew curls," shorn, so much so that some secretly picked up locks from the floor and hid them under their headscarves.³⁵ Sequestering hair locks becomes a symbol for preserving a cultural icon. In mentioning beauty in the locks' blackness, Winter reassigns a high worth to dark Romani features and defies longstanding racial prejudices by making the darkness valuable. Likewise, to counteract shame and preserve dignity, Franz Rosenbach tells of his traumatic attempt to pick up his mother's long braids from the floor after they were cut off in Auschwitz, only to have an SS officer hit him in the back.³⁶

In contrast, autobiographies contain few accounts of men's hair being shaved. Hanstein describes his own shaving explicitly, but he

---

32 "Vor allem für ältere Zigeunerfrauen war das eine kaum erträgliche Erniedrigung. Jetzt mussten sie sich im Beisein vieler anderer Männer und Frauen, Verwandten und Fremden, völlig nackt und breitbeinig hinstellen und sich unter der Oberaufsicht von jungen deutschen Rotznasen nackt rasieren lassen." Angeren-Franz, *Leben*, 83.
33 "Ich sehe Jesus vor mir, die ganze Leidensszene. Und dann fährt die Haarschneidemaschine über meinen Kopf, von einem Ohr zum anderen. Sie schneiden mir ein Kreuz." Franz, *Liebe und Haß*, 63.
34 "'Ach, du lieber Gott', rufen sie, 'liebes Kind, was haben sie mit dir gemacht~ Hier sind wir in der Hölle'" (ibid.).
35 "wunderschöne lange schwarze Haare, manche Korkenzieherlocken." Winter, *Z 3105*, 67.
36 Rosenbach, "*Der Tod*," 83.

"We were totally uprooted" 121

seems more ashamed at having to undress and run naked in front of women than by the hair shaving: "But the cold didn't matter to me on this day. Much worse was that I had to run by women and children. I could not imagine a larger humiliation."[37] Focus on the cultural significance of women's hair points to how women's bodies and sexuality proved particularly vulnerable to Nazi torment.

**Rape and Sexual Maltreatment**

Rape and sexual molestation were other disgraces befalling women in particular in the camps. Of course, men in the camps could also have been raped, but the stigma attached to such a shameful act could have rendered it too traumatic to reveal. Autobiographers talk only about women being raped. Otto Rosenberg confirms sexual mistreatment of Romani women, of "unsere Frauen" (our women), referring to them collectively: "The SS people mishandled our women. Not directly in the Block, but mostly behind the Block or elsewhere and then they shot them."[38] Even though everyone suffered, Rosenberg suggests the threat of rape made women suffer more than men: "More or less we all suffered the same. Some girls had maybe worse memories than I did because they were raped by the SS or by other soldiers."[39] Hanstein mentions so-called "bordellos" in Buchenwald.[40] Studies of prostitution in the camps have concluded that predominantly "German" women were prostitutes and that "No Jews worked at the brothels."[41] Of course, using "German" to characterize women prostitutes could apply to Romani women, many of whom would have been "German" citizens until April 1943, when Nazis revoked their citizenship. A lack of exact statistics and reporting makes evidence of the use of Romani women as sexual slaves inconclusive. Lily van Angeren-Franz talks about one Romani girl who Lily thought was a prostitute in the camp because the girl still had her beautiful, long hair. It turns out she was not, but even if

---

37 "Doch die Kälte an diesem Tag war mir egal. Viel schlimmer war, daß ich an Frauen und Kindern vorbei mußte. Eine größere Demütigung war kaum vorstellbar." Hanstein, *hundert Leben*, 48.
38 "Die SS-Leute haben unsere Frauen mißbraucht. Nicht direct im Block, sondern meistens hinter dem Block oder woanders, und anschließend haben sie sie erschossen." Rosenberg, *Brennglas*, 83.
39 "Mehr oder weniger hatten wir alle das gleiche Leid erlitten. Einige Mädchen hatten vielleicht noch viel schlimmere Erinnerungen als ich, weil sie von den SS oder von andern Soldaten vergewaltigt worden waren" (ibid., 127).
40 Hanstein, *hundert Leben*, 64.
41 Cf. "Nazi Camps Forced Women into Prostitution," March 2, 2009. http://www.instantnews.net/nazi-camps-forced-women-into-prostitution.aspx; "Forced Prostitution in WW II Camps Highlighted in Hamburg Exhibit," October 31, 2007. http://www.haaretz.com/news/forced-prostitution-in-wwii-camps-highlighted-in-hamburg-exhibit-1.232197.

she had been, Lily states, this woman would not have been alone. Lily asserts women in Auschwitz could register to be prostitutes, and many women did so mostly to save their relatives. A piece of bread could be a reward for services and could save a family member.[42]

Although sexual favors in realms outside the bordello might not surface in official records, coercion of women into unwanted sexual acts occurred unofficially. Lily has her own personal story.[43] When her brother was dying in the clinic, he had one last desire: to taste a potato. To fulfill his request, Lily promised a man working in the kitchen she would exchange sexual favors for a potato. She obtained the potato, and her brother had his last wish before dying. She dreaded returning to the kitchen to pay her dues. Instead, she enlisted the help of three other women who satisfied the man together while Lily further scrounged around in the kitchen for more provisions. Her story demonstrates not only the horrendous expectations placed on women, as sexual favors were exchanged for a family member's dying wish, but also the sense of solidarity among women to help each other out in such degrading situations. Not just one woman bore the shame; power came in numbers. The three women's sacrifices for Lily allowed her to pay them back by surreptitiously finding food for all of them.

Women's experiences in camps also differed from men's in the violent treatment of pregnant women and women with children. Long after the war, Angeren-Franz testified against Ernst August König, the SS private and "Blockführer," infamous for sadistically kicking pregnant Auschwitz prisoners until they died.[44] His trial in 1988 was considered the first related to Nazi crimes against Roma. The jury found him guilty of killing three people, and the judge sentenced him to life imprisonment. He hanged himself in 1991. When interrogated, Lily admitted she had not seen the murders, but they had been the talk of the whole camp for days. The other prisoners were horrified, not only by the sadistic murder of the pregnant women, but also by the fact that the women's other children had to witness the murders.[45] Mettbach describes the pregnant women who entered the camps. Often their children were stillborn, and when the children were born alive, the camp doctor Mengele forbade the mothers from nursing them. Mettbach refers to some mothers taking power over their childrens' destiny by holding the children so close that the infant was smothered to death. This rapid, horrific death, Mettbach opines, was better than

---

42 Angeren-Franz, *Leben*, 81.
43 Ibid., 70–82.
44 Ibid., 154–6.
45 An eyewitness, Angela Hudorivic, corroborates stories about violence against pregnant women (Rose, *Den Rauch*, 195).

slow death by starvation. The women who killed their children defied Mengele on their own, implying a kind of possible, albeit gruesome resistance. These women received punishment, usually a beating, not because they had killed their children, but because they had defied an order, preventing their children from becoming victims in "research" projects.[46]

## Solidarity

Women's closeness to children in the face of such danger could create more solidarity among women than among men. The concentration camp environment socialized men and women into distinct gender roles, a process that scholars and autobiographers have noted. Zimmerman, for example, claims that female Roma in Ravensbrück displayed more solidarity among themselves, receiving more help from influential people in the camps than male Roma in Buchenwald, Dachau, Mauthausen, or Sachsenhausen appeared to have. He attributes that solidarity to the presence of Romani children in Ravensbrück.[47]

Philomena Franz relates the tragic story of the selection occurring after her arrival with a group of women and children in Auschwitz-Birkenau from Ravensbrück.[48] As Franz stood in one line, the small, five-to-six-year-old daughter of a Polish Romani woman crawled in between Franz's legs. Franz hid the girl under her skirt and clung onto her. Because Franz was able to tell the officer she herself was a German, she was saved with the girl hiding under her skirt, whereas the Polish mother went on to her death in the "shower." A bond developed between Franz and the young girl; Franz describes sleeping together with her, stroking her at night as they lay in the cramped bunk, fantasizing about food they would like to cook and eat. But after some four weeks, Franz was transported to Wittenberge an der Elbe to work, whereas the girl stayed behind. For adult women, the presence of children could create hope and security. The same seemed true for the children, too. Ceija Stojka tells stories about her aunt, her mother, and a Polish woman who surrounded Ceija with physical warmth, stories, music, and thereby with promise and support.[49]

Solidarity among women often contrasts sharply with the feelings of autonomy that men express, a difference that could influence their survival strategies. Otto Rosenberg continually emphasizes how he survived in the camps and then afterwards by himself: "I was alone

---

46 Mettbach/Behringer, "*Wir wird ...*" 43.
47 Zimmermann, *Rassenutopie*, 123.
48 Franz, *Liebe und Haß*, 86–8.
49 Ceija Stojka, *Verborgenen*, 32.

and had to make all decisions alone in my young years."⁵⁰ Again, this tendency for self-sufficiency and autonomy arose not organically from some biological, innate drive but rather socially from situations in the camps whose main mission was to tear families apart. After Rosenberg talks about the Nazis' tactics to disband familial bonds, he observes how destruction of the family bred extreme individualism, so much so that a father finds himself stealing a child's bread.⁵¹ The men take no pride in their forced individualism as they see the fatal consequences for others.

Of course, had they been given the choice, not all males would have gone their own solitary ways. Ceija Stojka tells about her mother hearing about the fate of Mongo and Karl after the Auschwitz "Gypsy Camp" was liquidated and males separated from females. An older man, also with the last name "Stojka," took the brothers under his wing, claiming they were his grandchildren. Ceija asserts: "That was their salvation."⁵² Some men stuck together, some did not. Rosenberg, for example, notices how Sinti did not stick together in the camps as much as Russians did.⁵³ Philomena Franz, in contrast, claims that the solidarity among Roma and Sinti in the camps was much higher than among other groups. She observes differing degrees of solidarity among groups—the "Germans," she claimed, hit one another, stole each other's bread, and denounced each other. In contrast, "we Gypsies stuck together."⁵⁴ For her, ethnicity, and not sex, acted as a main determining factor for different reactions towards terrors. She also distinguishes ethnicity from nationality. As part of a Sinti family living and working in Germany for centuries, she could have called herself a "German"; instead, she consciously separated Sinti and "Gypsies" from Germans. Her perspective reminds researchers of the complexities in analyzing intersections of ethnicity and gender under traumatic conditions.

### Injustices Against Men

Men frequently found themselves in situations women did not experience. Hanstein talks about Nazis using male inmates for boxing tournaments to entertain guards, with extra rations promised to the winners. Regular inmates were not allowed to watch.⁵⁵ Romani men were famous for their boxing skills. The tragic fate of the German

---

50 "Ich war allein und mußte in meinen jungen Jahren alle Entscheidungen alleine treffen." Rosenberg, *Brennglas*, 142.
51 Ibid., 74.
52 "Das war ihre Rettung." Ceija Stojka, *Verborgenen*, 33.
53 Rosenberg, *Brennglas*, 101.
54 "wir Zigeuner hielten immer zusammen." Franz, *Liebe und Haß*, 74–5.
55 Hanstein, *hundert Leben*, 56.

Sinto boxer Johann "Rukeli" Trollmann, who won the 1933 German light-heavyweight title, however, shows the dangers awaiting male athletes. In June 1942 he was interned in the Neuengamme concentration camp, where he was a trainer for troops. He perished seven months later in the adjacent camp of Wittenberge as a result of a boxing match he won against a hated Kapo, a prisoner given privileges for helping oversee the camp. The Kapo was so humiliated by the defeat that he forced Trollmann to work to the point of exhaustion, and then the Kapo killed Trollmann with a shovel.[56]

Although being an athletic man could prove "useful" and "entertaining" to the Nazi guards, playing sports was not a guaranteed survival tactic. Stories of Nazi manipulation prove Romani inmates were not participating in sports for the love of the game, but rather for their lives and those of their teammates. Walter Winter tells about playing on a team for the "Gypsy Camp" in games against a team from the "Auschwitz-Stammlager" (Auschwitz-Regular Camp). As with boxing tournaments, games occurred to entertain the guards, who cheered for their own camps. The stakes were high for players, however, including increased punishment or even death for players whose guards felt humiliated by their team's loss. The winning team, by contrast, could also receive extra rations. When Walter Winter's team won and received extra rations, he saw women and children as more needy than the players and gave them the extra food. Winter was relieved when a tournament came out tied so that no one suffered the consequences.[57]

Such examples demonstrate the divergent experiences of men and women when faced with tactics that racialized ethnicity. Neither sex, however, possessed an advantage over the other in the face of such terror. Ultimately, divisions created solitariness and not solidarity, as the attempted extermination of an ethnic group took its toll on families and friends. Survivors found themselves destitute, alone, and traumatized. Memories of shared persecution became a main unifying force for ethnic identity.

## Post-*Porrajmos*/Holocaust Treatment

Immediate postwar years were marked by hardship for all Roma trying to build a "normal" life in a war-torn country. Modernization made finding an economic means of existence more difficult. Even before the war, industrialization had begun to hinder the profitability of traditional livelihoods. Karl Stojka describes the will of the Roma to build a stable economic basis, independent of the Allies' help. Stojka says Roma

---

56 Cf. Manuel Trollmann, *Johann (Rukeli) Trollmann*. http://www.johann-trollmann.de/
57 Winter, *Z 3105*, 84.

often felt like beggars when they picked up the Allies' food packages. He is proud of becoming a self-sufficient, self-educated businessman: "We did business. From our earnings we paid for the apartment and food, with the rest we paid for further education and training. We always educated and trained ourselves."[58] His pride coincides with his previously cited assertion of being "eternally proud to be a Gypsy."[59] His business acumen depends on his education, another debunking of generalizations about uneducated Roma.

Despite these achievements, attitudes towards Roma at this time often still reflected centuries-old stereotypes portraying them as vagrants, thieves, and swindlers. In the years directly after the war prejudicial citizens demanded Roma in their towns be removed.[60] Victims report the Allies treated them with respect—distributing food and clothing, allowing them to move around freely, trading with them, and playing music with them. After 1948, however, when the Allies handed over administration to German authorities, and the Federal Compensation Law came into effect, the situation worsened.[61] The main reason for deteriorating conditions was that the German criminal police, bureaucrats working in the German welfare system and the compensation units for victims of Nazism, and the general public did not acknowledge racial grounds for Roma's persecution.[62] This meant German authorities and legal systems often developed policies to fight what they saw as widespread "vagrancy" among Roma rather than help Roma economically and socially. While officials knew they could not reissue decrees from Nazi times, they argued laws enacted during the Weimar Republic were still valid. One such law, for example, was from 1926, allowing officials to imprison in workhouses those individuals who had so-perceived "moral faults" making them a "public burden."[63] In attempting to issue a law awarding compensation to all Nazi persecuted groups, authorities did not refer specifically to Roma as victims until March 1946. Thereafter, states began to establish stipulations for Roma even to apply for compensation—including proof of permanent living accommodations and a steady job—conditions an ethnic group having suffered severe economic hardship and social ostracism for centuries found hard to meet. Later, Roma had to demonstrate they

---

58 "Wir hatten gehandelt. Von dem Verdienten bezahlten wir Wohnung und Essen, das andere wurde für die Weiterbildung ausgegeben. Wir haben uns auch selbst untereinander weitergebildet." Karl Stojka, *Kindheit*, 35.
59 Ibid., 52.
60 Margalit, *Germany*, 58–9.
61 Knesebeck, *Roma Struggle*, 73.
62 Ibid., 23; Margalit, *Germany*, 61.
63 Margalit, *Germany*, 64.

"We were totally uprooted" 127

had democratic antifascist beliefs and citizenship, also preconditions not required of other groups asking for compensation.[64] The largest legal and economic struggles appearing in autobiographies are those regarding restitution for lost possessions and compensation for inhumane treatment such as forced labor, sterilization, reoccurring poor health conditions, and psychological trauma. Finally in 1956 and 1963, West German Supreme Court rulings required authorities to recognize Roma as Nazi victims.[65] Glaringly absent from all documents concerning restitution and compensation to Roma from 1945 until 1956 are Romani voices proving their suffering. In fact, some authorities discounted the validity and reliability of evidence offered by afflicted Roma outright. From all the wranglings, only accounts contained in Nazi documents remained for courts to consider.[66] Courts heard many cases of Roma requesting compensation from the 1950s to the 1980s, resulting in infrequent or inadequate awards of payments. Categorical denial that persecution had been racially motivated lay at the root of most rejections.

The early 1980s showed progress towards granting compensation and restitution, although by then Romani inmates of concentration camps were aging and beginning to die. Three events led to heightened attention to Roma as a persecuted group in West Germany and thereby to reconsideration of restitution laws. The first was a ceremony in memory of Romani victims of Nazism held at the site of the Bergen-Belsen concentration camp on 27 October 1979; the second was a hunger strike by 13 Sinti at the site of the Dachau concentration camp beginning in April 1980; the third was the convention of the World Romani Congress held in Göttingen in 1981. Consequently, Romani Rose—a Sinti on the hunger strike—founded the "Central Council of German Sinti and Roma" in 1982. Increased media attention to these actions caused then West German Chancellor Helmut Kohl to issue a public statement in 1982 recognizing the genocide of Roma, expressing his desire for a "moralische Wiedergutmachung" (moral correction of past wrongdoings), which eased the requirements for restitution funds.

The discrimination Roma faced in requesting restitution receives repeated attention in autobiographies. "Bernhard Reinhardt" first requested restitution in 1949 for the ill health he suffered from being in Auschwitz beginning in March 1943, his forced sterilization in Ravensbrück, as discussed earlier, and lingering health effects from a wound he received while in compulsory military service on the front in

---

64 Ibid., 97–101.
65 Ibid., 84.
66 Knesebeck, *Roma Struggle*, 161–94; Margalit, *Germany*, 102–16.

the "Strafkolonie Dirlewanger."[67] Behringer explains the case's 18-year-long bureaucratic complexities. Referring specifically to Reinhardt's forced military service with the Dirlewanger company, one judge questioned "whether this has to do with a racial persecution or whether the applicant was enlisted to work as an element that was asozial or work-shy."[68] The judge chose the final option, which justified refusing compensation. As Behringer points out, and as was the case with the grounds upon which the judge argued against restitution for "Bernhard Reinhardt's" sterilization, in denying restitution, the judge employed the same language the Nazis used to justify the persecution and deportation of Roma to concentration camps—namely, he calls them "asozial" (asocial) and "arbeitsscheu" (work-shy). The judge thus denied the *Porrajmos*. The language here reflects deeply ingrained racism; the judge did not even use the German word for a human being when referring to Reinhardt, but merely talked about him as an *Element*.

Hildegard Lagrenne was deported in May 1940 and, along with her family, was interned in many camps she calls the "SS-Sammellagern für Sinti" (SS-depot camp for Sinti).[69] As recompense for the five years she spent in camps, she received 2,000 Marks, minus 250 Marks she had to pay the lawyer.[70] Only those in camps designated as death camps after 1943, such as Auschwitz, were eligible for more restitution funds.[71] Likewise, Lily van Angeren-Franz relates with disbelief the many times she was questioned about the veracity of her deportation to Auschwitz. After the war, she found herself with other refugees in Bohemia in then Sudetenland. Those who had not been in camps continually asked her about her status and her wartime experiences, unable to believe what she had gone through.[72] When she was living in the Netherlands in 1966, she decided to request restitution funds. As evidence, she needed a doctor's verification that her nightmares, psychological trauma, and physical illnesses after the war were direct consequences of her time in the concentration camps. She lamented how difficult that task was because doctors in the Netherlands did not believe her and often

---

67 For the "Strafkolonie Dirlewanger" see footnote 18 above (pages 115–16).
68 "ob es sich um eine rassische Verfolgung gehandelt, hat, oder ob der Antragsteller als asoziales oder arbeitscheues Element zur Arbeit herangezogen wurde." Mettbach/Behringer, "*Wer wird ...*" 98.
69 Krausnick, "*Da wollten wir frei sein*," 37.
70 Ibid., 43. 2,000 DM in the 1950s and 1960s has an approximate buying power of $250 in 2014 as calculated from the following: "Entwicklung der Kaufkraft in Deutschland (DM Basis)," http://www.lindcom.de/Lindcom/Home/Statistik/kaufkraft.pdf and from 2014 currency conversion tables.
71 "*Da wollten wir frei sein*," 38.
72 Angeren-Franz, *Leben*, 100.

thought she was crazy.⁷³ When the courts asked her to spend a week under observation in a German clinic to determine the extent of her trauma, all she could recall was Dr Mengele's clinic in Auschwitz. She could not bring herself to face such an ordeal in another hospital facility. Philomena Franz describes another restitution debacle. She finally received 15,000 DM and a pension as compensation. She never saw any of the money, however; from this sum she had to pay all expenses for her ill husband who had been denied compensation.⁷⁴

Treatment of Roma regarding compensation and restitution in the German Democratic Republic (GDR—East Germany) does not seem any better than in the Federal Republic of Germany, as evidenced by Joseph Muscha Müller's aforementioned story of his sterilization's aftermath. Not until he was 20 and expressed a desire to get married and have a family did his parents reveal to him that he had been sterilized. A series of traumatic incidents began whereby women he wanted to marry rejected him once they learned he could not father a child. In 1947, his parents asked the state to acknowledge he had suffered Nazi persecution. He became the youngest person to be recognized as such in the city of Halle. In 1953, the newly formed GDR also officially admitted Müller had been a victim of Nazi persecution. But, Müller stated, recognition carried no advantages. He did not need the apartment he was offered because he lived with his parents. Instead of margarine, he received 50 grams of butter and a ration for more meat, which was not enough for a dog, he claimed.⁷⁵ Even more devastating was the prejudice he experienced as many thought he was a foreigner because of his darker complexion. He also faced blatant discrimination when searching for a job. Nazi terrors continued to haunt Roma long after the end of the war. Nazi policies meant to rip Roma asunder eventually formed Roma's shared history and the memory thereof. Roma consciously view this history as distinguishing them from non-Roma. In defining their ethnic identity, Roma attempt to balance omnipresent, externally inflicted history with multifaceted, internally created cultural markers.

## Assimilation and Nationality

From early records chronicling the arrival of Roma in Germanic lands in the fifteenth century, to national socialist racial profiling, to the denial of victims' requests for restitution, to Chancellor Helmut Kohl's public acknowledgment of Nazi persecution of Roma, few have addressed differences among Romani groups. While enumerating

---

73  Ibid., 141.
74  Franz, *Liebe und Haß*, 102. 15,000 DM in the 1950s and 1960s has the approximate buying power of $2,000 in 2014. See footnote 70 above (page 128).
75  Müller, *"Und weinen,"* 133.

distinct and shared traits among the various groups is impossible, rich diversity needs recognition to avoid dangerous generalizations. Despite differences, autobiographers display concerted efforts to build a positive, effective solidarity in tandem with political, social, and cultural changes. Philomena Franz perceives the common origin and history of migration as influential factors for Romani perspectives and values. Her explanation is a prime example of Spivak's concept of "strategic essentialism": in trying to balance the effects of historical persecution and socialization with possible innate traits Franz attempts to unite Romani groups. For Franz, a shared history relying on migrations from Inda and subsequent repeated expulsion brings Roma together as do customs she identifies as hospitality and freedom in nature. Total integration into non-Roma society, she states, would erase these traits.[76] As with Mišo Nikolić, Franz views diaspora and marginalization as bonding elements. Few, if any, autobiographers who survived Nazi persecution look back to Roma's roots in India, however, for the origin of this solidarity. Instead, memories of more immediate and recent persecution figure more significantly in coalescing them as an ethnic group. The younger generation seems more fascinated with Indian roots, as in Dotschy Reinhardt's autobiography.[77]

Other autobiographers express nostalgia for earlier times, predicated on the fear Roma are losing cultural markers defining them for centuries. Karl Stojka admits his anxiety about forfeiting identity through forced settlement, because he connects cultural identifiers characterizing Roma—nomadism and language—with survival.[78] He talks uncomfortably about Roma being in between times of stability and transformation—in a "Zwischenzeit" (in-between time).[79] That sentiment surfaces again in younger generation's narratives, as when Dotschy Reinhardt states: "It's a kind of life in conflict, between two worlds."[80]

Autobiographers feel strongly against assimilating totally into the dominant culture, but instead express clear desires to share any remaining customs, beliefs, lifestyles, and legacies. Walter Winter proclaims: "I always say that one must master the instruments of the other, but one must not necessarily always play them."[81] Again, Adelson's position "against between" may best reflect the wishes of

---

76 Franz, *Liebe und Haß*, 17–18.
77 Regarding younger generations searching for Romani roots in India see Harri Stojka's film *Gypsy Soul: Harri Stojka*. http://www.harristojka.at/hs/
78 Stojka and Pohanka, *Auf der ganzen Welt*, 8.
79 Ibid., 9.
80 "Es ist eine Art Leben im Zwiespalt, zwischen zwei Welten." Reinhardt, *Gypsy*, 211.
81 "Ich sage immer, man muss die Instrumente der anderen beherrschen, aber man muss sie nicht unbedingt immer spielen." Winter, *Z 3105*, 29.

many Roma to be able to live, work, and play flexibly and fluidly in many worlds without being fixed in any one. As much as Roma desire to hold onto cultural artifacts and show ethnic pride, many writers also emphasize they are "Austrian" or "German," whichever the case may be. Designation of nationality, as Karl Stojka asserts, should preside over racial categorization, but also should exist in tandem with ethnic identities as human beings. He proclaims a person's race makes no difference; Viennese Roma are integrated, even though they have different cultural backgrounds. He is adamant about claiming Austrian citizenship: "I am an Austrian, this is my country, this is my earth, this is my everything. Only here do I want to live and die. I cannot imagine anything else, but I grew up differently."[82] He asserts everyone—Roma, Sinti, Jews, Viennese, Germans—all live differently, and yet all as humans should find a home on this earth.

Hildegard Lagrenne, too, wishes for other Germans to see her as a fellow citizen so that she may live in Germany without relinquishing her customs and heritage: "We want to be together with the Germans, we are Germans, too. We have already been here for centuries. We only want to preserve our customs!"[83] She points out that groups frequently distinguish themselves from others: Bavarians from Prussians; Protestants from Catholics. No one has to give up everything to assimilate. To Lagrenne, Roma's main distinguishing and solidifying factor is language, whose destruction would mean Roma's demise. The language's oral nature, however, endangers Romany, yet also makes it fascinating in its diversity. Although Roma are now writing more of their songs and poetry down in Romany as the language becomes more codified, each version is different, creating puzzles to decipher meanings.

Indeed, a poem by Ceija Stojka epitomizes the deep relationship she honors between herself, her Lovara heritage, nature, and Austria, her home country:

> I am a root
> from Austria
> my roots lie deep
> yes, deep in the earth
> and my trunk is robust and healthy.
> And the earth

---

82 "Ich bin ein Österreicher, das ist mein Land, das ist meine Erde, das ist mein Alles. Ich möchte nur hier leben und sterben. Ich kann mir nichts anderes vorstellen, aber ich bin halt anders aufgewachsen." Karl Stojka, *Kindheit*, 20.
83 "Wir wollen mit den Deutschen doch zusammensein, wir sind doch auch Deutsche. Wie [sic] sind doch schon Hunderte von Jahren hier. Wir wollen nur unsere Sitten bewahren!" Krausnick, *"Da wollten wir frei sein!"* 48–9.

of our Austria
is without a core
and yet healthy to the core.[84]

Ceija's use of the tree metaphor with deep Austrian roots is reminiscent of Philomena Franz's aforementioned feelings of being totally "ausgerissen," (uprooted/torn out) by Nazi discrimatory laws. Constant denials of citizenship have provoked Roma's insistence on citizenship.[85] Ceija's poem and Philomena's emotions imply that Roma's history is, indeed, inextricably linked to the histories of German-speaking countries. Vice versa, Roma's experience as a marginalized ethnic group is tightly bound to the dominant culture in these countries. The pleas of Karl Stojka, Hildegard Lagrenne, and Ceija Stojka to have national identities and ethnicity stand side-by-side signal attempts to move fluidly across boundaries, and not be entrapped in a static "in-between" time. Their voices show awareness of ethnic identity as integral to a shared national past and present in their countries. By revealing their perspectives on aspects of that identity—customs, family, work, storytelling, language, nomadism, education, diversity, and a common history of persecution—such voices make Roma's status as a vibrant ethnic group part of a shared future as well.

---

84 "ich bin eine Wurzel aus Österreich meine Wurzeln liegen tief ja tief in der Erde und mein Stamm ist kräftig und gesund. Und die Erde von unserem Österreich ist ohne 'Kern' und doch kerngesund." *Ceija Stojka: Bilder und Texte. 1989–1995* (Vienna: Graphische Kunstanstalt Otto Sares Ges., m.b.H., 1995). The poem contains two wordplays: "Stamm" means both "tree trunk" and "tribe/clan" of Lovara. "Kern" means "core" as well as "kerngesund" for "healthy to the core."
85 Margalit, *Gypsy*, 39, 78–80.

*Five* "I live with my deceased":
Trauma, Gender, and Ethnicity
in Autobiographies by Ceija,
Karl, and Mongo Stojka

In her anthropological study on attitudes towards respect, death, and the elopements of Sinti living today in the Italian provinces of Alto Adige in Southern Tirol and Trentino, Tauber observes a special connection women make towards remembering the dead. In the three-and-a-half years she lived with Sinti,[1] Tauber noticed how women's everyday activities inspired them to conjure up more memories of deceased relatives and friends than men's did. Women had been the main travelling salespeople in families. As such, they often drove together on the same routes. Seeing places where they would go selling with other women who had since died led them to developing stories about such-and-such a village where they had stolen a hen, or a farmhouse where they had received milk, or a field where they had stationed their wagons. Even when women had gone *manghél* alone, they had lived in the presence of the deceased through contact with spaces provoking memories. Tauber writes that men did not have those memories and shared experiences as much.[2] Ceija Stojka's quote above, "I live with my deceased" (*Ich lebe mit meinen Verstorbenen*), corroborates Tauber's observations. Do Romani men and women have differing experiences affecting how and how much they remember? If so, how do these differences manifest themselves in situations and spaces?

---

1   Tauber married a Sinti man from the group in Southern Tirol in 1997; she states her research is largely based on her experiences living for the next three-and-a-half years with him and his family in the settlement (*Du wirst*, 15).
2   Tauber, *Du wirst*, 120.

The autobiographies of three Stojka siblings help answer these questions.[3] As members of the same family who experienced Nazi persecution, including being interned in Auschwitz-Birkenau together, their testimonies are invaluable for investigations into the effect of *Porrajmos*/Holocaust trauma on individual and collective memories. The devastation of so many families during the *Porrajmos*/Holocaust often precludes exploring memories of family members simultaneously. Individual survivors' accounts frequently stress how many family members they lost under Nazi persecution. The phenomenon that five of the six siblings and their mother, Maria "Sidi" Rigo Stojka, survived—75 per cent of the family—is amazing in light of historical evidence demonstrating that some 9,000 out of more than 11,000 Austrian Roma were killed during Nazi times, placing the survival rate at 18 per cent.[4] Autobiographies by a woman and two men provoke further inquiry into the significance of gender roles for remembering and recounting traumatic events.

However, the three Stojka siblings' autobiographies, while clearly written and readily accessible, do not always present a simplified account of shared family stories. They all differ in their evolution and contents. My analysis concentrates on two incidents with noticeable discrepancies. The first concerns inconsistencies surrounding the date and circumstances of their father's deportation; the second entails Ceija's account of a gruelling act against their mother in Auschwitz; the third relates to renditions about the selection process in Auschwitz where all three survived extermination. Several questions about memory formation arise due to these discrepancies. How does the reader and scholar handle issues of silence, truth, and veracity in cases where dissonance between family members' accounts of a supposedly shared situation arises? What impact might trauma have on shared and separate experiences as related in the individual autobiographical testimonies of each sibling? What role does gender as a major social construct in the lives and persecution of the three siblings play in relating that trauma? Ultimately, what does each individual story contribute to the collective history of the family and the social and collective memories of the plight of Roma under Nazi persecution?

---

3 Ceija Stojka's account of her internment in Bergen-Belsen, *Träume ich, dass ich lebe?: Befreit aus Bergen-Belsen*, her third book, appeared in 2005 (Vienna: Picus, 2005). She was in Bergen-Belsen with her mother during the last few months before the camp was liberated. At the same time, her brothers Karl and Mongo were in Buchenwald and Flossenbürg. In the interest of comparing all three siblings' autobiographies during the time that they were together in Auschwitz, I do not analyze Ceija's third book.

4 Freund, Baumgartner, and Greifeneder discuss the difficulties in assessing exactly how many Roma perished (*Vermögensentzug*, 53).

Major concepts from the vast research on memory in the fields of sociology, psychology, literature, cultural studies, and gender studies provide frameworks to help answer these questions and to test how well praxis bears out theoretical claims.[5]

Initial inspiration for such a theoretical framework comes from the work of Maurice Halbwachs, and those using his ideas as springboards for further research. Over 80 years have passed since Halbwachs wrote his pioneering sociological study on memory in which he coined the term "collective memory," but his observations are still relevant. In his 1925 work *Les cadres sociaux de la mémoire*, Halbwachs states that the collective memory is a fundamental element upon which all individuals base their memories and their personalities. Most of our memories arise when others provide an impetus for recall, or in reaction to stories we hear from others. Halbwachs recognizes that while individuals do remember, "it is in society that people normally acquire their memories. It is also in society that they recall, recognize, and localize their memories."[6] The "collective memory" becomes the composite of all the individual memories passing down through generations, thus forming an intrinsic part of community identity and history. Within this social realm of memory gathering, the family unit plays a major role in forming collective memory.[7] Every family group feels the urge to tell its story and thereby ensure its perpetuity.[8]

Family survival is certainly a theme occurring repeatedly in the Stojka siblings' writings. Ceija expresses this sense of urgency to have the Roma's group story told when she talks about the need to share her narrative publicly so that Roma do not disappear entirely.[9] She uses the collective "we" in her statement to imply both Romani people and her own family, given their prominence in Austrian culture. The cover story for the Austrian newsmagazine *Falter* in May 2004 testifies to the presence the Stojkas as a family unit has maintained in Vienna, stressing the family's status as creators of another side to Austrian culture one does not encounter in the canonical works of literature and classical music.[10]

Karl "Wackar" Horvath and Maria "Sidi" Rigo Stojka had six children:[11] Maria/"Mitzi", Katharina/"Kathi", Johann/"Mongo,"

---

5 Markus Fauser, "Gedächtnistheorien," *Einführung in die Kulturwissenschaften* (Darmstadt: Wissenschaftliche Buchgesellschaft, 2003), 116–38.
6 Maurice Halbwachs, *On Collective Memory*, ed. and trans. with an introduction by Lewis A. Coser (Chicago: University of Chicago Press, 1992), 38.
7 Ibid., 54–83.
8 Ibid., 75.
9 Ceija Stojka, *Verborgenen*, 154.
10 Paterno, "Die Stojkas," 72–3. See Illustration 2 (page 16).
11 The parents were wed only according to Romani law; thus, the mother and children kept her maiden name Rigo, along with the name Stojka, as is the custom.

Karl/"Karli," Ceija, and Josef/"Ossi." They belonged to a long line of travelling Lovara Roma, in the clan of the Bagareschtschi paternally and Giletschi maternally; their births occurred all over Austria—Karl in the Burgenland, Ceija in Styria, Mongo close to Vienna. In 1938 the family had to convert their travelling wagon into a small wooden house to become sedentary year round as mandated by Nazi laws. In 1940 their father was taken custody and then in 1941 sent to concentration camps in Dachau, Mauthausen, and then Hartheim, where he was killed.[12] Shortly thereafter, Kathi was brought to the concentration camp in Lackenbach in the Burgenland. On 3 March 1943 the rest of the family was deported to Auschwitz-Birkenau, when they met Kathi as they were loading into the train. In Auschwitz-Birkenau they all stayed together in the so-called "Gypsy Camp." The youngest child Ossi died there in 1943.

When the "Gypsy Camp" was liquidated in August 1944, males were separated from females. Ceija stayed together with her mother and sisters in Birkenau, where they were eventually transported through Auschwitz to the Ravensbrück women's concentration camp, then to Bergen-Belsen. After the British freed them, they returned to Vienna, where Ceija began second grade as a 12-year-old. Karl and Mongo went into the main camp in Auschwitz after the separation, and then, in September, to Buchenwald. In February 1945 they were sent to Flossenbürg. From there they embarked on the "Todesmarsch" (death march), until the Americans freed them on 27 April 1945. The brothers stayed around Flossenbürg until 1946, when they made their way to Vienna and found their mother and three sisters.

To return to Halbwach's assertion that the family unit is a font of information for studying collective memory, the Stojka family, with its long, shared history, offers an excellent case in point. Tragically, Halbwachs was never able to finish his work on collective memory; deported to Buchenwald, he died there shortly before the end of the war. Scholars recognize the unevenness of his posthumously published work, while also remaining cognizant of its significance. Aleida and Jan Assmann attribute much of the impetus for their research to Halbwachs's pioneering work.[13] They set out to address a major shortcoming in his

---

12 Ceija later discovered her father had been killed at Schloss Hartheim, Austria, which was known since the nineteenth century as a home for physically and mentally challenged children. Between 1940 and 1944 it was a "Euthanasieanstalt" (Euthanasia Institute); approximately 30,000 people were killed there. *Schloss Hartheim*, http://www.schloss-hartheim.at/index.php/en/

13 Aleida Assmann, *Erinnerungsräume: Formen und Wandlungen des kulturellen Gedächtnisses* (Munich: Beck, 1999); Jan Assmann, *Das kulturelle Gedächtnis: Schrift, Erinnerung und politische Identität in frühen Hochkulturen* (Munich: Beck, 1992).

ideas, namely, he postulated a broad category for "collective memory," not recognizing gradations or divergences. The Assmanns' observations expand the range of categories for memory dissemination. Jan Assmann, for example, differentiates *kulturelles Gedächtnis* (cultural memory) from *kommunikatives Gedächtnis* (communicative memory). The former manifests itself through more organized, ceremonial long-term processes of remembrances, such as texts, rites, rituals, and memorials, which thereby turn history into myth.[14] The latter forms more a part of the group's short-term memory—including recitations, oral storytelling, and observations—that span only three or four generations.[15] Both the "cultural" and "communicative" memories are important for identity formation. Particularly enlightening in the Assmanns' studies is their explanation of the complex way in which orality, literacy, and media interact to create cultural memory. As with any complex tool, writes Jan Assmann, the move from orality to written script contains dialectical forces of expansion and reduction. Writing enables ideas and information from all kinds of sources to develop. Reliance on the written text, however, can reduce natural memory capacities and abilities.[16] Despite the value many Western cultures award to written texts, orality—in the form of rituals, festivities, speeches, storytelling, musical performances—is still significant in constructing and maintaining memory texts.

The relationship of orality to the published text is important for the Stojkas' autobiographies. Readers and scholars might note that Ceija and Mongo are first and foremost singers and musicians; Karl and Ceija are visual artists; all three were not necessarily professional writers making a living from their books alone. As noted in Chapter One, each had assistance in writing their autobiographies. Still, following the oral tradition in which they grew up, all three are carrying forth the values of storytelling into an era and social context dependent on print media. The Assmanns' research shows oral culture has played no less a role than the print media in forming cultural memory. All three Stojkas—in interviews, essays, forewords, and autobiographies—also emphasize writing in their journals regularly. They thereby demonstrate a perpetual need to write, a process denied to them in their younger years when they were excluded from obtaining a formal education.[17] Their difficulties in writing down their own experiences

---

14 Jan Assmann, *Das kulturelle Gedächtnis*, 52.
15 Ibid., 50.
16 Ibid., 23.
17 See, for example, Ceija's interview with Berger ("Du darfst," 97–8), where she talks about first writing down stories about the concentration camps. When I visited her, Ceija showed me her journals, full of writing and drawings. She and Mongo were also avid correspondents with many people throughout the world.

without assistance from other writers mirror the hesitations of many *Porrajmos*/Holocaust survivors who remained silent due to shame, fear of further persecution, or a need to repress the horrors so as to continue to live. The literary talents of all three also emerge in their poems and song lyrics. Their texts' variety and hybridity attest to their abilities as writers in the broadest sense of the term.

This blurring of distinctions between orality and literacy has provoked scholarship on memory blending after the Assmanns. Concurrently, scholars have begun to call for more examples from a variety of historical periods and sociological circumstances to support theoretical claims. Welzer's *Das soziale Gedächtnis* points to the need to demonstrate how notions of collective, cultural, and communicative memory play themselves out in life situations. Besides being largely indebted to Halbwachs's and the Assmanns' studies, essays in Welzer's collection share the desire to "do history" by applying theoretical concerns to everyday cultural practices.[18] The studies focus on the Assmanns' differentiation between "cultural" and "communicative" memory, but the resulting scholarship also blurs that definition and creates new categories of investigation. In Welzer's collection, Keppler's essay on transmission of family stories through a variety of venues—conversations at the dinner table and slide-show evenings—is relevant for a collective analysis of the Stojkas' autobiographies. Keppler demonstrates how the everyday process of "communicative" memory building often spills over into institutionalized "cultural" memory. When those processes by which families share stories become rituals involving public forms of media, and in turn those public media enter into private households, then the boundaries coalesce and break down demarcations in memory formation.[19] The Stojkas' published individual autobiographies demonstrate how public "cultural" and private "communicative" memory realms can transition and blend into each other.

Welzer's plea to apply theory to practice inspires analysis of three stories that stand out in particular for their varying renditions in the Stojkas' autobiographies. The first story concerns the deportation, murder, and mourning rituals related to their father's death. Initially, what is most striking about the versions is that, in writing about their father's deportation, the siblings rely on different dates. In the

---

For an analysis of the relationship between Roma, literacy, and orality, and the different kinds of texts attesting to Roma literacy, see Toninato.

18 Harald Welzer, ed., *Das soziale Gedächtnis: Geschichte, Erinnerung, Tradierung* (Hamburg: Hamburger Edition, 2001), 19.

19 Angela Keppler, "Soziale Formen individuellen Erinnerns: Die kommunikative Tradierung von (Familien-) Geschichte," in Welzer, *Das soziale Gedächtnis*, 158.

first edition of Ceija's account in *Wir leben im Verborgenen* in 1988, the reader learns that the father was picked up by the Gestapo in 1941. Karl, in contrast, places the date in one publication in 1940[20] and in another publication at the end of 1941 or beginning of 1942.[21] Mongo supplies yet another date, namely 1940.[22] Such discrepancies may not seem important, and may actually be due to publishing mistakes. Still, the inconsistencies could lead to other deviations and muddy the chronology of occurrences. In all accounts, the date of the entire family's deportation then relies on dates and events surrounding the father's deportation. Ceija, for example, in her first rendition, claims the Gestapo picked up the family in 1941 in the Paletzgasse in Vienna on the day of their father's funeral; in the fourth edition published in 2003, she changes the date to 1943. The reader is not sure how much time has elapsed between the father's and the family's deportation. Both Karl and Mongo claim the family was picked up in March 1943, when Karl was in school and Mongo on his way to school. A historian insisting on total accuracy might question this date and the circumstance of the boys going to school, for Roma in Vienna were forbidden to attend school in 1938 and afterwards.[23] In any case, these differences in dates also cause variances in the length of time of the concentration camp internment, from up to four years, by Ceija's first account, or two and a half years, by Karl's and Mongo's accounts, and in Ceija's second account. What does one do with varying interpretations of personal histories? Do these variances really matter?

On the one hand, readers could surmise such variances may be due to the "fragile power" of individual memory, a power having the ability to recall, revise, distort, and forget.[24] Study of memory is just as much a study of forgetting. For literary studies, Olney poses relevant questions about autobiography, life-writing, or "periautography," the term he prefers, meaning "writing about or around the self."[25] Can the self be remembered accurately, he asks, and, just as important, can the self be narrated accurately? On the other hand, the trauma of the *Porrajmos*/Holocaust often exceeds our frame of reference regarding tensions between truth and history. Recent years have seen artistic and

---

20 Ceija Stojka, *Verborgenen*, 16; Karl Stojka, *Wo sind sie geblieben? Geschunden, gequält, ggetötet—Gesichter und Geschichten von Roma, Sinti und Juden aus Konzentrationslagern des Dritten Reiches*, eds Sonja Haderer-Stippel and Peter Gstettner (Vienna: Bundesministerium für Bildung, 2003), 23.
21 Karl Stojka, *Kindheit*, 22.
22 Mongo Stojka, *Papierene Kinder*, 78.
23 Zimmermann, *Rassenutopie*, 105.
24 Schacter, *Searching for Memory*, 308.
25 James Olney, *Memory and Narrative: The Weave of Life-Writing* (Chicago: University of Chicago Press, 1998), xv.

theoretical directions to redefine individual, collective, and historical experience related to trauma. "History is what hurts," Jameson asserts, suggesting the omnipresence of trauma in public events.[26]

Scholars have investigated intersections between trauma, memory, narrative, history, and politics. Caruth defines trauma as "an overwhelming experience of sudden or catastrophic events in which the response to the event occurs in the often delayed, uncontrolled repetitive appearance of hallucinations and other intrusive phenomena."[27] She asks provocatively: "Is the trauma the encounter with death, or the ongoing experience of having survived it?"[28] Trauma is a "double wound" because it "is not locatable in the simple violent or original event in an individual's past, but rather in the way that its very unassimilated nature—the way it was precisely *not known* in the first instance—returns to haunt the survivor later on."[29] Friedman, who has examined hundreds of survivor testimonies in the Shoah Archive for insights into sexuality and gender during the *Porrajmos/Holocaust*, points out that "non-Holocaust-connected studies on the effect of trauma and positive and negative stresses on the human psyche reveal that memories of cataclysmic events tend to be more accurate than those of ordinary ones, at least in a broad sense."[30] One must note a major difference between Caruth and Friedman. Caruth argues that those who experience traumatic experiences always "miss" those experiences when they happen; "forgetting" thereby becomes an anathema to memory in some sense. Friedman seems to assert the opposite, namely memory kicks in strongly at the time of traumatic experiences. Still, whether the trauma releases memories immediately or later, for both the essence of traumatic experience is almost always remembered well. Friedman refers to Schacter's studies where subjects under study have experienced trauma. The emotional impact persists, whereas any recorded distortion occurs mostly in the recounting of specific details. Schacter has found the unusually accurate recall of large traumatic events is due to the release of stress-related hormones

---

26 Frederic Jameson, *The Political Unconscious: Narrative as a Socially Symbolic Act* (Ithaca, NY: Cornell University Press, 1981), 102. Thomas Vogler describes Jameson's reference to the traumatic occurrence as a paradigm for the historical event in his "Introduction," in *Witness and Memory: The Discourse of Trauma*, eds Ana Douglass and Thomas A. Vogler (New York and London: Routledge, 2003), 5.
27 Cathy Caruth, *Unclaimed Experience: Trauma, Narrative, and History* (Baltimore and London: Johns Hopkins UP, 1996), 11.
28 Ibid., 7.
29 Ibid., 4.
30 Jonathan C. Friedman, *Speaking the Unspeakable: Essays on Sexuality, Gender, and Holocaust Survivor Memory* (Lanham, MD, New York and Oxford: University Press of America, 2002), 97.

"I live with my deceased"  141

that the brain's "emotional computer," the amygdala, triggers.³¹ One could say dates belong to some of those specific details, especially for narrators who at the time were children facing a horrendous event scarring their lives forever. Langer, having analyzed numerous literary texts and live testimonies of *Porrajmos*/Holocaust survivors, talks about such distortions of time in narratives. Survivors' memories are working on at least two planes of chronology: "experienced time" of the original trauma and "re-experienced time" in the narration. This may cause survivors to feel "out of time," which in turn may create chronological leaps, gaps, and falsities.³² Nevertheless, these distortions should not make one deny that the event occurred.

In light of these observations on how trauma can affect narrative, a comparative reading of the Stojkas' autobiographies in the aftermath of the father's death reveals a second major discrepancy. According to all three accounts, after learning Wackar had been killed in a concentration camp, Maria "Sidi" Rigo Stojka, the siblings' mother, asked for his bones back. Ceija writes when her mother received the urn in the mail, she shook it and asked in Romany: "'*Wackar, ande san du katte?*'" (*Wackar, are you in there?* Author's italics.) Ceija continues to describe the gruesome scene: "The urn opened up by itself and a couple bones fell out. She sewed a small sachet, put the bones in, and strung this sachet around her neck"³³ Later in Auschwitz, according to Ceija, an SS officer tore this sachet from the mother's neck and threw it in the drainage ditch. He then hit her face. The children rescued the sachet and wiped it off with their clothes. The event's trauma is reflected subsequently in the mother's dream: "She dreamed that we were brought into a crematorium and that we all only appeared dead."³⁴ In contrast, both Karl and Mongo talk of the father's bones and his clothing being sent back to the family upon the mother's request, but neither mentions the sachet or the incident of the SS officer tearing it from her neck in Auschwitz.³⁵

A first possible reason for this discrepancy and a possible link between gender, trauma, and memory might be that Ceija knew more about the neck sachet, and especially about the SS guard's brutality in the camp, because Ceija spent more time with her mother there,

---

31  Schacter, *Searching for Memory*, 217.
32  Lawrence Langer, *Admitting the Holocaust: Collected Essays* (New York, Oxford: Oxford University Press, 1995), 15.
33  "Die Urne öffnete sich, und ein paar Knochen fielen heraus. Sie nähte sich ein kleines Täschchen und gab die Knochen hinein. Dieses Täschchen band sie sich um den Hals." Ceija Stojka, *Verborgenen*, 19.
34  "Sie träumte, man hätte uns in das Krematorium gebracht und daß wir alle nur scheintot gewesen wären" (ibid., 26).
35  Stojka and Pohanka, *Auf der ganzen Welt*, 35; Mongo Stojka, *Papierene Kinder*, 84.

whereas the boys were separated from her more. That does not seem to be the case, however. Until their separation and the liquidation of the "Gypsy Camp" on August 2–3, 1944, the family lived, slept, and ate together. During daily activities, males and females worked separately under a division of labor by sex, but even if the SS guards ripped the mother's sachet off when the boys were working elsewhere, the boys would have had opportunities to hear about the incident when the family was together.

A second reason involves the complex role gender socialization plays in memory formation. Any study of the family must account for possible gender relationships between its members, as evidenced by psychological experiments that have drawn on the different events males and females remember, on the various ways the two sexes recount their memories, and on the influence of gender socialization on emotional recall.[36] First, psychologists have looked at the extent to which gender-differentiated socialization processes influence the degree to which men and women value emotions in their lives. Males show a socialization emphasizing "such qualities as independence, assertion, activity, self-confidence, and dominance," whereas females "are socialized into expressive roles, and are expected to be emotional, warm, nurturant, altruistic, and interpersonally sensitive."[37] Second, psychologists have examined how socialization processes manifest themselves in memory recall and narratives, whereby, "females consistently recalled more childhood memories than males did and were generally faster in accessing the memories recalled."[38] A possible reason for that difference surfaces in parents' interactions with their children: "parents are more likely to use an elaborative narrative style

---

36 Penelope Davis, "Gender Differences in Autobiographical Memory for Childhood Emotional Experiences," *Journal of Personality and Social Psychology*, 79.3 (1999): 498–510; Robyn Fivush, "Constructing Narrative, Emotion, and Self in Parent-Child Conversations about the Past," in *The Remembering Self: Construction and Accuracy in the Self-Narrative*, eds Ulric Neisser and Robyn Fivush (Cambridge: Cambridge University Press, 1994), 136–57; Robyn Fivush and Janine P. Buckner, "Creating Gender and Identity Through Autobiographical Narratives," in *Autobiographical Memory and the Construction of a Narrative Self: Developmental and Cultural Perspectives*, eds Robyn Fivush and Catherine A. Haden (Mahwah, NJ: Lawrence Erlbaum Associates, 2003), 149–67; Robyn Fivush and E. Reese, "The Social Construction of Autobiographical Memory," in *Theoretical Perspectives on Autobiographical Memory*, eds M. A. Conway, D. C. Rubin, H. Spinner, and W. A. Wagenaar (Dordrecht: Kluwer Academic, 1992), 115–32; Selma Leydesdorff, Luisa Passerini, and Paul Thompson, eds, *Gender and Memory*. Vol. IV of the *International Yearbook of Oral History and Life Stories* (Oxford: Oxford University Press, 1996).
37 Davis, "Gender Differences," 499.
38 Ibid., 498.

"I live with my deceased" 143

when conversing about past events with their young daughters than with their sons."[39] In light of these findings, the emotional content of the bone sachet story could cause a different reaction for Ceija than for Mongo or Karl.

In other research, gender becomes linked to trauma in *Porrajmos*/ Holocaust studies in a historical context. On one side, researchers point to the differing circumstances of persecution that women and men had to endure in concentration camps.[40] Whereas persecutory methods that I look at in the previous chapter affected Roma particularly intensely—sterilization, sanitation, shaving of hair, sexual mistreatment—these researchers mostly focus on how all women had to deal with different hardships related to biological factors—menstruation, pregnancy, the ability to bear children—than those that men experienced. But both sexes may also have devised differing survival tactics, including reliance on individualism or solidarity, which I also look at in the previous chapter. On the other side, scholars stress their ultimate concern with even asking whether gender ultimately does matter in the face of horrors befalling both men and women. As Holocaust survivor Ruth Bondy states: "Cyclon B did not differentiate between men and women; the same death swept them all away."[41] Again, sensitive scholars must proceed circumspectly so as not to privilege the experiences of one sex above the other.

Still, without denying that all the Stojkas, male and female, faced grave danger, gender does seem to be a factor in what the three Stojkas chose or did not choose, advertently or not, to relate. First, circumstances under which the three siblings lived, wrote, and then published their works reveal the influence gendered socialization exerted on writing practices. The barriers that Ceija encountered as a woman when she decided to publish her autobiography, including the initial lack of support she received from family and her husband, distinguish her writing process from that of her brothers.[42] As with other Roma groups, Austrian Lovara show vestiges of patriarchal structures.[43] With their highest value placed on family, each member

---

39 Fivush, "Constructing Narrative," 143.
40 Cf. Friedman, *Speaking the Unspeakable*; Marlene Heinemann, *Gender and Destiny: Women Writers and the Holocaust* (New York, Westport, CT, and London: Greenwood, 1986); Judith Tydor Baumel, *Double Jeopardy: Gender and the Holocaust* (London/Portland, OR: Vallentine Mitchell, 1998).
41 Ruth Bondy, "Women in Theresienstadt and the Family Camp in Birkenau," in *Women in the Holocaust*, eds Dalia Ofer and Lenore J. Weitzman (New Haven and London: Yale University Press, 1998), 310.
42 Ceija Stojka, "Du darfst," 97; Prüger, *Zigeuner*, 105.
43 Cf. Eder-Jordan, "'Traditionen'" and Ursula Hemetek, *Mosaik der Klänge: Musik der Minderheiten und religiösen Minderheiten in Österreich* (Vienna: Böhlau, 2001).

has his or her role in that unit, and each family has its patriarch. The *Falter* article evokes the strong image of patriarch Mongo at the time. Ceija, when asked whether she feared having her first book appear in public, hints at her precarious position as a female Roma, a "Romni," who has taken the step towards publication: "I have no fear, absolutely not. Although, when I present myself to the public as a Romni then it is a big venture, a risk, because it is clear that people have oppressed Roma and Sinti for centuries."[44] The final part of her answer shows she sees oppression of Roma as gender neutral. But her specific use of the term "Romni," when she could have employed the word "Rom"— which may be used both generally to refer to any Roma member and specifically to refer to a male—when talking about her own risk in publishing, points to her awareness of limiting gender norms. The brothers, in contrast, do not mention obstacles against writing down or publishing their stories.

As noted in Chapter Three, Mongo and Karl remark several times about gender roles they observed in their own family and Lovara group. Separate gender roles did not always mean inequity in valuing men's and women's activities, however, especially in the areas of work outside and inside the family, storytelling, and music-making. Hemetek observes that Ceija heard many of the songs she sings from her grandmother and aunt. Those songs' stories reveal rather ambivalent gender roles, whereby the woman is both the object of the man's desire and an active subject in choosing her mate, and, in many of the songs, in deceiving the man. Within the strong patriarchal family structure, in which family holds the highest worth, the woman assumes a major role as mother and transmitter of culture.[45] The main media for that transmission are the Romani language, songs, and storytelling.

Hence, in the story of the bone sachet, as Tebbutt observes, it is noteworthy that Ceija repeats her mother's words in Romany at this particularly tense and emotional moment of touching the bones. The use of Romany ties the mother's love, distress, and spiritual convictions strongly to her daughter through narration.[46] Also significant in the passage Ceija relates about the SS tearing the sachet from her mother's neck is the statement that the children only had their clothes, "our clothes" (*unsere Kleider*), to dry off the sachet.[47] Here, the father's

---

44 "Ich hab keine Angst, überhaupt nicht. Obwohl, wenn ich als Romni von Wien mich der österreichischen Oeffentlichkeit präsentiere, dann ist es für mich ein großes Wagnis, ein Risiko, denn es ist klar, daß man die Rom und die Sinti unter dem Volk seit Jahrhunderten drückt." Ceijka Stojka, "Du darfst," 154.
45 Hemetek, *Mosaik*, 321.
46 Tebbutt, *Sinti and Roma*, 138.
47 Ceija Stojka, *Verborgenen*, 26.

bones survive Nazi brutality through the collective effort of the family's clothing. As the narrator, Ceija inserts herself into the mother's efforts to preserve the family unit through maintaining the father's continual presence—in the form of both his physical bones and Ceija's story. Indeed, like her mother, Ceija shows in most of her writings an intense interest in keeping alive memories of deceased family members through certain rituals and artifacts. Hence, a third reason behind Ceija's inclusion of the bone sachet story could be the existence of a particularly gender-related mourning ritual to which Ceija and her mother subscribed.[48] Ceija's title, "I live with my deceased" (*Ich lebe mit meinen Verstorbenen*), suggests a special need to maintain a relationship between herself and dead family members. In Berger's film *Ceija Stojka: Porträt einer Roma*, an image similar to that of her mother's neck sachet occurs in a scene when Ceija describes a necklace she likes to wear, one assembled from family keepsakes. On screen she carefully dons the necklace and then touches each artifact on the chain, recounting its origin and significance. She shows objects from her deceased sisters Kathi and Mitzi; gifts from her children and grandchildren; a locket containing her most prized object—a lock of hair snipped from her son Jano on his deathbed—declaring: "The whole family is on here and it accompanies me and protects me."[49] Just as her mother clung to the bone sachet, so Ceija cherishes the presence of the dead in her life.

Lévi-Strauss, in his work on funeral and mourning rituals, provides a social anthropologist's viewpoint applicable to my analysis here. In his *Tristes Tropiques* he comments: "The image a society evolves of the relationship between the living and the dead is, in the final analysis, an attempt on the level of religious thought, to conceal, embellish or justify the actual relationships which prevail among the living."[50] Okely has used that observation as a basis for examining death rites and beliefs of English Roma. Her findings reveal rituals, however, that stand in marked contrast to Ceija's.[51] Instead of clinging to the remains of the dead person, as Maria "Sidi" Rigo Stojka and Ceija did, English Roma felt compelled to destroy the property of the deceased or give it away to Gadže, for death is associated with pollution, taboos related to the body, and even ethnic boundaries separating Roma from the Gadže. As discussed earlier, Lily van Angeren-Franz and Marianne Rosenberg, too, talk about the Sinti

---

48 I thank Karen Remmler for suggesting this idea in response to an earlier version of this chapter.
49 "Die ganze Familie ist dadrauf und das begleitet mich und schützt mich." Karin Berger (dir.), *Ceija Stojka: Porträt einer Roma* (Vienna: Navigator Film, 1999).
50 Claude Lévi-Strauss, *Tristes Tropiques*, translated by J. and D. Weightman (London: Cape, 1973), 246.
51 Okely, *Traveller Gypsies*, 192–6.

custom of burning the wagon in which someone had died.[52] To retain the possessions might invite the *mulo*, or spirit of the dead, to come back and cause misfortune and bad luck. Those observations have been confirmed for other countries, as in Stewart's study on Hungarian Roma.[53]

Hence, to say Ceija's observances of mourning rituals represent those of all Romani people, and especially of Romni and their beliefs, would be incorrect. As Fraser remarks, Roma living in Western Europe since the nineteenth century have acquired unique rituals, often associated with Christianity.[54] For Ceija and her family in Austria, rituals obviously have a basis in Catholicism with a strong Madonna worship and observance of regular Catholic masses for the dead. In this way, Ceija is, to return to Lévi-Strauss's assertion, embellishing and justifying her own relationship between the living and the dead, one having roots both in her adoption of a Christian belief in eternal life and in her desire to connect to her Romani matrilineage. As in the account of her mother dreaming about the family being "scheintot" (dead in appearance only) in the crematorium, Ceija also writes about dreams, but her dreams are good ones encompassing kind spirits and assuring her the dead are not to be feared, as in other countries: "we are not scared of our dead."[55] Consequently, Ceija builds her own rituals on ones similar to those she has observed of her mother, thus establishing a strong relationship to maternal lineage. That relationship most likely stems from the time she spent with her mother due to the gender roles that she, Karl, and Mongo observed in their family.

The significance of gender roles in deciphering possible reasons behind inclusion and exclusion of memory-stories raises the question about what to do with varying testimonies and whether their differences really matter. In his often-cited essay on survivor testimonies, Laub describes the differing reactions of a historian and a psychoanalyst (whom the reader later learns is Laub himself) upon hearing the testimony of an Auschwitz survivor about the Sonderkommando, or the Jewish prisoners who worked in death camps in exchange for certain privileges, uprising that took place in the camp on October 7, 1944. The historian questions the accuracy of testimony, stating the woman survivor who says she witnessed "4 chimneys" blowing up that day was wrong. Historians know there was only one chimney that blew up. The historian averred: "It was utterly important to remain accurate least the revisionists in history discredit everything."[56] The

---

52  Angeren-Franz, *Leben*, 134. Marianne Rosenberg, *Kokolores*, 50.
53  Stewart, *Time of the Gypsies*, 218–21.
54  Fraser, *Gypsies*, 313.
55  "wir fürchten uns nicht vor unseren Toten." Ceija Stojka, "Verstorbenen," 307.
56  Shoshana Felman and Dori Laub, MD, *Testimony: Crisis of Witnessing in Literature, Psycholanalysis, and History* (New York: Routledge, 1992), 61.

"I live with my deceased" 147

psychologist disagreed, insisting "the woman was testifying ... not to the number of the chimneys blown up, but to something else, more radical, more crucial: the reality of an unimaginable occurrence."[57] In merely talking about the occurrence, the woman survivor was "breaking out of Auschwitz even by her very talking."[58] She was testifying to an inconceivable event.

Discrepancies between history and personal recollection—and the reactions from two professionals—incite one to revisit the role of gender socialization in the three siblings' autobiographies. Ceija brings up patterns of female solidarity, and the story of the bone sachet seems to fit into those patterns. She talks about the mother's activities to help the family survive—saving food, stealing a turnip from a cart, and scrounging for any food or clothing possible. The mother's will to help extended beyond the family to others in the camp: she divided up among many women the contents of a care package that Kathi Stojka received from a friend in Vienna; she shared food with Polish women in the camp; and she cooperated with other mothers in strategies of survival. "The mothers banded strongly together," Ceija observes.[59] They sang songs together, often ones expressing resistance through a change in wording.[60] The women's solidarity, Ceija stresses, harks back to the solidarity she may have seen in her mother's connection with the father's bones, one in which even the dead and the living remain conjoined in a struggle against the powers of extermination. In portraying the SS guard ripping the sachet from her mother's neck, Ceija stands as a witnessing daughter. In solidarity with her mother, she depicts the will of the family and Roma to stand as a collective against evil. To Ceija, her mother's desire to maintain a collective within the family under such duress was the kind of "unimaginable occurrence" to which Laub referred, as was the SS guard's brutal act in trying to destroy that collective. The former seems unimaginable in its impossibility, the latter in its reality.

Likewise, Karl's stress on the fact that he was in school at the time of his father's arrest underlines the significant theme of education. His emphasis on schooling mirrors his determination to show independence and ability to survive on his own, characteristics he also attributes to

---

57 Ibid., 62.
58 Ibid.
59 "Die Mütter hielten sehr stark zusammen." Ceija Stojka, *Verborgenen*, 35.
60 Ceija talks about her sister changing the words to the song "Es wird ein Wunder geschehen" ("A Miracle Will Happen") by adding "und dann werden wir nach Hause gehen" ("and then we will go home.") (*Reisende auf dieser Welt*, 151). She thereby expressed hope to leave Auschwitz (*Verborgenen*, 151). For a discussion of music and performance as resistance, see Grobbel, "Contemporary Autobiography."

Roma in general and their efforts to break down stereotypes of being uneducated and uneducable. In contrast with Ceija's autobiography, however, Karl's does not often portray his mother as a focal point for his own education. He also does not relate stories and songs from his mother—as cultural transmission from one generation to the next—as Ceija does. When narrating about his time in Auschwitz, he portrays mainly a highly independent, autonomous existence among the inmates.[61] Several stories depict how he and others steal bread from other prisoners;[62] he trades stolen goods with other prisoners;[63] he observes "cannibalism" among prisoners eating other prisoners. These survival tactics, he surmises, sometimes worked, but mostly did not. He mentions saving his family through his kitchen duties, smuggling scraps out for them to eat: "During this time I as a child carried my family through."[64] Stories by Otto Rosenberg, Walter Winter, and Ewald Hanstein, as related in Chapter Four, corroborate Karl's strong feelings of independence and autonomy.

Similarly, although Mongo also recounts the story of receiving their father's bones back from Mauthausen, no mention is made of the sachet.[65] Mongo stresses in his recollections about Auschwitz his survival tactic of keeping his sense of humor through thick and thin.[66] Whether the two boys did or did not know about their mother making the sachet, wearing it around her neck, and then having the SS guard rip it off, both could have chosen not to relate the story based on their survival tactics, which seem to focus more on the individual than on the group's solidarity, or, in the mother's case, the family's solidarity. The differing foci in the three narratives match gender-differentiated socialization processes psychologists Fivish and Davis observe whereby the socialization of males emphasizes independence and activity, and that of females stresses emotions and nurturance. Gender differences are not biological or innate, but, like ethnicity, constructed by both externally imposed circumstances and socially formulated environments.

Besides the bone sachet story, differing renditions of the selection process in Auschwitz surface. In the night of August 2–3, 1944, the "Gypsy Camp" was liquidated. Karl was 13 and Ceija was 10; they thus would have been too young to live, for, as all three siblings explain, most children under 14 were considered too young to work and thus

---

61   Stojka and Pohanka, *Auf der ganzen Welt*, 38.
62   Ibid., 41.
63   Ibid., 48.
64   "Damals habe ich als Kind meine Familie durchgebracht," (ibid., 43).
65   Ceija states her father was in Dachau; she later learned he died in Hartheim. See footnote 12 above (page 136).
66   Mongo Stojka, *Papierene Kinder*, 140.

"I live with my deceased" 149

were gassed. Karl writes in his autobiography that their mother saved the two younger children by claiming they were dwarves, and thus looked young for their age.[67] He alludes to the fact that as dwarves they would have at least had the chance to survive as subjects for Mengele's medical experiments.

Ceija has a slightly different account, one involving a Polish woman who consoles her. According to Ceija, her mother saved her alone, for Karl was already in the right line with the older children and adults, along with her mother and Mongo, because they could work. Ceija stresses how she was in the left line—with those who were too young, old, or sick to work—when her beloved old Polish guardian takes her hand in comfort. Meanwhile, Ceija's mother and siblings try to convince the guard that Ceija is 16 years old and can work. The guard comes over to her and asks how old she is. "I said what my mother had instructed me to say. 'I can work well, I am already 16 years old.' After that he said to me that I should fetch the wheelbarrow and the much too big shovel."[68] Ceija did as she was told, proved she had the strength of a 16-year old, and survived.

Mongo claims to cite from Karl when he writes about the mother saving Karl and Ceija. Whereas Karl had said nothing about the person who let them pass, Mongo states clearly—after claiming to cite Karl—Dr Mengele had permitted Mongo and Ceija to stay with the others. For Mongo, the entire family is in the right line together from the beginning. Their mother held Mongo with her right hand and Ceija with her left hand. The mother's number gets called, and all three are instructed to go see Dr Mengele. Mongo writes: "Then he said to our mother: 'The children really are not 14 years old.' My mother answers: "Dr Mengele, they have lagged behind in their growth. They are dwarves.' Dr Mengele ordered his SS-man: 'Let them pass.'"[69]

In all three siblings' cases, the mother is the agent of survival, despite varying renditions of how she managed to save them. As Mongo writes: "Mother saved me and Ceija by her lie."[70] Unlike in the brothers' narratives, however, Ceija brings in another female figure to console her in her stress. Through renewed solidarity and calmness, Ceija is able to repeat her mother's words that she is old enough to

---

67 Stojka and Pohanka, *Auf der ganzen Welt*, 45.
68 "Ich sagte, was meine Mama mir beigebracht hatte. 'Ich kann gut arbeiten, ich bin schon 16 Jahre alt.' Darauf sagte er, ich soll die Schiebtruhe und die viel zu große Schaufel nehmen." Ceija Stojka, *Verborgenen*, 30–1.
69 "Dann sagt er zu unserer Mutter: 'Die Kinder sind doch keine 14 Jahre alt.' Mutter antwortet: 'Herr Dr. Mengele, sie sind im Wachstum zurückgeblieben. Es sind Zwerge.' Dr Mengele befiehlt seinen SS-Mann: 'Laß' sie passieren.'" Mongo Stojka, *Papierene Kinder*, 151.
70 "Mutter hat durch ihre Lüge Ceija und mir das Leben gerettet" (ibid.).

work. The role of the Polish woman in helping save Ceija, or at least in offering her support in matters of life and death, coincides with other instances of female solidarity in the camps that Ceija reports. What then might be the consequences of such comparisons between, on the one hand, survival tactics of solidarity and community Ceija observes, and, on the other hand, those of autonomy and individual will and humor Mongo and Karl present? Could they, too, be gender related? Scholars who interview women concentration camp survivors and examine their testimonies often point to females' general desire for solidarity with other women in the camps, their willingness to help each other, and their transferal of certain "maternal instincts" into building communities under duress.[71] These features are seen as different from men's experiences, which, as already mentioned, are often portrayed as more solitary and autonomous. What such studies risk, however, is a certain valorization of women above men in their abilities to survive monstrosities. One does not want to be "valorizing oppression," against which Ringelheim warns in her work on Jewish women and the Holocaust.[72] Am I implying suffering makes women better than men in their abilities to devise coping mechanisms and survival tactics? Am I letting "gender pride" get in the way of truth, another question Ringelheim and others have raised when examining the relationship between gender and traumatic violence?[73]

To avoid gender valorization, a more productive argument would continue to weave in findings on the "fragile" essence of individual memory, collective memory, and traumatized memory, all often influenced by perspective and socialization. In her analysis of Renais's film *Hiroshima, mon Amour*, Maclear confronts assumptions that history as a life story can be told in one version and sheds light on the different "ways of seeing" manifesting themselves in discrepancies between multiple tellings of an event.[74] Maclear references the film's opening, when the Japanese male character asks his French female lover if she has "seen everything" in Hiroshima after the atomic bomb dropped.

---

71 See Freund, Baumgartner, and Greifeneder, *Vermögensentzug*, 114; Elmer Luchterhand, "Social Behavior of Concentration Camp Prisoners: Continuities and Discontinuites with Pre- and Postcamp Life," in *Survivors, Victims, and Perpetrators*, ed. J. Dimsdale (New York: Hemisphere Publishing, 1980), 259–83; Joan Ringelheim, "Women and the Holocaust: A Reconsideration of Research," in *Different Voices: Women in the Holocaust*, eds Carol Rittner and John K. Roth (New York: Paragon House, 1993), 373–420; and Zimmermann, *Rassenutopie*, 123.
72 Ringelheim, "Women and the Holocaust."
73 Ronit Lentin, *Gender & Catastrophe* (London and New York: Zed Books, 1997).
74 Kyo Maclear, "The Limits of Vision: Hiroshima Mon Amour and the Subversion of Representation," in Douglass and Vogler, *Witness and* Memory, 233–47.

The lover persists in claiming she has, indeed, seen everything. Only later does she clarify her answers by saying what she has "seen" has been in the form of photos, films, newspaper articles, and accounts, not as an eyewitness. To describe this phenomenon of different ways of seeing, Maclear uses the term "transmemoration" in reference to our understanding of "experience, perception and knowledge as historically contingent."[75] This concept may prove useful in interpreting the divergent memories Ceija, Karl, and Mongo display in the events concerning the bone sachet and the selection process in Auschwitz. The siblings' related memories rely on their own ways of seeing, contingent on a socialization process that should account for gender and trauma.

The story behind one of Ceija's paintings exemplifies the "transmemoration" process, whereby media inspired a "different way of seeing" and a different way of remembering. The painting depicts a little girl with a flowered dress and an apple, lying on the ground in front of her as she faces an SS guard with a gun. On the back of the painting, Ceija describes how one day she was watching a television interview with a Holocaust survivor on ORF, the Austrian public broadcasting channel. The witness told of a guard who went to shoot a little girl in a flowered dress who had been selected because she was too young and small to work. Before shooting her, the guard rolled an apple to her on the ground. The guard then shot her, picked up the apple, and ate it. Ceija recalls how listening to this witness's story, and especially hearing about the flowered dress, sparked her own memories. She then remembered the little girl arriving in Auschwitz with a dress that was too big for her; Ceija, in contrast, had a dress that was too small for her. The two girls exchanged dresses. Had the witness not mentioned the flowered dress, Ceija claimed, she would not have remembered seeing this girl and the shooting. Just as the lover in Renais's film claims to have "seen everything" through exposure to outside media, so, too, does Ceija "see" or "re-see" the images of the dress, the girl, the apple, the guard, and the horrible murder after viewing the television broadcast. The images are so vivid that she creates an artwork from her perspective.[76]

Besides being stimulated by outside media images, ways of seeing are highly dependent on family dynamics, as Keppler notes. After examining numerous family conversations in a variety of settings, Keppler found that rarely does a family story become narrated in one sitting or in one piece. In fact, Keppler's final thesis is that family stories never exist in a totality. Bits and pieces of stories come together

---

75 Ibid., 245.
76 I thank Andrea Driendl for this reference and story. The painting hangs in her apartment in Vienna.

at different times, in different contexts, and from different family members. The collective family story is an ongoing, living one that circulates over and over among family members to formulate their identities as individuals and as a group.[77]

Thus, the Stojkas' autobiographies, with all their complexities and discrepancies, call for theoretical models that account for a number of influential factors. The categories of "individual" and "collective" memory that Halbwachs defines are not always distinguishable within a family whose members publish their life stories individually and as part of an ethnically persecuted group. Likewise, the individual stories of three members of a Romani family interned together in Auschwitz blur the boundaries that the Assmanns establish between the more private "communicative" and the more public "collective" memory. In such a context, gender and trauma, as born out in the collective, become variables influencing individual memories. In cases of ethnic persecution, scholars in their research must not ignore the possible consequences of victimization for both genders. The reader must also not judge whether one rendition is more truthful than another, or one survival or recounting method is more effective than another. The relationship between gender and memory becomes situationally determined in traumatic contexts.[78] It is difficult to assess when trauma may have affected the actions one person sees and another may not have seen, or the emotions one person experiences and the other does not, or the stories one person decides to tell and another person does not. With the Stojkas, readers truly have autobiographical, historical, and narrative treasures whereby members of a family are, as Fivush and Buckner remark, "both constructing their own independent life stories and creating a shared history based on family membership."[79] The siblings' individual autobiographies are remarkable in and of themselves. As a collective, however, they become even stronger, composing individual memories and ultimately a private family story to live on in public history.

---

77 Keppler, "Soziale Formen," 156.
78 Fivush and Buckner, "Creating Gender," 164.
79 Ibid., 155.

# Six "It was, because it wasn't": Gender and Ethnicity in Folk Tales, Fairy Tales, and Wonder Tales

My exploration into the intersections between gender and ethnicity in the world of Romani folk tales, fairy tales, and wonder tales in the German-speaking world begins with a recounting of Philomena Franz's story "Der reiche Kaufmann und die schöne Danuscha" (The Rich Businessman and the Beautiful Danuscha).[1] One day, a rich businessman went into the woods to find his forester brother. The businessman heard beautiful music emanating from a group of Romani musicians in the forest. He was so entranced with the music that he asked them to play at the festival of his name day. When he went home and told his wife what he had done, she was upset he had invited a "dirty pack of scoundrels" (*schmutziges Lumpenpack*) into their house.[2] Still, despite the wife's admonishments, the businessman followed his wishes, and the musicians came and played.

After the performance, the beautiful Danuscha stayed behind alone, only to have the businessman discover her when he began to sing, and she accompanied him in her sweet voice. The businessman immediately began speaking with her. His wife became angry, and Danuscha ran back to her family. But the businessman did not forget her. He searched for her and finally found her with her family and their travelling wagon. Her father did not want to let the businessman see his daughter; he feared that if the businessman decided to marry his daughter she would be ostracized in the non-Roma world. From the father's perspective, the attitudes of Gadže towards Roma, and not the Romani's wish to live separately from Gadže, posed the major threat to any possible union between Roma and non-Roma.

---

1 Franz, *Zigeunermärchen*, 65–72.
2 Ibid., 71.

Finally the father conceded and let the businessman stay with them. In the middle of the night, however, the businessman snuck off with Danuscha, and, as the ensuing lines imply, the two consummated their union under the stars. Both found what they had been looking for all their lives. Love prevails over money and reputation for the non-Romani man. For the Romni Danuscha, love takes precedence over the possibility of ostracization. Love is the ultimate value that holds them together.

The next day, the "Gypsies" travelled on, taking Danuscha with them, and the businessman returned to his life, which he found so unbearably sad and empty that he eventually died. All the townspeople, knowing that he had had an extramarital affair with a Romani girl, deemed him so disreputable that the priests refused to speak at his funeral, and the church musicians did not play in homage to him. On the day of his burial, however, his coffin opened, and a white figure resembling the businessman appeared and then disappeared. At the same time, Danuscha, who was still travelling with her family, gave birth to a son on a stormy night.

The years went by, and Danuscha continued to go out at night, much to her father's consternation. Her father, wanting to prevent her wanderings, decided to try and lock her up in the wagon. Still, at night he saw a dark figure going into the wagon. He finally confronted his daughter about the strange figure, and she admitted the ghost of the rich businessman had been visiting her. She then died a year later so that both lovers were united in death. The father was incredibly sad at losing his only child and remained sad the rest of his days. The story ends with a saying Franz states is well known among Roma: "In moments of despair what counts is not only what is right or wrong, but what helps us to live on."[3] Here, life and love prevail over judgments of right and wrong.

Surprisingly, this final message seems to condone the adulterous relationship between the businessman and Danuscha and the birth of a child out of wedlock, two occurrences contradicting traditional moral codes of fidelity. Yet the story does not totally defy certain standard images of Roma persisting for centuries—the inextricable link between Roma and music; the irreparable split between the Roma and the non-Romani world; and the dangers caused by the beautiful, seductive, mysterious "Gypsy" woman Danuscha, who attracted the businessman in life and afterwards.[4] These contradictory messages

---

3   "In Augenblicken der Verzweiflung zählt nicht nur das, was richtig oder falsch ist, sondern das, was uns hilft weiter zu leben" (ibid., 72).

4   For accounts of the stereotypes of Roma in literature by non-Roma, see Bogdal, *Europa*; Breger, *Ortlosigkeit*; and Solms and Strauß, *Zigeunerbilder*.

are puzzling, mostly because they differ from those in many other tales Franz tells where she presents images of Roma different from traditional ones espousing "Gypsies" as dirty, stealing bands of male musicians and seductive female fortune tellers aimlessly roaming. In *Zwischen Liebe und Haß* Franz portrays her own life of travel, music, family ceremonies, and traditions before, during, and after World War II in Germany. Sometimes she depicts that life with nostalgia but also with care not to over-romanticize and stereotype. Belonging to a family troupe of travelling musicians in high demand in the early decades of the twentieth century, Franz states she was better off than many Sinti, who slept in tents and had few possessions.[5] As much as she praises the travelling life for its heightened connections with nature, family, and Sinti, she also acknowledges the fear of possible danger travellers frequently experienced when they came to a new area.[6] Even some customs, such as a couple eloping without the father's consent to marry, end up "less romantic than novels often portray."[7] Franz walks the fine line between stressing worthy traits in the Romani lifestyle and preventing exotic views of that lifestyle.

Most of the folk tales and fairytales in *Zigeunermärchen* do not romanticize "Gypsy life" as one of only song, nature, and fortune telling. While Franz continues to stress what she views as the Sinti's love of music, nature, and travelling, she also depicts possible negative consequences of those affinities. Her Sinti characters are often poor and wear rags, reflecting a severe life. Images of summer travelling evoke idyllic scenes of freedom in woods and fields, but descriptions of winter months turn harsh, as in the tale about Snogo, a poor Roma who must brave the cold without a roof over his head.[8] Instead of perpetuating stereotypes, many stories didactically explain customs and rituals.

The final adage in "Der reiche Kaufmann und die schöne Danuscha," however, with the narrator dispelling the absolute need to know only what is right or wrong in the face of survival, is a telling reminder of the tensions that Roma face. On the one hand, storytellers attempt to maintain traditions; on the other hand, they try to live with and integrate into non-Romani society. At times, Romani storytellers rely on stereotypical images; at other times, they abruptly break stereotypes. In *Why Fairy Tales Stick,* Jack Zipes investigates the power of fairy tales to construct social change and critique, pointing out the integrative,

---

5  Franz, *Liebe und Haß,* 15.
6  Ibid., 28.
7  "weniger romantisch, als es in Romanen oft dargestellt wird" (ibid., 32).
8  Franz, *Zigeunermärchen,* 47–8.

transformative nature of fairy tales.⁹ Likewise, folk tales, fairy tales, and tales of wonder offer Roma a means to contrast truth and falsity, right and wrong, male and female, magic and reality, and Roma and non-Roma, in order to display values and customs comprising their ethnic identities while exploring possibilities for changes in gender roles and norms.

The tales I investigate represent a small, selective sample of those by prolific Romani storytellers.¹⁰ Romani stories often open with the standard fairy-tale beginning of "Once upon a time" (*Es war einmal*) or "Many years ago" (*Vor vielen Jahren*). Yet several tales commence with the paradoxical saying "It was because it wasn't (*Es war, weil es nicht war*) or "Just as it was not, so was it still" (*So wie's nicht war, so war es eben*). First, contrasting beginnings and endings reflect beliefs in a connection between ephemeral life on earth and ethereal spiritual life after death. Second, they demonstrate the continual contradictions Roma have encountered in their everyday lives. Likewise, several tales end with the expression "Here the good, there the bad" (*Hier das Gute, dort das Schlechte*), suggesting varying outcomes and interpretations every situation potentially encompasses. Not every story concludes with a happy ending. Even *tertenetura*—stories recounting actual occurrences or ones believed to be true—begin or end with a statement questioning their veracity, such as: "And this story, whether true or not, so it goes." (*Und diese Geschichte, ob sie wahr ist oder nicht, so geht sie!*)¹¹ Opening and closing proclamations reflect the tales' ambiguous nature and address the concerns of sceptics who might view events or characters as too fantastical to be true.

"Der geizige Bettler" (The Greedy Beggar) weaves together the real and the fantastical to recount the antics of a greedy Romani beggar.¹² The story begins with the ambiguous sentence: "Just as it was not, so it was; there was no blanket, just a cloth. Nobody can say whether it

---

9   Zipes, *Why Fairy Tales Stick.*
10  I am working from five main sources: Philomena Franz's *Zigeunermärchen*, which she wrote down; Reinhold Lagrene, "Anhang: Die Geschichte von Chinto Mari, " in Solms and Strauß, *Zigeunerbilder*, 101–12, which Lagrene wrote down; and three bilingual collections in German and Romany, transcribed directly from oral recordings that Heinschink and other researchers made from hundreds of tales that Romani storytellers recited to them from 1960 to 2000: 1. *Der Rom und der Teufel/O rom taj o beng: Märchen, Erzählungen und Lieder der Roma aus dem Burgenland/Romane pararistscha, phukajiptscha taj gila andar o Burgenland*, eds Dieter W. Halwachs, Emmerich Gärtner-Horvath, Michael Wogg (Klagenfurt: Drava, 2000); 2. *Fern von uns im Traum ...*; and 3. *Kerzen und Limonen/Momelja hem limonja: Märchen der Arlije./Arlijengere paramisja*, eds Petra Cech, Mozes F. Heinschink, Dieter W. Halwachs (Klagenfurt: Drava, 2009).
11  *Fern von uns*, 23.
12  *Rom und der Teufel*, 62–7.

is true or whether someone made it up. Roma told this story in earlier days."[13] Veracity contrasts with falsity. Emphasis on the Romani world as the source for the story creates a distinction from the non-Roma.

The Rom protagonist in the story was so greedy he refused to share his food first with a rabbit and then with a wild pig. One day he came to a farm, where the farmer woman asked him to help her take in the hay. The beggar refused unless she compensated him. She asked him why he needed payment because he already had something to eat. She knew this from the animals with which he did not share. She agreed to let him drink goat's milk as payment for his work. When she gave him the milk, he drank it up so greedily that he became sick. He returned to his home and told everyone there was a witch's house in the forest. Subsequently, everyone who went to find the witch and the house did not find anything and thus did not believe him. When he finally went back to see for himself, he met the pig and the rabbit again, who this time refused him their food. He wandered around looking for the house for years. Finally, some women looking for mushrooms found him dead in the forest.

The moral, so the story ends, is God punished the Rom because the Rom was so mean to the animals and did not give them something to eat when they were hungry. The story ends with an adage implying one must be willing to give more than just a small share: "Did not give a blanket, only a cloth."[14] This expression could have two meanings, depending on the subject, which is perhaps purposely missing. If the subject were "*Es*," then the expression would mean: "There was no blanket, just a cloth." If the subject were "*Er*," then the sentence would mean: "He did not give a blanket, just a cloth." In either case, the implication is that to give more is better than presenting less.

While the moral of the story—to share and share alike—seems ethically sound in any culture, in the context of Roma and Gadže relations this tale is significant. As a people who have been stereotyped as perpetual robbers and beggars, many Roma autobiographers admit to petty theft, justifying such as only occurring during hard times.[15] The usual behavior was to buy or exchange goods. The occasional small theft should in no way incriminate all Roma as hardened criminals, Elizabeth Kreutz claims.[16] The concept of stealing food also belongs to

---

13 "So wie's nicht war, so war es eben; hat Decke nicht, nur Tuch gegeben. Niemand kann sagen, ob sie wahr ist oder ob man sie erfunden hat: Die Roma haben früher diese Geschichte erzählt" (ibid., 63).
14 "Hat Decke nicht, nur Tuch gegeben" (ibid., 67).
15 Karl Stojka describes hardships forcing Roma to steal chickens during Nazi times: *Kindheit*, 18.
16 Kreutz argues the pettiness of such crimes as stealing made them less harmful than other crimes such a sexual offenses, child murders, prostitution, and

a larger system of etiquette advocating sharing food. Anna Mettbach talks about the hospitality her family showed in taking in anyone less fortunate than themselves.[17] Hancock describes this etiquette as part of purity and pollution beliefs: "Not offering something to eat—and for that matter refusing to accept something offered—is a serious breach of etiquette, because it suggests that the person slighted in this way is not clean.[18] The great pride Philomena Franz and Ceija Stojka take in the high quality of Romani cuisine reflects desires to share delicacies.[19] The fantastical contexts these tales provide mediate this message to share and share alike.

Regarding gender norms, "Der geizige Bettler" questions the stereotype of the female Romani witch. Only the greedy male Rom claims the woman is a witch; others cannot confirm his perceptions. The mixture of magical talking animals with human nonbelievers who produce a reality check leaves the story open-ended as to whether the female is really a witch or not. The story thus ambiguously provokes a reading defying harmful generalizations about all Romani women being witches while at the same time not denying that some of them may, indeed, have magical powers.

The fairy tale genre relies on magic and superstition. Theories about the genre of magical realism prove useful in determining how effectively mixing magic with reality debunks stereotypes. Mellen provides an overview of the various definitions of magical realism, distinguishing the genre from fantasy, "the marvelous," Surrealism, and magic realism.[20] Regardless of how one defines magical realism, most theorists note the genre's potential for allowing subversive, alternative voices to emerge, allowing, as Mellen states, "dissident ideas to emerge as couched in myth and legend and, hence, [granting] them a validity denied to them in social reality. In both Latin American and European novels, magic realism has been a means for authors

---

robbing banks (Krausnick, *"Da wollten wir frei sein!"* 21). Sway concludes that the belief in *mulo*, or the after-death spirits, and the fear that the spirits will come back to haunt them, prevents Roma from murder. She also states: "Wife beatings, child abuse, fist fights, and other violent behavior hardly exist among Gypsies" (*Familiar Strangers*, 11).

17  Mettbach/Behringer, *"Wer wird ..."* 22.
18  Ian Hancock, *We are the Romani people/Ame sam e Rromane dzene* (Hatfield, Hertfordshire: University of Hertfordshire Press, 2002), 81.
19  Franz, *Zigeunermärchen*, 25, 28. For an analysis of food metaphors in Ceija Stojka's stories, see Lorely French, "How to Cook a Hedgehog: Ceija Stojka and Romani ('Gypsy') Cultural Identity Through the Culinary Literary Arts," in *Cuisine and Symbolic Capital: Food in Film and Literature*, ed. Cheleen Ann-Catherine Mahar (Newcastle upon Tyne: Cambridge Scholars Press, 2010), 102–26.
20  Joan Mellen, *Magic Realism*, vol. 5 of *Literary Topics* (Farmington Hills, MI: The Gale Group, 2000).

"It was, because it wasn't" 159

to break through the stultifying confines of the status quo with ideas challenging accepted notions of politics, literature, and the nature of human existence."[21] While not all Romani tales fall into the category of magical realism, the magic Roma often introduce into their stories belongs to what Faris terms the "irreducible element," adding surprise and unpredictability that "tend to destabilize habitual structures of order and authority, a destabilization that makes room for new voices to emerge as transculturation proceeds."[22] Roma can thereby manipulate widely held stereotypes about their connection with mystical forces to produce equivocal interpretations, as in "Der geizige Bettler."

Reinhold Lagrene's "Die Geschichte von Chinto Mari" (The Story of Chinto Mari) proves the significant role magic plays in tales, even if making non-Roma appear laughable. A leitmotif relying on the relationship between the oppressed and the dominant culture reveals a self-inflicted identification of Sinti with evil forces. According to Lagrene, Sinti stories ironically turn around this prejudicial identification of Roma with evil to unveil the ignorance and superstition of the dominant culture.[23] In Lagrene's story, the character of the young trickster Chinto Mari injects whimsy into the plot while Chinto Mari's mother creates the ultimate twist.

When Chinto Mari refuses to take a bath, he runs away from home naked and tries to hide in a barrel. The first barrel he climbs into is full of tar, and the second is full of feathers. When he tries to remove the tar and feathers first from his head, his hair stays sticking up, so that he looks like he has horns. When he searches for food in a farmer's house, the farmer spies him and thinks he is the devil. The farmer offers a truckload of food to any person who can exorcize the devil from the farmhouse. The local priest tries to accomplish this task by spraying the house with holy water, but Chinto Mari stays in the house. When Chinto Mari's mother hears about the commotion, she knows immediately her son must be at the root of the brouhaha. She feigns possession of secret powers and offers to use them to rid the house of the devil.

The narrator tells the audience of her plan, which accomplishes its exact intention; namely, her scheme makes the non-Roma appear comic in their ignorance and unfounded superstition. She goes to the farmers with a whole wagon full of food, drink, and money and advises them they should let her try to free them from the bad spirits because she

---

21  Ibid., 63, 135.
22  Wendy B. Faris, *Ordinary Enchantments: Magical Realism and the Remystification of Narrative* (Nashville: Vanderbilt University Press, 2004).
23  Reinhold Lagrene, "Mündliche Erzählkunst als Volkskultur—Betrachtungen aus der Innensicht," in Solms and Strauß, *Zigeunerbilder*, 94.

knows an age-old curse her great grandmother had once told her while on a pilgrimage to Rome, which she herself had received from the Pope. In parentheses, the narrator adds the mother's thoughts: "(which naturally was not true, but out of fear for her son she saw no other possibility than to claim this in order to enter the house.)"[24] The mother thus reveals her intentions to use non-Roma's stereotypical beliefs about Roma—travelling in wagons bearing items the Gadže need; connecting with supernatural forces; wandering on pilgrimages; and legitimating her powers based on spiritual beliefs—to gain entrance into the non-Roma world. In her actions, one detects what Bhabha defines as mimicry, namely "the desire for a reformed, recognizable Other, *as a subject of a difference that is almost the same, but not quite.*"[25] She accomplishes what Bhabha identifies as *"splitting"* the discourse "so that two attitudes towards external reality persist; one takes reality into consideration while the other disavows it and replaces it by a product of desire that repeats, rearticulates 'reality' as mimicry."[26] The mother's images mimic non-Roma stereotypes about Roma; the family assumes characteristics non-Roma have foisted upon them, and in doing so they trick non-Roma into believing a reality that is not. "It was because it wasn't."

From outside the house, Chinto Mari's mother communicates in Romany with Chinto Mari as if he was the devil; of course, no one else understands. She tells him of the danger he is in and warns him that if he does not respond, then someone will burn the house down with him in it. The father, whom the narrator says has purposely remained distant from the entire scene, realizes Chinto Mari cannnot expose himself yet to the crowd, for then the farmers would become the laughingstock of the town for having believed he was the devil. That reaction could have grave consequences for Chinto Mari's parents, whom the townspeople would blame for making them look like fools. Consequently, the father sneaks around into the back of the house and helps his son dress in his regular clothes. The son and the father then walk out through the crowd as if neither of them has been involved in the whole calamity. The mother, in the meantime, goes into the house, moves the furniture and throws dishes around as if she is chasing away the devil. She emerges from the house dishevelled, and the crowd cowers before her in fear of her magical powers in ridding the house of the devil. The story's ending is quick, however. Subsequently, instead

---

24 "(was natürlich nicht stimmte, aber aus Angst um ihren Sohn sah sie keine andere Möglichkeit, als dies zu behaupten, um in das Haus zu gelangen)." Lagrene, "Anhang," 108.
25 Author's emphasis. Bhabha, *Location of Culture*, 86.
26 Author's emphasis, ibid., 91.

of praising and thanking the Sinti family, the townspeople avoid them, believing they consort with the devil. Eventually the ostracized family moves away. The woman becomes the savior for the son, but ultimately she cannot save the family from ostracism. Again, an ambiguous ending leaves the Romani woman as rescuing the town from what it believed were evil supernatural forces only to face alienation for herself and her family because she supposedly possessed magical powers. Such tales ultimately question stereotypes dividing the world into good and bad and the places Roma and non-Roma men and women assume in that schema, harking back to the centuries-old equation of Romani women with malevolent magical powers and the consequences of such connections. The amusing story of trickery creates a snowball effect tragically resulting in the family's forced departure from the town. The ultimate irony is that the woman merely feigns having such powers and thus does not really stand on either side of the dichotomy.

As with "Der geizige Bettler"—displaying stereotypes while dispelling them—the metaphor of truth and veracity in "Die Geschichte von Chinto Mari" discloses Roma's attempts to straddle their cultures with mainstream ones.[27] Romani storytellers adapt ideas from their own cultural contexts to fit the worlds where they have lived and are living. Conversely, they transform ideas and stories from non-Romani cultures through the use of materials from Romani cultures. Hence, Bhabha's concept of "cultural hybridity" applies to the double position of Romani culture, as Grobbel shows in her essay on Romani autobiographies, in that Romani culture forms part of the dominant culture at the same time that it remains outside. Romani tales reflect, according to Bhabha, "a movement away from a world conceived in binary terms, away from a notion of the people's aspirations sketched in simple black and white."[28] Avoidance of a black-and-white model opens doors for questioning norms and moral codes of behavior. But again, Roma do not stand merely "between" cultures, to borrow from Adelson's argument "against betweenness." In contrast, individual narrators' storytelling performances remain flexible and fluctuating. Lagrene emphasizes the important role that Romani storytellers play

---

27 Michael Wogg, "Märchen, Erzählungen und Lieder der Burgenland-Roma," in *Der Rom und der Teufel*, 237–49; Petra Cech and Christiane Fennesz-Juhasz, "Märchen, Erzählungen und Lieder der Lovara," in *Fern von uns im Traum*, 397–424; Petra Cech, Mozes F. Heinschink, and Dieter W. Halwachs, "Herkunft der Texte, Quellen und Reihung," in *Kerzen und Limonen*, 241–80; Antti Aarne, *The Types of Folktale: A Classification and Bibliography*, translated and enlarged by Stith Thompson, 2nd edn (Helsinki: Suomalainen Tiedeakatemia Academia Scientiarum Fennica, 1964).

28 Bhabha, *Location of Culture*, 14–15.

in building and transforming stories, continually devising twists and turns, making audiences reflect. The oral nature and the mixture of the real and the fantastical help to explain many tales' nonlinear, open-ended, ambiguous natures, characteristics that readers of more canonical tales might find confusing and illogical.

One story by Ceija Stojka plays especially with ambiguous relationships between the sexes and erotic references. "Warum der Rom bei seiner Frau blieb" (Why the Rom Stayed with His Wife)[29] tells about an eternally sad and serious princess whose father promises to offer her in marriage to any man who can make her laugh. This tale has many variations in collections of Western storytelling.[30] In Ceija's version, the king offers money for the winner, and her protagonist is a poor, dirty Rom with a wife and many children. Financial necessity spurs him to try his luck. He is able to make the princess laugh through performing a kind of striptease on top of an old oven he has transported with him to the castle. Both father and daughter are delighted; the father is so impressed that he asks the Rom to marry his daughter along with receiving the riches. The Rom is already married, and knows that his wife and seven children are waiting for him to return with the riches he has won. Thus, instead of agreeing to marry the princess right away and move into the castle, the Rom asks to live with her in a container on the water so they can swim together.

For six weeks the two swim in the water and eat and sleep in the container, leaving the reader to wonder how such an adulterous relationship fits into Roma's moral system of marital fidelity. The Rom eventually begins thinking about his wife and children, however, seeing them in his dreams, with his wife sewing and taking care of the children. To prevent the Rom from leaving the King locks him up in the castle. But the Rom manages to escape back to his wife, who prepares for him a meal of fried beans and semolina. He relishes the dinner and compliments her on the delicious, crunchy cracklings from the meal's fat. The final irony, however, is that the scrumptious crunchiness was not from cracklings but rather from beetles crawling into the food, a fact the wife reveals to her husband in a final note of retribution for his adulterous actions.

The tale's sexual innuendoes threaten to defy the usual gender norms in many Romani cultures, such as the taboo on sexual references and insistence on loyalty between husband and wife. The man performs a striptease whose underlying intent is to seduce the princess. He commits a form of adultery by absconding with her in a barrel. He eventually returns to his wife, who gains the upper hand by informing

---

29 *Fern von uns*, 10–17.
30 Aarne, *Types of Folktale*, 559.

him of his folly in mistaking insects for food. In the end, humor lightens the message of marital fidelity. As in "Der geiziger Bettler," food plays a major role, whether as ultimate reward or punishment.

In several stories sexual body parts are actual characters, adding fantasy and humor to otherwise gruesome endings. "Die 'Tochter'" (The 'Daughter'), for example, involves women's genitalia as a farcical means to reinforce the husband's loyal love for his wife.[31] A husband does not want to leave his wife, but she insists he go out into the forest and earn some money. In response to his unwillingness to leave her, she cuts off her "Tochter" (daughter) and puts her in a box for him to take with him. Obviously, "daughter" is a euphemism for vulva, for later in the story she refers to her " Geschlecht" (sexual part). Venturing into the forest with the box, the husband cuts wood diligently, soon yearning for the "daughter." He opens the box and a mouse (*die Maus*, which is also feminine) springs out.[32] His penis (*sein Pimmel*) beckons her not to run away, but she runs home, and he follows her. When his wife asks what happened he explains about the mouse running home and his yearnings for his wife. His wife reassures him the mouse has returned to her place, and indeed, when the man checks, he sees that "she" is again at home.

Such stories reveal both bawdy and body humor surfacing often in Romani folk tales. As the editors of the tales state, frequent humorous use of sexual organs is not obscene or vulgar but rather straightforward and matter-of-fact.[33] The ease with which the Romani female narrators reference the sexual organs in playful, often fantastical manners suggests storytelling may originally have been a means to counterbalance strict social and moral pressures present in conservative Romani groups. In "Der Priester und der Teufel" (The Priest and the Devil) sexual jokes connect with the common theme of outwitting the devil.[34] Here, a priest cavorts with women and girls, and for that reason the devil comes to fetch him. The priest asks for one more chance, which the devil gives him, stipulating the priest has to show the devil something the devil has never seen before. The priest surveys his goat and his servant girl, who weighs 120 kilos. He undresses the servant girl, brings her into the goat's stall, and takes the goat out. He asks her to get down on her hands and knees in the goat's stall, and then lays a chain around her neck. The devil arrives at the promised time, and the priest tells him to look around. The devil is amazed because he has never seen a goat

---

31 *Kerzen*, 56–7.
32 The mouse is also a literary sexual symbol, as prominently appearing in the *Walpurgisnacht* scene in Goethe's *Faust*.
33 Cech and Fennesz-Juhasz, "Märchen," 409–10.
34 *Fern von uns*, 38–9.

looking like the one he sees in the stall, and he exclaims "'She has the udders in front and the beard in back!'"[35] He lets the priest live and says goodbye.

In "The Rom besiegt den Teufel" (The Rom Defeats the Devil), a Rom hears about a church possessed by the devil.[36] He tells the priest he can exorcize the devil. The priest agrees, and the Rom begins to wait for the devil. At precisely midnight, the devil appears, only to hear the Rom playing beautiful music on his violin. The devil is so impressed he asks the Rom if he would teach him how to play the violin. The Rom answers affirmatively, but says he first must cut the devil's long claws and to do so, the devil has to stick his hands into stocks. The devil does so, and, of course, the Rom closes the stocks on his hands. Realizing his fate, the devil flies away from the church, taking the stocks with him. The Rom receives his payment for the exorcism and buys clothes, a wagon, and horses. The devil, however, eventually finds him again. The Rom spies the devil and tells his wife they are doomed. He instructs her to get on all fours and to put her head on the ground and her posterior in the air. The devil sees her and exclaims: "'You don't believe that I can hold my paws in there again, do you?'"[37] The devil leaves and is never seen again.

The foci of these tales are the woman's sexual anatomical parts, but they deceive the devil. The tales contain a two-sided view of women's sexuality, mirroring dual reasoning behind the purity and pollution taboos. On one side stand perceptions of indecent and impure women; on the other side exist depictions of powerful and supernatural women. Characters in stories perform acts whose mention in public would be taboo; according to the claims of autobiographers, Roma, and especially women, are usually not allowed to mention sexual matters in public. Perhaps this is the reason why a man, Karl Nitsch, narrated the stories.

Comedy, according to Henderson, offers "a vicarious victory of the individual against society and of the average man against superior authority."[38] The effectiveness of the humor depends on the three-sided constellation of the storyteller, the object of ridicule, and the audience. By having the target of humor be a recognizable superior power—a king, monster, or devil—the storyteller and audience can take uninhibited pleasure in what would usually be considered shameful and prohibitive

---

35 "'Sie hat die Euter vorne und den Bart hinten!'" Ibid., 39.
36 Ibid., 34–7.
37 "'Du glaubst doch nicht, daß ich meine Pfoten wieder dort hineinhalte!'" Ibid., 37.
38 Jeffrey Henderson, *The Maculate Muse: Obscene Humor in Attic Comedy* (Oxford: Oxford University Press, 1991), 34.

"It was, because it wasn't" 165

language, acts, or events. Use of obscene and vulgar humor brings escalated degradation to the targeted subject of ridicule. The audience "could in the theater safely watch someone *else* being exposed, someone *else* losing his protective cover of modesty and shame."[39] Victims could be either characters on stage or groups whom those characters represented. In Romani tales, aristocracy, devil, clergy, and Gadže—social, economic, religious, and political powers-that-be—are the victims. Women stand on both ends of the spectrum—as objects of jokes and ultimate rescuers.

Henderson argues that the Greeks enjoyed sexual and vulgar humor in Attic comedy exactly because "in their private lives they took uninhibited pleasure in the acts to which the obscenities referred."[40] Uninhibited pleasure surfaces in the Ancient Greeks' open depictions of sexual acts in art, descriptions of their everyday lives, and literature. Many of the comic elements related to sexual humor disappeared in the Roman era, which showed less public openness about private sexual acts. For Roma, Mozes Heinschink, in a discussion with Beate Eder-Jordan, predicts if strict customs begin to loosen, as with sexual norms, then sexual openness in their stories will disappear.[41] Whether Heinschink's predictions will come true as Roma assimilate into German-speaking countries is difficult to say. For Roma, assimilation and the loosening of strict codes of behavior may not threaten the kind of sexual openness observed in stories, especially as more stories appear in written, published form. Romani culture has changed and will continue to change. In publishing their tales Romani seem more concerned with processing memory and identity than with fixing static representations.

As with jokes focusing on self-criticism and self-deprecation, raucous humor can also become a mechanism of self-defense placing storytellers in positions of owning their own stories, not constantly serving as the brunt of stories and jokes someone outside the group tells. Besides the outlet sexually explicit language and stories provide to Roma, bawdy humor and sexually provocative tales, when told in a straightforward manner, serve as mechanisms to diffuse restrictions. Humor in Romani folk tales also frequently relies on self-deprecation. While the stories often contain individual heroes, no universal heroes emerge. As Yoors notes, the prevalence of humor often mitigates the heroic acts with a self-deprecation that can endear the audience to the storyteller and protagonist.[42]

Lest readers think women's sexuality and genitalia serve only as targets of jokes in the narrations, several tales focus on clever women

---

39 Ibid., 10.
40 Ibid.
41 Eder-Jordan, "'Traditionen,'" 183.
42 Yoors, *Gypsies*, 155.

outwitting authority figures, mostly males, in a sexual manner. In "Und ich, wohin?" (And I, Where Do I Go?), a Romni gathers money for her family by inviting a hairdresser, grocer, and mayor to her house, leading them to believe they will enjoy sexual relations with her while her husband is at work.[43] Instead, she tricks them into jumping out of the window when they think her husband is coming home, leaving their pants and money behind for her to keep. As they leap from the window, she brands them with the iron. When the hairdresser and grocer go to the mayor to complain, they discover from the iron mark on his behind that he, too, has been duped. The tale concludes with the assertion, "Above all, she is a clever woman."[44] Here, the woman is not a victim but rather an active agent in gaining money for her family to survive.

In all her flirting and invitations to engage in extramarital affairs, the Roma wife here again suggestively breaks with the moral and ethical codes of gender behavior characterizing many Romani groups, which often demand marital fidelity from both the wife and the husband. In the end, of course, this wife remains true to her husband and acquires the necessary money to feed her family. Thus her behavior suggests circumstances in which the woman can at least bend such codes, especially when women's actions involve family welfare. The woman does not need to stand by passively while her family languishes. When the survival of the family is at stake, the woman may gain honor by distorting sexual taboos. She may also play with the boundaries that dictate her sexual behavior without overstepping those boundaries.

Some tales contain blatant role reversal, especially as women readily don male clothing to accomplish a task impossible for women to undertake. "Die zwei Becher" (The Two Cups), related by a man, is a long, complicated tale with many twists and turns.[45] Plot details unveil action-packed, sometimes noncohesive, nonlinear configurations and fluctuating, often ambiguous social mores and gender relationships. Mixing fantasy with reality, the tale challenges structures of dominant linear, authoritative narratives, which allows for imagining possibilities. The tale begins in the usual ambiguous manner: "It was because it was, a fairy tale."[46] A couple had a child, but neither the mother nor the father had work. The father had a fishing rod, and every day he went fishing. But one day the father died, and the ten-year-old son had nothing to do so he went fishing with his father's rod. On the first day he caught a fish and sold it to the local priest, making his mother very

---

43 *Kerzen*, 46–53.
44 "'Schwamm drüber, sie ist eine schaue Frau,'" (ibid., 53).
45 Ibid., 166–79.
46 "Es war weil es war, ein Märchen" (ibid., 167).

happy. On the second day, the boy caught an even bigger fish and sold it to the priest, again making his mother very happy, but this time she asked the boy to bring the next fish he caught home to eat. On the third day, the boy caught a fish and brought it home. When they cut the fish open, they found two cups. They decided to drink water from the cups, but when the son drank, gold pieces fell from his mouth. The more he drank, the more gold pieces fell out of the cups.

With these newly acquired riches, the son decided to leave home to find a wife. He went to stay at an inn, but the innkeeper refused him service because he looked so poor. He found a place to stay with an old woman, but then he saw the innkeeper's daughter. He went to the well to fetch water with his cup, out of which fell gold pieces, which he gave to the poor people. The innkeeper's daughter spied him with his cup and the gold pieces. She instructed her servant to summon the boy to her. He went to her, and she contemplated ways to take his money. The narrator then just relates how "after a while he seduced her."[47] She became pregnant, but she had the boy's money and the cup. The girl's parents found out that she was pregnant and ordered her to go to the judge to be condemned to death for carrying an illegitimate child. To help her out, the girl's brother saw a dog, which he killed. He then soaked the girl's shirt in the dog's blood and told the girl to leave. The brother then showed his parents the blood-soaked shirt as evidence of the girl's death.

The girl travelled long and far and came to the house of an old woman. The girl told the woman she was pregnant and needed a room. The woman provided her with a room and something to eat, but then, when the girl said she was thirsty, the woman only offered her own urine as drink because a dragon had drunk up all the water in town. The girl decided to travel on and asked the woman if she wanted to come with her, which the woman did. They went into town together and came to a hotel. The girl offered to buy the hotel with the money from the cup, and the hotel owner sold it to her. The girl then donned men's clothing, appearing as if she were a waiter, and offered everyone free food, drink, rooms, and clothes for a month in her hotel.

Among all the guests who came for a month to take advantage of this offer, the girl constantly looked for the father of her child. He finally arrived in the third month, unshaven and hungry. She commanded the other workers to bathe, shave, and dress him. She then appeared before him in men's clothing and asked if he recognized her. He did not, and then she revealed who she was. She explained that she had a son by him. She also continued to offer free food, drink, room, and clothes to guests until her parents finally came. The girl asked the

---

47 "Nach und nach verführt er sie" (ibid., 171).

waiters to shave her father and bring him to her. Dressed in men's clothing she told her father that she had something to sell to him. She showed him the cup, which spouted forth gold in front of the father. The father greedily asked what she, still in men's clothing, wanted for the cup. She said she wanted only to have sex with him. The father said he would allow himself to have sex with a man. The father undressed, and the daughter spat at him. The father quickly got dressed again, only to have his daughter scold him for prostituting himself for money, implying that homosexual relations were prohibited.[48] She then compared her own decision to sleep with the young boy for money, for which her father had wanted to have her condemned to death, and revealed herself as his daughter by taking off her men's clothing. She called in her servants to murder her mother and father. The story ends with an image of the good and bad: "She lived with her man in the inn, there the bad, here the good."[49] The ambiguous nature of the girl's deeds and sexuality provokes an equally equivocal dual point of view whereby good co-exists with bad.

Here is a story of greed, revenge, prejudice against an unwed mother, cross-dressing, potential incest, and parental murder. Readers and listeners might be surprised such base, vulgar events occur in a tale by Roma, whose social mores have usually called for sharing, honoring elders, maintaining virginity before marriage, and prohibiting murder. Because the story lacks Romani characters, one could interpret the tale as criticizing a lack of moral grounding in non-Romani society. Still, the final statement suggests ambiguous social mores pertaining to Romani and non-Romani cultures alike. Again, mixing reality with fantasy allows for testing out relationships and acts that might otherwise be prohibited.

Not all stories with women cross-dressing end in such horror though, thus substantiating the diversity of Romani tales. In "Das Märchen von den drei Schwestern" (The Fairy Tale of the Three Sisters), as told by a female storyteller, a king had three daughters.[50] One day a messenger reported that another king had declared war on him, making the first king very angry. His oldest daughter asked him what was wrong, but he told her not to ask because she was not a man and would not

---

48 This is one of the few references to homosexual relationships in all the texts I have read. One character in Simone Schönett's novel re:mondo is gay, as discussed in Chapter 8, but he is not Roma. Heterosexual relationships seem to be the norm for the writers in general, as interactions between the daughter and father in "Die zwei Becher" suggest, and yet I see no outspoken intolerance of homosexuality.
49 "Sie lebte mit ihrem Mann in der Herberge, dort das Schlechte, hier das Gute." Kerzen, 179.
50 Ibid., 136–45.

understand. The daughter retorted with "Tell me, I can do everything like a man."[51] When the king told her about the war declaration, she demanded he give her a sharp knife, let her sew some men's clothing, and give her a horse, and then she would go to war. The father did not grant her request. When she attempted to go to war anyway, her father appeared to her as a large, three-headed monster and scared her so much she retreated. The second daughter attempted the same as the first, but then her father appeared to her as a six-headed monster, so that she was scared and returned home. The third daughter then demanded her father allow her 40 days to get supplies and armaments so that she could help him. He allowed her to nourish the horse for 40 days, and then she set off. Her father appeared to her as a nine-headed dragon, but the girl recognized him as her father and told him to go home. She proceeded and met a wolf in the forest with a child in its mouth. She hit the wolf on the mouth so that the child fell out. She took the child with her, and he grew up with her.

After a while, the daughter rode with the child into a kingdom. While staying in the inn, she heard people talking about a wolf absconding with all the sons born to the queen. The daughter fetched the boy and brought him to his father king. The king asked what she wanted for the boy, and she said the king's health. Claiming that his health meant nothing to her, he asked again. She answered she wanted his black horse and his black dog. At first the king did not want to give her these, but then he acquiesced.

The daughter then travelled to another kingdom. She heard whoever could jump over a big fire would become the king's son-in-law. She hopped on her horse and jumped over the fire. She was then taken to the king, who arranged for a wedding with his daughter. In the night in which the daughter was supposed to sleep with the bride, the daughter took out her sword, stuck it in the middle of the bed, and told the bride: "When you touch me, my sword with rise up and cut you in pieces. When I touch you, it will cut me to pieces."[52] The sexual implications of the double-edged sword in bed are clear, as is the metaphorical connection with the ambiguous cross-dressing actions.

The next morning the king went to his daughter to celebrate the consummation of the marriage, but his daughter told him nothing had happened between the married couple. After a week, still nothing had happened, and the king became angry. He summoned the "groom"—the girl dressed as a man—and told her/him to bring him back the fairies' water to help them consummate their marriage. The "groom"

---

51 "Sag es mir, ich kann alles wie ein Mann" (ibid., 137).
52 "Wenn du mich berührst, wird mein Schwert aufstehen und dich zerhacken. Wenn ich dich anrühre, wird es mich zerhacken" (ibid., 143).

rode with her horse, found the water, and brought it back. Again, when the king heard nothing had happened, he demanded the "groom" bring the fairies' mirror. When the same happened yet again, the king asked her/him to fetch the fairies' wands. The "groom" acquired three wands from the fairies, but just as s/he was escaping with her/his booty, the fairies hexed her/him with yet another twist to her/his sexual identity: "If you are a man, you shall become a woman. If you are a woman, you should become a man."[53] The girl quivered and turned into a man. Happily, s/he rode back to the king and told him they could celebrate a real wedding with her/him and the king's daughter. They celebrated for 40 days and 40 nights, as characters and audience flow together in the end: "They there, we here, there they, here we."[54]

Here is a wild tale whose happy end implicitly condones crossdressing and sexual transformation. This positive outcome contrasts with the previous tale "Die zwei Becher," in which the girl's crossdressing ultimately led her to kill her parents, a reprehensible act for Roma, who not only hold family and elders in high esteem, but also demonstrate a high respect and fear of the dead. The final message about the good and bad side of the girl's actions concludes the first tale, whereas in this latter one, gender fluidity inspires characters and audience to intermingle. In both stories, the protagonist is a clever female able to fight supernatural and human forces, carry on actions that defy social mores, and ultimately survive in a positive relationship.

Scholars have demonstrated how binary opposites prevalent in fairy tales—good and evil, men and women, children and adults, animals and humans, country and city—have served as models for countries in the process of building national, and often nationalistic identities. Such construction often involves developing racial, sexual, ethnic, or national traits differentiating one nation from another.[55] In Roma fairy tales, binary opposites exist—between Roma and non-Roma worlds, men and women, animals and humans, lower and upper classes—but the equation of good and bad to individual sides is not always clear. From opening tales with lines such as "It was because it wasn't," listeners and readers are warned to expect paradoxes, inconsistencies,

---

53 "Wenn du ein Mann bist, sollst du eine Frau werden. Wenn du eine Frau bist, sollst du ein Mann werden!" Ibid., 145.
54 "Sie dort, wir hier, dort sie, hier wir" (ibid.).
55 For the role of literature in creating a national and nationalistic identity see Klaus Amann and Karl Wagner, eds, *Literatur und Nation. Die Gründung des Deutschen Reiches 1871 in der deutschsprachigen Literatur* (Vienna, Cologne and Weimar: Böhlau, 1996); Benedict Anderson, *Imagined Communities: Reflections on the Origin and Spread of Nationalism* (London: Verso, 1991); and Gabi Kathöfer, *Auszug in die Heimat: Zum Alteritäts(t)raum Märchen* (Hildesheim, Zürich and New York: Georg Olms Verlag, 2008).

and open-endedness. By concluding with an equally equivocal proclamation—"There the bad, here the good"—storytellers fulfill those expectations. No clear message surfaces, leaving room to contemplate the tales' many meanings. Storytelling offers Roma, a people excluded from the process of nation building, a familiar resource to fantasize and envision a world lacking in binary opposites. Storytelling becomes a means to break down limiting stereotypes, assert social critique, and sustain hope for cultural connections.

# Seven "The emotions are autobiographical, the story is fictional": Violence in Mariella Mehr's Trilogy

Mariella Mehr is a Jenisch author of novels, essays, dramatic pieces, and poems concerning her own personal history and that of Jenisch in Switzerland. Jenisch history proves how misconstrued monolithic interpretations of Romani cultures can be. As an ethnic subgroup, Jenisch have historically shared with Roma the tendency towards travelling lifestyles; hence officials have often labelled them "Fahrende" (Travellers). Along with that tradition comes possible intermingling between the different subgroups. Thus, many Jenisch most likely share Romani biological roots. The first records of Roma entering Europe from the fourteenth century reveal hybridization among Romani subgroups, whereby nomadic groups travelling from one town to another intermingled with other nomadic groups, resulting in new ethnic groups, including Jenisch.[1] Likewise, Mišo Nikolić includes descriptions of various travelling subgroups from former Yugoslavia—for example, Jenisch and Lovara—who "mixed" together. Categorizing one individual Romani subgroup as explicitly distinct from another is difficult.[2]

Tragically, racial mixing also proved dangerous for Jenisch during Nazi times. Robert Ritter concluded from his "research" that Roma who were not "pure," but rather had "mixed" with other races, posed the largest threat to a desired German "Aryan" nation. His proposed "solution" to the threat from "mixed-raced" Jenisch included collection in labor camps and prevention of "breeding of this population of mixed

---

1 Donald Kenrick, *Gypsies: From the Ganges to the Thames* (Hatfield, Hertfordshire: University of Hertfordshire Press, 2002), 43.
2 Nikolić, *... und dann...*, 117.

blood."³ Ironically, the one factor hindering Jenisch from automatic inclusion with other Romani subgroups—namely, the history of intermingling and thus a possible lack of biological origins in India—also justified their status as a persecuted population under Nazi ideology. The history of Jenisch in Switzerland contains violent measures to abolish them and their way of life.⁴ The early years of modern Switzerland in the nineteenth century coincided with a dark side in Jenisch history. Just two years after its founding in 1848, the liberal Swiss nation issued a law to naturalize so-called "Heimatlose" (homeless people), travellers with no country. In this category fell mobile, often poor, migrant workers without a permanent residence. Jenisch were among the most prevalent victims.⁵ The Swiss officials saw Jenisch as opposing a more desirable bourgeois, stable order. To enforce policies of residence, the federal government turned to local, often poverty-stricken communities that could not provide Travellers with the economic or social means to settle permanently. Many Travellers continued to live a nonsedentary existence, and thus were viewed as criminals, instigating increased police surveillance. Coupled with deteriorating economic situations, such actions made financial and social conditions for Jenisch even more difficult.

Faced with what Swiss officials perceived as a growing menace to the social order, the country invited its four neighbors in 1909 to establish an international mechanism to exchange information on Roma. When that invitation received no response, the Swiss Justice Department began officially recording the numbers and location of travelling groups. Pro Juventute, the country's largest and most respected children's charity, agreed to help abolish the travelling life in Switzerland. In 1926 the foundation decided to resettle Jenisch children in order to rescue innocent youngsters from what was perceived as harmful biological and social influences on their lives.⁶ Thus began a system of

---

3   "Fortpflanzung dieser Mischlingspopulation." Original German in Müller-Hill, *Tötliche Wissenschaft*, 60; English from Müller-Hill, *Murderous Science*, 57.
4   See Huonker, *Fahrendes Volk*, and Meier and Wolfensberger, *"Eine Heimat."*
5   Bernhard Schär, "Mariella Mehr als Inspiration für eine postkoloniale Geschichte der Schweiz—Einige Überlegungen," *Liebchen*, 8–16. Discrimination and persecution against Jenisch, Travellers, and "Homeless" peoples occurred in the sixteenth century in Switzerland and intensified in the nineteenth century as the Jenisch became increasingly more defined as different from the other subgroups. Not until 1843–4 do court records mention Jenisch as a language and a major determinant group characteristic (Meier and Wolfensberger, *"Eine Heimat,"* 190).
6   Pro Juventute stood in close contact with other state organizations taking children deemed in a state of "Verwahrlosung" ("neglect") away from their parents and placing them in foster homes and institutions. Different criteria determined what constituted "neglect," including conditions of upbringing,

taking children from their parents without parental consent, changing the children's names, placing them in foster homes, and even sterilizing them. Institutionally condoned abductions, undertaken under the auspices of the state-sanctioned program "Relief Agency for Children of the Road," continued until 1973, with, eventually, over 600 children forcibly removed. Pro Juventute still exists today as a mission to help children, youth, and parents in Switzerland, Austria, and Germany.

Mehr's history and that of her family are tightly interwoven with this Swiss Jenisch history. In a 1973 autobiographical essay, Mehr traces the beginnings of her ancestral lineage back to her great grandfather, the head of the "clan," who travelled into eastern Switzerland in the late nineteenth century. This great grandfather and his brother perished in prison after being convicted of murder, while others in the clan "moved around the country begging."[7] Mehr was born in 1947, when approximately 20,000 travelling and nomadic people lived in Switzerland, unsupported by any governmental assistance.[8] She was one of the "Children of the Road," separated from her mother at birth, and then placed in an orphanage. Her life story includes numerous acts of violence wrought against her, including placement in foster homes and mental institutions—where she received electroshock treatment—the removal of her son by the authorities, and prison sentences. Mehr refers to herself as Roma and has published bilingual volumes of poetry in German and Romany. At the center of her writings stand disenfranchised people—many Roma, female, homeless, and mentally unstable—who have experienced physically violent acts. In a conversation with the Swiss newspaper the *Neue Züricher Zeitung* in 1997, she stated her focus on violence stems from her own violent experiences as a child, both as victim and perpetrator. Still, she claims she cannot comprehend why such injustices occur. She needs to create "new languages" to portray and understand the horrors.[9]

The roots of the violence preoccupying Mehr cannot be divorced from her own personal history and the collective one of the peoples

---

      personality traits, licentiousness, alcoholic consumption, livelihood (especially if the mother was a prostitute), mental capacity, delinquency, marriage relationships, and household practices. The nature of these criteria, however, remained nebulous. Nadja Ramsauer, *"Verwahrlost": Kindswegnahmen und die Entstehung der Jugendfürsorge im schweizerischen Sozialstaat 1900–1945* (Zürich: Chronos Verlag, 2000), 189–92; 219–42.

7    "bettelnd durchs Land zogen." Mariella Mehr, "Autobiographisches einer Jenischen," *focus*, 39 (März, 1973): 10.

8    Mariella Mehr, "E. Xenos 1922, Einer von 600," *RückBlitze* (Bern: Zytglogge, 1990), 14.

9    Mehr, "Die Lust an der Selbstpreisgabe: Mariella Mehr im Werkstattgespräch," *Neue Züricher Zeitung* (25 November 1997), 35; cited in Finnan, "From Survival," 154.

involved—again, in most cases Roma. While such a statement may seem indisputable and obvious, centuries-old stereotypical images of Roma project essential qualities outside of any historical context. Roma become perceived as living in a kind of "time capsule,"[10] which ignores their rich historical past, or, as in the case of Mehr, denies the dark historical shadows the Gadže have cast. Besides existing "outside of time," Roma become "placeless," to echo once again Breger's concept of "Ortlosigkeit" (Placelessness). The disconnection between images of nomadic, free-spirited Roma travelling around in wagons and real-life situations often fraught with violence has caused government agencies to mistreat Roma and misunderstand them as deviant and degenerate.[11] Perceived deviance, in turn, became the prime reason for disciplinary actions, coinciding with Foucault's observation that "one of the primary objects of discipline is to fix; it is an anti-nomadic technique."[12]

Without understanding this past, readers may have difficulty comprehending the violence in Mehr's works. This is not to defend or justify that violence, but merely to point out that the violence involving Roma in Mehr's prose is far more removed from and much more complex than the gratuitous kind one often sees in Hollywood action films. Mehr further problematizes the ambiguous, linguistically historical nature of the German term for violence, namely "*Gewalt*," which can hold two main meanings depending on the context. Etymologically, the word traces its origins back to the Indo-Germanic root "*val*," or in Latin "*valere*," which as the verb "*gewalten*" and the noun "*Walden*" mean "to possess the ability to make decisions and decrees," or, in essence, "to have power."[13] In the case of legally sanctioned laws, for example, the expression "Gewaltenteilung" refers to the division of powers or the system of checks and balances between two branches such as the executive and the judicial in a government. In this positive sense then, "*Gewalt*" can mean "power" or "force," as in the expression "*höhere Gewalt*"—designating an "act of God"—or "*Naturgewalt*," meaning "force of nature." Even today, the verbs "*walten*," meaning "to rule," and "*verwalten*," meaning "to administer," share this root. In Latin and Anglo-Saxon, two separate words came to connote "power" and "violence," namely "*potentia/ potestas*" and "*vis/volentia.*"

Thus, historically, the German language poses an exception to other Latin-based and Germanic languages; in the Middle Ages and early

---

10   Lemon, "Telling Gypsy Exile," 34.
11   David Sibley, *Outsiders in Urban Society* (New York: St. Martin's Press, 1981): 19.
12   Michel Foucault, *Discipline and Punish*, translated by Alan Sheridan (New York: Vintage, 1978), 207.
13   Peter Imbusch, "Der Gewaltbegriff," in *Internationales Handbuch der Gewaltforschung*, eds Wilhelm Heitmeyer and John Hagan (Wiesbaden: Westdeutscher Verlag, 2002), 29.

Modern period, the term *"Gewalt"* came to hold four different meanings with varying values. First, *"Gewalt"* referred to a public authority tied to a certain legal system; second, *"Gewalt"* was a neutral term for a territorial ruling figure, that is, the physical holder of a geographically designated area; third, *"Gewalt"* indicated the possession of an ability to rule or issue decrees; and fourth, the substantive *"Gewalt"* and the adjective *"gewaltig"* acquired the meaning of physical violence or force for both a political entity and an individual. For this reason, until the end of the sixteenth century, the term *"Gewalt"* swung between the Latin *"potentia/potestas"* and *"vis"/"volentia."*[14] The term was codified in the sixteenth century and came to mean largely an action that physically harmed a body or objects without legal recourse. Still, certain expressions connoting the original idea of power have remained in use, such as the above-mentioned *"höhere Gewalt"* (act of God) and *"Naturgewalt"* (act of nature), as well as *"Civil-Gewalt"* (civil power) *"weltliche Gewalt"* (world power), *"geistliche Gewalt"* (intellectual power), and *"Staatsgewalt"* (authority or government).

Being victim to state-sanctioned violence, Mehr witnessed the dual meanings of the word *"Gewalt"* as both the "power that possesses the ability to make decisions and decrees" and "physical violence meant to harm a body or object." The dual nature of the term "violence" provokes what Lawrence identifies as:

> diverse questions and conflicting answers ... . Is violence an outrage of necessity? An enemy of freedom and social order or their indispensable foundation? A rational means or a self-frustrating instrument? Is it the outcome of perverted learning or a normal, instinctual need? Is violence a pathological or a voluntary form of behavior for which agents bear full responsibility? Can societies prevent its occurrence or must they resign themselves to an order including it?[15]

Comprehending possible controversial roots of violence necessitates reformulating the questions. The double meaning of the term *"Gewalt"* transfers itself onto the protagonists in Mehr's trilogy, creating questions and conflicts intrinsic to the nature of violence itself.

Mehr certainly does not claim to answer the questions Lawrence poses. She does, however, provide a new perspective from which to ask the questions based on her experiences as a member of an oppressed

---

14   Peter Imbusch, *Moderne und Gewalt: Zivilisationstheoretische Perspektiven auf das 20. Jahrhundert* (Wiesbaden: Verlag für Sozialwissenschaften, 2005), 26.
15   John Lawrence, "Violence," *Social Theory and Practice* 1.2 (Fall 1970), 31–49. Quoted in Imbusch "Der Gewaltbegriff," 27.

ethnic group facing state-sanctioned violence. Analysis of Mehr's works reveals three main messages. First, violence against individuals and groups of people serves only to perpetuate more violence. Second, writing about violence can become an effective means to reinsert the victims of that violence into history. Third, through unabashed portrayal of violence—with its inexpressible pain and suffering—the "self" (and I place this loaded term in parenthesis knowing there may be many diverse and divided "selves") becomes better understood as the interconnected, inextricably linked forces of both the mind and the body. By carrying forth these three messages in the portrayal of her protagonists' violent acts, Mehr subversively challenges the dualism between mind and body, rational and irrational, and male and female permeating Western thought since at least the eighteenth century.

Elaine Scarry's pathbreaking study *The Body in Pain* offers an apt theoretical model for analyzing the violence and pain in Mehr's novels.[16] Especially cogent here are Scarry's observations on pain's ability to destroy the victim's language, and on the power the violence of war and torture in particular have to "unmake" a person's world. That process of unmaking occurs through an act of splitting "the human being into two," that is, into "a self and a body," or "a 'me' and 'my body.'" Scarry defines that split and the significant role language plays in that "unmaking" and, potentially, in the "making":

> The "self" or "me," which is experienced on the one hand as more private, more essentially at the center, and on the other hand as participating across the bridge of the body in the world, is "embodied" in the voice, in language. The goal of the torturer is to make the one, the body, emphatically and crushingly *present* by destroying it, and to make the other, the voice, *absent* by destroying it.[17]

The tension between presence and absence of bodies and voices pervades Mehr's works. Where Mehr's works diverge from Scarry's analysis, however, is in Mehr's attention to the individual and collective histories out of which destructive violence and the ensuing pain arise. Scarry distinguishes pain from other human emotions by pointing out that such emotions have referents, as in "love of x, … fear of y, … ambivalence about z … . [P]hysical pain—unlike any other state of consciousness—has no referential content. It is not *of* or *for* anything. It is precisely because it takes no object that it, more than any other phenomenon

---

16   Elaine Scarry, *The Body in Pain: The Making and Unmaking of the World* (New York: Oxford University Press, 1985).
17   Ibid., 48–9.

resists objectification of language."[18] Mehr, in contrast, shows pain does indeed come *from* something, that is, from her own personal history of violence and pain as well as from the collective Jenisch history. From those contexts Mehr branches out to demonstrate other abusive situations from which pain does arise. In an effort to make her voice present and to mend the split between her "me" and "her body," she exposes the referential context from which pain and violence can originate.

Mehr's earliest works help understand her depiction of violence. In the 1984 narrative *Das Licht der Frau* (*The Light of the Woman*), Mehr reflects on the months she spent in Madrid observing the "mujeres toreros," the female bullfighters, and their motives and aspirations in participating in ritualized human violence against an animal—the bull, the "Torito," protectorate of the goddess Diana.[19] On the one hand, Mehr recognizes women have been absent in the long history of Spanish bullfighting. Hence, she acknowledges the female bullfighters' wish to defy that history and its intendant stereotypes of woman as the so-deemed "weaker sex." In performing that task in a theatrical arena, the female bullfighters protest publicly against the machismo of the Spanish man. On the other hand, Mehr cannot understand the desire to advocate killing as an art form. She discerns an irony in female bullfighters' enthusiasm as they participate in the ritualized demise of their own principles. On the beds of these women Mehr finds plastic dolls sitting innocently and prettily in feminine skirts and makeup. Female bullfighters talk about the bull in connection with the goddess Diana and the feminine principle. But, Mehr assures, no feminine principle would allow meaningless destruction. Female bullfighters' desires to appear innocent, naïve, and feminine contrast with their destructive tendencies. Ironically, these bullfighters threaten to destroy a life force from which they claim to derive their existence.

Still, self-ironically, Mehr cannot help but recognize herself in the women bullfighters she interviews. She confirms she has experienced such violence on two levels, namely in her work and in her life experiences. Writing about the legitimation of violence and ritualized violence, she concedes, comprises just another step towards understanding one's self, a step one hopes will ultimately lead to a certain freedom. But the price for these steps is the infliction of pain, wounds, and sadness, the same price to pay ultimately for violence. The implication that writing is yet another form of violence will surface later in her trilogy of novels.

In a 1990 interview, entitled "Frauenmut"[20] (Woman's Courage), Mehr connects her own Romani background, collective Romani history

---

18  Ibid., 5.
19  Mariella Mehr, *Das Licht der Frau* (Bern: Zytglogge, 1984).
20  Mariella Mehr, "Frauenmut," in *Rückblitze* (Bern: Zytglogg, 1990), 175–84.

and culture, and her interest in ritualistic violence related to bullfighting. She explains how writing *Das Licht der Frau* was a logical development in her confrontation with a ritualistic kind of violence inflicted on her and a group perceived as racially inferior. She claims the book is her favorite, even though she recognizes she still does not comprehend the phenomenon of violence. In hindsight, she sees the work as an interim report on her search for that understanding begun 20 years prior with her coming-of-age. In attempting to connect gender and ritualized violence, she thus paves the way for her later writings focusing on both individual and collective histories of Romani peoples. Just as women bullfighters concurrently use violence to struggle against machismo and to submit to patriarchal systems, so, too, do Romani characters employ violence as a self-defense mechanism and a threatening self-destructive force. The dual nature of the word "Gewalt"—switching between meanings of "power" and "violence"—continues to haunt her stories.

This complex combination of power, violence, and gender provokes further investigation into concepts of female sadism and masochism, especially in the context of the women bullfighters' response to violence, namely revenge, the perpetuation of violence, and self-punishment. Sadism is an active form of wounding, hurting, humiliating, or even destroying others to derive pleasure in oneself. Masochism is a state of experiencing enjoyment in suffering from being wounded, hurt, or humiliated. While psychologists debate the exact causes and motivations for the pleasure derived from both, many do agree that in sadism and masochism pain symbolizes power and control over the victim.[21] While both sexes engage in practices of sexual sadomasochism, psychologists see sadism "evident most often in males."[22] In turn, this observation might imply masochistic tendencies are most evident in women, and yet the evidence remains inconclusive. In social-psychological theories, masochistic practices represent for men and women "an escape from self."[23] This means that as submissive victims, "masochists can absolve themselves of responsibility for their own behaviors while acting at the demand of their dominent partners."[24] The masochists then feel a

---

21 Pamela M. Yates, Stephen J. Hucker, and Drew A. Kingston, "Sexual Sadism: Psychopathy and Theory," in *Sexual Deviance: Theory, Assessment, and Treatment*, eds Richard D. Laws and William T. O'Donohue (New York and London: The Guilford Press, 2008), 213.
22 Drew A. Kingston and Pamela M. Yates, "Sexual Sadism: Assessment and Treatment," in Laws and O'Donohue, *Sexual Deviance*, 231.
23 Roy E. Baumeister, "Masochism as escape from self," *Journal of Sex Research*, 25.1 (February 1988): 28–9.
24 Stephen J. Hucker, "Sexual Masochism: Psychopathology and Theory," in Laws and O'Donohue, *Sexual Deviance*, 258.

certain release from any restrictions, fears, or anxieties they may have experienced in their "true selves" devoid of masochistic inclinations.[25]

Second-generation feminist theories emerging in the 1980s viewed sadomasochism in which males played out sadistic fantasies on submissive masochistic females as indicative of patriarchal norms of male dominance and female submissiveness—noting that sadomasochism could also involve women as sadists and men as masochists in heterosexual and homosexual relationships. They pointed to the prevalence of men who engaged in sadistic activities against women as masochists. While not subscribing to a belief in innate masochistic tendencies in women, or, in what Caplan defined as "the myth of women's masochism,"[26] they nevertheless saw female masochism as a "logical response to social circumstances that leave women only limited options."[27] Second-generation feminist responses to masochism have become contentious for some third-generation feminists, however. Rather than critique female masochistic or sadistic practices, some newer feminists have defended those practices as a means for women to pursue erotic pleasures as they see fit. These proponents see masochism and sadism as potentially rebellious acts against what the newer generation sees as overly politically correct social norms.[28] Masochism and sadism can offer ways to engage in productive fantasies that bring women pleasure outside restrictive prescribed gender norms.

Mehr's characters, however, are not engaging in masochistic or sadistic fantasies. Instead, they are the young female bullfighters struggling with macho norms, children witnessing violence, adolescent girls entangled in ambiguous and complex histories and roles, and grown women with painful and abusive backgrounds. They frequently face limited options to express their reactions to traumatic backgrounds. Their own abuse of others has roots in reality, an abuse that "results in fear, anxiety, and physiological and behavioral reactions to the stress induced by abuse."[29] In response to her own abuse as a persecuted Jenisch, Mehr creates thematically and stylistically difficult, at times even "incomprehensible" works whose characters' actions and reactions reflect their fears, anxieties, and stress.

No subject is taboo for Mehr, including rape, child abuse and abduction, illness, and electroshock treatments. Her first works—her

---

25  Ibid., 258.
26  Paula Caplan, *The Myth of Women's Masochism* (New York: E. P. Dutton, 1985).
27  Rita Felski, "Redescriptions of Female Masochism." *Minnesota Review* 63/64 (Spring/Summer 2005): 132.
28  Ibid., 138.
29  Yates, Hucker, and Kingston, "Sexual Sadism," 223.

novel *steinzeit*, her drama *Kinder der Landstrasse*, and her novel *Zeus oder der Zwillingston (Zeus or the Twin Sound)*[30]—break with traditional narrative aesthetics to create nonlinear, abruptive, discomforting stories connecting and disconnecting with each other. Mehr's writing reflects what Scarry analyzes as a "text in pain"—mirroring Mehr's own "body in pain"— intersecting personal issues and public records.[31] They explore connections and disconnections between insiders and outsiders, privileged and oppressed, sane and insane, oppressed and oppressors, perpetrators and victims, and males and females. These dualisms manifest themselves in violent actions in all the works. On the one side emerges the violence related to abuse and isolation through institutionalization, psychological examination, electroshock therapy, lobotomies, sterilization, sexual mistreatment, and public humiliation by those in positions of power. On the other side surface the violent reactions of self-inflicted wounding, lacerations, inhumane treatment towards animals, and murder by those in positions of subjugation. Of all Mehr's works, her trilogy—comprised of *Daskind (Thechild)*, *Brandzauber (Firemagic)*, and *Angeklagt (Accused)*—presents her most controversial confrontations with the violence in both her personal and her Jenisch history.[32] Each work highlights female protagonists perpetuating through extreme measures the violence they have experienced.

The main character in *Daskind* is an adopted child whose origins are unknown to the townspeople. In reality, as the reader learns by piecing together the evidence throughout the book, the child comes from an incestuous relationship between her so-deemed adoptive father and his hermit sister who lives alone in the woods and practices natural healing arts, or, as some in the town believe, witchcraft. The child has no name and is referred to merely as "Daskind," all written as one word. Daskind is called by other names, such as "Saumädchen, Hürchen" (ugly slut, little whore), or "Dreckigerbalg" (filthy brat). Without a proper name, however, Daskind has no identity that fits the

---

30  Mariella Mehr, *steinzeit*, 7th edn (Bern: Zytglogge, 1980; 1990); Mariella Mehr, *Kinder der Landstrasse: Ein Hilfswerk, ein Theater und die Folgen* (Bern: Zytglogge, 1987); Mariella Mehr, *Zeus oder der Zwillingston* (Zürich: Edition RF, 1994).

31  The original inspiration for looking at Mehr's work *Kinder der Landstrasse* in conjunction with Scarry's ideas of "texts" and "bodies" in pain came from Maratte C. Denman, "Homeless in Heidi-Land—Figuring Gypsies in Mariella Mehr's Play *Akte M. Xenos ill. *1947-Akte C. Xenos ill. *1966.*" Paper at the 1998 conference of the Pacific Ancient and Modern Language Association, San Jose, California, 1998.

32  Mariella Mehr, *Angeklagt* (Zürich: Nagel & Kimche, 2002); *Brandzauber* (Zürich and Frauenfeld: Nagel & Kimche, 1998); *Daskind* (Zürich and Frauenfeld: Nagel & Kimche, 1995). (Berlin: Ullstein, 1997).

norm. Therefore, she stands "little chance of being accepted" in the close-knit provincial community.[33] Daskind cannot speak; the story oscillates between relaying her inner thoughts, the townspeople's opinions, and the narrator's observations on all the characters' interior lives, hidden emotions, and intentions. Daskind's life is full of beatings by her adoptive family, ostracism by the community, and rape by respected town fathers. The story ends after she uses her slingshot to kill the "Sigrist" (Sexton), who has spoken out vehemently against her presence in the town.

In *Brandzauber*, the protagonist Anna is an arsonist and a Romani girl whom authorities take away from her family when she is young. Anna escapes from confining institutions and sets the trailer where her mother still lives on fire. The young Anna misplaces the blame for the state taking custody of her on her alcoholic Romani mother whose position as a social outcast serves to perpetuate either passive resignation or extreme violence. Anna's mother survives the fire badly burned; Anna's father comes under suspicion for having set the trailer on fire, and he subsequently commits suicide. Anna's personal childhood story is framed by her interactions with a Jewish girl, Franziska, who also belongs to a historically oppressed ethnic group, and whose family has felt Nazi persecution. Anna and Franziska meet in an orphanage, and their relationship develops into a sadomasochistic one, with Anna as the sadist and Franziska the masochist. Around these two stories and their intersections, Mehr sets up yet another frame, namely in the voice of the older Anna, when she later works in a clinic and encounters a patient who reminds her of Franziska.

In *Angeklagt* the protagonist, Kari Selb, has grown up in an upper-class, Caucasian family, which appears "normal" on the outside, but whose alcoholic, stay-at-home mother and abusive, philandering architect father have made Kari a self-described arsonist and murderer. Rather than accept total guilt for her crimes, however, Kari conjures up a "guardian angel," an "Engel fürs Grobe," (angel for the horrible), called "Malik." Malik becomes Kari's accomplice for the crimes that Kari feels she cannot undertake herself, but that she feels necessary in order for her to face her everyday life in a dysfunctional family. At the age of 26, Kari, with Malik's "help"—and then the aid of a second figure, Seraphim, a disenfranchised hunchback—has already set over 100 fires and murdered three people. After finally being accused, Kari narrates the heinous details of some of those crimes to the court psychologist. Kari's explanations of emotions and occurrences form the novel's content. As the book progresses, Kari's confession gathers momentum and, by the end, becomes quick and breathless to echo the

---

33   Fordham, "Fear," 76.

escalating violence. Violence appears as existential, and the novel's portrayal of such is direct, uncensored, and unforgiving. Indeed, the book is the slimmest one in the trilogy, yet the most brutal in the sheer number of violent crimes and the psychological analysis of the criminal's possible motives.

The protagonists in all three books share at least four characteristics. First, all are females who have survived extreme abuse, whether physical or mental, and whether as victims or witnesses of such abuse. The recurring scenes of the physical beatings in *Daskind* are especially harsh. Kari Kenel, the adoptive father, continually brings Daskind to the bathroom and lashes her with his leather belt; she "Hears the hesitant removal of the leather belt from the beltloops, then the sizzling of the leather in the air."[34] Imagining another world, one with "rainbow-colored ornaments" (*regenbogenfarbene Ornamente*), and waiting until "the pain goes into its flesh so that it transforms" are the only ways Daskind can survive the pain.[35] Poignant in Mehr's sentences is the loss of the subject as related from the child's perspective mixing colorful fantasy with dark reality. Daskind cannot imagine a world where she is a subject of her own fate.

In *Brandzauber* the narrator describes the beatings she witnessed her father giving her mother, causing the child Anna to react violently against her father: "He did not feel the small fists of the girl who drummed on his back and pulled on his jacket."[36] For the mute child, reciprocal violence becomes a main communication device, with violence ultimately becoming "a universal language."[37] Unfortunately, the less powerful remain helpless as Anna's pounding on her father's back is futile.

In *Angeklagt* the narrator reflects on how arguments and conflicts belonged to everyday life at home "like the daily bread" (*wie das tägliche Brot*).[38] Verbal confrontations between her parents, often when they were drinking, resolved themselves eventually with loud groans the child heard coming from the bedroom. The implication that sexual gratification can settle domestic conflict coincides with Scarry's

---

34 "Hört das zögernde Herausziehen des Ledergurtes aus den Hosenschlaufen, dann das Zischen des Leders in der Luft." Mehr, *Daskind*, 20.
35 "bis der Schmerz in sein Fleisch eingeht, daß es sich verwandle" (ibid.).
36 "Er spürte nicht die kleinen Fäuste des Mädchens, die auf seinem Rücken trommelten und an seiner Jacke zerrten." Mehr, *Brandzauber*, 181.
37 "Gewalt ist eine Universalsprache." Friedhelm Neidhardt, "Gewalt, Soziale Bedeutungen und sozialwissenschaftliche Bestimmungen eines Begriffs," in *Was ist Gewalt? Auseinandersetzungen mit einem Begriff*, Band 1: Zum Gewaltbegriff im Strafrecht, ed. V. Krey (Wiesbaden: Bundeskriminalamt, 1986), 134.
38 Mehr, *Angeklagt*, 16.

observations on how for victims and observers of violence, "special wants like sexuality are made ongoing sources of outrage and repulsion. Even the most small and benign of bodily acts becomes a form of agency."[39] The link between violence and sexuality also becomes visible in interactions between the narrator in *Angeklagt* and her father. She associates the attic in the house with her father's assaults on her dog and "everything between my legs. The childchild legs."[40] Use of the singular word "Kindkind" (childchild) to describe the young legs resembles the nameless, one-word designation "Daskind." Resentment against the child leads to violence against animals, likewise implying sexual violence against the child. The impact of such violence surfaces when the child kills a blackbird directly after this beating.[41]

A second characteristic of all three works is that all three protagonists feel the heavy weight of silence and muteness. When the father beats Daskind, the reader learns he abuses her because she shames him for not being able to speak.[42] The first descriptions of the protagonist tell how Daskind has never spoken, but instead cried and tossed about.[43] The narrator makes clear how doctors have determined that Daskind has nothing physically wrong that would prevent her from speaking. This muteness and its diagnosis occurred after going home with her (foster) father and becomes the cause for a vicious circle of violence.[44] Muteness shames him, inciting his beatings, which, in turn, enforce the silence.

In *Angeklagt* the protagonist remembers remaining silent, even when she needed to defend her actions and fight for her life. Her life is replete with continual silence and cover-ups about the abuse she received at home. For example, no one is supposed to talk about the incident when her father, in an alcoholic rage, knocked out her teeth, necessitating false teeth at a young age. The cover-up required much money and silence. When speaking about her parents' continual drinking and abuse she admits somebody should have called the police. Instead, everyone remained mute. No one on the outside wanted to know about what was going on inside, and thus they chose to hear only silence: "Only silence forces itself outside, icey silence."[45]

Scarry deals with silence erupting when violence consumes everyday life. Just as literary characters such as Sophocles' Oedipus,

---

39 Scarry, *Body in Pain*, 48.
40 "und alles zwischen meinen Beinen. Den Kindkind Beinen." Mehr, *Angeklagt*, 115.
41 Mehr, *Daskind*, 21.
42 Ibid., 90.
43 Ibid., 5.
44 Ibid., 88.
45 "Dringt nur das Schweigen nach draußen, eisiges Schweigen." Mehr, *Angeklagt*, 95.

Shakespeare's Lear, and Beckett's Winnie need to talk to live, so, too, does pain cause an entire breakdown of talk: "Intense pain is also language-destroying: as the content of one's world disintegrates, so the content of one's language disintegrates; as the self disintegrates, so that which would express and project the self is robbed of its source and its subject."[46] As in the case with Anna in *Brandzauber*, when she hits her father's back while he hits her mother, silence threatens to engender more violence. Lack of communication becomes the only recourse.

A third commonality is that all three protagonists live in small, closed communities where everyone thinks they know everything about everyone, and where appearances of so-called "normalcy" are important. In *Angeklagt*, the narrator describes the village as one showing no sympathy for the misfortunate. Rather, the townspeople delight in others' misfortune to the point of hypocrisy. People are gleeful when they discover the person whom they had respectfully greeted at the shopping center one week earlier was just caught shoplifting. One hint of the violence permeating the reputable architect's house would bring demise through such *Schadenfreude*. In provincial communities, outsiders threaten any possible harmony. Fear of the outsider in *Daskind* manifests itself at numerous times in the villagers' reactions to certain characters and events.[47] *Daskind*'s adoptive father, Kari Kenel, has worked in Idaho for a few years, and thus the townspeople no longer view him as a "local" (*Einheimische[r]*). Even the townspeople's reactions to various plants and foods reveal their fear of the unfamiliar, such as village inhabitants' unwillingness to eat from Kari's fig tree, which was not from the area and therefore too exotic for them.[48]

Similarly exotic, a travelling exhibit of a whale cadaver constitutes a main cultural event for the village.[49] A lengthy description of how the adults and their children fearfully examine the preserved whale indicates the villagers' limited perspectives. The community's president describes the whale in exotic and racist human terms, comparing the massive creature to a "huge, black-tarred Negro" (*riesig, schwarzgeteerter Neger*).[50] He gives tribute to the "brave men" (*tapfere Männer*) risking their lives to kill the 23-meter-long, 55-ton monster

---

46  Scarry, *Body in Pain*, 35.
47  Fordham, "Fear," 78–9.
48  The fig tree also "reminds the villagers of original sin and of their own repressed sexuality" (ibid., 79). Kari attempts to give his wife, Frida Kenel, a fig, but as much as she reached out for the fruit, she ultimately pulled back her hand and allowed the fruit to splatter at Kari's feet (*Daskind*, 144–5).
49  Mehr, *Daskind*, 93–5.
50  Ibid., 93.

"The emotions are autobiographical, the story is fictional"  187

with only harpoons.⁵¹ Whereas most of the children scream in fright and excitedly mimic throwing harpoons at the whale, Daskind remains silent; instead, she looks into the whale's eyes. There, Daskind expects to find the whale's homeland, filled with light, colors, peace, and animals, strongly resembling the rainbow-colored fantasy world Daskind had envisioned while her foster father was beating her. But Daskind cannot find this idyllic homeland in the whale; instead, Daskind sees its "adversaries" (*Widersacher*) and its killers (*Töter*) having existed for millions of years.⁵² Fantasy does not match reality. Outer peaceful appearances do not coincide with inner turmoil. Violence is generations old and continually self-perpetuating.

The contrast between appearances and reality in the small village in *Daskind* surfaces during the carnival time. Heavy drinking, beatings, debauchery, and sexual abuse fill the festivities. Costumes and masks provide the necessary cover to remain anonymous while letting one's violent side surface. The narrator informs readers that during these few raucous days of the year every pub in the village reported beatings and violence. The inhabitants' disguises, however, cover up their heinous actions. The narrator also makes clear that carnival time was a "man's thing" (*Männersache*), when "an archaic drive sucked the men in hoards through the streets and pubs, until nothing remained."⁵³ The women, disgusted by the men, were forced to succumb, "laid on the cross and gruffly handled."⁵⁴ Sexuality and violence converge as the men in drunken stupors do not care who their partners are: "because when copulating one is not selective, even the woman right next to him enjoyed no respite on these days."⁵⁵ The neighbor's wife, one's own wife, the servant girl, the adolescent girl—no one is spared from the free-for-all—and nightmares continued to haunt them long after the carnival was over. Portraying men as perpetrators of the public festival's debauchery coincides with Mehr's ideas on the patriarchal connection between machismo and bullfighting in *Das Licht der Frau*.

Just as outer, public appearances of the peaceful village do not reflect its inhabitants' inner, private turbulence, neither do the outside emotional reactions of the three main characters to their heinous deeds belie any internal regrets. A fourth common feature of the trilogy's three protagonists is that they all view their violent actions in a distant,

---

51   Ibid., 95.
52   Ibid., 94.
53   "ein archaischer Trieb schletzte die Männer in Horden durch die Straßen und Kneipen, bis nichts mehr ganz blieb" (ibid., 69).
54   "die Frau mit Gewalt aus Kreuz gelegt" (ibid.).
55   "denn beim Kopulieren war man nicht wählerisch, auch des nächsten Weib genoß an diesen Tagen keine Schonzeit" (ibid.).

cool, nonengaged, unremorseful manner. *Angeklagt* presents the most chilling reflection in this regard, beginning with the narrator Kari's statement about her existential violent nature: "I am in the condition of mercy. I kill. I am."[56] Murder becomes portrayed as a morally accepted act requiring no justification. Underlying such statements are skeptical comments towards the state-sanctioned justice system that does not consider the motives of the killer anyway. The narrator admits her own hardened reaction to death and violence, pointing to an upbringing that desensitized her. At one point she references her father's cruelty towards animals as located in a weighted potato sack—most likely filled with kittens—he brings to the river to drown. That scene becomes a precursor to her own animal abuse. From her father she has also learned about the possibility of evil existing outside of time and space: "I always understood destruction as his independent force."[57]

Mehr's protagonists become desensitized to violence and murder through patterns and actions they observe and then learn from their parents or others with authoritarian power. Daskind has even become oblivious to the regular beatings her foster father gives her. Daskind must not only accept the beatings, but she also must prepare for them herself.[58] A passage soberly describes how just before her father beats her, Daskind finds the chair next to the window, clears it of the dirty wash lying on there, carries the chair to the middle of the room, pulls her nightgown up over her behind, lays her stomach down on the chair, and waits for Kari Kenel to pull the belt out from his beltloops on his pants. She has been conditioned to accept the violence faithfully.

Models of violent perpetrators such as Kari Kenel possess "*Gewalt*" in the initial etymological sense of the word—derived from the Indo-Germanic root "vall," meaning to possess the ability to make decisions or decrees. In the modern age, however, power merges with violence, in the same manner the meaning of "*Gewalt*" transformed over time to encompass both connotations. After Daskind has hit the Sigrist with the slingshot, she feels no remorse, but rather sadistically, senses happiness and observes nature's beauty. The novel ends with a description of Daskind rubbing up against the chalet's wall with her right shoulder as she passes the lilies and roses, described as "mild-and-modern skin."[59] The lush flowers—lilies for death, roses for love—contrast with the macabre image of the fried lung awaiting the child at home for lunch. The Sigrist is now silent, and Daskind assumes

---

56  "Ich bin im Zustand der Gnade. Ich tote. Ich bin." Mehr, *Angeklagt*, 7.
57  "Ich habe Zerstörung immer als seine selbständige Kraft verstanden" (ibid., 61).
58  Fordham, "What leads a child to kill? Violence and its effects in selected works of Mariella Mehr," in *Liebchen*, 49.
59  "Milch und moderne Haut." Mehr, *Daskind*, 223.

a superior position as she uncaringly steps over him. The following lines conclude the novel: "Daskind has found peace. Continues to smile, Daskind."[60] This horrific ending leaves Daskind and reader alike speechless. The smile seems to stand in for missing emotions that may never find a voice.

*Brandzauber* also leaves readers with the question of whether appropriate linguistic expressions even exist to describe experienced violence. Anna, in relating the state-sanctioned process of taking Jenisch children away from their families, conveys the mechanisms Jenisch needed to create in dealing with the losses. They were incensed, but no one stood up and defended themselves. Anna, in turn, is angry at her father for not protecting her; she is angry at her people for not calling this a catastrophe; she is angry at everyone for just standing by and playing the part of Job. Her extremely mixed emotions in reaction to the individual and collective trauma of such horrific actions range from hopelessness, to patience, to acceptance, but eventually ineffectiveness. Devising concrete ways to deal with the tragedy is impossible. In the end, she returns to direct her hate towards her father: "She despised her father who did not succeed in protecting her."[61] Her mother, too, does not come to her defense. Instead her mother lies drunk on the floor, smashing bottles against the wall and window: "The sound of breaking glass as the last greeting. This will later find a place of honor in the Xenos files—a welcome justice."[62] The reference to Xenos files as the code name for files of so-deemed vagrant children abducted from their families had also formed a key layer in Mehr's drama *Kinder der Landstrasse*.[63] Xenos files stand as written evidence for incidents—the words of the perpetrators—while victims' voices remain mute. Anna, in contrast, wants to leave behind a "signature," (*Handschrift*), referring to her own written evidence of her existence and voice, but in violent terms.[64] For her as Jenisch, few models rely on writing to break the cycle. Instead, physical violence is the norm.[65]

---

60   "Hat Daskind einen Frieden gefunden. Lächelt wieder, Daskind" (ibid., 224).
61   "Sie verachtete ihren Vater, dem es nicht gelungen war, sie zu schützen." Mehr, *Brandzauber*, 50.
62   "Das Klirren der Scheibe als letzter Gruß. In der Akte Xenos würde es später einen Ehrenplatz erhalten—eine willkommene Rechtfertigung" (ibid., 73).
63   Mehr, "E. Xenos;" 10–23.
64   Mehr, *Brandzauber*, 117.
65   In the context of *Zeus oder der Zwillingston*, Sälzer connects violence and writing in the documents of the scientists who diagnosed Roma and then submitted them to violent psychiatric treatment. Anna-Lena Sälzer, "Vom Fixieren in Aktenprosa und metrischen Gesängen. Schrift und Gewalt in Mariella Mehrs Roman *Zeus oder der Zwillingston*," in Patrut, Guțu and Uerlings, *Fremde Arme*, 207–9.

Writing can counteract violence at the same time that it can also be infused with violence. The French writer Monique Wittig postulates that writing can be a violent act. Her works challenge categories of man and woman from a materialist approach, analyzing sexual norms in terms of political economy. While a full discussion of Wittig's writings is not possible here, her theories and words on textual violence apply to the connection between violence and writing in Mehr's works.[66] In "Some Remarks on *The Lesbian Body*," Wittig emphasizes the inevitability and necessity of this connection.[67] Writing changes; writing instills new meaning into the old. Words "must bring a shock to the readers. If the readers don't feel the shock of words, then your work is not done. That is true for any work of literature you are producing. So from the start there is a violence to the reader. And a good reader could be blasted in the process."[68] One of the most poignant words Wittig coined in French is "bourreleuse," or "torturer, executioner," as in Wittig's statement: "I [written in French as the split "j/e"] am the mad tormentor galvanized by torture and your cries intoxicate m/e m/y best beloved the more that you restrain them."[69] Wittig characteristically splits her first-person signifier with a slash—j/e—and describes her reasoning for doing such through textual violence: "J/e is the symbol of the lived, rending experience which is m/y writing, of this cutting in two which throughout literature is the exercise of language which does not constitute m/e as subject."[70] She creates a "third term" for gender: "a term that would not be neuter, genderless, but gender-undecidable (or better still, gender-multiple)."[71]

Such a "third term" mirrors Mehr's use of "Daskind" for one of her most violent protagonists entrapped in tortured prose and a text in pain. The syntax and stylistics of *Daskind* evince fragmentariness and woundedness. The novel opens with the following distorted phrases: "Has no

---

66  Mehr did meet Monique Wittig at the Solothurner Literaturtagen and Mehr has in her library a copy of Wittig's 1969 novel, *Les Guérillères*. However, Mehr most likely did not intensively engage in Wittig's theories and the two most likely did not have any personal interactions: Ueli Ellenberger, e-mail message to Lorely French, November 26, 2008.
67  Monique Wittig, "Some Remarks on *The Lesbian Body*," in *On Monique Wittig: Theoretical, Political, and Literary Essays*, ed. N. Shaktini (Urbana and Chicago: University of Illinois Press, 2005), 44–8.
68  Ibid., 45.
69  Shaktini, "Introduction," in Shaktini, *On Monique Wittig*, 6, note 6.
70  Shaktini notes that Wittig included this remark in the Le Vay translation of *Le corps lesbien/The Lesbian Body* (ibid.).
71  Susan Rubin Suleiman, "(Re)Writing the Body: The Politics and Poetics of Female Eroticism," in *The Female Body in Western Culture: Contemporary Perspectives*, ed. Susan Rubin Suleiman (Cambridge, MA and London: Harvard University Press, 1986), 23.

name, Thechild. Called Thechild. Or Smallboy, although it is a young girl. When the women in the village feel like it, it is called Smallboy, or Smallbrat, affectionately. Also Naughtybrat, when Thechild has needs to go to the bathroom, or Piggirl, Littlewhore, Dirtybrat."[72] Sentences twist verbs and subjects around; passive constructions leave active subjects empty and helpless; incomplete sentences have no verbs or subjects. Focus is on the object, Daskind, whose identity in a multitude of forms always assumes a "third term," deriding and fracturing. Textual violence prohibits having a first and last name and disallows Daskind to stand as subject and agent of her actions.

A striking example of Mehr's tortured prose occurs when Daskind goes shopping at Bruno Keller's grocery store. The narrator hints at what might happen during the visit. Before Daskind arrives at the store, Bruno Keller is observing his neighbor, Gotthold Schätti, bringing the milked cows out of the stall. The reader learns Bruno has spent a sexually unsatisfying night with his wife, wooing her in vain and ultimately sleeping "in sheets stinking of sweat and unsatisfied desires."[73] When Daskind enters the door, Bruno Keller attempts to molest her. Once again she stands helpless as the object, and not the subject of her actions, or as an afterthought following the verb referring to another person's actions:

> Can't move, Thechild.
> Has no air in the lungs, Thechild.
> Is pinned to the door frame by Keller's hands, Thechild.
> Is a scream in Thechild.
> Has anger, Thechild.
> Screams.[74]

Even when Daskind finally screams, she is totally invisible as the subject of her actions. Out of that scream, however, with its unknown

---

72 "Hat keinen Namen, Daskind. Wird Daskind genannt. Oder Kleinerbub, obwohl es ein Mädchen ist. Wenn den Frauen im Dorf danach zumute ist, wird es Kleinerbub genannt, oder Kleinerfratz, zärtlich. Auch Frecherfratz, wenn Daskind Bedürfnisse hat, oder Saumädchen, Hürchen, Dreickigerbalg." Mehr, *Daskind*, 5.
73 "im nach Schweiß und unbefriedigten Gelüsten stinkenden Bettzeug" (ibid., 61).
74 "Kann sich nicht mehr bewegen, Daskind.
Hat keine Luft in den Lungen, Daskind.
Wird von Kellers Händen am Türrahmen festgenagelt, Daskind.
Ist ein Schreien im Kind.
Hat einen Zorn, Daskind.
Schreit." Ibid., 62.

agent, comes a "will to survive" (*einen Willen, nicht unterzugehen.*)[75] The reader is not sure if the scream warded off Keller's attack or not. In the next section, the character Gotthold Schätti is carrying Daskind home from outside Keller's store, where Schätti had seen her lying unconscious. Daskind cannot speak to tell what has happened.

The narrative voice in *Daskind* remains in the third person, sometimes able to read characters' thoughts and report on their actions, but not always. In Mehr's other works, varying narrative voices—sometimes reliable, sometimes not—and cyclical imagery unveil her tortured style. *Brandzauber* begins with a detailed description in the third person of Anna's obsession with observing her carnivorous plant devouring an ant. Anna has timed the event, triumphantly recording that the plant's and insect's struggle had not even lasted a minute. The narrator conveys Anna's pleasure indirectly, reporting her thoughts matter-of-factly. "A good day" (*Ein guter Tag*).[76] Descriptions of Anna's meticulous documentation of the date and time of the event continue, as well as her ruminations on other such devourings. Anna sticks her own finger in the plant's clutches—an attempt at self-inflicted wounding—only to see the tiny jaws close in vain. The narrator conveys how Anna anthropomorphizes the plant's disappointment in finding Anna's finger inedible; in distaste, the plant opens and closes its "lips" (*Lippen*).[77] In response, Anna sticks her finger in her mouth and feels the plant's sticky digestive secretions slide over her tongue. The next two lines jar the reader as they jump into the first person: "I am Anna. Anna Priska Kreuz. Death."[78] The curt sentence structure contrasts with previous long sentences describing the plant's destructive actions and the insect's helplessness. First-person narration makes the torture more real and present. Anna's self-identification with death illuminates her sadism. The narrator has both described and shown the violence permeating the novel.

Confluence of third-person protagonist with third-person narrator emerges in other key spots, as when Anna begins to kill birds after the authorities have taken her father to prison on suspicion he set the trailer on fire. Her father had taken care of birds by feeding them, claiming they were heaven's ambassadors destined to accompany people to the other world. The description of the father's arrest is in the third person. Anna's chronicle of her murders then moves to the first person: "The first bird was a blackbird. I pressed her wings to her body, tried to

---

75 Ibid., 62.
76 Mehr, *Brandzauber*, 7.
77 Ibid., 10.
78 "Ich bin Anna. Anna Priska Kreuz. Der Tod" (ibid.).

stick my fingers into her eyes."[79] The narration continues in the first person to detail how she nails the bird to the wall. The third-person narrator jumps in to reveal Anna conflicted by her cruelty. The violent act has not satisfied her. In contrast, she sees herself defying feminine masochistic tendencies, as she is lacking an "inalienable measure of destructive volition to which feminine desire is understood to be subordinate."[80] The killings become "her vain attempts to return to the security of a comprehensible world."[81] In the end, her actions appear in the third person: "Anna buried her head and cried awkwardly."[82] Caught in a web of societal and familial violence, Anna becomes both victim and perpetrator by misreporting the arson, concurrently emotionally detached and attached to her own and others' torture. Likewise, words and images circle around in never-ending cyclical torture. The image of Anna nailing the blackbird to the wall corresponds with other instances of crucifixes and crucifixions. Franziska, Anna's partner in sadomasochism, noticed crucifixes—a sign of eternal suffering—everywhere in the orphanage where they live. Franziska's favorite saying was "Sometimes birds fall from heaven,"[83] reminiscent of the blackbird's killing. Anna's and Franziska's favorite "game" was called "Kreuzigen" (crucifixion), whereby Anna nailed Franziska's hands to the wall, symbolic of a crucifixion, a macabre twist on Franziska's Jewishness. References to body parts appear in incomplete or fragmented sentences: "Franziskas silent mouth, her silent hands, the silent eyes."[84] Language fractures and tortures the body and the self.

Similarly, *Angeklagt* begins with short, yet complete sentences as Kari Selb tells the stories of her killings to a psychologist: "I am in the state of grace. I kill. I am."[85] While disjointed sentences remind one of Descartes's famous dictum that formulated a personal human connection with knowledge—"I think, therefore I am"—Kari Selb's statement indicates no cause and effect. She fails to see the effects of her violence, disconnected from the self and power. As with Daskind, Kari Selb has a genderless name; she informs the psychologist that she

---

79  "Der erste Vogel war eine Amsel. Ich presste ihr die Flügel an den Körper, versuchte, ihr meine Finger in die Augen zu stoßen" (ibid., 52).
80  "zerstörerischem Willen, dem sich weibliche Lust unterzuordnen versteht" (ibid., 53).
81  "ihre vergeblichen Versuche, in die Geborgenheit einer verständlichen Welt zurückzukehren" (ibid., 54).
82  "Anna verbarg den Kopf in ihren Händen und weinte ungeschickt" (ibid.).
83  "Manchmal fallen Vögel vom Himmel" (ibid., 48).
84  "Franziskas schweigsamer Mund, ihre schweigsamen Hände, die schweigsamen Augen" (ibid., 121).
85  "Ich bin im Zustand der Gnade. Ich töte. Ich bin." Mehr, *Angeklagt*, 7.

knows no other female person with this first name, although she does know others with Selb as a last name. Unlike Daskind, she can split her name in two, a fracture giving her an individual and collective identity. The novel's narrative structure reflects potential disjointedness. In initially having Kari tell the court psychologist her story, Mehr sets up expectations for a dialogic novel. But the reader hears only Kari's voice. The reader never hears the psychologist's questions, answers, or explanations; they only surface indirectly through Kari, who remains in her own world, her words dominating.

As in the other two novels, sentences frequently have no subjects, leaving the image of a protagonist not totally in control of her own story. Images circulate, such as the color red of Malik's shoes, fire, and blood. Body parts, too, appear unattached and dismembered. Kari relates her dreams about teeth, stating she grinds her teeth in her sleep. When she was living at home, her mother could not stand the sound and had always bound a towel around Kari's head when she slept to prevent her from gnashing. The story of gnashing teeth arises later in the book when Kitte, another inmate in the psychological institute where Kari is staying, also grinds her teeth. When the other inmates cannot stand the sound any more, instead of binding a cloth around her head, the house personnel extract her teeth. In a matter-of-fact manner, Kari connects the violence wrought against Kitte with the violence Kitte wields against her daughter's rapist when she shot him in the courtroom. Abuse leads to abuse. Sentence structures portraying dismemberment, wounds, separations, fractures, and torture mirror cyclical violence that characters endure and perpetuate. Torturous prose creates selves split between subjects and objects. Rupturing affords them the distance to commit and then reflect on their violent acts. By the end, Kari Selb's short, distinct sentences have turned into run-on, incoherent statements, devoid of grammar and syntax. In her final words she finds herself imprisoned for life:

> because sometime
> everyone only after peace if possible still before the demise
> yes now your heart will finally open
> stop with the ostracism
> thank you thank you
> really heartfelt thanks[86]

---

86   "weil irgendwann
    jeder nur nach Frieden wenn möglich noch vor dem Ableben
    ja jetzt geht dir endlich das Herz auf
    Schluss mit dem Scherbengericht
    danke danke
    also wirklich herzlichen Dank" (ibid., 139–40).

Kari's hopeless situation and unremorseful description of her crimes make her final thanks ironic, reminiscent of Mehr's irony in the narrative about the female bullfighters. Still, the trilogy, which began with the description of Daskind as an afterthought—"Has no name, Thechild"[87]—ends with Keri Selb's plea—addressed in the second person—to end ostracism, abuse, and violence. Whereas the protagonists in *Daskind* and *Brandzauber* pose only more violence as a solution, Kari suggests peace.

To return to Mehr's Jenisch roots, admittedly only Anna in *Brandzauber* is identified as Roma. The commonalities between the three protagonists, however, make the influence of Mehr's own experiences with violence apparent. In speaking about *Daskind*, Mehr admits the story is fiction: she has never killed a sexton or witnessed or committed many of the other acts in the book. But the village is real, she states: she spent the most important years of her life—between ages five and ten—there, and she has described it just as she remembers it. She, too, did not speak until she was over four years old, and thus suffered ostracization because of her silence. She quotes from an interview with Josef Heller: "The emotions are autobiographical, the story is fictional."[88] The emotions in the trilogy are helplessness, insensitivity, and muteness.

*Brandzauber* provokes the question as to whether any real option other than violence exists for Roma who have been persecuted. The danger is, of course, a generalized stereotyping of all Roma as violent, even if that violence is understood as a reaction to a history of persecution and justified as a self-defensive survival mechanism. By including the non-Romani figure of Daskind in the trilogy's first book and then Kari in the final book, Mehr demonstrates the dangers of abuse against individuals, regardless of ethnic background.[89] Depictions of a female child and adolescents as the main receptors and then perpetrators of the violence raise theoretical concerns about the dangers of violence becoming self-inflicting and self-perpetuating. The simplest interpretation of that violence would be to view each protagonist on her own self-destructive trajectory. This analysis would mirror historical interpretations of such violence. Mehr, however, has detected the irony in similar diagnoses for her own life. In a speech to the

---

87  "Hat keinen Namen, Daskind." Mehr, *Daskind*, 5.
88  "Die Gefühle sind autobiographisch, die Geschichte ist Fiktion." Döbler, "Nachwort," 232.
89  This is not to say that *Angeklagt* is ahistorical in its treatment of violence. When talking about Malik as her twin, Kari refers to Nazi experiments showing how twins not only complement each other, but are also capable of committing the same actions without the other knowing about their affinity (Mehr, *Angeklagt*, 44). *Angeklagt* also references Kari's grandfather who had overseen a military pack of dogs during the war (ibid., 15, 94, 133).

psychiatric clinic at St Urban in 1996, standing in front of an audience of doctors and psychiatrists, she cites from her file from 1963, in which she was described as an "annoyable, weak, impulsive, and egotistical psychopath with neurotic mechanisms and a strong tendency towards high self-estimation, which her desire to become an author proves."[90] As a prolific published writer, she recognizes how ironically her life has defied the diagnosis of "experts." Their language receives respect and attention for its roots in a scientific context claiming objectivity and rationality. What such language and perceptions discredit, however, are the subjective wishes of the "object" under study. The body in such a description becomes solely the result of hereditary destiny, with no consideration for the complex relationship between body and the psyche.

Finnan interprets Mehr's portrayal of self-perpetuating violence—especially in *Brandzauber*—as potentially subversive in its connection between gender and Jenisch history, which is riddled with attempts to silence and depersonalize subjectivity.[91] Okely speaks of an inherent subversion of stereotypes when Romani women actually cultivate violence in their communities.[92] Cyber-ethnographers Nemeth and Gropper note the frequent use of rough language in American Romani blogs as a "successful defense of territory," concluding: "Mostly harmless, yet capable of using physical force if necessary, [Gypsy, Romany, and Traveller] peoples typically pose as rough characters in appropriate situations as an adaptive response to their constant need to protect their social space and fend off unwanted intruders."[93] Mehr's protagonists demonstrate similar raw emotional reactions to protect and defend themselves.

Historical records show how perpetrators viewed Jenisch women as posing the largest threat to the dominant culture with their potential to carry on the group's culture and ethnicity through childbearing. In the writings of Alfred Siegfried, the initiator and, until 1959, leader of the "Relief Agency for the Children of the Road," belief in the notorious connection between genetics, social milieu, and women's influential role in both becomes apparent, as he wrote in 1964: "Vagrancy is, like

---

90 "verstimmbare, haltlose, impulsive und geltungsbedürfige Psychopathin mit neurotischen Mechanismen und einem starken Hang zur Selbstüberschätzung, was ihr Wunsch, Schriftstellerin zu werden, beweist." Mariella Mehr, "Von Mäusen und Menschen: Vortrag an der psychiatrischen Klinik St. Urban LU, 19. Dezember 1996," in *Blickwechsel: Die multikulturelle Schweiz an der Schwelle zum 21. Jahrhundert*, ed. Simone Prodilliet (Lucern: Caritas-Verlag, 1998), 155.
91 Finnan, "From Survival," 153.
92 Okely, *Own or Other Culture*, 80.
93 David J. Nemeth and Rena C. Gropper, "A Cyber-Ethnographic Foray into GR&T Internet Photo Blogs," *Romani Studies*, 18.1 (June 2008): 65.

certain especially dangerous hereditary diseases, for a fact passed on by women."[94] Eugenic measures that the agency took to eradicate Jenisch ways of life—prohibition against marriage, sterilization, abortion, and euthanasia of unborn children—reflect violence and discrimination directed specifically against women.[95]

Mehr's essay on "Frauenmut" further illuminates these ideas; Mehr explicitly states she does not want to fall into the trap of characterizing all women as "peaceful, conformist, non-rebellious, consolers and lovers."[96] Her own background has prevented her from assuming such roles. Indeed, *Angeklagt* begins with a quote—supposedly from Foucault—about the subversive potential violence holds for women: "Feminine killing is a step out of feminine silence. It means nothing other than: I am talking. Now I am talking."[97] Whether or not Foucault said or wrote these words, many of his texts on the relationship between violence, power, and history relate directly to Mehr's philosophy here. In *Discipline and Punishment*, for example, he observes "the metamorphosis of punitive methods on the basis of a political technology of the body in which might be read a common history of power relations

---

94  "Die Vaganität wird, wie gewisse besonders gefährliche Erbkrankheiten, in der Hauptsache durch die Frauen weitergegeben." Alfred Siegfried, *Kinder der Landstrasse. Ein Versuch zur Sesshaftmachung von Kindern des fahrenden Volkes* (Zürich, Stuttgart: 1964), 13.

95  Ramsauer outlines gender-related reasons as to why "neglected" children, but not specifically Jenisch children, were removed from their homes in Switzerland in the early twentieth century. Excessive alcohol consumption was largely related to men, whereas suspicion of prostitution and "immoral" activities always fell on women. Any employed woman, no matter what the work, often raised suspicions about the parents' ability to provide proper financial and social conditions for the children's upbringing. Statistics show more women than men were sterilized for their so-deemed incapacities to raise children. Ramsauer found only one case where a man was considered to be psychologically disturbed and had to consent to sterilization before he married a woman (Ramsauer, *"Verwahrlost,"* 219–39.)

96  "friedfertige, angepasste, unaufmüpfige Trostspenderinnen und Liebende." Mehr, "Frauenmut," 179.

97  "Weibliches Töten ist ein Schritt aus der weiblichen Sprachlosigkeit. Es heißt nichts anderes als: Ich spreche. Jetzt spreche ich." Efforts to find the exact source of this quote in Foucault's writings have been futile. Nancy Goebel, Head Library at Augustana Faculty, University of Alberta, asks for the source on the Foucault-L mail-list, but replies indicate the quote does not sound like Foucault, or they supply similar passages by Foucault, but no one finds this exact quote: Nancy Goebel, "Source needed for quote," Foucault-L mail-list, 2 March 2005. http://foucault.info/Foucault-L/archive/msg09605.shtml. My own e-mail correspondence with Mehr's partner, Uehli Ellenberger, also failed to reveal a source.

and object relations."⁹⁸ Power and cultural perceptions of the body are inextricably linked, and changes in the one manifest themselves in changes in the other. Such was the case, Foucault points out, at the end of the eighteenth century: as the body became more objectified, so, too, did punitive methods become more distanced, inflicting less physical pain, but with a "'higher' aim" to enforce systems of power.

Mehr's portrayal of violence thus becomes a way to insert herself and those peoples who share a history of being victims of violence—Roma, children, women—into history. Violence serves as a mnemonic device reminiscent of Jameson's observation "History is what hurts."⁹⁹ As Mehr grapples with the relationship gender and ethnicity have to violence, she depicts the female body as disrupting the dichotomy of mind and body. Perpetuation of violence in her works becomes a reaction against the dualism between mind and body. She creates what Elizabeth Grosz proposes as a "corporeal feminism," breaking away from dichotomies of mind and body, matter and form, soul and nature, male and female.¹⁰⁰ Mehr's fractured style represents voices of tormented women as subjects of their own texts. The three female protagonists in her trilogy and their ultimate or possible fates reveal that when the violence becomes too harsh, the danger for women lies in expressing extreme aggressiveness.

Complex questions remain, however. While each protagonist may have learned to defend herself and "speak out" against violence wrought against her, where will that process lead her in a world that might not yet comprehend the historical forces behind her actions as a woman, or, as in Anna's case, a Romani woman? What will Daskind have left in her life after killing the town clergyman in a small, rural town that has never accepted her anyway? What does Anna have to look forward to besides meticulously observing and taking notes on her carnivorous plants? Kari ultimately finds herself imprisoned for life in the cell next to where another inmate named "Seppvrenivogel" has been incarcerated for killing her husband. When all Kari can hear is "Seppvrenivogel" masturbating all day, one wonders whether Kari had envisioned this situation for her life? Does the violence each woman has wrought lead to power, or are power and violence, in Foucault's terms, inherently separable and different?¹⁰¹ Does the removal of the external impediment to their freedom lead to internal empowerment?

---

98   Foucault, *Discipline*, 24.
99   See Chapter 5, footnote 26 (page 140).
100  Elizabeth Grosz, *Volatile Bodies: Toward a Corporeal Feminism* (Bloomington: Indiana University Press, 1994). For ideas on the mind/body split in literature and performance as related to Grosz's idea of "corporeal feminism," see Michaela Grobbel, *Enacting Past and Present: The Memory Theaters of Djuna Barnes, Ingeborg Bachmann, and Marguerite Duras* (Lanham: Lexington Books, 2004).
101  See Monique Deveaux, "Feminism and Empowerment: A Critical Reading

Or, in perpetuating the violence, does each protagonist contribute to what Audre Lorde characterizes as "that piece of the oppressor" within herself?[102] Mehr leaves readers to ponder these questions. She presents some possibly controversial, ambiguous answers, but also inquires from a perspective having personally experienced publicly sanctioned violence. Instead of letting that "piece of the oppressor" lay mute within her, she calls for women to develop more effective dialectical thought mechanisms and modes of actions. Those would best manifest themselves in creative, alternative expressiveness outside of mainstream political and social systems, thereby developing effective methods of confronting and overcoming violence in personal and public histories. Writing and speaking publicly have become her outlets, and self-expressive acts deal with pain resulting from a lifetime of violence. As Scarry observes, pain by its very nature "does not simply resist language but actively destroys it."[103] Documents recording personal injury and violence allow "pain to enter into a realm of shared discourse that is wider, more social, than that which characterizes the relatively intimate conversation of patient and physician."[104] Expressing the pain "is a necessary prelude to the collective task of diminishing pain."[105] Violence unmakes, disintegrates, and destroys. Were Mehr to have remained silent, she would have displayed how language induced by terror and trauma destroys the objectified and marginalized body. Through writing she rejects such destruction, defies objectification of pain and violence, and contributes not to "the deconstruction of the world but that world's construction and reconstruction."[106] Employing a kind of "strategic violence"—whereby materialistic and discursive violence are inseparable—she combats the mind/body dualism marking Western civilization.[107] She thereby not only adds voice to the nature of pain, but re-presents both the voice and the body.

---

of Foucault," in *Feminist Interpretations of Michel Foucault*, ed. S. J. Hekman (University Park, PA: The Pennsylvania State University Press, 1966), 211–37.
102   Lorde, "Age, Race, Class, and Sex," 539.
103   Scarry, *Body*, 4.
104   Ibid., 9.
105   Ibid.
106   Ibid., 161.
107   The term "strategic violence" comes from Hanssen's essay on Elfriede Jelinek, whose works also contain violent acts by men and women, showing how dominant groups perpetuate violence and oppressed groups use violence in strategic ways: "Elfriede Jelinek's Language of Violence," *New German Critique*, 68 (Spring/Summer 1996): 79–112.

# Eight    "It is a kind of life in conflict, between two worlds": Voices of the Post-*Porrajmos*/Holocaust Generation

How have the younger generation of Romani writers defined their ethnicity? How do gender and ethnicity intersect in their works. Do the same themes—extended family, storytelling, language, work practices, shared history of persecution, violence, and trauma, diversity, purity and pollution practices—surface? Do any additional issues concern younger writers? Have views on ethnicity and gender changed? If not yet, do writers anticipate future changes? If so, what effect might transformations have on the future of Romani cultures and ethnicity? Dotschy Reinhardt's autobiography *Gypsy: Die Geschichte einer großen Sinti-Familie* (*Gypsy: The Story/History of a Large Sinti Family*), Simone Schönett's novels *Im Moos* (*In the Bog*) and *re:mondo*, and Stefan Horvath's narrative *Katzenstreu* (*Kitty Litter*) provide responses from three unique, diverse writers.[1]

---

1    These three authors continue to be prolific, and I had to limit my analysis to these books. In 2014, Dotschy published a second book, *Everyone's Gypsy*, which looks at global images of Roma. Simone Schönett has three other novels, *Nötig* (2006), *Oberton and Underground* (2012), and *Der private Abendtisch* (2014), but they do not concentrate on Jenisch. Stefan Horvath published *Atsinganos: Die Oberwarter Roma und ihre Siedlungen* in 2013, which looks at the return of Oberwarter Roma to their settlement after the *Porrajmos*/Holocaust and the reactions they received from non-Roma inhabitants. Despite extensive research and personal inquiries, I have not discovered any writings by the younger generation in Switzerland to analyze. Lotty Wohlwend's works on "Verdingkinder," literally "Children things," or "children used as cheap labor," includes reports on Roma in Switzerland from a journalist's perspective: *Gestohlene Seelen: Verdingkinder in der Schweiz*. Frauenfeld, Stuttgart and Vienna: Huber, 2009; *Silas: gejage—geschunden—gedemütigt. Ein Report*. Frauenfeld, Stuttgart and Vienna: Huber, 2006.

Illustration 7: Dotschy Reinhardt. Copyright by Uwe Hauth.

"It is a kind of life in conflict, between two worlds"  203

Illustration 8: Simone Schönett. Copyright by Eva Asaad.

Illustration 9: Stefan Horvath. Photo by Horst Horvath.

## Gypsy: Die Geschichte einer großen Sinti-Familie

By using "Gypsy" as the first word in her autobiography's title, Dotschy Reinhardt and Fischer, her publishers, globalize her story and attempt to reach a wide audience.[2] The subtitle prepares readers for a story centering on an illustrious musical family. When asked to delineate her exact relationship to Django Reinhardt, she spoke less about specific, individual family connections and more about one large extended family, as concepts applying to other musical German Sinti families—Rosenberg, Rose, Weiß, to name a few.[3] When travelling or on tour, Dotschy Reinhardt is always either accompanied by family and friends, or she encounters them along the way. Her autobiography begins with her on tour sitting in the back seat of a van with her cousin Lancy, who plays bass in her band. Her narrative describes numerous road trips with her family and her band.

Living in Berlin and visiting her family in southwest Germany regularly, she speaks affectionately about seeing her maternal grandmother "Gali." As a child, Dotschy Reinhardt spent much time with Gali while her parents were selling on the road, or, as they were, "auf Geschäft gehen" (going out on business).[4] Dotschy also regularly accompanies her family on pilgrimages, especially her uncle Stromeli, who became an evangelical preacher after his son had died of cancer. As a young girl she viewed and sang her first concerts in tents the missions set up for services. During the school year the family had a stationary residence, either in a camper in her grandmother's garden or later in an apartment. Summers were spent travelling around the countryside in the camper.

Close-knit connections to family inspired Dotschy to write her book. On one particular day, Gali, born in 1934, told horrendous stories of Nazi persecution, stories she had not wanted to tell until she was close to the end of her life. Gali talked about her aversion to public monuments that listed names of Romani victims.[5] In the village

---

2   In a personal interview, Reinhardt admitted that using the word "Gypsy" was a compromise with the publisher, who believed that "Gypsy" would be more recognizable even to German readers than "Sinti" and would make the book more marketable. She definitely did not want to use the word "Zigeuner." She realized that "Gypsy," too, has negative connotations, but she believed it did not connote persecution as strongly as "Zigeuner" did for German Sinti (Personal interview with Lorely French, Berlin, July 6, 2010).
3   Personal interview with Lorely French. Berlin, July 6, 2010.
4   Reinhardt, *Gypsy*, 24.
5   The issue of memorials to Roma remains controversial; see: Stefan Berg, "The Unending Battle Over Berlin's Sinti and Roma Memorial," *Spiegel Online*, December 28, 2010. http://www.spiegel.de/international/germany/a-project-in-jeopardy-the-unending-battle-over-berlin-s-sinti-and-roma-memorial-a-736716.html. For the *Stolperstein* memorials, see Chapter 3, footnote 55 (page 83).

where the Reinhardts and other Sinti lived, non-Roma planning such a monument came around asking for the names of Sinti victims of the Nazi to engrave, a request Gali found reprehensible: "How dishonorable that is—first they kill us, and then they write down whom they have caught."[6] She alluded to the Romani custom against speaking the names of the dead—as Ewald Hanstein revealed when he visited the Auschwitz monument—by stating that some Sinti would get sick when passing the monument. Gali observed that officials were erecting monuments for themselves regardless of Romani customs, demonstrating Roma's historically induced voicelessness.

While respecting her grandmother's sentiments, Dotschy admits that she, as a member of the younger generation, has no objection to such monuments and is actually in favor of such remembrances. She recognizes her generation has rights and privileges that her grandmother's generation did not, and especially educational opportunities, which have brought Sinti some equality and freedom to struggle against wrongdoings. She feels obligated to fight against prejudices by writing a book from the perspective of a Sintezza with the ability to talk honestly about her and her family's life. Her personal and familial stories intertwine. Yet, the opinions of the younger and older generations differ. Dotschy respects her grandmother's viewpoint while realizing the need to keep memories alive, finding herself in the position of standing between two worlds—those of the older and younger generations.

Dotschy also stands between the two worlds of Roma and non-Roma, especially regarding her views on Romany. As with Ewald Hanstein, she is against non-Roma learning Romany and against the codification of Romany into a written language. First, she states, Roma have no country and no government of their own; Romani culture and language are the only possessions they have completely for themselves. Second, she recalls Nazi times, when so-called "Gyspy Researchers"—the most notorious being Eva Justin—learned Romany to gain the peoples' trust, only to betray them. In teaching Romany to non-Roma, Roma risk that betrayal again. Third, in opposing codification, Dotschy stresses the many dialectical variations based on geography, family, or subgroups. One written version would endanger this diversity. She emphasizes Romany's orality, and therein lies its beauty as a living language surviving on real personal interaction: "It needs speakers, storytellers. People who master this language so well that they think, dream, and fantasize in Romany. Then the language is alive, then it won't die out,

---

6   "Wie unwürdig das ist—erst bringen sie uns um, und dann schreiben sie noch auf, wen sie erwischt haben." Reinhardt, *Gypsy*, 32.

and I am going to devote myself to that."⁷ Finally, she has witnessed the shame and fear that the older generation has as a result of the dominant culture's prohibitions against speaking the language. Consequently, many Roma did not teach their children Romany. She sees revivalist sentiments to learn, use, and take pride in the language emerging in the younger generation. Non-Roma, having been averse to the language for so long, should not suddenly enjoy the privilege of learning Romany.

Besides extended family and language, a work ethic involving men, women, and children unifies Sinti. Travel is often at the heart of occupations. Dotschy Reinhardt's parents—who are antique dealers, mostly in old musical instruments—and many other Sinti still engage in business requiring travel. Self-employment, although exhausting, has allowed them independence, freedom, and options. As with the generation born in the 1920s and 1930s, both men and women in Reinhardt's parents' generation and in her own generation have worked outside the home. Extended family has usually cared for the children while the parents have been away. Likewise, many in the younger generation desire gender equality and independence. Dotschy Reinhardt is a singer, author, and researcher. Her relationship with her husband David Rose, also a singer, is one of equals, she states. When asked whether she sees competition between the two of them that might result in unequal treatment, she answered with a definitive "no." She is happy that she can turn to Rose as a competent, knowledgeable singer who offers her invaluable advice and support. Reciprocally, he relies on her competency and knowledge for his singing. There exists more of a "symbiosis" than a "competitive struggle" between them. Both are enormously pleased when they succeed.⁸

Living in Berlin and touring frequently, Dotschy also sees her lifestyle challenging the Sinti's highly regarded family values: "We Sinti are used to keeping our clans together. For us it is anything but self-evident that a member of the family goes so far away, certainly not a woman."⁹ Her final phrase here hints at gender norms believing women as still more tied than men to family responsibilities. She suggests that her career pursuits might sever norms. Her statement

---

7   "Es braucht Sprecher, Geschichtenerzähler. Leute, die diese Sprache so gut beherrschen, dass sie in Romanes denken, träumen und phantasieren. Dann ist diese Sprache lebendig, dann wird sie nicht aussterben, und dafür setze ich mich ein" (ibid., 48).
8   Reinhardt, personal interview with Lorely French, Berlin, July 6, 2010.
9   "Wir Sinti sind es gewohnt, unsere Sippen zusammenzuhalten. Für uns ist es alles andere als selbstverständlich, dass ein Familienmitglied so weit weg geht, schon gar nicht eine Frau." Reinhardt, *Gypsy*, 35.

evinces changing attitudes and the necessity to find new ways to juggle professional aspirations and family obligations. She makes clear, however, that she still abides by certain Sinti taboos, especially the one against talking publicly about sex and sexuality: "Concerning private matters, we Sinti are usually very closedmouthed contemporaries. One treasure that we guard well—everything that has to do with sexuality. I do not even like to type the word for that."[10] But one can talk about love, she emphasizes. She devotes an entire chapter comparing her mother and father's relationship to hers with David Rose. Her parents are cousins, and although that relationship was not unusual for the time, the family still disapproved. Against Gali's wishes, the couple met secretly until Dotschy's mother became pregnant with Dotschy. As was the custom, her parents never officially married, but still saw themselves as married according to Sinti customs.

Dotschy's father was born in 1947; her mother went to school seven years after him, belonging to what Dotschy calls "part of a transition generation" (*Teil einer Übergangsgeneration*).[11] Her mother wanted to learn a profession, which was not self-evident for Sinti women at the time, and wanted to go out into the world on her own. In her mother's generation women also began to wear pants for the first time, a major transformation in Romani culture. Her mother donned pants only in private, and not in front of her own parents. Dotschy, too, carries on this custom of wearing dresses and skirts in public and in front of her elders. She describes this dress code as respectful to the older generation. If her father had seen her in pants in front of other people then he would have felt ashamed for her. Aesthetically, Dotschy also prefers to wear skirts and dresses. With pants, one sees everything, all bodily curves and contours, which could be deemed sexually provocative. Having options, freedom, and understanding of diversity remain her main messages. She emphasizes that many families do not let norms dictate their roles, and that some families are stricter than others. Some families practice customs that others do not. Her aunt, for example, who has been married and has four children, wears pants. Wearing a skirt, Dotschy stresses, is not an absolute requirement. She does not see sexism at the root of fashion because clothing choices are hers and not those of a limiting patriarchal culture; the cultural context for these choices is not that simple. She justifies such norms for the same reason that she wants to keep their language secret, that is, so that Roma have

---

10 "Was private Dinge angeht, sind wir Sinti in der Regel sehr verschwiegene Zeitgenossen. Einen Schatz hüten wir besonders gut—alles, was mit dem Geschlechtlichen zu tun hat. Das Wort dafür mag mir nicht in die Tastatur kommen" (ibid., 213).
11 Ibid., 71.

customs to call their own. If the tradition of women wearing skirts is not hurting anyone else, she asks, why should anyone question that?[12] Her statements also imply that other, more significant incidents of oppression need more attention than women's clothing choices.[13] When asked about transforming gender roles, Dotschy Reinhardt explains first and foremost that roles have changed for all people since the 1950s, not only for Roma.[14] Sinti are not the only people who historically have had norms leaving few options for women besides childcare, cooking, and housekeeping. Most Western cultures have witnessed rapid generational shifts, just as in Dotschy's family. Her generation is living more liberally than her parents' generation, who lived looser than her grandparents' generation. In the contexts of sexual and social taboos, generational changes and diversity, a couple should not kiss each other in public or make out or hold hands in front of their parents. Some Sinti are stricter than others in following this taboo, she emphasizes. Some would gossip if they spotted public displays of affection, and some would not care. Personally, she wishes that more Sinti would adhere to age-old traditions, but she does not judge against others who do not.

As with her own parents and in several autobiographies, Dotschy's marriage to David Rose involved "elopement." Using negative constructions, she implies that virginity was not necessarily a requirement for women upon marrying: "When I got to know David it was not self-evident not to have any premarital relationships, but we did not live in the Middle Ages any longer."[15] Elopement remained standard practice, especially when parents might catch wind of the relationship before the couple made a public announcement. After the elopement, the couple decides whether they will officially marry or not, and thus, the parents choose to understand and accept their children's decision. Parents' approval is more a formality than a deciding factor for the marriage. Unlike with the older generation, where the birth of a boy usually incited more jubilation than the birth of a girl, Dotschy emphasizes that her own parents never made her or her sister feel inferior to a boy. They instilled in their girls self-confidence and self-worth, aiding in their professional and personal lives. But Dotschy also knows some less self-confident women who let themselves be beaten and deceived and then act as if nothing is wrong.

---

12 Reinhardt, personal interview with Lorely French, Berlin, July 6, 2010.
13 See Chapter 3, footnotes 169 and 170 (pages 107–8).
14 Reinhardt, personal interview with Lorely French, Berlin, July 6, 2010.
15 "Als ich David kennenlernte war es zwar nicht selbstverständlich, keine vorehelichen Beziehungen zu haben, immerhin lebten wir nicht mehr im Mittelalter." Reinhardt, *Gypsy*, 222.

"It is a kind of life in conflict, between two worlds" 209

A passage at the end of her book emphasizes some main wishes of her people, especially those of the younger generation. Many of these desires—citizens' rights, security, equality, and educational opportunities—are self-evident and shared by everyone, regardless of ethnicity or gender, Dotschy states. But her people want and need more than that. They pine for freedoms different from what non-Roma imagine the "carefree Gypsies" possess. Roma do not want the freedoms offered in racist folk songs or expulsions from geographical areas, but rather the freedom to seek out their own living spaces. Dotschy claims that her generation has found those freedoms: "Now I sing of the possibility for this freedom. Of the possibility that had become a reality for my people of my generation."[16] She concludes with hopes, desires, possibilities, and realities. Her understanding of ethnic identity involves a consciously shared ethnic identity and history of persecution. Rather than allow Roma's traumatic experiences to lead to despair, however, Dotschy focuses on positive characterizations helping Roma survive— family, language, storytelling, music-making, freedom of options, education, and diversity. Her autobiography lends an important voice to personal histories of those before her and those she hopes will follow.

## *Im Moos* and *re:mondo*

In an interview at the Leipziger Book Fair of 2011, Simone Schönett talks about her second novel, *re:mondo*.[17] From her experiences and observations, Schönett notes Jenisch characteristics, careful to avoid generalizations. Most distinguishing is the extended family bond (*Großfamilienverband*). The second is language, although she acknowledges the language is dying out. Third is the shared recognition of a common history of persecution. Fourth is the simple consciousness that one is Jenisch, a trait Schönett recognizes as nebulously indefinable and highly intuitive. A fifth is the art of storytelling (*die Kunst des Geschichtenerzählens*), which can conjure up myths of family origins. In the end, she explicitly links her motivation for writing her book with political measures to deport groups of Roma in France back to Romania and Bulgaria beginning in summer 2010.[18] Such human rights violations justify making public what had remained secret for so long:

---

16 "Nun singe ich von der Möglichkeit dieser Freiheit. Von einer Möglichkeit, die für meine Leute aus meiner Generation zur Realität wurde" (ibid., 284).
17 "AUFgelesen: Simone Schönett," Literradio, March 9, 2011.
18 Cf. BBC News Europe, "Q & A: France Roma Expulsions," *BBC News Europe*, October 19, 2010. http://www.bbc.co.uk/news/world-europe-11027288; and Matthew Saltmarsh, "Sarkozy Toughens on Illegal Roma." *New York Times*, July 29, 2010.http://www.nytimes.com/2010/07/30/world/europe/30france.html?_r=1

"My motivation is to arouse a public voice." (*Meine Motivation ist die öffentliche Stimme zu erheben.*) Her pressing desire falls in line with that of other Roma feeling the urge to make their voices heard.

Both Schönett's novels incorporate these five characteristics. Most importantly, the storylines depend on the extended family and are replete with relationships so complicated that readers have to construct family trees to comprehend the connections. In *Im Moos*, Konratio—referred to as the *Patrus*—is the dying patriarch of a five-generation Austrian Jenisch family. The younger family members have intermarried with non-Jenisch. Readers learn little about Konratio's parents and those of his wife Josefine, but several references to Josefine's mother Nana and father Anton arise. Konratio and Josefine have two daughters, Otti and Claudia; Otti and her Gadže husband Ralf have two children, Igor and Jana; and Claudia and her Gadže husband Dieter have two children, Daniel and Susi; Jana and her Gadže husband Pawel have one child, Nana; and Igor and his Gadže wife Tita have one daughter, Ruth.

With Konratio dying, the patriarchal structure of the Jenisch family is clearly transforming. Instead of describing the past life of the dying patriarch Konratio, however, the opening scene shows Igor, Konratio's grandson, preparing to host the family's Christmas Eve festivities. He is decorating the house and cooking before his wife Tita returns. Konratio does not come down to the family affair because he is too sick. Thus, implicitly, Igor is positioned to become the new patriarch, and yet he shows little interest in leading the family and carrying out its customs. While Igor is responsible for preparing the family celebration, his methods do not please his mother Otti, and she constantly checks up on him and reprimands him. Igor makes mulled wine and lights the candles while music from Mozart's *The Magic Flute* plays in the background. The fact that classical, and not Romani, music fills the house indicates another generational and cultural shift. Igor has pursued a musical career, not in the usual Jenisch way of learning from his ancestors, but rather through formal study at the conservatory in Vienna. Igor will also not follow in his grandfather's footsteps of selling goods door-to-door. Igor's ineptness at travelling surfaces later in the story: during a hiking trip in the mountains he gets lost and has to stay overnight in the threatening cold. Tita has to call the search team to rescue him. In losing his way, Igor shows he is not equipped with the wherewithal to lead a travelling salesman's life. When Konratio is on his deathbed, Igor's mother Otti thinks about Igor as the head of the family, "and shakes her head in doubt."[19] Igor's wife Tita shares his mother's skepticism about his potential success as the patriarch.

---

19 "und schüttelt zweifelnd den Kopf." Schönett, *Im Moos*, 117.

No, the central figure is not the older patriarch Konratio, and not even the younger, possible future patriarch Igor, but rather the female figure Jana, Igor's sister and Konratio's granddaughter. She is the one family member taking great interest in her Jenisch language and background. As a child, she noticed the strange language her family spoke. She questioned why her aunt Claudia's non-Jenisch husband Dieter could not comprehend what Jana later learned was a "secret language," "a language of selling door-to-door", or "a customer language."[20] To the family, the Jenisch language developed from their desire to possess something that the Gadže did not, just as Ewald Hanstein and Dotschy Reinhardt reasoned that Sinti should keep the language secret as a possession they could call their own.

Jana also assumes a major role as storyteller. She is the only family member to whom her grandmother Josefine, Konratio's wife, has told Jenisch stories, which now become precious as Josefine sits silently, licking her lips that can utter no word, thus attesting to how the patriarchal structure has silenced the older generation's women. Jana does not want to be silenced; she searches out other Jenisch communities by travelling to Switzerland to live with a group there; she meets with an Austrian Jenisch poet she hears on the radio; she learns from him about the Nazi persecution and the practices that continued even after the war, when Jenisch children were removed from their families to prevent what officials considered a harmful nomadic lifestyle.

To explore her Jenisch past, Jana becomes an artist, creating collages incorporating the Jenisch language. She begins to have questions about her Jenisch identity, including whether she was actually Jenisch, and, if so, what exactly made her so. Was it blood, she asks, or family secrets or language? She admits that she always romanticized what she perceived as the carefree lifestyle of children who were able to sit around the campfires, free and uninhibited. She recognizes, however, that she neglected to notice that even the smallest children were bound to a system that functioned only when all members contributed to the collective's survival. That meant that children often had to beg for their own food in the name of doing work. Her observation questions idyllic portrayals non-Jenisch might have painted of the travelling lifestyle.

Schönett's book is an important one for Roma because of its realistic portrayal of changes that have occurred in Jenisch families and the desire to transmit collective stories and memories to the younger generation. The shift from the older patriarch to the younger female family member intent on carrying on Jenisch language and stories is noteworthy. Schönett expresses an awareness of Austrian historical and social circumstances that have brought Jenisch to where they are

---

20 Ibid., 31.

today. At the same time, she remains cognizant that such circumstances can create transitions in family dynamics. Defining and maintaining ethnicity becomes that perpetual balance between self-fashioning from within and imposition from without.

When Jana travels to the Jenisch poet to talk about history, he tells her of the governmental measures to place children in special homes or schools. Jana has not known about these measures except that her mother, Otti, and other relatives who were over 50 years old, told her about living in "homes" away from home. Otti and others did not explain, however, that these "homes" were part of the systematic, state-sanctioned abduction of children from their families. Instead, Jana's relatives merely said that they had gone to such "homes" because the regular school had been too far away. After talking with the Jenisch poet, Jana recognizes her family's cover-up, noting that the school was not too far away, but really only ten minutes distant. From the younger generation's vantage point, Jana tries to comprehend the older generation's shame.

Likewise, Schönett's novel is significant for portraying customs and beliefs. When Jana and Pawel attend the funeral of an Austrian Sinti, everyone smokes continuously in order to keep dreadful *mulo* death spirits away. Jana's and Pawel's daughter Nana is baptized according to old Jenisch traditions: all the family members whisper a secret wish in the baby's ear, and the priest blesses an amulet with artifacts that family members contributed to protect the baby. Through the perspective of Otti's non-Romani husband Ralf, certain culinary specialties suggest stereotypes that non-Jenisch have of the Jenisch. When Ralf first met Otti, his mother warned him about "those in the bog" (*denen im Moos*)[21] and told him that Jenisch ate cats and dogs. Thus, when Otti's Jenisch family offered him rabbit or lamb to eat, he pretended he was not hungry instead of telling them that he suspected he was eating some house pet. The family never talked about Ralf's refusals to eat; they simply gave him something else to eat while they ate what was in the pot. When Ralf went outside after the meal, the family made fun of him in his absence for not eating what they ate. But the children, too, never really knew whether they had eaten a cat or dog, and Konratio and Josefine would never give them a straight answer when they asked. With a note of irony, the narrator concludes: "Sometimes it really was a rabbit, very often really a lamb."[22] From the Jenisch perspective, Gadže stereotypes about food belonged to the history of interactions between Roma and non-Roma. Josefine explains how in the war the Gadže were always happy to receive anything to

---

21 Ibid., 44.
22 "Manchmal war es wirklich ein Hase, sehr oft wirklich ein Lamm," (ibid.).

eat, and no one asked what it was. Konratio chimes in to state that after sharing such hospitality, Jenisch became known as the "dog and cat eaters."[23] Unfounded stereotypes thus arose from Jenisch generosity.

Just as Jana takes the greatest interest in preserving the Jenisch language and door-to-door salesmanship, so, too, does Josefine as the family's female head slowly begin to replace Konratio as the family's main storyteller. Josefine begins to tell stories to her granddaughter Nana. In doing so, Josefine is chagrined to discover that her ulterior motive is to prove that she is replacing Konratio as storyteller; she admits to telling stories not for entertainment, but rather to show Konratio that he had become superfluous.

For the generations of Jenisch in *Im Moos*, work has meant selling wares door-to-door (*Hausieren*). Yet, not everyone has followed this lifestyle with the same enthusiasm. Konratio's side of the family was always on the road and at markets, and Konratio and his five siblings were born while their parents were earning their livelihood as travelling salespeople. By the age of ten, Konratio was visiting houses by himself to carry on the trade. *Hausieren*, so he states, is in his blood, and his only inheritance from his ancestors. But this livelihood was not his "lifeblood" (*Herzblut*).[24] He would have preferred being a travelling horseshoe blacksmith, although he has been good at what he has done.

In contrast, Josefine's family travelled only during summer, taking up residence in winter, when they ran a village pub. Her brother Igor wanted to earn his living as a musician, and even had the opportunity to study at a music conservatory, but his father had insisted that he needed Igor to play dance music at the family inn. Konratio and Josefine continued to sell wares door-to-door until the late 1990s, much to Josefine's displeasure. In fact, Josefine would much rather have adopted norms she perceives in non-Romani culture, that is, ones where women do not need to work outside the home. For Josefine, *Hausieren* is "dirty" (*dreckig*) and stigmatizes Jenisch; she prefers a house and a "normal life."[25] Josefine is pleased and proud when her daughter Claudia marries Dieter, a Gadže, because then Claudia does not need to work because of Dieter's financial success as an antique dealer.

The daughters Claudia and Otti are caught in the middle between Konratio's demands to accompany him peddling his wares and Josefine's disgust at the occupation of travelling salesperson. But the daughters end up obeying their father and go *Hausieren*. Even though they had other work in the antique business and in running

---

23 "Hunde- und Katzenfresser" (ibid., 45).
24 Ibid., 80.
25 Ibid., 81.

the inn, they respected their father's wishes and accompanied him at five o'clock in the morning, following his explicit and implicit orders. Claudia is happy to move away from the "Bog," and when her marriage begins to turn sour, she does not want to leave Dieter because it would mean going back to the only professions she has learned from her parents: "selling door-to-door from my father and pub life from my mother."[26] When Jana wishes to learn the trade from Konratio, Josefine tries to dissuade her by stating that Jana does not have it in her blood to go *Hausieren*.

Josefine's characterization of *Hausieren* as dirty work and her wish for her daughters and herself not to work outside the home provide interesting perspectives on women's emancipation. Whereas early Western feminists clamored for opportunities for women to work outside the home, Josefine expresses disgust at the limited employment options she sees for Jenisch women. Her aversion to working and to having her daughters work presents a differing vantage point from which to consider women's occupational alternatives. Josefine has no romanticized notions about Jenisch women's world of work. In this way, Schönett's book debunks many preconceived notions about ethnicity and gender for Jenisch specifically and for Roma in general. Her characters want freedom of options for employment, expression, travel, and leisure just as Dotschy Reinhardt expressed.

Schönett's *re:mondo* also centers on family networks. The characters' lives intertwine more subtly than in the earlier work, causing readers to wonder whether the connections are coincidental or not. At the center stands Sara, from a Jenisch family with roots in Langfenn, in the mountainous area of Jenesien in Southern Tirol between Austria and Italy. The novel begins in this area with the narrator's prologue invoking the biblical tale of Noah, the flood, and Noah's ark. In the Jenisch version, however, Noah had a brother, Jakob, unknown to most, who was a musician, a traveller, and a free spirit. When Noah talked about the flood and building an ark, Jakob, too, believed the signs foreshadowing the flood, but could not resign himself to living in such an enclosed ark. He would rather die in freedom than imprison himself so. Instead, Jakob took his musical instruments, mounted his horse, and went travelling, happy he would somehow survive. Eventually a woman joined him, and together they encountered other musicians from all corners of the globe who accompanied them. When the flood began, they all found themselves in Langfenn, in the Jenesian mountains. They sought refuge in a rocky area that later became their church, and for 150 days and nights they stayed there "with the magic

---

26 "'Hausieren von meinem Vater und das Gasthausleben meiner Mutter'" (ibid., 54).

of their playing, with the force of their laughter and the power of their belief in the good and a life in freedom."[27] After the flood subsided, they came out and named themselves with the old word for "'Insiders, Those In The Know': Jenisch."[28] Having remained "Outsiders" for centuries, classifying themselves as "Insiders" is powerful. Exact Jenisch traits, however, remain nebulous and intuitive—focusing on music, humor, goodness, freedom, language, and shared knowledge. These traits, however, accord with Schönett's assertion that Jenisch intuitively recognize each other by unspecified, indefinable characteristics. Schönett seems to be practicing what Spivak identifies as "*strategic* use of positivist essentialism,"[29] just as other Roma talk about certain indefinable "innate traits." While Schönett has been thoughtful in describing other historical, social, cultural, and linguistic factors that define Jenisch, forming ethnic bonds through perceived essential characteristics brings increased solidarity in the right place at the right time.

This story of origin, the narrator claims, has never been written down, but rather passed on only from one mouth to another's ear, remaining a secret in Jenisch circles. Sara, too, vows to tell her own, yet unborn child this "true" (*wahre*) story one day and to take him or her on a pilgrimage to Jenesien to thank the goddess in the small church that stands on the rocky cliffs there. She does not want her offspring to forget "that the true stories of the Travelers also begin so: It was because it wasn't."[30] Thus, cleverly and not coincidentally, this "true" (*wahre*) story ends with the ambiguous saying "It was because it wasn't" that often opens Romani folk tales. The equivocal message reflects the continual tensions Roma have experienced and suggests that every situation causes varying outcomes and interpretations. Sara's emphasis on this opening line's importance for Jenisch stories sets the stage for subsequent complexities. Indeed, each character's story in *re:mondo* unveils ambiguous meanings and open-endedness.

Similar to Dotschy Reinhardt in her autobiography and Jana in Schönett's first novel, Sara stands between the Romani and Gadže worlds. Sara left her Jenisch family to study at the university, a decision that her mother in particular resented. Sara intended to study sociology to eventually help her people, but she ended her educational endeavors after three semesters, discovering she did not belong in the academic

---

27 "mit der Magie ihres Spiels, mit der Kraft ihres Lachens und der Macht ihres Glaubens an das Gute und ein Leben in Freiheit." Schönett, *re:mondo*, 6.
28 "'Eingeweihte, Wissende': Jenische'" (ibid.).
29 Spivak, "Subaltern Studies," 13.
30 "dass die wahren Geschichten der Fahrenden immer so beginnen: Es war, weil es nicht war" (Schönett, *re:mondo*, 7).

world. She now earns a living from reading tarot cards at open-air markets and over the phone. She is also in a relationship with a Gadže, Stephan, and wants to start a family, which Stephan does not. At the novel's beginning, she has just discovered she is pregnant and is contemplating how she will tell Stephan.

In fact, Stephan has severed all ties with his family and cannot understand Sara's longing for human connections, her inability to recognize his need for privacy, and her desire to be a parent. Stephan works the nightshift as a hospital aid. While on duty, he becomes fascinated with the stories of the patient Raymond Bovy, an elderly homosexual Dutch man facing a leg amputation. Coincidentally or not, Raymond was born in 1919, the same year in which Sara's grandmother, Anna, was born. Raymond also comes from Nijmegan, Holland, the same town where Anna had worked for one-and-a-half years as a maid until March 1938, when Austria became part of the "German Reich." Anna had gone to Holland to experience life outside of the Austrian Jenisch community where she had grown up. In 1938, as a "Reichsdeutsche," Anna was sent back "home" to Austria. Raymond tells Stephan stories about the three prison terms he served for attempts to escape Nazis in Holland. He also describes a stint with the Foreign Legion in France and the years he lived in Australia. His fears about the forthcoming amputation cause him to reveal a secret to Stephan: in the hopes of receiving better care, Raymond has lied to the hospital personnel that he is a medical doctor.

The reader never learns whether Anna and Raymond's paths may, indeed, have physically crossed in Holland, but the similarity of their traumatic situations as "Outsiders" becomes evident. Likewise, the novel's title, *re:mondo*, literally meaning "return to the world," unites them as "Insiders." References to returning and repeating surface constantly, beginning with Sara's wish to return to Jenesien with her child, and reinforced by Anna's favorite saying, which she repeats over and over: "*Everything that was will be again.*"[31] The narrator also reveals that Stephan secretly calls Raymond "Remondo," a variation on the title.

As with *Im Moos*, *re:mondo* revolves around the lives of many generations of Austrian Jenisch and their struggle to maintain their identity. *Im Moos* weaves together five generations; *re:mondo* includes six. The oldest character in *re:mondo*, Piero Nobbel, who lived from 1854 to 1941 and practiced natural medicine, was also the clan's leader during the years after the Nazis had assumed power in Austria. In 1900, Piero had saved the life of a Gadže General's daughter. In exchange, the General had promised to reward Piero with a favor. As that favor, Piero asked the General for advice on how Piero's clan could survive the Nazis.

---

31 "*Alles was war, wird wieder sein*" (author's italics, ibid., 27).

After learning about Nazi plans for Jenisch, the General assured Piero that neither Jenisch origins nor race would pose problems. The General reassured him that, in contrast to other Roma, Jenisch were considered European natives because of their fairer complexion and their years of residency in the German-speaking countries. The only problem, according to the General, was the Jenisch lifestyle, and mainly their reliance on travel for work, which the Nazis categorized as "asozial" (asocial). According to Robert Ritter's "research," Jenisch who had intermarried with Jews or with members of other Romani subgroups would encounter difficulties because of "racial impurity." The General recommended that Piero's clan assimilate to avoid persecution and eventual extermination. Young men should voluntarily register for the military; other members should find "regular" work in factories and abandon travelling; they should not speak Jenisch; and, most importantly, no more than two of them should be seen together. This meant no more tending horses, pulling wagons, and travelling together.

Piero discussed these recommendations around the campfire with his clan. Their initial reaction was anger, then fear, then anxiety. Piero reminded them of their oldest tradition: "the art of survival: A Jenisch person always survives."[32] As with autobiographers and Dotschy Rheinhardt, most Roma have stressed this characteristic, but whether that trait is a blessing or a curse continues to perplex them. Adaptability can also mean sacrifice of ethnic identity. The Jenisch's initial hostile reaction to Piero's adoption of the General's recommendations reflects this dilemma.

While the Jenisch were fervidly discussing Piero's proposed survival tactics around the campfire, Anna slipped off with Matteo, a young Jenisch man. The two consummated their love on a mossy bed under the moonlight and then returned to the campfire to await approval of their bond as marriage. In other times, according to traditions, their slipping out and then returning together would have been signals for their parents to declare them married, just as autobiographers talk about "elopement." But the gravity of the historical situation and the profundity of the conversation around the campfire that night prevented anyone from noticing the couple's actions. No one declared them married. Consequently, the couple could not call themselves husband and wife. The couple's story demonstrates the major impact history has had on Roma's private lives and traditions. Anna and Matteo would have to suffer the consequences of historical circumstances destroying traditions crucial to the ethnic group's survival.

Nine months later, Anna bore a daughter, Franziska (Franzi), in May 1940, and became a single mother. Matteo had joined the military, but

---

32 "die Kunst des Überlebens: Ein Jenischer überlebt immer" (ibid., 54).

eventually returned as a deserter to Anna. They publicly announced their union to the others and everyone celebrated their long-awaited marriage. The couple was able to live together in the family's house until September 1943, when two officials came looking for Matteo. Luckily, he had gone scrounging for food when they searched his house. After the officials left, Matteo returned, but the family then feared for their lives and forced him to go into hiding. Against her family's wishes, Anna decided to live with him and Franzi in a secluded cave where two of Matteo's cousins had been hiding for over a year. They all lived a few months together in the cave, but in the harsh winter Franzi fell ill, and Anna brought her to the hospital. Anna had her own identification papers, but not Franzi's birth certificate. Without such, Franzi came to the immediate attention of the doctors who said she must be stolen and must be placed in foster care. When officials scrutinized Anna's records, they accused her of not having been registered at home for months and not having served her required year of service work for the Reich. They claimed she had been living a vagabond's life, travelling aimlessly around, earning a living illegally selling unregistered wares, and begging. Consequently, they classified her as an "asocial." She spent the night in jail and then underwent a physical examination. The doctors said they had found a tumor in her abdomen, and they needed to operate. They promised her Franzi back after the operation. All turned out to be lies: Anna later learned she was sterilized and Franzi had been taken into foster care.

This synopsis demonstrates how Schönett astutely incorporates key elements of Austrian Jenisch history into her fictional account, including hiding from Nazis, classification as a vagabond, child abduction, and sterilization. Likewise, other Jenisch traits surface throughout the novel. Regarding language, Jenisch words occur not as prevalently as in *Im Moos*, but solidarity definitely arises around common linguistic usage. While at the university, Sara encounters a man called Langenpfeil and remembers that Anna had spoken often with mistrust and resentment about him. Langenpfeil was the first Jenisch who had systematically written down the Jenisch language, believing that only through writing could age-old knowledge survive. For Anna, her family, and most Jenisch, unveiling the language in writing constituted betrayal. Sara, however, admits she is not against preserving a written language, but she understands her people's concerns. She attempts to found an organization with Langenpfeil to help Jenisch, but finds only the loudest and the most ignorant members speak out at meetings. In history books for classes, she finds no trace of Austrian Jenisch, but she learns about Pro Juventute's actions in Switzerland and learns about the oppressor's language. She cannot forget the sentence by the Pro Juventute leader advocating tearing families apart to fight "vagrancy" among Travellers.

Faced with the historical threat of annihilating Jenisch through dismantling families, Sara confronts her own pregnancy. In a surprising twist of fate, when she finally tells Stephan she is pregnant, she learns he is not the father because, unbeknownst to her, he has had a vasectomy. She becomes enraged at Stephan and confused at the situation. First, because of the forced sterilizations in her family, she cannot understand how a man could voluntarily destroy his fertility, and, even worse, never talk to her about his decision. Second, she now knows that Serge, a Jenisch man she had met at a market and with whom she had slept one night, is the father. Sara and Serge had experienced an immediate bond with each other, one based not only on mutual attraction, but on their recognition of each other as Jenisch. Here, Schönett's fourth characteristic of Jenisch again comes into play, namely, an unconscious recognition of other Jenisch based on inexact, indefinable traits. The narrator refers to "invisible hats" that Jenisch wear and "insider knowledge" by which Jenisch instinctively recognize each other.[33] Again, "*strategic* use of positivist essentialism"[34] creates crucial bonds in the right place at the right time. Sara discovers "the invisible hats" that Serge and she have in common.[35]

Such coincidental ties evince Schönett's art of storytelling, whereby she intertwines numerous characters and plot lines, employing sophisticated literary devices. Many sentences begin with the conjunction "dass" (that) without a preceding clause, resulting in long strings of thoughts and actions depending on one another as in a chain-link fence.[36] This technique reinforces the apparent coincidental, linked nature of events. Most clever is the use of verb tenses. Stories in the past are narrated in the present and stories in the present are narrated in the past. This unexpected disjoining of tenses demonstrates the relativity of time. As with the opening story of Jakob and Jenisch origins, in which "Outsiders" become "Insiders," twists of time turn traditional views of Roma as being "out of time" and "out of place" into depictions of their history and stories existing everywhere in time.

Jenisch omnipresence over time emerges in customs even Sara continues to follow, many of which coincide with those in *Im Moos*. Regarding work, Sara comes from a long line of travelling male and female peddlers. At the beginning of the twentieth century, Anna's family still possessed the precious so-called "Maria-Theresien-Patente," the centuries-old traders license allowing them to sell goods at certain markets all over Austria. The licensed trader was allowed to train anyone

---

33 "'unsichtbare Hüte'" (ibid., 12).
34 Spivak, "Subaltern Studies," 13.
35 "die unsichtbare Hüte" (Schönett, re:mondo, 163).
36 Maria Slunsky, "Simone Schönett: re:mondo." *Literaturhaus Wien*, November 30, 2010. http://www.literaturhaus.at/index.php?id=8625

and pass the license to the next generation. Beginning in 1919, however, this license no longer permitted its holder to train others and then to pass the license on. Instead, those who wanted to learn the trade had to acquire their own licenses, which were available only to those who had lived and been registered in a place for the previous ten years. These conditions were almost impossible for any Jenisch to attain due to the history of expulsions and inability to be registered as residents. After the war, Matteo and Anna could still sell door-to-door and at markets with their old license, but hardly any travelling groups were left for solidarity. The fact that Sara reads tarot cards for a living and continues to travel to markets places her in the long line of female fortune tellers whose livelihood has caused a reputation for both the exotic and the deceptive. Ironically, in Sara's own relationship, Stephan welcomes the times when he sees her begin her telephone readings, not because he values her work in the same way that Roma value women working, but because he knows then that she will be busy and leave him alone for a while.

Believing in spiritual forces, Sara interprets dreams, mostly her own, and unveils symbols such as copper—meaning luck and happiness in love—and owls—signifying the necessity to do what one has vowed to do. Sara and her family vigilantly follow traditions surrounding death and afterlife spirits. When Piero Nobbel dies, his last wish is that no one should come to his funeral. Jenisch place high significance on death rituals; the clan fears that without rituals—staying with the corpse until the burial and laying his favorite foods and possessions next to him in the grave to accompany him into the afterlife—then the dead would find no peace in the afterlife. By not wanting the wake, music, final meal, schnapps, and final commemoration, Pierro had chosen to leave the ephemeral world as Gadže, not Jenisch, would. Still, as Anna lights a candle at noon on the day of her great-grandfather's funeral, a wind blows in through the closed windows, circles around in the house, and then disappears through the fireplace. Anna knows that the wind is her great-grandfather taking his leave, even without the rituals.

Sara later visits the grave of Piero Nobbel, her great-great-great-grandfather, and lays down bread, chocolate, and a handful of corn kernels. She sprinkles salt around in a circle and pours honey schnapps in the middle. She performs this ritual for his and the family's well-being. She feels a wind blow in the same way that Anna had felt it blow. And then the words come to her: *"The dead are present in memory. Only the spirit can continue on. The old secrets are better preserved in the hearts of those in the know than in books."*[37] Sara's thoughts express two strong

---

37 *"Die Toten sind in der Erinnerung anwesend. Nur der Geist kann weiterbestehen. Die alten Geheimnisse sind im Herzen der Wissenden besser aufbewahrt als in den Büchern"* (author's italics, Schönett: re:mondo, 118).

Jenisch and Roma beliefs: the existence of spirits that transcend the body and the importance of members' memories and feelings rather than the written word. She relies on "those in the know," the insiders. Many customs evoke these sentiments. Schönett's novels also prove rich in disclosing how gender and ethnicity intertwine. No official written document needs to sanctify marriage. Instead, rituals consist of "elopement" and then an official proclamation by the clan's head and any other witnesses to the "elopement." Anna's great-grandfather had married her father and mother in this manner with the group recognizing the bond publicly. Thus, when Anna and Matteo wanted to have the group acknowledge their "elopement," the group's unawareness devastated the couple. When Anna and Matteo finally do get married, they celebrate in a much more modest fashion than usual, reflecting the oppressive war years. For the second time, historical circumstances affect Jenisch customs.

Other changes also arise. Marrying a non-Jenisch was frowned upon in Anna's time, whereas in contemporary times, Sara's relationship with Stephan is more conceivable. Regarding the taboo against talking publicly about sexuality, when Sara attempts to convince her female relatives who had been forcibly sterilized to initiate court proceedings, they are too ashamed to take public action. Even among themselves they use the euphemism "operations" (*Operationen*) to refer to the sterilizations.[38] Anna almost overcomes her silence, however, and begins to follow Sara's advice, but Anna can proceed only so far in the process. When she learns she must undergo a complete gynecological examination as proof, she refuses what she sees as an invasive personal procedure and declaration. Against this background of forced sterilizations, however, abortion is not an option to Sara, even though she dreads Stephan's anti-family stance. Her child represents a circle to her. After Stephan beats her in reaction to discovering she is carrying another man's child, Sara's father and brothers come to retrieve Sara's belongings and take her home. As Sara is driving behind them away from Stephan, she takes another direction, leading her to the camp where Serge is staying. He greets her with open arms, claiming that he knew she would come. Sara's story ends with Serge making her coffee just how she prepares it.

Both protagonists Jana and Sara stand poised to carry on Jenisch traditions. They represent the younger generation's values as moving away from patriarchal structures esteeming a boy's life over a girl's and supporting a double standard for the sexes. Women's virginity upon marriage is no longer required. Purity and pollution taboos separating women from men are not present. Still, the two female characters

---

38  Ibid., 97.

belong to a long line of women who have worked inside and outside the home and have contributed financially to the family's well-being. Moreover, they are keeping the Jenisch language alive, researching, and raising awareness about historical persecution. They both recognize the induced silence afflicting women in previous generations. Jana and Sara become storytellers insuring that their families' stories and histories will endure. Likewise, Simone Schönett has become a storyteller for Jenisch.

## Katzenstreu

Stefan Horvath's works combine what he says are "reality and insanity" (*Realität und Wahnsinn*).[39] *Ich war nicht in Auschwitz* includes fictional stories and oral narratives about the sufferings of his parents' generation. *Katzenstreu* centers on the murder of his son, one of four Romani victims of a bomb planted in a roadside sign reading "Roma zurück nach Indien" (Roma go back to India) in Oberwart, Austria, on February 4, 1995.[40] When the four went to dismantle the sign, the bomb exploded. Horvath's narrative relays the incident through various perspectives, but mostly that of the perpetrator. *Ich war nicht in Auschwitz*, as the book jacket states, is the first work by a Rom from the major Romani settlement in Oberwart in the Austrian province of Burgenland. In the introduction, Horvath synopsizes Roma's history in Burgenland, stating already in the first line that the "Gypsy" history is also one of suffering.[41] He traces marginalization and persecution from the time Roma settled in Burgenland two to three centuries ago, through Nazi times, when the first deportations began in 1938 and systematically killed all but about 500 of some 10,000 Roma living in Burgenland, to his son's murder.

Whereas *Ich war nicht in Auschwitz* documents the Burgenland Roma's suffering, *Katzenstreu* shows Horvath confronting the personal trauma of his son's murder. To that end, he needs to find a structure different from that which other writers would use.[42] As he stares at the corpses of the four victims on the morning after the bombing, he sees his life and his son's life playing in his mind "as if in a film" (*wie in einem Film*)—his son's first smile, first steps, first days at school. Cinematic memories spark images of his Romani people suffering under

---

39  Stefan Horvath, *Katzenstreu: Erzählung* (Oberwart: edition lex liszt 12, 2007), 5.
40  "Roma Attentat in Oberwart," *ORF TVTHEK*, February 5, 1995. http://tvthek.orf.at/program/Archiv/7648449/Roma-Attentat-in-Oberwart/3229505. See Illustration 10 for the memorial to this tragic event.
41  Stefan Horvath, *Ich war nicht in Auschwitz: Erzählungen* (Oberwart: edition lex liszt 12, 2003).
42  Horvath, *Katzenstreu*, 97.

"It is a kind of life in conflict, between two worlds"  223

Illustration 10: Mahnmal für Roma und Sinti (Memorial for Roma and Sinti), Oberwart, Austria. Photo by Christian Ringbauer

Nazis—concentration camps, barbed wire, his people talking about their suffering and demanding he not look away as other Roma had done before. In emotional passages about the violent history connecting his son and Roma, Horvath as author and narrator does not embody an authoritarian father figure, but instead comes across as sensitive, caring, engaged, and historically conscious. Although he creates a very different written portrayal than Reinhardt and Schönett craft, like them he identifies his ethnicity with values of extended family, common language, shared history, cultural consciousness, and storytelling.

Horvath as author and narrator does not display authoritarian literary omniscience either. In finding a structure unlike any other, he contemplates a mixture of documentary and fictional scenes. The opening line emphasizes veracity: "This is a true story."[43] But immediately he throws shadows of doubt on that statement, desiring to relate highly personal experiences happening to him after the murder, "experiences that I did not invent although they seem unbelievable."[44] While writing his book, "reality and insanity were so close next to each other."[45] Subsequently, he takes readers through steps of figuring

---

43  "Dies ist eine wahre Geschichte" (ibid., 5).
44  "Erlebnisse, die ich nicht erfunden habe, obwohl sie unglaublich wirken" (ibid.).
45  "waren Realität und Wahnsinn so nah beieinander" (ibid.).

out how to combine these two conflicting forces. He first demonstrates how the murder became a motive for non-Roma to confirm their stereotypical suspicions of illegal behaviors among Roma. In the evening after the murder, some 100 policemen came to the Roma settlement in Oberwart, not looking for the murderer, but rather for weapons and drugs that the police had long, yet wrongfully, suspected the Roma had hidden there. Horvath also describes the deluge of reporters who came with preconceived notions about what happened. One journalist suspected Horvath of being an accomplice, claiming Horvath had altered the crime scene and had cleared away weapons and drugs in the Roma's houses before the police search. Horvath laments how his days and nights became consumed with speaking to the press, politicians, and other Roma there; eventually, he was only sleeping 20 hours a week. Until his son's murder, Horvath had been one of the quietest residents. From that day forward, he dared to speak more in public.

In October 1995 he realized he could not continue in such a frenzied, sleepless state of mind. When he was offered an apartment in the Oberwart hospital where he worked, which was located further away from the town's center, he accepted. He and his family knew this move would disrupt their bond. Still, he needed distance. Ironically, he discovered that the apartment was located on the site of the first barracks constructed to house Roma who returned to Oberwart after World War II and that he had actually been born in these barracks. Return to his origins brought him tranquility, but also spurred him to confront his son's murder head on. He followed the turn of events closely. First, the murder occurred; then came other letter bombs that the bomber, Franz Fuchs, sent to members of ethnic groups and to officials supporting "minority" rights; finally, Fuchs committed suicide in 2000.

Horvath makes clear how much writing became his therapy after losing his son. In his role as a mouthpiece for Roma he found relief, much needed sleep, and a writing plan.[46] He decided to write the story from the vantage points of those involved, choosing as main characters the murderous bomber Franz Fuchs (although he remains unnamed in the book); the bomber's parents; a group of locals who gather regularly in a pub; and the father of the murdered Rom. At times, Horvath refers to his piece as a drama, and, in fact, a performance reading is available on CD.[47] His multi-perspective rendition of a violent racist act with its

---

46 Ibid., 11–12.
47 Willi Spuller and Sebastian Schottke. *Katzenstreu: Hörspiel-Dokumentation von Willi Spuller und Sebastian Schottke nach dem Buch "Katzenstreu" von Stefan Horvath*, CD (Oberwart: blaubogen and edition lex liszt 12, 2008). The reading

intrinsic contradictions provokes numerous questions. In portraying the murderer as a man coming from a stable, middle-class family in Styria and an excellent pupil, the narrative incites inquiries into the murderer's motives: What would lead such a young man to commit such a violent act? Why would men sit playing cards at the local pub instead of acknowledging the violent event that occurred in their own backyards? What kind of racist attitudes lurk behind criminal investigations in which police search Roma houses for drugs and weapons, turning victims into perpetrators? And ultimately, how can Roma break away from age-old discrimination?[48]

In delving into the perpetrator's mind, the first-person narrator describes entering worlds bringing him to the border between truth and insanity. Struggling to comprehend the bomber's motives, the narrator experienced trancelike visions of Christ's birth and gladiator battles; he heard the cries of slaves and the stammerings of wounded people; he appeared in visions as a king, beggar, hangman and delinquent; he died in the Crusades and was reborn. The murderer accompanied the narrator through these scenes, trying to convince the narrator also to destroy and kill. Confrontation with violence in visions reminds readers of Mariella Mehr's experience in coming to terms with violence wrought against her and other Jenisch. She portrayed characters unable to overcome violent tendencies, figures compelled to perpetrate a violence begetting more violence. Horvath's narrator, in contrast, as the murder vicim's father, does not succumb to this vicious cycle. He conquers his adversary: "Yet ultimately my strength was stronger than his because in me hatred, destruction, and death do not stand in the foreground."[49] In the end, the narrator bestows forgiveness on the perpetrator rather than adopt his violent tactics.

This multitude of perspectives persists as a playscript, and individual narratives assume dramatic form. The first pub scene begins with a list of characters and a location identified as "Somewhere in Austria,"[50] representing the transcendence of time and space. The scenes with the bomber's parents, Josefa and Johann, describe—in the style of nineteenth-century realism—an idyllic landscape setting amidst southern Styrian wineries. Johann affectionately calls Josefa "Peperl." Their intelligent, perfectionist, yet socially challenged son has

---

only includes the characters of the murderer, the father (read by Stefan Horvath himself), and the figure of Death, but omits the author's foreword, the scenes in the pub, and those with the murderer's parents. The order of the individual chapters also varies, but the text in the individual scenes remains the same.
48 Horvath, *Katzenstreu*, 9.
49 "Doch schließlich war meine Kraft stärker als seine, weil in mir nicht Hass, Zerstörung und Tod im Vordergrund standen" (ibid., 16).
50 "Irgendwo in Österreich" (ibid., 21).

moved back home after having problems adjusting at the University of Graz. He has brought a cat home, and when his parents see him taking food, a litter box, and kitty litter into his small cottage in the back garden they hope caring for the cat will help their son socially. Instead, he increasingly spends more time awake at night and becomes even more reclusive, which begins to worry his mother. This portrait of the perpetrator's home life is a study in contradictions between idyll and strangeness, or, as Horvath would say, between truth and insanity.

Background details on the perpetrator and murder also lend insights into gender roles. The female characters come across as more astute and disturbed at the heinous crime than the males. First, the story's title connects the perpetrator's cat with a 13-year-old Romani girl's keen perceptions. As the narrator sits writing the book in his kitchen one night, the word "Katzenstreu" (Kitty Litter) circles around in his mind. Without explanation, he decides to give the book this title. One subsequent night, Hovarth and the Romani girl are driving back from a public reading of his first book when the girl explains to him how he might have arrived at the second book title; she points out that his son's murderer had used a kitty litter box to make the bomb's base. Horvath had seen the words "Katzenstreu" when he had examined the murder site on the morning after the explosion; those words had continued subconsciously to haunt him. Horvath marvels at the girl's ingenuity. Second, Franz's mother suspects that her son may be the bomber, an idea her husband dismisses. She notices their son's increasing reclusiveness and penchant for staying up late at night. When she reads in the paper that the water used to make the bomb came from the source near their house, she raises further suspicions about their son's activities. In response, her husband devises numerous counterarguments to defend their son. Ultimately, his wife relinquishes her suspicions. Third, the female pub owner, Daniela, offers continual retorts to the xenophobic and racist remarks she hears from the pub's non-Romani male customers. In reaction to the murder, Roland and Kurt express sympathy for the victims and find the still unknown perpetrator crazy, but Willi goes off on a tirade against foreigners in general, ranting about them stealing jobs from Austrians because they work for less money and under the worst conditions. Daniela retorts to Willi that many foreigners work diligently and pay their taxes, whereas the other men say nothing. She also later expresses her sorrow for the murdered men and criticizes government officials for turning the funeral into a celebration rather than a tragedy. Willi reacts: "'Who is interested in a Gypsy funeral?'"[51] After Daniela states that she cannot understand the men's xenophobia, Gerd replies that she need not understand because

---

51 "'Wen interessiert schon ein Zigeunerbegräbnis?'" (ibid., 83).

she is a woman: "'The head of a woman is not suitable for thinking. It is only for other pleasant things. Things that women can do better than thinking.'"[52] Significantly, Rom Stefan Horvath accepts the Romani girl's observations, whereas the non-Roma father Joseph and pubgoers categorically dismiss women's opinions. In portraying these reactions, Horvath implicitly questions generalizations about Roma being more patriarchal than non-Roma.

Horvath's narrative also stresses language as a prominent cultural marker. When watching a television broadcast on Burgenland Roma, the bomber identifies Roma negatively by their language. He becomes furious when the "dark-skinned" Roma speak Romany and German subtitles appear. He rails against the designation "Roma" and conjures up other stereotypes: "Roma. What an ugly word. Gypsies, thieves, knifers, work-shys, those are words that suit this breed of people. Roma, what a trendy word."[53] To him, Roma's use of Romany becomes a manipulative threat to the dominant culture. Others in the narrative also find Romany threatening. In the pub Willi becomes hostile towards the designation "Roma," after claiming that Roma do not want to work and want only to live from theft and scrapping.[54] The pubgoers then conflate Roma with foreigners, as Franz predicts foreigners will make the German language obsolete. Willi claims that foreigners do not even try to integrate or speak a word of German.[55] Such enraged reactions justify Roma's urgent desire to preserve their language, as do the hurdles and even dangers they face in speaking Romany.

Ultimately, Horvath cannot claim the same veracity of his story as he did at the beginning. In contrast to the book's opening sentence—asserting this is "a true story"—the final sentence reads: "The book makes no claim to truth. It just shows how it could have been or maybe also not."[56] The contrasting claim and then disclaimer are reminiscent of Romani fairy tales as well as Schönett's story about Jenisch origins—contradictory opening and closing lines portray complex ambiguities Roma continue to encounter. As a storyteller, Horvath composes a lasting record of what he identifies as truth and falsity, reality and

---

52 "'Der Kopf der Frau eignet sich nicht zum Denken. Er ist nur für andere angenehme Sachen. Sachen, die Frauen besser beherrschen als denken'" (ibid., 85).
53 "Roma. Was für ein hässliches Wort. Zigeuner, Diebe, Messerstecher, Arbeitsscheue, das sind Worte, die zu diesem Menschenschlag passen. Roma, was für ein Modewort" (ibid., 18).
54 Ibid., 86.
55 Ibid., 70.
56 "Dieses Buch erhebt keinen Anspruch auf Wahrheit. Es zeigt lediglich, wie es sein hätte können oder vielleicht auch nicht" (ibid., 98).

insanity. In his position as a nonauthoritarian male narrator, he presents a model challenging portrayals of Romani cultures as patriarchal.

## Gender and Ethnicity through the Generations

Undoubtedly, gender roles have changed from when autobiographers born between 1920 and 1940 were growing up to the present. Purity and pollution customs receive little attention in the works of the post-*Porrajmos*/Holocaust generation compared to works by writers born earlier, suggesting that the younger generation does not follow such customs or considers their usage too insignificant to mention. Patriarchal structures are also not as strong; both sexes make decisions independent of the family's patriarch. Accounts of children born out of wedlock and a disappearing insistence on women's virginity upon marriage document an increased acceptance that women are not required to be virgins when marrying, thus whittling away at sexual double standards. No one mentions how disappointing the birth of a girl is and no one claims that parents gave boys more opportunities than girls. All narrative includes strong female characters, some, as in *Katzenstreu*, who are more insightful than males.

Many roles however, have stayed the same, which may not be negative. A strong work ethic still recognizes the importance of both sexes in providing the family's economical livelihood. Women and men still both practice storytelling as a public, visible activity keeping shared stories alive. For some families, as in Schönett's *Im Moos*, the role of storyteller has switched from male to female. Additionally, the extended family is still highly valued, even though modern circumstances have induced family separations: Reinhardt lives in Berlin, miles away from her family; Schönett's female protagonists break away from their families to work or study; Horvath lives in a separate apartment away from his family while in personal mourning for his son. Despite caesuras, the writers intimate that the extended family, storytelling, and shared stories, plus memories, contribute most to maintaining ethnic identity. Language, too, is still a major building block of ethnic identity. Within the family, language will thrive best. Signs of a possible resurgence in learning and using the language emerge as writers become increasingly conscious of Romany's diminished usage. Reinhardt asserts her generation is showing more desire to learn Romany; Schönett's works contain untranslatable Jenisch words; and Horvath portrays Roma in the Burgenland speaking Romany in public forums, sometimes to the consternation of prejudicial non-Roma Austrians. The continued hostility reinforces the contradiction between wanting to learn Romany, yet often needing to hide that desire and knowledge. The family instills the desire for freedom that travel may bring as well. Although writings prove that German-speaking Roma

"It is a kind of life in conflict, between two worlds" 229

have not been exclusively nomadic, most yearn for travel opportunities uninhibited by laws and restrictions. Even the younger generation has fond memories of travel with family, especially Reinhardt's music tours, pilgrimages, and road trips; and Schönett's protagonist Jana selling wares door-to-door with her grandfather. Due to their collective memory of historical persecution, Roma today keep a watchful eye open for continued discrimination, prejudice, and violent actions. Several occurrences have sparked political debate and action: the first major one being the Oberwart bombing; the most recent one being a survey revealing that one in three Germans do not want to live in a neighborhood with Roma.[57] Reinhardt comments nonjudgmentally on the differences between older and younger generations' concerns. For her, the older generations have paved the way for the younger generation to have the "luxury" of focusing on "finer points" of discrimination and prejudice. In learning from the older generation about the advantages or disadvantages of transformations, the younger members can now make informed decisions on accepting or rejecting changes. Flexibility and adaptability receive constant reflection in these writings, and solidarity with one another will prove to be strengths that will keep Roma alive. Coincidentally or not, when talking about strong Sinti bonds, Reinhardt cites the same lines that Ceija Stojka does, which began my introduction: "And I already think that in many Sinti families this motto still always counts, that is, 'together we are strong.'"[58] I thus circle back to the beginning of my study and reinforce intersecting points between generations. Family, language, a work ethic focusing on collective success, common history, shared consciousness of ethnic identity, and storytelling are catalysts for unity. Both sexes' persistent striving for freedom of options emerges clearly in all generations. From Roma voices arises an optimism fostering solidarity.

---

57 Reports of violence and persecution appear regularly in European news. One particularly controversial piece was the title page of the Swiss newspaper *Weltwoche* on 10 April 2012, showing a child pointing a pistol with the headlines "Die Roma kommen: Raubzüge in der Schweiz" (The Roma are coming: Robber Bands in Switzerland). The Zentralrat deutscher Roma und Sinti denounced the coverage as falsely criminalizing Roma: "Sinti und Roma zeigen *Weltwoche* an," *Spiegel Online*, April 10, 2012. http://www.spiegel.de/kultur/gesellschaft/zentralrat-der-sinti-und-roma-zeigt-weltwoche-an-a-826666.html
58 "Und ich denke schon, dass bei vielen Sinti Familien immer noch dieses Motto zählt, also 'zusammen sind wir stark.'" Reinhardt, personal interview with Lorely French, Berlin, July 6, 2010.

# Epilogue: Writing as "the art of survival"

In her influential essay "Playfulness, 'World'-Travelling, and Loving Perception," the Latina feminist philosopher María Lugones poses a model for intersectional theories on racism and sexism.[1] In advocating for "travelling playfully" between "worlds," or among diverse social contexts and constructs, Lugones promotes cross-cultural loving and understanding that does not harm plurality. To move playfully, one must be at ease in a "world." She outlines four ways to feel that ease. The first is being a "fluent speaker" in that "world," knowing all the norms, words, and moves. The second is being "normatively happy," or in agreement with the norms. The third is being "humanly bonded" and love those in the "world." The fourth entails having "a shared history."[2] Knowing other people's "worlds" is "part of knowing them and knowing them is part of loving them."[3] She stresses, however, that many people belong to and travel to several "worlds." From her own experience as an Argentinian woman, Lugones finds marginalized groups, such as women of color, "are known in several 'worlds' and as 'world'-travellers." The only way to get to know them is to know and to travel to their diverse "worlds."[4]

Romani voices provide fascinating insights into the many "worlds" in which they travel. I have explored two major ones—ethnicity and gender—within yet another, the German-speaking "world." Non-Romani suppression and ignorance make their perspectives precious. Their writings reveal travels to other "worlds" with intersecting pathways, including work, family, history, language, storytelling, writing, publication, politics, and music. Lugones' suggested

---

1   María Lugones, "Playfulness, 'World'-Travelling, and Loving Perception," *Hypatia*, 2.2 (1987): 3–19.
2   Ibid., 12.
3   Ibid., 17.
4   Ibid., 18.

ways to be at ease in each "world" apply to any traveller wishing to move playfully into Romani "worlds" to understand them. Her observations support appreciating the Romany language, norms, human emotions, and shared history.

Unfortunately, not all those travelling to or observing Romani "worlds" have appreciated or understood them. Roma have more often than not encountered what Lugones terms "arrogant perception," from a non-Roma viewpoint systematically seeing outsiders' "worlds" as less valuable. Arrogance thereby intends to break the spirit of inhabitants of "other worlds." To move into a "world" inhabited by arrogance, outsiders must learn to balance maintaining traditions that define one's identity with adapting to the dominant "world." Dotschy Reinhardt speaks exactly of sustaining this equilibrium when she describes the advantages of family, traditions, and adaptability that have helped Sinti to survive.[5] Likewise, as Piero Nobbel—the Austrian Jenisch clan leader in Schönett's re:mondo—sits around the campfire with his group, he talks about how they will have to assimilate to survive Nazi persecution. He reminds them of their oldest trait: "the art of survival: A Jenisch person always survives."[6] All autobiographers have emphasized the art of survival.

Along with survival, however, has come sacrifice in adapting to the dominant culture, which for many has meant relinquishing time-honored ethnic traditions. Some, such as Bernhard Steinbach, have a less positive view of adaptability than Dotschy Reinhardt when survival is at stake: "I am proud that I am a Sinto. That we have to deny our identity as Sinti and assimilate—that cannot be the right way. I am what I am. I am not allowed to deny that. I do not need to hide myself."[7] The long history of persecution stands behind Steinbach's understandable skepticism of assimilation. Total assimilation is also not a goal of Roma's adaptability.

Fear of adaptability inducing total assimilation motivates Mozes Heinshink's question, as posed in a discussion with Beate Eder-Jordan, namely, will changes in gender norms and roles undermine Romani cultures?[8] This question, however, assumes Romani women and men have always accepted and adhered to patriarchal structures. This presupposes purity and pollution customs have always discriminated

---

5   Reinhardt, *Gypsy*, 180.
6   "die Kunst des Überlebens: Ein Jenischer überlebt immer." Schönett, *re:mondo*, 54.
7   "Ich bin so stolz darauf, daß ich Sinto bin. Daß wir unsere Indentität als Sinti verleugnen und uns anpassen—das kann nicht der richtige Weg sein. Was ich bin, das bin ich. Das darf ich doch nicht verleugnen. Ich brauch mich nicht zu verstecken." Krausnick, *"Da wollten wir frei sein!"* 70.
8   Eder-Jordan, "'Traditionen'," 183.

against women; restrictive codes of appearance and dress have confined women's choices; work inside and outside the home has posed a double burden to women; Romani cultures assign a higher value to boys than girls; and female voices have been suppressed. Romani writings have shown these assumptions are not always true.

Some purity and pollution customs are rooted in a belief in the impurity of women's bodily fluids, and thus allot women a lower status than men. More complex explanations, however, recognize such customs' symbolic significances. Purity laws can dispel stereotypes of the "dirty, squalid Gypsy." Pollution taboos can ward off undesired intrusions from potentially dangerous non-Roma. Women can choose to adhere to dress codes as they respect elders, prefer a certain aesthetic taste, and deem clothing choices minor aspects in the larger scheme of cultural coding, whereby criticism can distract from women's larger, more pressing issues. Work ethics can show Romani women have always worked, and, in many cases, controlled the finances in the family. The extended family can ameliorate any potential double burden for women as family and neighbors care for children while parents are on the road working. Valuing boys over girls at birth has applied mostly to the older generation, whereas the younger generation emphasizes parental encouragement for both sexes to pursue careers and personal goals. Related to making their voices public, some women relate instances of suppression—Ceija Stojka talks about her siblings and her husband discouraging her to publish[9]—but this opposition seems to have subsided. Romani females and males alike feel the urge to tell and publish their stories, and both have assumed major roles as storytellers for their peoples. Silencing has prevailed mostly from non-Roma and has affected Romani men and women alike.

The question about the relationship between adaptability, gender roles, and cultural assimilation also assumes a gender inequality holding the man's world as the standard. In other words, attaining equity mostly means women must aspire to be like men. In this regard, Western feminists have much to learn from the value Roma place on the extended family and the vital role women play in maintaining familial bonds. In Chapter One, I spoke of how theoretical insights gleaned from Black-American feminists and scholars of intersectionality can apply to Romani Studies. The exchange of ideas regarding intersections of gender and ethnicity should flow in both directions. Other scholars have advocated such communication between cultures.[10] American

---

9 Prüger, *Zigeuner*, 105.
10 Cf. Jonathan Warren and Christina A. Sue, "Comparative Racisms: What Anti-Racists Can Learn From Latin America," *Ethnicities*, 11, (2011): 32–58; they advocate for exchange between American and Latin American anti-racists.

feminist Naomi Wolf, for example, describes how she and another divorced, single-parent panelist, an Indian man living in the United States, were on a panel in India talking about juggling family and career.[11] The audience included some of the most progressive movers and shakers in India. Their questions afterwards, Wolf observes, reflected a certain sorrow on the Indians' part. Although the audience recognized freedom and equality had been priorities for Western feminists—"life, liberty, and the pursuit of happiness"—the Indians found something missing. They wondered how Western feminists could have wanted to transform the most important aspect of life, namely the family. Wolf later had an individual conversation with one audience member who confirmed this sadness, mixed with anxiety and questioning. Indian woman were excited about many aspects of Western feminism spreading in India, such as greater professional opportunities. But they also feared losing their deepest personal attachments. They wanted to welcome the best of Western feminism without harming family relationships. Fear of disbanding the family unit, too, seems to lie at the root of Heinschink's question regarding Romani women. While they, like the Indian women, want to embrace the greater opportunities and options Western feminism may have to offer, those changes may threaten the familial core of their ethnic identity. Again, Roma's strength at adapting may also prove to be their ultimate weakness if they succumb to assimilation.

One must also listen to Romani writers' constant and timeless pleas against overgeneralizations and interpretations out of context. Dotschy Reinhardt takes issue with portraying all Roma as nomadic and carefree, as in the German folksong "Lustig ist das Zigeunerleben" (Merry is the Gypsy Life).[12] Many Roma, she claims, did not live in the forest because they found it so merry, but because they had to flee from those wanting to imprison, beat, rape, or murder them. Roma desire to live uninhibited lifestyles, she stresses, and neither images nor realities should confine them. On the one hand, Roma have no inborn drive to travel from place to place; she knows many families who reside permanently in Germany. On the other hand, when spring comes around, many crave travelling in their campers. Mostly they hanker for freedom to congregate with other people in a life full of larger connections.[13]

Diversity plays a key role in all the writings. From autobiographies to fairytales to novels to narratives to experimental forms, writers

---

11  Naomi Wolf, "What Price Happiness," *More*, April 2010. http://www.more.com/news/womens-issues/what-price-happiness
12  Reinhardt, *Gypsy*, 11.
13  Ibid., 17.

explore a wide variety of themes and introduce multifaceted layers of history, personalities, and perspectives. Schönett's storytelling method is different from that in tales with roots in an oral tradition. Still, all rely on the ambiguous adage of being "true and therefore not true." The revengeful reactions Mehr's characters have to violence varies greatly from Horvath's willingness to forgive his son's murderer. Reinhardt's openness about expressing perspectives on controversial topics—non-Roma learning Romany; memorials commemorating Roma who died under the Nazis; and norms of dress—differs from the older generation's hesitation to publish their stories until decades after World War II. The trauma that Ceija, Mongo, and Karl Stojka experienced in concentration camps manifests itself uniquely in their respective narratives.

Despite differences, Romani writers have already found one possible solution to the dilemma of adaptability versus assimilation—storytelling. By writing, Roma create a public forum to explain the values of the extended family, language, storytelling, ethnic awareness, and a common history.[14] Hübschmannová concludes her 1991 essay on the rise of Romani literature in Czechoslovakia by stating that creating literature will be the main bulwark in keeping Roma together.[15] In a globalized context threatening to divide precious extended families so crucial to Romani culture, literature unites. Indeed, for the generation born between 1920 and 1945, while outside forces tore families and groups asunder, autobiographical accounts have helped unify Roma in their search for individual and collective ethnic identities. Through publishing, female and male writers are equally carrying on traditions of their generations and those before them. Writers of all generations pose new ways of constructing an ethnic identity beyond gender constraints in all their worlds. One only has to listen to their voices.

---

14 The International Romani Writers Association attempted to create a "Romani Library," resulting in a bibliography of more than 1,000 literary pieces. See "Romani Library Project," (2006), Next Page Foundation. http://www.npage.org/article89.html. The website "Schäft qwant: transnationaler Verein für jenische Zusammenarbeit und Kulturaustausch" provides information on Jenisch writers. www.jenisch.info.
15 Milena Hübschmannová, "Birth of Romani Literature," 91–7.

# Appendix: Biographies of Romani Writers

**Lily van Angeren-Franz** (1924–2011) was born on January 24, 1924 in a stall in Upper Silesia. Her father was respected in his travelling Sinti group, where he was a judge, mediator, and musician. Her mother peddled wares door-to-door. In March 1943 Lily and her family were deported from Hildesheim to Auschwitz. She was registered under her maiden name, Adele Franz, number Z-561. As a secretary in the office of the "Gypsy Camp" she survived Auschwitz and was also in Ravensbrück and its outer camp, Graslitz, in Sudetenland. After the war, she immigrated to Holland and married. She was a witness in one of the last trials in Germany of a camp SS officer, Ernst-August König, which took place in Siegen from 1987 to 1991. Her autobiography, *Polizeilich zwangsentführt: Das Leben der Sintezza Lily van Angeren-Franz von ihr selbst erzählt* (2004), was published originally in Dutch. She participated regularly in commemorations in honor of Auschwitz victims and was the main speaker at the fiftieth anniversary of the liberation of Auschwitz.

**Philomena Franz** (1922–) was born in Biberach an der Riss as part of a renowned travelling musical family group. She grew up in Stuttgart with ten siblings, all performing in Germany and Europe together. For seven years she earned her living as a folk singer and dancer. In 1939, when the family was returning to Germany after a performance in Paris, the Gestapo confiscated their belongings at the border. The family was forbidden to travel and perform. Philomena was ordered to work in an ammunition factory. In March 1943, she was deported to Auschwitz and then, in May 1943, to Ravensbrück, where she worked in an ammunitions factory for Siemens. After about a year, she was deported to Schlieben in Thüringen and was forced to make bombs during the night shift. She escaped, only to be caught eight days later and tortured. She was transported to Oranienburg, where she was interrogated and tortured. She was transported back to Auschwitz and was destined to be gassed. Instead, she was commanded to shovel corpses onto trucks. After three weeks she was sent to Wittenberge an der Elbe and forced to work in an airplane factory. Shortly before the end of the war, she escaped and remained in hiding with the Red Army. Her collection of folktales is entitled *Zigeunermärchen* (1989). Her autobiography *Zwischen Liebe und Haß* appeared in 1992. Today she lives in Rosrath near Cologne. She organizes readings and speaking engagements at schools and universities. In 1995, she was the first Sinti awarded the *Bundesverdienstkreuz* (Federal Cross for Merits), the highest civil honor in Germany. In 2001, she was awarded the honor of "Frauen Europas Deutschland" (Europe's Women in Germany).

**Ewald Hanstein** (1924–2009) was born in Breslau and spent his youth in Berlin. In 1936, he was confined to the ghetto "Berlin-Marzahn Rastplatz." In 1943, he was deported to Auschwitz, where his mother and six siblings were already detained. His father was deported to Sachsenhausen and died there. His mother and siblings died in Auschwitz. When the "Gypsy Camp" was liquidated, he was deported to Mittelbau-Dora, then to the outside camp Ellrich Juliushütte, and then to Harzungen. When that camp was liquidated, he was sent on a "death march" over the Harz to Börderland. The Americans liberated him in April 1945 in Eggersdorf. After the war, he was a member of the police force in the German Democratic Republic (GDR). In 1950, he was arrested according to a false accusation and imprisoned for ten months. In 1954, he fled to Bremen. He worked as a locksmith for the company Borgward. He also owned a clothing shop in the Harz. After 1979, he participated in the Bremen Sinti Organization and then in the Landesverband Deutscher Sinti und Roma. He was a member of the board of the Zentralrat der deutschen Sinti und Roma in Heidelberg. In 2006, he received the *Bundesverdienstkreuz* (Federal Cross for Merits), the highest civil honor in Germany. His autobiography, *Meine hundert Leben—Erinnerungen eines deutschen Sinto,* appeared in 2005.

**Stefan Horvath** (1949–) was born in a Romani settlement in Oberwart, Austria. The settlement was later taken down to build the town hospital where Horvath works today. He was the first Rom to attend grade school in Oberwart. From 1964 to 1982, he worked for construction companies in Vienna. From 1989 to 1994, he was a foreman for a construction company. On the night of February 4, 1995, his son, Peter Sárközi, was killed along with three other young Roma men while trying to dismantle a bomb that the letter bomber, Franz Fuchs, had set on a road outside of Oberwart. For years, Stefan Horvath suffered sleeplessness and trauma. Then he began to write. His book *Ich war nicht in Auschwitz. Erzählungen* appeared in 2003; *Katzenstreu. Erzählung* was published in 2007; *Atsinganos. Die Oberwarter Roma und ihre Siedlungen* appeared in 2013.

**Elisabeth Kreutz** (1896), **Hildegard Lagrenne** (1921–2007), **Friedrich Kreutz** (1922), and **Bernhard Steinbach** (1918) belong to the extended Sinti family who tell their story in *"Da wollten wir frei sein!" Eine Sinti-Familie erzählt* (1983). **Elisabeth Kreutz** was the mother of Hildegard Lagrenne and Friedrich Kreutz. She was a fortune teller in the interwar period, when she travelled. In 1928, the family set up a stand with games and fortune telling at markets, carnivals, and festivals throughout Germany. In 1940, she was deported to a concentration camp along with several of her family, who later perished there. The family's autobiographical narratives do not contain many details of their time in the camps. After the war, she lived around Mannheim and continued to tell fortunes and sell goods door-to-door. **Hildegard Lagrenne** was also in a concentration camp, where she bore her son Mohrle. After the war, she and her husband travelled around Germany selling wares and playing music. **Friedrich Kreutz** was a musician in the family's carnival stand; he was deported to camps in Cologne and Auschwitz, but then obtained a driver's license falsely that did not show his Sinti heritage. Consequently, he joined the Army and was a soldier in Berlin, Bromberg, Russia, Estonia, and Reval. When he was wounded and in the infirmary, officials discovered he was a Sinti. Still, he survived, went back to duty, but then was put in a camp in Kattowitz. He met his wife in 1945. After the war he sold goods door-to-door. When he tried to get a pension for the wounds he had received while fighting, he was denied with the excuse that he had voluntarily enlisted in the service. **Bernhard Steinbach** enlisted in the German army in 1940 without officials knowing he was a Sinti. His parents advised that he should tell the officers before he suffered grave consequences for hiding his heritage. He told his commander, who dismissed him 14 days later. In the meantime, some 30 family members had been imprisoned in a camp near Frankfurt. He joined them in the camp to stay close to them and met his future wife there. Their child was born there. In 1943 they were deported to Auschwitz. His child died shortly after their arrival. He was able to survive by playing music in the camp. He also was forced into military service in the Dirlewanger company. In 1948, he began a business with his wife selling textiles. He received some restitution for the trauma he suffered in Auschwitz. In total, he lost 45 family members in concentration camps.

**Mariella Mehr** (1947–) was born in Zürich, Switzerland, to a travelling Jenisch family. Pro Juventute's state-sanctioned program "Hilfswerk für die Kinder der Landstrasse" took her away from her family as an infant to prevent her from developing a "vagabond" lifestyle, placing her in a home for mentally ill babies. She spent over 18 years in homes, psychiatric clinics, and boarding schools, suffering sexual abuse, electroshock treatment, and moral degradation. In 1966, she was imprisoned for 19 months for "moral destitution and work-shyness." In 1973, she founded "Radgenossenschaft der Landstrasse," which exposed the scandal of Pro Juventute's "Kinder der Landstrasse" action, and began her journalistic, political, and documentary work. In 1981, she published her book *steinzeit*, followed by *Das Licht der Frau* (1984), *Kinder der Landstrasse* (1986), *Rückblitze* (1990), *Zeus oder der Zwillingston* (1994), *Daskind* (1995), *Brandzauber* (1998), *Nachrichten aus dem Exil* (1998), *Widerwelten* (2002), *Angeklagt* (2002), and *Im Sternbild des Wolfes* (2003) She has received literary prizes from the cantons of Zürich, Bern, and Graubünden. The University of Basel bestowed on her a PhD *honoris causa* of the faculty of philosophy and history for her work against discrimination. She has one son, Christian, who lives in Zürich. In 2005 she was Writer-in-Residence at Oberlin College. Today she lives in Tuscany, Italy.

**Anna Mettbach** (1926–) was born on January 26, 1926 in Ulfa, Germany. In spring and summer she travelled with her parents who sold willow baskets her father made. In fall and winter they resided in Heidelberg and its surroundings. In May 1940, her mother's family was deported to Poland. In 1942, her mother went to visit her uncle to find out where her family was. After three weeks, while on the train home, the police arrested her. She was deported to Auschwitz. When the "Gypsy Camp" was liquidated she was deported to Ravensbrück, where she worked in the Siemens factory. At the end of the war, she was on a "death march" from Wolfenberg to Dachau, where the Americans liberated her. Her efforts to gain restitution from the German government after the war were met with resistance. The narrative of her life before, during, and directly after the war appeared in *"Wer wird die nächste sein?": Die Leidensgeschichte einer Sintezza, die Auschwitz überlebte* (1999).

**Joseph Muscha Müller** (1932–) was born in Bitterfeld and grew up with foster parents. He never met his biological German Sinti parents or his twin brother. At the age of 12 he was forcibly sterilized through Himmler's decree and would have been deported directly to Bergen-Belsen. Members of the underground resistance group "Edelweiß," however, to which his foster father belonged, absconded with him from the hospital and kept him hidden in a garden shed for over four months until the end of the war. He worked in the German Democratic Republic (GDR) as a teacher in a youth home. In 1956, he moved to West Berlin and received a higher degree in remedial education (*Heilpädagoge*). He worked for many years in a well-known Berlin clinic for children and youth. For his work educating the public on the horrors of the

Nazi times and his engagement in assisting psychologically-troubled children he received a medal of honor from the German government. In 1992 the brochure "Das Kind Muscha" appeared at the "Gedenkstätte Deutscher Widerstand" (*Memorial to German Resistance*). Based on this brochure Anja Tuckermann wrote the children's book *Muscha*. Müller's autobiographical novel *Ausgegrenzt* appeared in 1999.

**Miroslav Nikolić (Mišo)** (1940–2008) was born on a country road between Požarevac and Petrovac na Mlavi in Serbia. His father was a horse trader and his mother a fortune teller. His family survived the Nazi invasion and subsequent occupation of Yugoslavia in 1941 by continually fleeing, hiding, and confronting official bureaucracy. In 1962, after serving in the Yugoslavian military with his brother, he immigrated to Western Europe. His journey brought him through Italy, France, Belgium, Germany, Poland, and eventually Vienna, where he met his future wife, singer Ruzsa Nikolić-Lakatos. He worked as a house painter, rug dealer, and musician. He played guitar and violin in his family ensemble "Nikolić-Lakatos," with Ruzsa as singer and his two sons as guitarists. In 1995, Mišo began participating in writing workshops organized by Christa Stippinger at the Amerlinghaus in Vienna. He began to write down his own and his family's stories, which resulted in two published autobiographies: ... *und dann zogen wir weiter: Lebenslinien einer Romafamilie* (with a foreword by Mariella Mehr, 1997) and *Landfahrer: Auf den Wegen eines Rom* (2000). His wife Ruzsa continues to live in Vienna and performs regularly as a singer at Romani festivals and events.

**Dotschy Reinhardt** (1975) was born near Ravensburg in Southern Germany. She belongs to one of the main musical Sinti families, the Reinhardts, whose circle includes jazz guitarist Django Reinhardt, guitar player Bobby Falta, and jazz musicians Schnuckenack Reinhardt and Zipflo Reinhardt. By listening to their music, rather than by formal training, she learned to sing and play the guitar. Today she tours with her band around Europe performing songs she has composed and her renditions of classic jazz songs, singing mostly in Romany and English. She lives in Berlin with her Sinti husband, David Rose, also a singer. Her CD *Sprinkled Eyes* appeared in 2006. Her book *Gypsy: Die Geschichte einer großen Sinti-Familie* was published in 2008, and her *Everybody's Gypsy: Popkultur zwischen Ausgrenzung und Respekt* appeared in 2014.

**Otto Rosenberg** (1927–2001) was born in Draugupönen in Eastern Prussia and grew up in Berlin. His father was a horse trader and musician, and his mother was a homemaker. His parents separated when he was an infant, and he lived with his grandmother in Berlin. In 1936, he was incarcerated in the ghetto "Berlin-Marzahn Rastplatz." In 1938, the male members of his family were deported to Sachsenhausen and Oranienburg concentration camps. Shortly before his sixteenth birthday, he was transported to Auschwitz. His 11 siblings perished in Auschwitz. Only he and his mother survived. When the "Gypsy Camp" was liquidated, he was transported to Buchenwald. He worked in Gawabau, installing water and gas pipes. He served in the forced military Dirlewanger company. He was later transported to Bergen-Belsen and participated in the "death march" shortly before the end of the war. After the war, he returned to Berlin to find his mother. He met his wife there, and they had seven children together. He later became chairman of the Landesverband Sinti und Roma Berlin. His memoir is entitled *Das Brennglas* (1998). His daughter, Marianne Rosenberg, is a performer and singer and published her autobiography *Kokolores* in 2006.

**Simone Schönett** (1972–) was born in Villach, Austria, to a Jenisch family. She studied Education and Media Communications at the University of Klagenfurt. *Im Moos* (2001) was her debut novel, followed by *Nötig* (2006), *re:mondo* (2011), *Oberton und Underground* (2012), and *Der private Abendtisch* (2014). Together with Harald Schwinger, she has also written dramatic pieces. She is a co-founder of the artistic collective WORT-WERK; an organizer for the "Nacht der schlechten Texte" (Night of the bad texts), an annual ironic forum for experimental literary forms; a columnist for *Liga*, the Austrian journal for human rights; and an activist for the rights of Roma and Jenisch in Europe. She has received literary prizes, including the Förderpreis des Carl-Mayer-Drehbuchwettbewerbs (together with Harald Schwinger) (2004) and an Austrian national grant for literature (2004/5).

**Ceija Stojka** (1933–2013) was born on March 23, 1933, in a small village inn in Kraubath in Styria, Austria, as part of a travelling Lovara family. On October 17, 1939, she and her family were travelling in Styria when they learned a decree had been passed forbidding all Roma from leaving their place of abode. They decided to move to live with friends in Vienna. In 1941, Ceija's father was arrested, deported in 1942 to Dachau, and murdered in Hartheim as a victim of the T4 euthanasia program. On March 31, Ceija, her mother, and her five siblings were taken from Vienna and eventually deported to Auschwitz. Ceija had the number Z6399 tattooed on her arm. In 1943, Ceija's youngest brother Ossi, aged eight, contracted typhus and died in Auschwitz. In late July 1944, all remaining inmates of the Auschwitz-Birkenau "Gypsy camp" who were able to work were transferred to other concentration camps. On August 1, 1944, Ceija, her mother, and an aunt were transferred to the Ravensbrück women's camp. On the night of August 2, 1944, the 3,000 Roma remaining in Auschwitz were gassed. In January 1944, Ceija was transferred to Bergen-Belsen. On April 15, 1945, British troops liberated Bergen-Belsen. After the war, Ceija and her family resumed the travelling life. She entered the second grade at the age of 12. Later, after her family no longer traded horses because cars became the main means of transportation, she travelled around and sold carpets and fabrics at markets. Eventually she settled in Vienna, married, and had three children and then many grandchildren. In the late 1980s she began to tell her life story in the autobiographies *Wir leben im Verborgenen: Erinnerungen einer Rom-Zigeunerin* (1988); *Reisende auf dieser Welt* (1992); and *Träume, dass ich lebe? Befreit von Bergen-Belsen* (2005). She released a CD of her singing in Romany, *Me Dikhlem Suno* (2000) and published a poetry book, *Meine Wahl zu schreiben—ich kann es nicht* (2003). Her artwork has been exhibited throughout Europe, and in Japan and the United States.

**Karl Stojka** (1931–2003) was born in Wampersdorf, in eastern Austria, on April 30, 1931. (See the entry on Ceija Stojka for their shared family history.) On March 31, 1943, Karl was deported with his family to Auschwitz, and received the number Z5742 tattooed on his arm. He was transported to Buchenwald to perform forced labor. He was considered too young to work, so he was sent back to Birkenau. He survived liquidation of the "Gypsy Camp" and was later sent to Flossenbürg. He took part in the "death march" shortly before the war ended, and in April 1945 the Americans freed him near Roetz, Germany. He returned to live in Vienna, where he began a rug business. He spent a year travelling around the United States. In 1985 he began to paint and started his career as an artist. His paintings depict the lives of persecuted Roma under the Nazis. He exhibited his artworks in Japan, the United States, and Germany. A catalogue of the works he exhibited in the United States, *Nach der Kindheit im KZ kamen die Bilder* (1992) includes his essay about his life. His autobiography *Auf der ganzen Welt zu Hause: Das Leben und Wandern des Zigeuners Karl Stojka* (with Reinhard Pohanka) appeared in 1994.

**Johann Mongo Stojka** (1929–2014) was born in Guntramsdorf in Lower Austria when his family was travelling. On March 31, 1943, he and his family were deported to Auschwitz. He received the number Z5740 tattooed on his arm. (See the entry on Ceija Stojka.) With his brother Karl, Mongo was transported to Buchenwald when the "Zigeunerlager" at Auschwitz was liquidated. Mongo was sent back to Birkenau, and was later in Flossenbürg. He survived the "death march" shortly before the war ended. Afterwards, he went into business with his brother selling rugs in Vienna, and was a well-known singer and storyteller. With his son, the jazz musician Harri Stojka, he published a CD, *Nevi Luma* (1997), singing renditions of traditional songs in Romany. In 1999 Mongo planted a chestnut tree on the "Hellerwiese," the location of a camp for travelling Roma during World War II. In 2003, the park was renamed "Barankapark" for the family's grandmother. His autobiography *Papierene Kinder. Glück, Zerstörung und Neubeginn einer Roma-Familie in Österreich* appeared in 2000. His book *Legenden der Lowara: Lieder und Geschichten der Roma von Wien*, a compilation of Lovara legends and songs, was published in 2004.

**Latscho Tschawo** (1932–) spent two years in Auschwitz, and was freed on January 28, 1945. He does not talk much about the details of his early life. Instead, his book *Die Befreiung des Latscho Tschawo: Ein Sinto Leben in Deutschland* (1984), recounts his travails in the Federal Republic of Germany (FRG) and the German Democratic Republic (GDR) after the war. He looked for family survivors, but most members, including his father in Sachsenhausen, had been murdered in concentration camps. Officials captured Latscho as an orphan and institutionalized him. He escaped, but was caught again. He escaped again, stole a bicycle, and was considered a delinquent. He found an uncle, who tried to assume custody of him, but officials denied the request, and Latscho was institutionalized again. At 18, he immigrated to the GDR. After 16 years, he found his mother, who lived in the FRG, and Latscho immigrated to her. He started a family and had ten children. His life in the FRG became riddled with hostile encounters with non-Roma and with the police. For a variety of petty crimes, he received a prison sentence of nine years and six months. The justice system characterized him as a "hardened, irreformable criminal." In his book he asks whether he really became "free" on January 28, 1945.

**Walter Winter** (1919–2012) was one of nine children in a Sinto family of fairground owners and workers. They travelled throughout Germany, and he attended various schools. He was conscripted into the German navy, but later discharged on "racial grounds." He was deported in 1943 to the "Gypsy Camp" at Auschwitz-Birkenau. Just before the "Gypsy Camp" was liquidated, he was deported to Ravensbrück and then Sachsenhausen. After the war he was employed in the family circus and amusement park. His first memoir, *Winterzeit: Erinnerungen eines deutschen Sinto, der Auschwitz überlebt hat*, edited by Thomas Neumann and Michael Zimmermann, appeared in 1999 and was translated as *Winter Time: Memoirs of a German Sinto who survived Auschwitz* by Struan Robertson in 2004. A second memoir appeared in 2009 under the title *Z 3105: Der Sinto Walter Winter überlebt den Holocaust*, edited by Karin Guth.

# Bibliography

Aarne, Antti. *The Types of Folktale: A Classification and Bibliography*. Translated and enlarged by Stith Thompson. 2nd rev. edn. Helsinki: Suomalainen Tiedeakatemia Academia Scientiarum Fennica, 1964.

Adelsberger, Lucie. *Auschwitz: Ein Tatsachenbericht. Das Vermächtnis der Opfer für uns Juden und für alle Menschen*. Berlin: Lettner Verlag, 1956.

Adelson, Leslie. "Against Between: A Manifesto." In *Unpacking Europe: Towards a Critical Reading*, edited by Iftikar Dadi and Salah Hassan, 244–55. Rotterdam, NL: NAi Publishers, 2002.

Amann, Klaus and Karl Wagner, eds. *Literatur und Nation. Die Gründung des Deutschen Reiches 1871 in der deutschsprachigen Literatur*. Vienna, Cologne and Weimar: Böhlau, 1996.

*Amerlinghaus*. http://www.amerlinghaus.at/

Anderson, Benedict. *Imagined Communities: Reflections on the Origin and Spread of Nationalism*. London: Verso, 1991.

Anderson, Siwan. "The Economics of Dowry and Brideprice." *Journal of Economic Perspectives*, 21.4, (Fall 2007): 151–74.

Angeren-Franz, Lily van. *"Polizeilich zwangsentführt": Das Leben der Sintizza Lily van Angeren-Franz von ihr selbst erzählt aufgezeichnet von Henny Clemens und Dick Berts*, ed. Hans-Dieter Schmid, and trans. from the Dutch by Martina den Hertog-Vogt. Quellen und Dokumentationen zur Stadtgeschichte Hildesheims, ed. Herbert Reyer, Stadtarchiv Hildesheim, vol. 15. Hildesheim: Verlag Gebrüder Gerstenberg, 2004.

Appell, Laura W. R. "Menstruation among the Rungus of Borneo: An Unmarked Category." In *Blood Magic: The Anthropology of Menstruation*, eds Thomas Buckley and Alma Gottlieb, 94–112. Berkeley: University of California Press, 1988.

Assmann, Aleida. *Erinnerungsräume: Formen und Wandlungen des kulturellen Gedächtnisses*. Munich: Beck, 1999.

Assmann, Jan. *Das kulturelle Gedächtnis: Schrift, Erinnerung und politische Identität in frühen Hochkulturen*. Munich: Beck, 1992.

"AUFgelesen: Simone Schönett." Literradio. March 9, 2011. http://archiv.literadio.org/get.php/766pr1606

*Avoiding the Dependency Trap: A Regional Human Development Report*. Bratislava: United Nations Development Programme and the Regional Bureau for Europe and the Commonwealth of Independent States. 2002.

Baeyer, Walter von. "Über die Auswirkungen rassischer Verfolgung von Konzentrationslagerhaft vom Standpunkt des Psychiaters." *Emuna. Horizonte.*, 5.1, (1970): 65–8.

Bahlmann, Lith and Mathias Reichelt, eds. *Ceija Stojka (1933-2013): "Sogar der Tod hat Angst vor Auschwitz." "Even Death is Terrified of Auschwitz." "Vi o Merimo Daral Katar o Auschwitz."* Nuremberg: Verlag für Moderne Kunst, 2014.

Barth, Fredrik, ed. *Ethnic Groups and Boundaries. The Social Organisation of Culture Difference.* Boston: Little, Brown, 1969.

Bauer, Yehuda. "Gypsies." Volume 2 of *Encyclopedia of the Holocaust*, ed. Israel Gutman, New York: Macmillan, 1990. 634–8.

Baumeister, Roy F. "Masochism as escape from self." *Journal of Sex Research*, 25.1, (February 1988): 28–59.

Baumel, Judith Tydor. *Double Jeopardy: Gender and the Holocaust.* London and Portland, OR: Vallentine Mitchell, 1998.

BBC News Europe. "Q & A: France Roma Expulsions." October 19, 2010. http://www.bbc.co.uk/news/world-europe-11027288

Bell, Michele Ricci. "Lyrical Redefinitions of Heimat in Mariella Mehr's *Nachrichten aus dem Exil* and *Widerwelten*." *German Quarterly*, 83.2, (Spring 2010): 189–211.

Benedik, Stefan, Barbara Tiefenbacher, and Heidrun Zettelbauer. *Die imaginierte "Bettlerflut": Temporäre Migrationen von Roma/Romnija—Konstrukte und Positionen.* Klagenfurt: Drava, 2013.

Berg, Stefan. "The Unending Battle Over Berlin's Sinti and Roma Memorial." *Spiegel Online*. December 28, 2010. http://www.spiegel.de/international/germany/a-project-in-jeopardy-the-unending-battle-over-berlin-s-sinti-and-roma-memorial-a-736716.html

Berger, Karin (dir.). *Ceija Stojka: Porträt einer Roma*. DVD. Vienna: Navigator Film, 1999.

Bhabha, Homi K., ed. *The Location of Culture.* London and New York: Routledge, 1994.

—"Culture's In-Between." In *Questions of Cultural Identity*, eds Stuart Hall and Paul Du Gay, 53–60. London, Thousand Oaks and New Delhi: Sage Publications, 1996.

—*Nation and Narration.* London: Routledge, 1994.

Blandfort, Julia. *Die Literatur der Roma Frankreichs.* Memesis: Romanische Literaturen der Welt. Ed. Ottmar Ette. Vol. 60. Berlin, Munich, Boston: de Gruyter, 2015.

Block, Martin. "Die Literatur der Zigeuner (Sinti und Roma)." *Kindlers Neues Literatur Lexikon*, vol. 20. Munich: Kindler Verlag, 2001. 569–75.

Bock, Gisela. *Zwangssterilisation im Nationalsozialismus: Studien zur Rassenpolitk und Frauenpolitik.* Opladen: Westdeutscher Verlag, 1986.

Bogdal, Klaus-Michael. *Europa erfindet die Zigeuner: Eine Geschichte von Faszination und Verachtung.* 4th edn. Berlin: Suhrkamp, 2013.

Bondy, Ruth. "Women in Theresienstadt and the Family Camp in Birkenau." In *Women in the Holocaust*, eds Dalia Ofer and Lenore J. Weitzman, 310–26. New Haven and London: Yale University Press, 1998.

Bott-Bodenhausen, Karin. "Kultursplitter." In Bott-Bodenhausen, ed., *Sinti in der Grafschaft Lippe*, 179–201.

—"Prosoziales Verhalten: Formen der Hilfe für Sinti." In *Sinti in der Grafschaft Lippe*, Bott-Bodenhausen, ed., 129–73.

Bott-Bodenhausen, Karin, ed. *Sinti in der Grafschaft Lippe. Studien zur Geschichte der "Zigeuner" im 18. Jahrhundert.* Munich: Minerva-Publikationen, 1988.

Breger, Claudia. *Ortlosigkeit des Fremden: "Zigeunerinnen" und "Zigeuner" in der deutschsprachigen Literatur um 1800.* Cologne: Böhlau, 1998.

Bibliography 247

Briel, Petra-Gabriele. *"Lumpenkind und Traumprinzessin": zur Sozialgestalt der Zigeuner in der Kinder- und Jugendliteratur seit dem 19. Jahrhundert.* Gießen: Focus, 1989.

Burleigh, Michael and Wolfgang Wippermann. *The Racial State: Germany 1933–1945.* Cambridge: Cambridge University Press, 1991.

Caplan, Paula J. *The Myth of Women's Masochism.* New York: E. P. Dutton, 1985.

Caruth, Cathy. *Unclaimed Experience: Trauma, Narrative, and History.* Baltimore and London: Johns Hopkins University Press, 1996.

Cech, Petra and Christiane Fennesz-Juhasz. "Märchen, Erzählungen und Lieder der Lovara." In *Fern von uns im Traum,* 397–424.

Cech, Petra, Mozes F. Heinschink, and Dieter W. Halwachs. "Herkunft der Texte, Quellen und Reihung. In *Kerzen und Limonen,* 241–80.

*Ceija Stojka: Bilder und Texte. 1989–1995.* Vienna: Graphische Kunstanstalt Otto Sares GmbH, 1995.

Cohen, Rich. *Israel is Real: An Obsessive Quest to Understand the Jewish Nation and its History.* New York: Farrar, Straus and Giroux, 2009.

Collins, Patricia Hill. *Black Feminist Thought: Knowledge, Consciousness, and the Politics of Empowerment.* New York: Routledge, 2000.

Crenshaw, Kimberlé. "Mapping the Margins: Intersectionality, Identity Politics, and Violence against Women of Color." *Stanford Law Review,* 43.6, (1991): 1241–99.

Cresswell, Tim. *In Place/Out of Place: Geography, Ideology, and Transgression.* Minneapolis and London: University of Minnesota Press, 1996.

Crowe, David and John Kolsti, eds. *The Gypsies of Eastern Europe.* Armonk, NY and London: M. E. Sharpe, Inc., 1991.

Danckwortt, Barbara. "Franz Mettbach—Die Konsequenzen der preußischen 'Zigeunerpolitik' für die Sinti von Friedrichslohra." *Historische Rassismusforschung. Ideologen—Täter—Opfer. Mit einer Einleitung von Wolfgang Wippermann,* eds Barbara Danckwortt, Thorsten Querg, and Claudia Schöningh, 273–95. Hamburg: Argument, 1995.

Davidson, Cathy N. and Jessamyn Hatcher, eds. *No More Separate Spheres!* Durham, NC and London: Duke University Press, 2002.

Davies, Owen. *Witchcraft, Magic and Culture 1736–1951.* Manchester and New York: Manchester University Press, 1999.

Davis, Penelope. "Gender Differences in Autobiographical Memory for Childhood Emotional Experiences." *Journal of Personality and Social Psychology,* 79.3, (1999): 498–510.

De Kock, Leon. "Interview with Gayatri Chakrovorty Spivak: New Nation Writers Conference in South Africa." *Ariel: A Review of International English Literature,* 23.3 (July 1992): 29–47.

Denman, Maratte C. "Homeless in Heidi-Land–Figuring Gypsies in Mariella Mehr's Play *Akte M. Xenos ill. *1947-Akte C. Xenos ill. *1966.*" Paper at the 1998 conference of the Pacific Ancient and Modern Language Association, San Jose, California, 1998.

Deveaux, Monique. "Feminism and Empowerment: A Critical Reading of Foucault." In *Feminist Interpretations of Michel Foucault,* ed. Susan J. Hekman, 211–37. University Park, Pennsylvania: The Pennsylvania State University Press, 1966.

Dill, Bonnie Thornton and Ruth Enid Zambrana. "Critical Thinking about Inequality: An Emerging Lens." In *Emerging Intersections: Race, Class, and Gender in Theory, Policy, and Practice,* eds Bonnie Thornton Dill and Ruth Enid

Zambrana. 1–21. New Brunswick, NJ and London: Rutgers University Press, 2009.

Djurić, Rajko. *Roma und Sinti im Spiegel der deutschen Literatur: ein Essay*. *Mit einem Vorwort und Einleitungskapitel von Joachim S. Hohmann*. Studien zur Tsiganologie und Folkloristik 13. Frankfurt a. M.: Lang, 1995.

Döbler, Katharina. "Nachwort." In Mariella Mehr, *Daskind*. 227–38.

*Dokumentations- und Kulturzentrum deutscher Sinti und Roma*. http://www.sintiundroma.de/

Döring, Hans-Joachim. *Die Zigeuner im nationalsozialistischen Staat*. Kriminologische Schriftenreihe aus der Deutschen Kriminologischen Gesellschaft 12. Hamburg: Kriminalistik Verlag 1964.

Douglas, Mary. *Purity and Danger: An Analysis of Concept of Pollution and Taboo*. 1966. New York: Routledge, 2002.

Douglass, Ana and Thomas A. Vogler, eds. *Witness and Memory: The Discourse of Trauma*. New York and London: Routledge, 2003.

Durrant, Jonathan B. *Witchcraft, Gender and Society in Early Modern Germany*. Leiden, Boston: Brill, 2007.

Eder, Beate. *Geboren bin ich vor Jahrtausenden ... Bilderwelten in der Literatur der Roma und Sinti*. Klagenfurt: Drava, 1993.

Eder-Jordan, Beate. "Ausbruch aus der Anonymität: Roma-Literatur im historischen und kulturellen Kontext." In Ceija Stojka, *Meine Wahl zu schreiben*, 65–75.

—"'Traditionen wurden weitergegeben wie die Märchen': Eine Sintiza gewährt Einblick in ihr Leben." *L'Homme: Zeitschrift für feministische Geschichtswissenschaft*, 7.1 (1996): 170–83.

El-Tayeb, Fatima. "Foreigners, German, and German Foreigners: Constructions of National Identity in Early 20th Century Germany." In *Unpacking Europe: Towards a Critical Reading*, eds Salah Hassan and Iftikhar Dadi, 72–81. Rotterdam: Museum Boijmans Van Beuningen and NAi Publishers, 2001.

Emigh, Rebecca Jean, Eva Fodor, and Iván Szelényi. "The Racialization and Feminization of Poverty?" In *Poverty, Ethnicity and Gender*, eds Emigh and Szelényi, 1–32.

Emigh, Rebecca Jean and Iván Szelényi, eds. *Poverty, Ethnicity and Gender in Eastern Europe during Market Transition*. Westport, CT and London: Praeger Publishers, 2001.

"Emils Ring." Journalists of the Henri-Nannen-Schule, August 21, 2014. http://www.zeit.de/zeit-magazin/leben/2014-07/sinti-hamburg-emil-weiss

Engbring-Romang, Udo. "Glossar." In *"Wer wird die nächste sein?"* eds Mettbach and Behringer, 117–26.

"Entwicklung der Kaufkraft in Deutschland (DM Basis)." http://www.lindcom.de/Lindcom/Home/Statistik/kaufkraft.pdf

Enzensberger, Ulrich. "Anmerkungen." In Otto Rosenberg. *Das Brennglas*, 146–59.

Erich, Renata M. "Roma in Österreich." In *Die Sprache der Roma*, eds Dieter W. Halwachs and Florian Menz, 13–16.

*Farbe bekennen: Afro-deutsche Frauen auf den Spuren ihrer Geschichte*, eds Audre Lorde, Katharina Oguntoya, May Opitz, and Dagmar Schultz. Berlin: Orlando Verlag, 1986.

Faris, Wendy B. *Ordinary Enchantments: Magical Realism and the Remystification of Narrative*. Nashville: Vanderbilt University Press, 2004.

Fauser, Markus. "Gedächtnistheorien." In *Einführung in die Kulturwissenschaften*. Darmstadt: Wissenschaftliche Buchgesellschaft, 2003. 116–38.

Bibliography 249

Felman, Shoshana, and Dori Laub, M.D. *Testimony: Crisis of Witnessing in Literature, Psycholanalysis, and History.* New York: Routledge, 1992.

Felski, Rita. "Redescriptions of Female Masochism." *Minnesota Review,* 63/64, (Spring/Summer 2005): 127–39. http://minnesotareview.dukejournals.org/content/2005/63-64/127.full.pdf

*Fern von uns im Traum… /Te na dikas sunende… : Märchen, Erzählungen und Lieder der Lovara./Lovarenge paramiči, tertenetura taj gjila,* eds Petra Cech, Christiane Fennesz-Juhasz, Dieter W. Halwachs, and Mozes F. Heinschink. Klagenfurt: Drava, 2001.

Ficowski, Jerzy. "Supplementary Notes on the Mageripen Code Among Polish Gypsies." *Journal of the Gypsy Lore Society.* Series 3, 30, (1951): 123–32.

—"Die Vernichtung." In *Auschwitz vergast, bis heute verfolgt: Zur Situation der Roma (Zigeuner) in Deutschland und Europa,* ed. Tilman Zülch. Reinbek: Rowohlt, 1979.

Finnan, Carmel. "From Survival to Subversion: Strategies of Self-Representation in Selected Works by Mariella Mehr." In *The Role of the Romanies,* eds Saul and Tebbutt, 145–55.

Fivush, Robyn. "Constructing Narrative, Emotion, and Self in Parent-Child Conversations about the Past." In *The Remembering Self: Construction and Accuracy in the Self-Narrative,* eds Ulric Neisser, Robyn Fivush, 136–57. Cambridge: Cambridge University Press, 1994.

Fivush, Robyn and Janine P. Buckner. "Creating Gender and Identity Through Autobiographical Narratives." In *Autobiographical Memory and the Construction of a Narrative Self: Developmental and Cultural Perspectives,* eds Robyn Fivush and Catherine A. Haden, 149–67. Mahwah, NJ: Lawrence Erlbaum Associates, 2003.

Fivush, Robyn and E. Reese. "The Social Construction of Autobiographical Memory." In *Theoretical Perspectives on Autobiographical Memory,* eds M. A. Conway, D. C. Rubin, H. Spinner, and W. A. Wagenaar, 115–32. Dordrecht: Kluwer Academic, 1992.

Fonseca, Isabel. *Bury Me Standing: The Gypsies and Their Journey.* New York: Vintage, 1995.

"Forced Prostitution in WW II Camps Highlighted in Hamburg Exhibit." October 31, 2007. http://www.haaretz.com/news/forced-prostitution-in-wwii-camps-highlighted-in-hamburg-exhibit-1.232197

Fordham, Kim. "Fear of Difference and its Consequences in Selected Works of Mariella Mehr." In *Crossing Over: Redefining the Scope of Border Studies,* eds Antonio Medina-Rivera and Diana Orendi, 75–86. Newcastle: Cambridge Scholars Publishing, 2007.

—"What leads a child to kill? Violence and its effects in selected works of Mariella Mehr." In *Liebchen, sag,* 49–53.

Foucault, Michel. *Discipline and Punish.* Trans. Alan Sheridan. New York: Vintage, 1978.

—"The Subject and Power." *Critical Inquiry* 8 (Summer 1982). 777–95.

Frank, Michael. "'… dass hochdero Lande und Unterthanen davon rein und unbeschwert bleiben sollen'—Lippische Obrigkeit und Sinti in der frühen Neuzeit." In *Sinti in der Grafschaft Lippe,* ed. Bott-Bodenhausen, 43–65.

Franz, Philomena. *Zigeunermärchen.* Bonn: Europa Union Verlag, 1989.

—*Zwischen Liebe und Haß: Ein Zigeunerleben.* Freiburg, Basel and Vienna: Herder, 1992.

Fraser, Angus. *The Gypsies.* Oxford and Cambridge, MA: Blackwell, 1995.

French, Lorely. "An Austrian Roma Family Remembers: Trauma and Gender in

Autobiographies by Ceija, Karl, and Mongo Stojka." *German Studies Review*, 31.1 (February 2008): 65–86.

— "How to Cook a Hedgehog: Ceija Stojka and Romani ('Gypsy') Cultural Identity Through the Culinary Literary Arts." In *Cuisine and Symbolic Capital: Food in Film and Literature*, ed. Cheleen Mahar, 102–26. Newcastle upon Tyne: Cambridge Scholars Press, 2010.

— "'If we didn't have this story, we would not have this day': Roma 'Gypsy' Stories as Sustenance in Difficult Life Stages." *Pacific Coast Philology*, 49.1 (2014). University Park, PA: Penn State University Press, 2014: 5–24.

— "LIVE-DANCE-PAINT-WRITE: A Multi-Media Project on Romani ('Gypsy') Artist, Writer, Singer, and Educator Ceija Stojka. " *Interface: The Journal of Education, Community, and Values*, 10.3, (April 2010). http://commons.pacificu.edu/cgi/viewcontent.cgi?article=1015&context=inter10

French, Lorely, Louise Stoehr, and Gudrun Sherman, "Berlin als interkultureller Text." DVD. Philadelphia: American Association of Teachers of German, 2012.

Freund, Florian, Gerhard Baumgartner, and Harald Greifeneder. *Vermögensentzug, Restitution und Entschädigung der Roma und Sinti*. Veröffentlichungen der Österreichischen Historikerkommission. Vermögensentzug während der NS-Zeit sowie Rückstellungen und Entschädigungen seit 1945 in Österreich, 23.2. Vienna and Munich: Oldenbourg, 2004.

Fricke, Thomas. *Zigeuner im Zeitalter des Absolutismus. Bilanz einer einseitigen Überlieferung. Eine sozialgeschichtliche Untersuchung anhand südwestdeutscher Quellen*. Pfaffenweiler: Centaurus, 1996.

Friedman, Jonathan C. *Speaking the Unspeakable: Essays on Sexuality, Gender, and Holocaust Survivor Memory*. Lanham, New York and Oxford: University Press of America, 2002.

Gajarawala, Toral Jatin. *Untouchable Fictions: Literary Realism and the Crisis of Caste*. New York: Fordham University Press, 2013.

Geertz, Clifford, ed. *Old Societies and New States: The Quest for Modernity in Africa and Asia*. New York: The Free Press, 1967.

Gellner, Ernest. *Nations and Nationalism*. Introduction by John Breuilly, 1983. 2nd edn. Ithaca: Cornell University Press, 2008.

Gilman, Sander L. *Difference and Pathology: Stereotypes of Sexuality, Race, and Madness*. Ithaca and London: Cornell University Press, 1985.

Gilsenbach, Reimar. *Weltchronik der Zigeuner. 2500 Ereignisse aus der Geschichte der Roma und Sinti, der Luri, Zott und Boza, der Athinganer, Tattern, Heiden und Sarazenen, der Bohémiens, Gypsies und Gitanos und aller Minderheiten, die "Zigeuner" genannt werden*. Vol. I: Von den Anfängen bis 1599. Studien zur Tsiganologie und Folkloristik 10. Frankfurt a. M.: Peter Lang, 1994.

Giorgianni, Erika. "Der Mut des Wortes: Zeitgenössische Zigeunerliteratur in Österreich." Tesi die Laurea, Universita' ca' Foscari di Venezia. 2002.

Goebel, Nancy. "Source needed for quote." Foucault-L mail-list. March 2, 2005. http://foucault.info/Foucault-L/archive/msg09605.shtml

Gosewinkel, Dieter. "Die Nationalisierung der Staatsangehörigkeit im Deutschen Kaiserreich." *Das Deutsche Kaiserreich in der Kontroverse*, eds Sven Oliver Müller and Cornelius Torp, 392–405. Göttingen: Vandenhoeck & Ruprecht, 2009.

Grellmann, Heinrich Moritz Gottlieb. *Die Zigeuner. Ein historischer Versuch über die Lebensart und Verfassung, Sitten und Schicksahle dieses Volks in Europa, nebst ihrem Ursprunge*. Dessau/Leipzig: n.p., 1783.

Grobbel, Michaela. "Contemporary Romany Autobiography as Performance." *German Quarterly*, 76.2 (2003): 140–54.

—"Crossing Borders of Different Kinds: Roma Theater in Vienna." *Journal of Austrian Studies*, 48.1, forthcoming (Spring 2015).

—*Enacting Past and Present: The Memory Theaters of Djuna Barnes, Ingeborg Bachmann, and Marguerite Duras*. Lanham: Lexington Books, 2004.

Gronemeyer, Reimer. *Zigeuner im Spiegel früher Chroniken und Abhandlungen. Quellen vom 15. bis zum 18. Jahrhundert*. Gießen: Focus, 1987.

Gronemeyer, Reimer and Georgia A. Rakelmann. "Rom Zigeuner auf dem Weg in die Postmoderne." In *Roma: Das unbekannte Volk: Schicksal und Kultur*, eds Mozes F. Heinschink and Ursula Hemetek, 14–28. Vienna, Cologne and Weimar: Böhlau Verlag, 1994.

Grosz, Elizabeth. *Volatile Bodies: Toward a Corporeal Feminism*. Bloomington: Indiana University Press, 1994.

Guy, Will. *Between Past and Future: The Roma of Central and Eastern Europe*. Hatfield, Hertfordshire: University of Hertfordshire Press, 2001.

Hackl, Erich. "Vorwort." In Eder. *Geboren bin ich vor Jahrtausenden…* .

Halbwachs, Maurice. *On Collective Memory*, ed. and trans. with an introduction by Lewis A. Coser. Chicago: University of Chicago Press, 1992.

Hall, Kim F. *Things of Darkness: Economies of Race and Gender in Early Modern England*. Ithaca and London: Cornell University Press, 1995.

Halwachs, Dieter W. "Romani in Österreich." In *Die Sprache der Roma: Perspektiven der Romani-Forschung in Österreich im interdisziplinären und internationalen Kontext*, eds Dieter W. Halwachs and Florian Menz, 112–46. Klagenfurt: Drava, 1999.

Hancock, Ian. "The Eastern European Roots of Romani Nationalism." In *The Gypsies of Eastern Europe*, eds Crowe and Kolsti, 133–50.

—"Gypsy History in Germany and Neighbouring Lands: A Chronology Leading to the Holocaust and Beyond." In *The Gypsies of Eastern Europe*, eds Crowe and Kolsti, 11–30.

—"On the Interpretation of a Word: Porrajmos as Holocaust." 2006. The Romani Archives and Documentation Center. http://www.radoc.net/radoc.php?doc=art_e_holocaust_interpretation&lang=ry&articles=true

—"'Uniqueness' of the Victims: Gypsies, Jews and the Holocaust." In *Without Prejudice: The EAFORD International Review of Racial Discrimination*, 1.2 (1988): 45–67.

—*We are the Romani people/Ame sam e Rromane dzene*. Hatfield, Hertfordshire: University of Hertfordshire Press, 2002.

Hanssen, Beatrice. "Elfriede Jelinek's Language of Violence." *New German Critique*, 68 (Spring/Summer 1996): 79–112.

Hanstein, Ewald. *Meine hundert Leben: Erinnerungen eines deutschen Sinto*. Aufgezeichnet von Ralf Lorenzen. Mit einem Geleitwort von Henning Scherf. Bremen: Donat Verlag, 2005.

Haraway, Donna Jeanne. *Simians, Cyborgs, and Women: The Reinvention of Nature*. London: Free Association Books, 1991.

*Harri Stojka*. http://www.harristojka.at/hs/

Harris, Melvin. *Patterns of Race in the Americas*. New York: W. W. Norton, 1964.

Haupt, Gernot. *Antiziganismus und Religion: Elemente einer Theologie der Roma-Befreiung*. Vienna and Berlin: LIT Verlag, 2009.

—*Antiziganismus und Sozialarbeit: Elemente einer wissenschaftlichen Grundlegung, gezeigt an Beispielen aus Europa mit dem Schwerpunkt Rumänien*. Berlin: Frank & Timme, 2006.

# Bibliography

Heinemann, Marlene. *Gender and Destiny: Women Writers and the Holocaust*. New York, Westport, CT, and London: Greenwood, 1986.

Heinschink, Mozes. "E Romani Čhib—Die Sprache der Roma." In *Roma: Das unbekannte Volk: Schicksal und Kultur*, eds Mozes F. Heinschink and Ursula Hemetek, 110–28. Vienna, Cologne, and Weimar: Böhlau Verlag, 1994.

Heller, Wilfried. "Zur Bedeutung von Ethnizität in Transformationsländern unter dem Einfluss von Globalisierung." In *Ethnizität in der Transformation*, eds Heller, Jordan, Kahl, and Sallanz, 9–25.

Heller, Wilfred, Peter Jordan, Thede Kahl, Josef Sallanz eds. *Ethnizität in der Transformation*. Vienna and Berlin: LIT Verlag, 2006.

Hemetek, Ursula. *Mosaik der Klänge: Musik der ethnischen und religiösen Minderheiten in Österreich*. Vienna: Böhlau, 2001.

Henderson, Jeffrey. *The Maculate Muse: Obscene Humor in Attic Comedy*, Oxford: Oxford University Press, 1991.

Herbert, Ulrich, ed. *National Socialist Extermination Policies: Contemporary German Perspectives and Controversies*. New York: Berghahn Books, 2000.

Hilberg, Raul. "Gypsies." In *The Holocaust Encyclopedia*, ed. Walter Laqueur, 271–7. New Haven: Yale University Press.

Hohmann, Joachim H. *Geschichte der Zigeunerverfolgung in Deutschland*, revised edn. Frankfurt a. M.: Campus, 1988.

—*Verfolgte ohne Heimat: Geschichte der Zigeuner in Deutschland*. Studien zur Tsiganologie und Folkloristik 1. Frankfurt a. M., Bern, New York and Paris: Peter Lang, 1990.

—*Zigeuner und Zigeunerwissenschaft: Ein Beitrag zur Grundlagenforschung und Dokumentation des Völkermords im "Dritten Reich."* Marburg and Lahn: Guttandin & Hoppe, 1980.

hooks, bell. *Feminism is for Everybody: Passionate Politics*. Cambridge, MA: South End Press, 2000.

—*Yearning: Race, Gender, and Cultural Politics*. Boston: South End, 1990.

Horvath, Stefan. *Atsinganos: Die Oberwarter und Roma und ihre Siedlungen*. Oberwart: edition lex liszt, 2013.

—*Ich war nicht in Auschwitz: Erzählungen*. Oberwart: edition lex liszt 12, 2003.

—*Katzenstreu: Erzählung*. Oberwart: edition lex liszt 12, 2007.

Hübschmannová, Milena. "Birth of Romani Literature in Czechoslovakia. Social and Political Background." *Cahiers de Littérature Orale*, 30 (1991): 91–7.

Hucker, Stephen J. "Sexual Masochism: Psychopathology and Theory." In Laws and O'Donohue, *Sexual Deviance*, 250–63.

Huonker, Thomas. *Diagnose: "moralisch defekt". Kastration, Sterilisation und Rassenhygiene im Dienst der Schweizer Sozialpolitik und Psychiatrie 1890–1970*. Zürich: Orell Füssli, 2003.

—*Fahrendes Volk—verfolgt und verfemt: Jenische Lebensläufe*. Zürich: Limmat Verlag, 1987.

Imbusch, Peter. "Der Gewaltbegriff." In *Internationales Handbuch der Gewaltforschung*, eds Wilhelm Heitmeyer and John Hagan, 26–57. Wiesbaden: Westdeutscher Verlag, 2002.

—*Moderne und Gewalt: Zivilisationstheoretische Perspektiven auf das 20. Jahrhundert*. Wiesbaden: Verlag für Sozialwissenschaften, 2005.

Jameson, Fredric. *The Political Unconscious: Narrative as a Socially Symbolic Act*. Ithaca, NY: Cornell University Press, 1981.

*Jenischer Kulturverband Österreich*. http://members.aon.at/jenisch.at/

Karamehic-Oates, Adna. "European Roma Learn from African American Rights Struggle." *Open Society Foundation.* http://blog.soros.org/2010/06/european-roma-learn-from-african-american-rights-struggle/

Karpati, Mirella. "Geschichtliches." In *Zigeuner*, ed. Anno Wilms, 7–24. Zürich/Freiburg im Breisgau: Atlantis Verlag, 1972.

Kathöfer, Gabi. *Auszug in die Heimat: Zum Alteritäts(t)raum Märchen.* Hildesheim, Zürich, and New York: Georg Olms Verlag, 2008.

Kelley, Robin D. G. "Interview with Robin D.G. Kelley. Edited Transcript." California Newsreel. 2003. http://www.pbs.org/race/000_About/002_04-background-02-05.htm

Kenrick, Donald. *Gypsies: From the Ganges to the Thames.* Hatfield, Hertfordshire: University of Hertfordshire Press, 2002.

—"Romanies without a Road." *Contemporary Review*, 232 (1978): 153–6.

Kenrick, Donald and Grattan Puxon. *The Destiny of Europe's Gypsies.* London: Chatto-Heinemann for Sussex University Press, 1972.

Keppler, Angela. "Soziale Formen individuellen Erinnerns: Die kommunikative Tradierung von (Familien-)Geschichte." In Harald Welzer, ed. *Das soziale Gedächtnis: Geschichte, Erinnerung, Tradierung.* 137–59. Hamburg: Hamburger Edition, 2001.

Kertész Wilkinson, Irén. *Vásár van előttem : egyéni alkotások és társadalmi kontextusok egy dél-magyarországi oláhcigány lassú dalban/The Fair is ahead of me. Individual creativity and social contexts in the performances of a south-east Hungarian Vlach Gypsy slow song.* Budapest: Institute of Musicology of the Hungarian Academy of Sciences, 1997.

*Kerzen und Limonen/Momelja hem limonja: Märchen der Arlije./Arlijengere paramisja.* Petra Cech, Mozes F. Heinschink, and Dieter W. Halwachs eds. Klagenfurt: Drava, 2009.

King, Deborah. "Multiple Jeopardy: The Context of a Black Feminist Ideology." In *Feminist Frameworks*, 3rd edn, eds Alison M. Jaggar and Paula S. Rothenberg. New York: McGraw-Hill, 1993.

Kingston, Drew A. and Pamela M. Yates. "Sexual Sadism: Assessment and Treatment." In *Sexual Deviance*, eds Laws and O'Donohue, 231–49.

Knesebeck, Julia von dem. *The Roma Struggle for Compensation in Post-War Germany.* Hatfield, Hertfordshire: University of Hertfordshire Press, 2011.

Kóczé, Angéla. "Gender, Ethnicity and Class: Romani Women's Political Activism and Social Struggles." PhD dissertation, Central European University, Budapest, Hungary. 2011. www.etd.ceu.hu/2012/sphkoc01.pdf

König, Ulrich. *Sinti und Roma unter dem Nationalsozialismus: Verfolgung und Widerstand.* Bochum: Studienverlag Dr. N. Brockmeyer, 1989.

Krausnick, Michail, ed. *"Da wollten wir frei sein!": Eine Sinti-Familie erzählt.* Mit Fotos aus dem Familienalbum, aus dem Bundesarchiv Koblenz und von Klaus Fark. Weinheim and Basel: Beltz Verlag, 1983.

—*Die Zigeuner sind da. Roma und Sinti zwischen Gestern und Heute.* Würzburg: Arena, 1981.

—*Wo sind sie hingekommen? Der unterschlagene Völkermord an den Sinti und Roma.* Gerlingen: Bleicher Verlag, 1995.

Kristov, Nicholas D. and Sheryle WuDunn. *Half the Sky: Turning Oppression into Opportunity for Women Worldwide.* New York: Vintage, 2009.

Lacková, Ilona. *A False Dawn: My Life as a Gypsy Woman in Slovakia.* Hatfield, Hertfordshire: University of Hertfordshire Press, 1999.

Lagrene, Reinhold. "Anhang: Die Geschichte von Chinto Mari." In *Zigeunerbilder*, eds Solms and Strauß, 101–12.
—"Mündliche Erzählkunst als Volkskultur—Betrachtungen aus der Innensicht." In *Zigeunerbilder*, eds Solms and Strauß, 91–100.
Langer, Lawrence. *Admitting the Holocaust: Collected Essays*. New York and Oxford: Oxford University Press, 1995.
Laws, D. Richard and William T. O'Donohue, eds. *Sexual Deviance: Theory, Assessment, and Treatment*. New York and London: The Guilford Press, 2008.
Lemon, Alaina. "Telling Gypsy Exile: Pushkin, India, and Romani Diaspora." In *Realms of Exile: Nomadism, Diasporas, and Eastern European Voices*, ed. Domnica Radulescu, 29–48. Lanham, Boulder, New York and Oxford: Lexington Books, 2002.
Lentin, Ronit. *Gender & Catastrophe*. London and New York: Zed Books, 1997.
Lévi-Strauss, Claude. *Tristes Tropiques*. Trans. J. and D. Weightman. London: Cape, 1973.
Lewy, Guenter. *The Nazi Persecution of the Gypsies*. Oxford and New York: Oxford University Press, 2000.
Leydesdorff, Selma, Luisa Passerini, and Paul Thompson, eds. *Gender and Memory*. Vol. IV of *the International Yearbook of Oral History and Life Stories*. Oxford: Oxford University Press, 1996.
*Liebchen, sag/Vitamia, dimmi: 60 Jahre Mariella Mehr/A Mariella Mehr per I suoi 60 anni*. Fondazione Franco Beltrametti. Lugano: Arti Grafiche Veladini, 2007.
Liégeois, Jean-Pierre. *Roma in Europe*. Strasbourg: Council of Europe Pub. 2007.
Lorde, Audre. "Age, Race, Class, and Sex: Women Redefining Difference." In *Sister Outsider: Essays and Speeches*. 114–23. Freedom, CA: The Crossing Press, 1984.
—"Apartheid U.S.A." In *A Burst of Light: Essays by Audre Lorde*, 27–38. Ithaca, NY: Firebrand Books, 1988.
—"The Master's Tools Will Never Dismantle the Master's House." In *Sister Outsider: Essays and Speeches*, 110–13. Freedom, CA: The Crossing Press, 1984.
Luchterhand, Elmer. "Social Behavior of Concentration Camp Prisoners: Continuities and Discontinuites with Pre- and Postcamp Life." In *Survivors, Victims, and Perpetrators*, Joel Dimsdale, ed., 259–83. New York: Hemisphere Publishing, 1980.
Lugones, María. "Playfulness, 'World'-Travelling, and Loving Perception." *Hypatia*, 2.2, (1987): 3–19.
Maclear, Kyo. "The Limits of Vision: *Hiroshima Mon Amour* and the Subversion of Representation." In *Witness and Memory*, eds Douglass and Vogler, 233–47.
"*mahrime* (ritually unclean)" *Rombase*. http://ling.kfunigraz.ac.at/~rombase/
Malinowski, Krimhilde. *Das Schweigen wird gebrochen: Erinnerungen einer Sintezza an den Nationalsozialismus*, ed. Norbert Aas. Bayreuth: Bumerang-Verlag, 2003.
Margalit, Gilad. *Germany and its Gypsies: A Post-Auschwitz Ordeal*. Madison: University of Wisconsin Press, 2002.
"Maria Theresia and Joseph III: Policies of Assimilation in the Age of Enlightened Absolutism." *Rombase*. http://ling.kfunigraz.ac.at/~rombase/cgi-bin/art.cgi?src=data/hist/modern/maria.en.xml
Matras, Yaron. *Romani: A Linguistic Introduction*. Cambridge: Cambridge University Press, 2002.
Mayall, David. *Gypsy Identities 1500–2000: From Egipcyans and Moon-men to the Ethnic Romany*. London and New York: Routledge, 2004.
Mayerhofer, Claudia. *Dorfzigeuner: Kultur und Geschichte der Burgenland-Roma von der ersten Republik bis zur Gegenwart*. Vienna: Picus, 1987.

Mehr, Mariella. *Angeklagt*. Zürich: Nagel & Kimche, 2002.
—"Autobiographisches einer Jenischen." In *focus*, 39 (March 1973). 10.
—*Brandzauber*. Zürich/Frauenfeld: Nagel & Kimche, 1998.
—*Daskind*. Zürich/Frauenfeld: Nagel & Kimche, 1995; Berlin: Ullstein, 1997.
—"E. Xenos 1922, Einer von 600." In *RückBlitze*, 10–23. Bern: Zytglogge, 1990.
—"Frauenmut." In *RückBlitze*, 175–84. Bern: Zytglogge.
—*Kinder der Landstrasse: Ein Hilfswerk, ein Theater und die Folgen*. Bern: Zytglogge, 1987.
—*Das Licht der Frau*. Bern: Zytglogge, 1984.
—"Die Lust an der Selbstpreisgabe: Mariella Mehr im Werkstattgespräch." *Neue Züricher Zeitung* (November 25, 1997): 35.
—*RückBlitze*. Bern: Zytglogge, 1990.
—*steinzeit*. 1981. 7th edn. Bern: Zytglogge, 1990.
—"Von Mäusen und Menschen: Vortrag an der psychiatrischen Klinik St. Urban LU, 19. Dezember 1996." In *Blickwechsel: Die multikulturelle Schweiz an der Schwelle zum 21. Jahrhundert*, Simone Prodilliet, ed., 155–69. Lucern: Caritas-Verlag, 1998.
—*Zeus oder der Zwillingston*. Zürich: Edition RF, 1994.
Meier, Thomas Dominik and Rolf Wolfensberger. *"Eine Heimat und doch keine". Heimatlose und Nicht-Sesshafte in der Schweiz (16.–19. Jahrhundert)*. Zürich: Chronos Verlag, 1998.
Meiners, Christoph. "Über die Farben, und Schattierungen verschiedener Völker." *Neues Göttingisches historisches Magazin*, I, (1792): 611–72. http://www.ub.uni-bielefeld.de/diglib/aufkl/neugoemag/neugoemag.htm
—"Über die Verschiedenheit der cörperlichen Grösse verschiedener Völker." *Neues Göttingisches historisches Magazin*, I, (1792): 697–726. http://www.ub.uni-bielefeld.de/diglib/aufkl/neugoemag/neugoemag.htm
Mellen, Joan. *Magic Realism*. Vol. 5 of *Literary Topics*. Farmington Hills, MI: The Gale Group, 2000.
Mettbach, Anna and Josef Behringer. *"Wer wird die nächste sein?" Die Leidensgeschichte einer Sintezza, die Auschwitz überlebte*. Frankfurt a. M.: Brandes & Apsel, 1999.
Michaels, Jennifer. "The Impact of Audre Lorde's Politics and Poetics on Afro-German Women Writers." *German Studies Review*, 29.1 (February 2006): 22–40.
Miklosich, Franz. *Ueber die Mundarten und die Wanderungen der Zigeuner Europas*. Denkschriften der kaiserlichen Akademie der Wissenschaften, Philosophisch-historische Klassen. Vols 21–31. Vienna: n.p., 1872–80.
Miller, Carol. "American Rom and the Ideology of Defilement." In *Gypsies, Tinkers, and Other Travellers*, ed. Farnham Rehfisch, 41–54. New York: Academic Press, 1975.
—"Respect and Rank Among the Machvaia Roma." *Journal of the Gypsy Lore Society*, Series 5, 4.2 (August 1994): 75–94.
Miller, Carolyn R. "Genre as Social Action." In *Genre and the New Rhetoric*, eds Aviva Freedman and Peter Medway, 23–42. London: Taylor and Francis, 1984.
Milton, Sybille. "Context of the Holocaust." *German Studies Review*, 13.2, (May 1990): 271–3.
—"Sinti and Roma in Twentieth-Century Austria and Germany." *German Studies Review*, 23.2, (May 2000): 317–31.
"Moral Relativism." *Stanford Encyclopedia of Philosophy*. http://plato.stanford.edu/entries/moral-relativism/
Müller, Joseph Muscha. *"Und weinen darf ich auch nicht…" Ausgrenzung, Sterilisation, Deportation—Eine Kindheit in Deutschland*. Berlin: Parabolis, 2002.

Müller-Hill, Benno. *Murderous Science: Elimination by Scientific Selection of Jews, Gypsies, and Others, Germany 1933–1945.* Trans. George R. Fraser. Oxford: Oxford University Press, 1988.

—*Tötliche Wissenschaft: Die Aussonderung von Juden, Zigeunern und Geisteskranken 1933–1945.* Reinbek bei Hamburg: Rowohlt, 1984.

Münster, Sebastian. *Cosmographia.* Basel: Henrichum Petri, 1550.

"Nazi Camps Forced Women into Prostitution." March 2, 2009. http://www.instantnews.net/nazi-camps-forced-women-into-prostitution.aspx

Neidhardt, Friedhelm. "Gewalt, Soziale Bedeutungen und sozialwissenschaftliche Bestimmungen eines Begriffs." In *Was ist Gewalt? Auseinandersetzungen mit einem Begriff.* Band 1: Zum Gewaltbegriff im Strafrecht, ed. Volker Krey, 109–47. Wiesbaden: Bundeskriminalamt, 1986.

Nemeth, David J. and Rena C. Gropper. "A Cyber-Ethnographic Foray into GR&T Internet Photo Blogs." *Romani Studies*, 18.1 (June 2008): 39–70.

*Nevipe—Rundbrief des Rom e.V.* http://www.romev.de/wp-content/uploads/2013/PDF/Rundbrief_42.pdf

Nikolić, Mišo. *Landfahrer: Auf den Wegen eines Rom.* Klagenfurt: Drava, 2000.

—. *. . . und dann zogen wir weiter: Lebenslinien einer Romafamilie.* Mit einem Vorwort von Mariella Mehr. Klagenfurt: Drava, 1997.

Nirenberg, Jud, ed. *Gypsy Sexuality: Romani and Outsider Perspectives on Intimacy.* Mesa, AZ: Clambake Press, 2011.

Nyman, Lynette Marie. "A Complex Relationship: Menopause, Widowhood, and the Distribution of Power Among Older Rom Women." *Journal of the Gypsy Lore Society*, Series 5, 7.2 (August 1997): 97–117.

Okely, Judith. "Gypsy Women." In *The Traveller-Gypsies*, 201–14.

—"Gypsy Women: Models in Conflict." In *Perceiving Women*, ed. S. Ardener. 55–86. London: Malaby, 1975.

—"Kontinuität und Wandel in den Lebensverhältnissen und der Kultur der Roma, Sinti und Kalé." In *Europäische Roma—Roma in Europa*, eds Reetta Toivanen and Michi Knecht. Berlin: Berliner Blätter: Ethnographische und ethnologische Beiträge, 39, (2006): 25–41.

—*Own or Other Culture.* London and New York: Routledge, 1996.

—*The Traveller-Gypsies.* 1983. Cambridge, MA: Oxford University Press, 1998.

Olney, James. *Memory and Narrative: The Weave of Life-Writing.* Chicago: University of Chicago Press, 1998.

Opfermann, Ulrich F. *"Dass sie den Zigeuner-Habit ablegen." Die Geschichte der "Zigeuner-Kolonien" zwischen Wittgenstein und Westerwald.* Frankfurt a. M.: Peter Lang, 1996.

Pankok, Moritz, ed. *Ort des Sehens. Kai Dikas. Place to See 2*, with a foreword by Ceija Stojka and introduction by André J. Raatzsch. Berlin: Kai Dikas, 2012.

Paterno, Wolfgang. "Die Stojkas: Eine spezielle Wiener Familie. Ihr Patriarch Mongo Stojka im Porträt." *Falter* 20/04 (14–20 May, 2004): 72–3.

Patrut, Iulia-Karin, George Guțu, and Herbert Uerlings, eds. *Fremde Arme—arme Fremde: "Zigeuner" in Literaturen Mittel- und Osteuropas.* Inklusion/Exklusion: Studien zu Fremdheit und Armut von der Antike bis zur Gegenwart 3. Frankfurt a. M.: Peter Lang, 2007.

Péter, László. "How Extreme Marginalization Generates Ethnicity." In *Ethnizität in der Transformation*, eds Heller, Jordan, Kahl, and Sallanz, 99–118.

Piasere, Leonardo. "Quanto può esere plurietnico uno stato?" In *Un mondo di mondi: Antropologia delle Culture Rom*, 11–20. Naples: l'ancora, 1999.

# Bibliography 257

Pott, Augustus F. *Die Zigeuner in Europa und Asien. Ethnographischlinguistische Untersuchungen, vornehmlich ihrer Herkunft und Sprache nach gedruckten und ungedruckten Quellen.* Halle: E. Heynemann, 1845.

Prüger, Heidelinde. *Zigeuner Sein.* Klagenfurt: Hermagoras/Mohorjeva, 2001.

*Radgenossenschaft der Landstrasse: Dachorganisation der Jenischen der Schweiz.* http://www.radgenossenschaft.ch/

Ramsauer, Nadja. *"Verwahrlost": Kindswegnahmen und die Entstehung der Jugendfürsorge im schweizerischen Sozialstaat 1900–1945.* Zürich: Chronos Verlag, 2000.

Reemtsma, Katrin. *Sinti und Roma. Geschichte, Kultur, Gegenwart.* Munich: Beck, 1996.

Reinhardt, Dotschy. *Gypsy: Die Geschichte einer großen Sinti-Familie.* Frankfurt a. M.: Scherz/S. Fischer Verlag, 2008.

—*Everybody's Gypsy: Popkultur zwischen Ausgrenzung und Respekt.* Berlin: Metrolit, 2014.

Reinhardt, Lolo. *Überwintern: Jugenderinnerungen eines schwäbischen Zigeuners. Ergänzt von seiner Schwester Märza Winter. Mit einer Erzählung von Richar Scherer.* Ed. Monika Döppert. Gerlingen: Bleicher Verlag, 1999.

"Relativism," *Stanford Encyclopedia of Philosophy.* http://plato.stanford.edu/entries/relativism/

Renner, Erich, ed. *"Und wir waren auch Naturmenschen:" Der autobiographische Bericht des Sinti-Musikers und Geigenbauers Adolf Boko Winterstein und andere persönliche Dokumente von und über Sinti und Roma.* Studien zur Tsiganologie und Folkloristik. Ed. Joachim S. Hohmann. Vol. 22. Frankfurt a. M., Berlin, Bern, New York, Paris and Vienna: Peter Lang, 1997.

Riegler, Roxane. *Das Verborgene sichtbar machen: Ethnische Minderheiten in der österreichischen Literatur der neunziger Jahre.* Austrian Culture 43. Margarete Lamb-Faffelberger, General Editor. New York, Washington, D.C., Baltimore, Bern, Frankfurt, Berlin, Brussels, Vienna, and Oxford: Peter Lang, 2010.

Ringelheim, Joan. "Women and the Holocaust: A Reconsideration of Research." In *Different Voices: Women in the Holocaust,* eds Carol Rittner and John K. Roth. New York: Paragon House, 1993.

*Der Rom und der Teufel/O rom taj o beng: Märchen, Erzählungen und Lieder der Roma aus dem Burgenland/Romane pararistscha, phukajiptscha taj gila andar o Burgenland,* eds Dieter W. Halwachs, Emmerich Gärtner-Horvath, and Michael Wogg. Klagenfurt: Drava, 2000.

"Roma Attentat in Oberwart." ORF TVTHEK. February 5, 1995. http://tvthek.orf.at/program/Archiv/7648449/Roma-Attentat-in-Oberwart/3229505

*Roma und der Arbeitsmarkt: Berufs-und Bildungsförderung für Sinti und Roma in Deutschland.* Berliner Institut für Vergleichende Sozialforschung. Berlin: Edition Parabolis, 2007.

"Romani Library Project." 2006. Next Page Foundation. http://www.npage.org/article89.html

*[romani] Projekt.* http://romaniprojekt.uni-graz.at/index.en.html

*Romano Centro.* http://www.romano-centro.org

*Rombase: Didactically edited information on Roma.* http://ling.kfunigraz.ac.at/~rombase/

Rose, Romani, ed. *"Den Rauch hatten wir täglich vor Augen": Der nationalsozialistische Völkermord an den Sinti und Roma.* Heidelberg: Wunderhorn and Dokumentations- und Kulturzentrum Deutscher Sinti und Roma, 1999.

# Bibliography

Rosenbach, Franz. *"Der Tod war mein ständiger Begleiter": Das Leben, das Überleben und das Weiterleben des Sinto Franz Rosenbach. Von ihm selbst erzählt und dokumentiert von Norbert Aas.* Munich: Bayerische Landeszentrale für politische Bildungsarbeit, 2005.
Rosenberg, Marianne. *Kokolores: Autobiographie.* Berlin: Ullstein. 2006.
Rosenberg, Otto. *Das Brennglas.* Aufgezeichnet von Ulrich Enzensberger mit einem Vorwort von Klaus Schütz. 1998. Munich: Knaur, 2002.
Rroma Foundation/Rromani Fundacija. http://foundation.rroma.org/
Rudiger, Johann. *Von der Sprache und Herkunft der Zigeuner aus Indien.* Hamburg: Buske, 1790.
Said, Edward. *Orientalism.* New York: Vintage Books, 1979.
Saltmarsh, Matthew. "Sarkozy Toughens on Illegal Roma." *New York Times.* 29 July 2010. http://www.nytimes.com/2010/07/30/world/europe/30france.html?_r=1
Sälzer, Anna-Lena. "Vom Fixieren in Aktenprosa und metrischen Gesängen. Schrift und Gewalt in Mariella Mehrs Roman *Zeus oder der Zwillingston.*" In *Fremde Arme,* eds Patrut, Guţu and Uerlings, 203–17.
*Samudaripen-Porrajmos: Roma Holocaust.* https://groups.yahoo.com/neo/groups/Roma_Holocaust/info
Saul, Nicholas. *Gypsies and Orientalism in German Literature from Realism to Modernism.* London: Legenda, 2007.
Saul, Nicholas and Susan Tebbutt. *The Role of the Romanies: Images and Counter-Images of "Gypsies"/Romanies in European Cultures.* Liverpool: Liverpool University Press, 2004.
Scarry, Elaine. *The Body in Pain: The Making and Unmaking of the World.* New York: Oxford University Press, 1985.
Schacter, Daniel L. *Searching for Memory: The Brain, the Mind, and the Past.* New York: Basic Books, 1996.
"Schäft qwant: transnationaler Verein für Jenische Zusammenarbeit und Kulturaustausch." http://www.jenisch.info/
Schär, Bernhard. "Mariella Mehr als Inspiration für eine postkoloniale Geschichte der Schweiz—Einige Überlegungen." In *Liebchen, sag/Vitamia, dimmi: 60 Jahre Mariella Mehr/A Mariella Mehr per I suoi 60 anni.* 8–16. Fondazione Franco Beltrametti. Lugano: Arti Grafiche Veladini, 2007.
*Schloss Hartheim.* http://www.schloss-hartheim.at/index.php/en/
Schönett, Simone. *Im Moos. Roman.* Weitra/Plöchl: Bibliothek der Provinz, 2001.
—*re:mondo.* Klagenfurt: Edition Meerauge, Verlag Johannes Heyn, 2010.
*Schriftenreihe des Dokumentations- und Kulturzentrums Deutscher Sinti und Roma.* Heidelberg: Dokumentations- und Kulturzentrum Deutscher Sinti und Roma, 1995.
Schultz, Dagmar. *Audre Lorde: The Berlin Years 1984–1992.* DVD. New York: Third World Newsreel, 2012.
Sennett, Richard. "The Rhetoric of Ethnic Identity." In *The Ends of Rhetoric: History, Theory, Practice,* eds John Bender and David Wellbery. Stanford: Stanford University Press, 1990.
Shaktini, Namascar. "Introduction." In *On Monique Wittig,* ed. N Shaktini, 1–6.
Shaktini, Namascar, ed. *On Monique Wittig: Theoretical, Political, and Literary Essays.* Urbana and Chicago: University of Illinois Press, 2005.
Sibley, David. *Outsiders in Urban Society.* New York: St. Martin's Press, 1981.
Siegried, Alfred. *Kinder der Landstrasse. Ein Versuch zur Sesshaftmachung von Kindern des fahrenden Volkes.* Zürich/Stuttgart: Pro Juventute, 1964.

Silverman, Carol. "Music and Power: Gender and Performance among Roma (Gypsies) of Skopje, Macedonia." In *Music, Language and Literature of the Roma and Sinti*, ed Max Peter Baumann, 247–62. Intercultural Music Studies 11. Berlin: Verlag für Wissenschaft und Bildung, 2000.
—*Romani Routes: Cultural Politics & Balkan Music in Diaspora*. Oxford: Oxford University Press, 2012.
"Sinti und Roma zeigen *Weltwoche* an." *Spiegel*. April 10, 2012. http://www.spiegel.de/kultur/gesellschaft/zentralrat-der-sinti-und-roma-zeigt-weltwoche-an-a-826666.html
*Sinti Allianz Deutschland*. http://sintiallianz-deutschland.de
Slunsky, Maria. "Simone Schönett: *re:mondo* Literaturhaus Wien. November 30, 2010. http://www.literaturhaus.at/index.php?id=8625
Smith, Anthony D. *National Identity*. Reno and Las Vegas: University of Nevada Press, 1991.
Smith, Sidonie and Julia Watson. *Reading Autobiography: A Guide for Interpreting Life Narratives*. 2001. 2nd edn. Minneapolis and London: University of Minnesota Press, 2010.
Sollors, Werner, ed. *The Invention of Ethnicity*. Oxford: Oxford University Press, 1989.
Solms, Wilhelm and Daniel Strauß, eds. *"Zigeunerbilder" in der deutschsprachigen Literatur*. Schriftenreihe des Dokumentations- und Kulturzentrums Deutscher Sinti und Roma. Heidelberg: Dokumentations- und Kulturzentrum Deutscher Sinti und Roma, 1995.
Spivak, Gayatri Chakravorty. "Afterword." *Imaginary Maps: Three Stories by Mahasweta Devi*, 197–205. New York and London: Routledge, 1995.
—"Can the Subaltern Speak?" In *Marxism and the Interpretation of Culture*, eds Cary Nelson and Lawrence Grossberg. Urbana and Chicago: University of Illinois Press, 1988.
—"Subaltern Studies: Deconstructing Historiography." In *Selected Subaltern Studies*, eds Ranajit Guha and Gayatri Chakravorty Spivak, 3–32. Oxford: Oxford University Press, 1988.
—"Translator's Preface." In *Imaginary Maps: Three Stories by Mahasweta Devi*, xxiii–xxix. New York and London: Routledge, 1995.
Spuller, Willi and Sebastian Schottke. *Katzenstreu: Hörspiel-Dokumentation von Willi Spuller und Sebastian Schottke nach dem Buch "Katzenstreu" von Stefan Horvath*. CD. Oberwart: blaubogen and edition lex liszt 12, 2008.
Stewart, Michael. "Brothers in Song: The Persistence of (Vlach) Gypsy Community and Identity in Socialist Hungary." PhD dissertation, London School of Economic and Political Science, 1987.
—"Conclusions: Spectres of the Underclass." In *Poverty, Ethnicity and Gender*, eds Emigh and Szelényi, 191–203.
—*The Time of the Gypsies*. Boulder, CO/Oxford: Westview Press, 1997.
Stippinger, Christa, ed. *Ceija Stojka: Auschwitz ist mein Mantel: Bilder und Texte*. Vienna: Edition Exil, 2008.
Stojka, Ceija. "Amenca ketane." In *Romane Ġila: Lieder und Tänze der Roma in Österreich*, ed. Ursula Hemetek, with Walter Deutsch, Mozes Heinschink, Albena Pantchev, Ulrich Goebel, and Hans Reister. 45–6. Vienna: Österreichische Dialektautoren und Institut für Volksmusikforschung an der Hochschule für Musik und darstellende Kunst, 1992.
—"'Du darfst keine Andere sein.' Ceija Stojka im Gespräch mit Karin Berger." In *Wir leben im Verborgenen*, Ceija Stojka, 97–155.

—"Ich lebe mit meinen Verstorbenen." In *Fern von uns im Traum*, 303–7.
—*Meine Wahl zu schreiben—ich kann es nicht: Gedichte (Romanes, deutsch) und Bilder*. Landeck: EYE: Literatur der Wenigerheiten, 2003.
—*Reisende auf dieser Welt: Aus dem Leben einer Rom-Zigeunerin*. Vienna: Picus, 1992.
—"Sie waren Rom vom Stamm der Lowara." In *Ceija Stojka*, Stippinger, 11–32.
—*Träume ich, dass ich lebe?: Befreit aus Bergen-Belsen*. Vienna: Picus, 2005.
—"Unsere Seele war krank." In *Fern von uns im Traum*, 308–17.
—*Wir leben im Verborgenen: Erinnerungen einer Rom-Zigeunerin*. 1st edn. Vienna: Picus, 1988; 4th edn, 2003.
Stojka, Karl. *Nach der Kindheit im KZ kamen die Bilder*, ed. Gerald Grassl. Vienna: VIDO—Verein zur Information der Öffentlichkeit zu Kunst, Wissenschaft und Kulturpolitik, 1992.
—*Wo sind sie geblieben? Geschunden, gequält, getötet—Gesichter und Geschichten von Roma, Sinti und Juden aus Konzentrationslagern des Dritten Reiches*, eds Sonja Haderer-Stippel and Peter Gstettner. Vienna: Bundesministerium für Bildung, 2003.
Stojka, Karl and Reinhard Pohanka. *Auf der ganzen Welt zu Hause: Das Leben und Wandern des Zigeuners Karl Stojka*. Vienna: Picus, 1994.
Stojka, Mongo. *Papierene Kinder: Glück, Zerstörung und Neubeginn einer Roma-Familie in Österreich*. Vienna: Molden, 2000.
—"Unsere alte Welt." In *Fern von uns im Traum*, 246–71.
"Stolpersteine." http://www.stolpersteine.com
Suleiman, Susan Rubin. "(Re)Writing the Body: The Politics and Poetics of Female Eroticism." In *The Female Body in Western Culture: Contemporary Perspectives*, ed. S. R. Suleiman, 7–29. Cambridge, MA and London: Harvard University Press, 1986.
Surdu, Laura and Mihai Surdu, eds. *Broadening the Agenda: The Status of Romani Women in Romania. A Research Report Prepared for the Roma Participation Program*. New York: Open Society, 2006. http://www.opensocietyfoundations.org/reports/broadening-agenda-status-romani-women-romania
Sutherland, Anne. *Gypsies: The Hidden Americans*. Prospect Heights, IL: Waveland Press, Inc, 1975. Reissued 1986.
Sway, Marlene. *Familiar Strangers: Gypsy Life in America*. Urbana and Chicago: University of Illinois Press, 1988.
"Taboo and Shame (Ladž) in traditional Roma communities." *Rombase*. October 2003. http://ling.kfunigraz.ac.at/~rombase/cgi-bin/art.cgi?src=data/ethn/belief/ladz.en.xml
Tauber, Elisabeth. *Du wirst keinen Ehemann nehmen! Respekt, Bedeutung der Toten und Fluchtheirat bei den Sinti Estraixaria*. Forum Europäische Ethnologie, ed. Dorle Dracklé, Thomas Hauschild, Wolfgang Kaschuba, Orvar Löfgren, Bernd Jürgen Warneken, and Gisela Welz. Nr. 8. Berlin: Lit Verlag, 2006.
Tebbutt, Susan. "Disproportional Representation: Romanies and European Art." In Saul and Tebbutt, *The Role of the Romanies*, 159–77.
—"Marginalization and Memories: Ceija Stojka's Autobiographical Writing." In *'Other' Austrians: Post-1945 Austrian Women's Writing*, ed. Allyson Fiddler, 141–52. Bern: Peter Lang, 1998.
—"'My Name in the Third Reich was Z:5742': The Political Art of the Austrian Rom, Karl Stojka." *Scholarship and the Gypsy Struggle: Commitment in Romani Studies*, ed. Thomas Acton, 69–80. Hatfield, Hertfordshire: University of Hertfordshire Press, 2000.

—"Stolen Childhood: Austrian Romany Ceija Stojka and her Past." In *Holocaust Studies: A Journal of Culture and History*. Children of the Holocaust, special issue, ed. Andrea Reiter. II.2 (Autumn 2005): 37–61.
Tebbutt, Susan, ed. *Sinti and Roma: Gypsies in German-Speaking Society and Literature*. New York and Oxford: Berghahn, 1998.
Thurner, Erika. *National Socialism and Gypsies of Austria*. Tuscaloosa: University of Alabama Press, 1998.
Tong, Rosemarie Putnam. *Feminist Thought: A More Comprehensive Introduction*, 3rd edn. Boulder: Westview Press, 2009.
Toninato, Paola. *Romani Writing: Literacy, Literature and Identity Politics*. Routledge Research in Literacy 4. New York/London: Routledge, 2014.
Trollmann, Manuel. *Johann (Rukeli) Trollmann*. http://www.johann-trollmann.de/
Trumpener, Katie. "The Time of the Gypsies: A 'People without History' in the Narratives of the West." *Critical Inquiry*, 18, (1992): 843–84.
Tschawo, Latscho. *Die Befreitung des Latscho Tschawo: Ein Sinto-Leben in Deutschland*. Bornheim-Merten: Lamuv Verlag, 1984.
Tuckermann, Anja. *"Denk nicht, wir bleiben hier!": Das Lebensgeschichte des Sinto Hugo Höllenreiner*. Munich/Vienna: Carl Hanser Verlag, 2005.
"Udienza al rappresentanti di diverse etnie di Zingari e Rom." Speech by Pope Benedict XVI to Roma and Sinti in Europe. June 11, 2011. http://www.vatican.va/holy_father/benedict_xvi/speeches/2011/june/documents/hf_ben-xvi_spe_20110611_rom_it.html
Uerlings, Herbert. "Fremde Blicke. Zur Repräsentation von 'Zigeunern' in der Schweiz seit dem 19. Jahrhundert (Gottfried Keller, Carl Durheim, Mariella Mehr)." In *Fremde Arme*, eds Patrut, Guṭu, and Uerlings, 143–202.
"UN Presses Czech Republic on Coercive Sterilization of Romani Women." *European Roma Rights Center (ERRC)*. September 4, 2006. http://www.errc.org/cikk.php?cikk=2626See
Vermeersch, Peter. *The Romani Movement: Minority Politics and Ethnic Mobilization in Contemporary Central Europe*. New York and Oxford: Berghahn Books, 2006.
Vidal-Naquet, Pierre. *The Jews: History, Memory, and the Present*, trans. and ed. David Ames Curtis. New York: Columbia University Press, 1996.
Vogler, Thomas. "Introduction." In *Witness and Memory*, eds Douglass and Vogler, 1–54.
Warren, Jonathan and Christina A. Sue. "Comparative Racisms: What Anti-Racists Can Learn From Latin America." *Ethnicities*, 11 (2011): 32–58.
Welzer, Harald, ed. *Das soziale Gedächtnis: Geschichte, Erinnerung, Tradierung*. Hamburg: Hamburger Edition, 2001.
Willems, Wim. *In Search of the true Gypsy. Gypsies as Object of Study during the Enlightenment, Romanticism and Nazism*. London: Frank Cass, 1997.
Wing, Adrien Katherine, ed. "Introduction." *Critical Race Feminism: A Reader*, 1–19. New York and London: New York University Press, 2003.
Winter, Walter Stanosk. *Winter Time: Memoires of a German Sinto Who Survived Auschwitz*. Trans. and annot. by Struan Robertson. Hatfield, Hertfordshire: University of Hertfordshire Press, 2004.
—*Winterzeit: Erinnerungen eines deutschen Sinto, der Auschwitz überlebt hat*, eds Thomas W. Neumann and Michael Zimmermann. Hamburg: Ergebnisse Verlag, 1999.
—*Z 3105: Der Sinto Walter Winter überlebt den Holocaust*, ed. Karin Guth. Hamburg: VSA-Verlag, 2009.

Wittig, Monique. "Some Remarks on *The Lesbian Body.*" In Shaktini, *On Monique Wittig*, 44–8.
Wogg, Michael. "Märchen, Erzählungen und Lieder der Burgenland-Roma." In *Der Rom und der Teufel*, 237–49.
Wohlwend, Lotty. *Silas: gejage—geschunden—gedemütigt. Ein Report.* Frauenfeld, Stuttgart, and Vienna: Huber, 2006.
—*Gestohlene Seelen: Verdingkinder in der Schweiz*. Frauenfeld, Stuttgart, and Vienna: Huber, 2009.
Wolf, Naomi. "What Price Happiness," in *More* (April 2010). http://www.more.com/news/womens-issues/what-price-happiness
Wright, Emily. "To be Roma means to be a traveler and thief." Swissinfo.ch. 7 Sept 2010. http://www.swissinfo.ch/eng/-to-be-roma-means-to-be-a-traveller-and-thief-/28286556
Wright, Margaret. "I Want the Right to Be Black and Me." In *Black Women in White America*, ed. Gerda Lerner, 607–8. New York: Pantheon Books, 1972.
Yates, Pamela M., Stephen J. Hucker and Drew A. Kingston. "Sexual Sadism: Psychopathy and Theory." In *Sexual Deviance*, eds Laws and O'Donohue, 213–30.
Yoors, Jan. *The Gypsies*. Prospect Heights, IL: Waveland Press, 1967. Reissued 1987.
Zantop, Susanne. *Colonial Fantasies: Conquest, Family, and Nation in Precolonial Germany, 1770–1870*. Durham, NC and London: Duke University Press, 1997.
*Zentralrat deutscher Sinti und Roma*. http://zentralrat.sintiundroma.de
Zimmermann, Michael. *Rassenutopie und Genozid: Die nationalsozialistische "Lösung der Zigeunerfrage."* Hamburger Beiträge zur Sozial- und Zeitgeschichte, Vol. 33, ed. Michael Wildt. Hamburg: Hans Christians Verlag, 1996.
—*Verfolgt, vertrieben, vernichtet: die nationalsozialistische Vernichtungspolitik gegen Sinti und Roma*. Essen: Klartext, 1989.
Zipes, Jack. *Breaking the Magic Spell: Radical Theories of Folk and Fairy Tales*. Lexington, KY: University of Kentucky Press, 1979. Revised and expanded edition 2002.
—*Why Fairytales Stick: The Evolution and Relevance of a Genre*. New York and London: Routledge, 2006.
Zwicker, Marianne C. "Journeys into Memory: Romani Identity and the Holocaust in Autobiographical Writings by German and Austrian Romanies." PhD Dissertation, University of Edinburgh, 2009. https://www.era.lib.ed.ac.uk/bitstream/1842/6201/1/Zwicker2010.pdf
*Zwischen Gleichgültigkeit und Ablehnung: Bevölkerungseinstellungen gegenüber Sinti und Roma* (Berlin: Zentrum für Antisemitismusforschung and Institut für Vorurteils- und Konfliktforschung, e.V., 2014), 155–7. http://www.antidiskriminierungsstelle.de/SharedDocs/Downloads/DE/publikationen/Expertisen/Bevoelkerungseinstellungen_Sinti_und_Roma_20140829.pdf?__blob=publicationFile

# Index

abortion, eugenic measures and 197
  in literature by Roma 221
  Roma attitudes towards 89
adaptability 97, 217, 229, 232–3, 235
Adelson, Leslie 39, 39n. 120, 130, 161
African-Americans, and feminist theory 3, 31–3, 233–4
  historical similarity to Roma 33n. 97, 37–8
  slave trade and colonialism 56–7
Allies 125–6
American Roma 12, 69, 75, 78, 196
Amerlinghaus 21, 25, 241
Angeren-Franz, Lily van,
  biography 25, 43, 237
  *"Polizeilich zwangsentführt": Das Leben der Sintizza Lily van Angeren-Franz* 59, 64, 66, 73–4, 78, 81, 82, 83, 85–6, 88n. 73, 89, 91, 94–5, 97, 101, 106n. 164, 117, 120, 122, 128, 146, 237
appearance, physical of Roma 49, 54–5, 70, 233 *see also* stereotypes
Arnim, Achim von 20
art, artist, artistic, artwork vii–viii, 1, 4, 9n. 17, 70, 103, 108, 137, 211, 243

"asocials," ("Asoziale"), Roma considered 19, 114n. 10, 114–15, 128, 217–18
*Asozialenerlaß* (Asocial Decree) 112n. 3
assimilation, definition of 62n. 94
  integration and 34, 48–58
  in the interwar period 58–63
  national identity and 4, 129–32
  policies in the Age of Enlightened Absolutism 55–6
  resistance to 48
  Roma attitudes towards 4, 165
  skepticism towards 232
  versus adaptability 232–5
Assmann, Aleida and Jan 136–8, 152
Athinganoi, etymology of "Zigeuner" 6
Auschwitz, Auschwitz-Birkenau, concentration camp 1n. 3, 2, 27, 61, 70, 73, 83, 91n. 86, 112n. 4, 113, 113n. 7, 114n. 10, 117–20, 122–5, 127, 128, 129, 132, 134, 134n. 3, 136, 141, 146, 147, 147n. 60, 148, 151, 152, 205, 222, 237, 238, 239, 240, 242, 243, 244
*Auschwitz-Erlaß* (Auschwitz Decree) 112
Austria, Austro-Hungarian 11

264  Index

history of Roma in 7, 11, 15–17, 41, 216
Jenisch in 210–12, 214–19
laws against beggars in 17n. 19
Lovara Roma in 143
numbers of Roma in 112
numbers of Roma murdered during Nazi time from 134
prejudices against Roma in 226–8
Pro Juventute in 175, 218
Roma claiming citizenship in 130–2
Romani families in 15, 135–6
Romani organizations in 21
[romani] Projekt 18
see also Oberwart; Vienna
autobiography, motivations for Roma to publish 27–8, 31, 143–4
relationship with fiction 30
theories of 22–31, 105–6, 139–40

Barth, Fredrik 52
Bavaria 52, 57, 61, 131
begging, beggars 13n. 11, 17n. 19, 19, 48, 51, 54, 55n. 66, 96, 126, 175
in literature by Roma 156–7, 218, 225
Behringer, Josef 115–16, 128
Bergen-Belsen, concentration camp 127, 134n. 3, 136, 240, 242, 243
Berger, Karin 145
Berlin 32, 58, 59, 65, 83n. 55, 90n. 86, 204, 206, 228, 239, 240 see also Berlin-Marzahn
Berlin-Marzahn 92, 92n. 93, 100, 109, 111, 117, 118, 119, 238, 242
Bhabha, Homi 5, 38–9, 50, 160, 161
birth, birthing 4, 13, 73–4, 77, 80–2, 84, 98, 102, 104, 136, 154, 175, 208, 218, 228, 233

Black Americans see African-Americans
Block, Martin 19n. 27
Bock, Gisela 114–15
Breger, Claudia 20, 26, 176
brideprice 84, 104
Buchenwald, concentration camp 121, 123, 134n. 3, 136, 242, 243
*Bundesentschädigungsgesetz* (BEG-S, Federal Law of Restitution) 116
burial rituals 220 see also death rituals

Caruth, Cathy 140
children, assimilation of 58–9
care of 92, 206
persecution in Nazi time 27, 122–3, 148–9
removal of Romani from families 5, 16, 55–6, 174–5, 189, 196–7, 197n. 95, 211–12
roles and values in Romani culture of, 65–6, 70, 88–9, 93, 101–3, 109 112, 117–18, 123
violence and 198
Christian, Christianity 51n. 42, 52–4, 56, 57, 146,
clothing 49, 70, 79–80, 107–8n. 170, 126, 141, 145, 147, 166–9, 207–8, 233, 238 see also dresses
concentration camps see *individual camps* (Auschwitz; Buchenwald, etc.)
cooking, customs in Romani culture about 13, 37, 76–79, 81, 88, 88–9, 94, 103–5, 208
courtship 4, 74, 84–6, 102, 106–7
Crenshaw, Kimberlé 35–6
cross-dressing, in Romani tales 168–70
culinary rituals see food

Dachau, concentration camp 111, 123, 127, 136, 148n. 65, 240, 242
dance, dancing 13n. 11, 54, 97–9
  death, rituals 4, 5n. 6, 13, 22–3, 74–5, 81–4, 94, 105, 145–6
  in literature by Roma 154, 156, 158n. 16, 167–8, 188, 192, 210, 212, 213, 220, 225
  of Roma from persecution 51, 113, 118, 122–3, 125, 128, 133–4, 138
  trauma and 140–3
deportation of Roma 55, 61, 90, 112n. 4, 117, 128
Dirlewanger, SS-Kompanie 115, 115–16n. 18, 128, 239, 242
diversity, of Roma 4, 6, 30, 35–6, 56, 68, 71–2, 85, 97, 99, 130–2, 168, 201, 205, 207–9, 234–5
*Dokumentations- und Kulturzentrum deutscher Sinti und Roma* (Documentaion and Cultural Centre of Sinti and Roma) 21
"*Dorfzigeuner*" (village Gypsies) 61, 61n. 90, 96
Douglas, Mary 74
dresses, Romani women wearing 80, 88, 151, 207 *see also* clothing
Dutch 43, 85, 88n. 73, 216, 237

Eder, Eder-Jordan, Beate 13n. 11, 19n. 27, 165, 232
education, educational opportunities 3, 4, 14, 25, 27, 62, 69–71, 88, 101–2, 108, 126, 132, 137, 147–8, 205, 209, 240
Egypt, origin of word "Gypsy" and 6, 50n. 38
Eichendorff, Joseph Freiherr von 20
England 12, 44, 50n. 38, 51n. 42

*Erlaß zur Errichtung von Sammellagern* (Policy for the Construction of Camp Depots) 112n. 4
essentialism
  criticism of 35
  G. Spivak's notion of "strategic use of positivist essentialism" 46, 130, 215, 219
ethnicity, ethnic identity, theories about 63
  construction of 66, 69, 115
  definitions of 43–8
  gender and 30–9, 73, 109, 113, 124–5, 148, 196, 198, 214, 221, 231, 233
  national identity and 132
  Romani writers perspectives on 3, 4, 6, 41–72, 124, 153, 201, 209, 212, 214, 221, 223, 228–30
*ethnies* 24–5, 47, 111n. 2

family, family life, of Roma 4, 6, 13, 59–60, 64–6, 70–1, 77–9, 84–109, 232
  collective memory and 133–52
  importance of for Roma 27, 44, 59, 60–1, 113, 122–4, 129, 132, 204–2, 223–4, 228–9, 231–5
  in literature by Roma 155, 158, 160–1, 166, 170, 183, 201, 204–22
  men's roles in 144–5, 228 *see also* patriarchy
  prominent Romani and Sinti 15–16, 135
  women's roles in 15, 84–92, 94–109, 143–4, 228 *see also* work
Federal Republic of Germany (FRG), West Germany 67, 129

feminism, feminist theories 3, 31–6, 181, 214, 231–4
*Festsetzungserlaß* (Arrest Decree) 112n. 4
Ficowski, Jerzy 78n. 22
finances *see* money
folk tales, wonder tales, fairytales, definitions of 5n. 6
gender and ethnicity in Romani 153–72
individual tales
"Der geizige Bettler" (The Greedy Beggar) 156–9, 161, 163
"Die Geschichte von Chinto Mari" (The Story of Chinto Mari) 159–62
"Das Märchen von den zwei Schwestern" (The Fairy Tale of the Three Sisters) 168–70
"Der Priester und der Teufel" (The Priest and the Devil) 163–4
"Der Reiche Kaufmann und die schöne Danuscha" (The Rich Businessman and the Beautiful Danuscha) 153–5
"Der Rom besiegt den Teufel" (The Rom Defeats the Devil) 164
"Die Tochter" (The Daughter) 163
"Und ich, wohin?" (And I, Where Do I go?) 166
"Warum der Rom bei seiner Frau blieb" (Why the Rom Stayed with His Wife) 162–3
"Die zwei Becher" (The Two Cups) 166–8
magic in 30
folklore, images of Roma in 52, 54, 209, 234
food *see* cooking

fortune telling, fortune tellers 13, 20, 50–1, 51n. 42, 56, 61, 93–5, 112n. 4, 155, 220, 239, 241
Foucault, Michel 6, 176, 197, 197n. 97, 198
France 68, 90, 96, 109, 216, 241
Roma expulsions 209
*see also* Paris
Frankfurt am Main 52, 54, 61n. 90, 239
Franz, Philomena, biography 237–8
*Zigeunermärchen* 153–5, 158, 238
*Zwischen Liebe und Haß* 60, 70–1, 79, 82, 86, 91n. 86, 109, 118, 120, 123–4, 129, 130, 155, 238
Fraser, Angus 44, 45n. 17, 55, 146
Friedman, Jonathan C. 140
funeral practices 82, 139, 145, 154, 212, 220, 226 *see also* burial rituals; death rituals

Gadsche, Gadže, non-Roma, relationships and attitudes towards Roma 6, 13, 17, 19–20, 22, 26, 29, 33n. 97, 35, 41, 45, 48–9, 51–2, 55, 57–8, 60–2, 98–9, 145, 153, 157, 160, 165, 176, 210–13, 215–16, 220, 224, 226–8, 231, 233
Gajarawala, Toral Jatin 28–9
Geertz, Clifford 45–6
Gellner, Ernest 48, 56
gender norms, in Romani autobiographies 74–109
*see also* clothing; dresses; family; ethnicity; marriage; patriarchy; sexuality; work; women
genocidal/genocide 34, 111, 111n. 2, 127
German Democratic Republic (GDR)/East Germany 67, 82, 129, 238, 240, 244

Germany, history of Roma in 11–12, 49–55, 57–8 *see also* interwar period; National Socialism
  linguistical studies in 18–19
  numbers of Roma in 12
  Romani organizations in 21
*Gesetz für Verhütung erbkranken Nachwuchses* (Law for Prevention of Offspring from People Suffering with Hereditary Illnesses) 112n. 4
*Gewalt*, meanings of 176–7, 180, 188
Gilsenbach, Reimar 51n. 42
Goethe, Johann Wolfgang 20
Grellmann, Heinrich 17
Grimmelshausen, Hans Jakob Christoffel von 20
Gypsy, negative connotations of 6–7, 35, 45, 52–4, 59, 61n. 90, 79, 233
  origin of term 50n. 38, 54
  use of the term by Roma 7, 35, 41–2, 204
"Gypsy Camp" (*Zigeunerlager*) 113n. 7, 124, 125, 136, 142, 148, 237, 238, 240, 242, 243, 244

"Habsburg Monarchy/Empire 55–6, 68n. 124
Halbwachs, Maurice 135–6, 138, 152
Halwachs, Dieter 12n. 4
Hamburg 52, 90, 121n. 41
Hancock, Ian 44–5, 112–13n. 6, 158
Hanstein, Ewald, biography 237–8
  *Meine hundert Leben—Erinnerungen eines deutschen Sinto* 42, 53n. 53, 58, 64, 67, 69, 83–4, 88–9, 91n. 86, 93, 97, 103, 106n. 164, 109, 118, 119, 121, 124, 131, 238

Hartheim 136, 136n. 12, 148n. 65, 242
Heinschink, Mozes 25, 156n. 10, 165, 234
Hilfswerk für die Kinder der Landstrasse (Relief Agency for Children of the Road) 5, 15, 175, 196, 239
Himmler, Heinrich 112n. 4, 240
Hitler, Adolf 74, 111
Holocaust *see Porrajmos*/Holocaust
hooks, bell 31–3, 35
Horvath, Stefan, biography 238–9
  *Ich war nicht in Auschwitz. Erzählungen* 222, 238
  *Katzenstreu. Erzählung*;
  *Atsinganos. Die Oberwarter Roma und ihre Siedlungen* 201, 222–8, 239
humor 148, 150, 163–6
Hungarian Roma, 13n. 11, 33n. 97, 71, 99, 146
hybridity 3, 5, 38–9, 138, 161

identity, identities, construction of 3, 62–4, 68–9, 137
  ethnic 13, 34–5, 41–8, 59, 72, 76, 125, 209, 228–9, 234–5
  individual and collective 28, 67, 135
  in literature by Roma 165, 170, 182, 191, 194, 211, 216–17, 228
  national 4, 24–5, 50, 56, 170
  Romani perceptions of 57, 129, 130, 132, 165, 209, 232
illiteracy 41, 62, 69, 111
illness 4, 13, 74–5, 80–4, 128–9, 181
in-betweenness, condition of 39
  Roma expressing 130–2
India, Indian, Indic, Dalit "untouchable caste" 28–9
  origin(s) of Roma 6, 24n. 55; 43–5, 130, 174

# 268  Index

Roma searching for roots in 130, 130n. 77
of Romani language 18
stereotypes of Roma origins in 222
widow sacrifice in and Spivak's theory of the subaltern 38
women's roles in 233–4
integration *see* assimilation and integration
International Romani Writers Association (IRWA) 235n. 14
intersectionality 3, 35–9, 233
interwar period, integration and assimilation in 58–63
Israel 34

Jameson, Frederic 140, 140n. 26, 198
jazz 241, 244
Jenisch, as Roma 7–8, 12, 20–1
characteristics and customs 209–10, 212–15
history 103, 173–6, 179, 182, 189, 195–7, 212, 216–19
language 209, 211
*Jenischer Kulturverband Österreich* 21
Jew, Jewish history, in comparison with Roma 33–5, 52, 53n. 53, 55n. 66, 57, 115, 121, 131, 150
interactions with Roma 58–60, 183, 193, 217
Justin, Eva 27, 68, 118–19, 205

Kalderaš, Kalderash Roma 11, 71–2, 78, 81, 86–7
Kertész Wilkinson, Irén 99–100
Kleist, Heinrich von 20
Kohl, Helmut 127, 129
Krausnick, Michail 19, 64n. 98
Kreutz, Elisabeth, biography 239
writing in *"Da wollten wir frei sein!": Eine Sinti Familie erzählt* 89, 90n. 86, 94, 157–8, 106–7
Kreutz, Friedrich, biography 239
writing in *"Da wollten wir frei sein!": Eine Sinti Familie erzählt* 90n. 86, 116n. 18

Lackenbach 112n. 4, 136
Lacková, Elena (Ilona) 89
Lagrene, Reinhold 156n. 10
"Die Geschichte von Chinto Mari" ("The Story of Chinto Mari") 159–61
Lagrenne, Hildegard, biography 239
writing in *"Da wollten wir frei sein!": Eine Sinti Familie erzählt*, 66–7, 69, 70–1, 77, 80, 82, 84, 86–7, 90, n. 86, 91, 94, 105, 128, 131, 132
laws, against Roma under National Socialism *see individual laws* (Nürnberger; Rassengesetz, etc.)
Lévi-Strauss, Claude 145–56
Liégeois, Jean-Pierre 7
linguist, linguistic 6, 17–18, 37, 43, 69, 176, 189, 215, 218
literacy, illiteracy 4, 25, 41, 48, 56, 62, 69–7, 72, 111, 137–8
Lorde, Audre 31–3, 199
Lovara 5n. 6, 11, 71, 78, 87, 88, 93, 131, 132n. 84, 136, 143, 144, 173, 242, 244
Lübeck 52
Lugones María 231–2

magical realism 5, 158–9
*"mahrime"* (ritually unclean) 13, 75, 76, 81, 103
Malinowski, Krimhilde 42n. 7, 117n. 24
Margalit, Gilad 52, 111n. 1
marginal, marginalized, marginalization 3, 8, 28–33,

35–6, 41, 44–52, 66, 76, 115, 130–2, 199, 222, 231
Maria Theresia, Empress 15, 55, 61
marketing, of Roma culture 38–9, 54
markets, Roma trading at 65, 94, 97, 106, 219, 239, 243
in literature by Roma 213, 216, 220
marriage; arranged 13, 84–5
customs 4, 13, 74, 84–90, 99, 101–2, 104, 108, 207–8, 217–18, 221, 228
endogamous and exogamous 87–8, 210, 217
in literature by Roma 162, 168–9, 217, 221
loyalty in 90, 162–3
policies forbidding 55, 197
masochism 180–1
Matras, Yaron 68
Mauthausen, concentration camp 123, 136, 148
Mehr, Mariella, biography 239–40
*Angeklagt* (Accused) 182, 183–6, 188, 193–5, 197, 240
"Autobiographisches einer Jenischen" 175
*Brandzauber* (Firemagic) 182, 183, 184, 186, 189, 192–6, 240
*Daskind* (Thechild) 182–3, 184, 185, 186–9, 190–2, 193, 194, 195, 198, 240
"E.Xenos 1922, Einer von 600" 175, 189
"Frauenmut" 179, 197–8
*Kinder der Landstrasse: Ein Hilfswerk, ein Theater und die Folgen* 182, 189, 240
*Das Licht der Frau* 179–81, 187, 240
*Rückblitze* 8, 179, 240
*steinzeit* 182, 240
"Von Mäusen und Menschen: Vortrag an der psychiatrischen Klinik St. Urban LU, 19. Dezember 1996" 196
*Zeus oder der Zwillingston* (Zeus or the Twin Sound) 182, 189n. 65, 240
Meiners, Christoph 49n. 32, 50
memorials to Sinti and Roma 83, 85, 137, 204n. 5, 223, 235, 242
memory 4–5, 29, 44, 52, 83, 129, 134–5, 165, 220
collective 47–8, 135–8, 152, 229
communicative 137–8, 150
family 142
gender and 142–6, 152
individual 139–40, 150, 152
men, in feminist theory 33
injustices against in
concentration camps 124–5
sterilization of 114–17
*see also* gender norms; patriarchy; work
Mengele, Josef 122–3, 129, 149
Mettbach, Anna, biography 240
"Wer wird die nächste sein?": *Die Leidensgeschichte einer Sinteza, die Auschwitz überlebte* 42, 65, 79, 90, 95, 116, 128, 158, 240
Middle Ages 52, 76, 208
migration *see* travelling
mimicry 5, 160
minority 8, 44, 68, 224
money 52–3, 82, 84, 89, 92–3, 95–6, 99, 129, 154, 159
in literature by Roma 162–3, 166–8, 185, 226
Müller, Joseph Muscha, biography 240–1
*Ausgrenzung* 42, 53n. 53, 116–17, 129
*mulo* spirits 5n. 6, 15, 81–4, 94, 101, 146, 158n. 16, 212

multilingualism *see* polyglotism
Munich 52, 61
music making/musicians 4, 9, 15, 17, 20, 21, 33n. 97, 35, 38–9, 54, 57, 66, 70, 74, 79, 82, 93–4, 97–101, 105, 123, 126, 135, 137, 144, 153–5, 164, 204, 206, 209, 210, 213, 214, 215, 220, 229, 231, 237, 239, 241, 244 *see also* singing

nation, nationalism, nationhood, notions of 29
　assimilation and 129–32
　building of 24, 34, 37–8, 49–50, 62–3, 170–1
　identity 4, 24, 47–8, 56, 111, 124
　role of literature in 24–5, 48, 54, 170–1
　Romani 24n. 55, 111n. 2
National Socialism, National Socialist, Nazi, persecution of Roma 4, 15, 18–19, 27, 34, 43, 46, 58–62, 68, 73–4, 82, 90–1, 93, 103, 109, 111–32, 134, 136, 173–4, 183, 194 n. 89, 204, 205, 211, 216–18, 222–3, 232 see also individual laws against Roma (*Asozialenerlaß*; *Auschwitz-Erlaß*, etc.)
nature 26, 63, 130, 131–2, 155, 176, 188
Neuengamme, concentration camp 125
Nikolić, Jovan 8n. 16
Nikolić, Mišo, biography 241
　*... und dann zogen wir weiter: Lebenslinien einer Romafamilie* 25, 42, 71, 93, 173, 241
　*Landfahrer: Auf den Wegen eines Rom* 25, 42, 68–9, 71, 78, 81, 87, 90, 96, 100, 104, 105, 109, 241

Nikolić-Lakatos, Ruzsa 71, 87, 98, 104, 105, 241
nomadism 52, 62–6, 69, 111, 130, 132 *see also* travelling
non-Roma *see* Gadsche, Gadže
*Nürnberger Rassengesetze* (Nuremberg Race Laws) 112n. 4

Oberwart bombing of Roma in 6, 222–4, 229, 238
Okely, Judith 14, 45, 75, 145, 196
orality, oral 5, 5n. 6, 17, 19, 26, 29, 34, 37, 66, 131, 137–8, 162, 205–6, 222, 235

Paris 51, 237
patriarchy, patriarchal, perception of Roma and 13–16
　norms 4, 89, 143–4, 180–1, 187
　norms, mitigation and transformation of 3–4, 14, 74, 78–80, 101–9, 207–8, 210–11, 221–2, 227–8, 232–3
pilgrim, pilgrimage 54, 63, 160, 204, 215, 229
place, placelessness, in place/out of place ("*Ortlosigkeit*") 54
poetry of Roma 8n. 16, 131, 175, 243
politics, identity representation and 35–6, 56, 231
　intersections with trauma, memory, narrative, and history 140
　of persecution against Roma 26
　Romani and European 24
　in Romani writing 29–30, 158–9
　ritual, 98–9
polyglotism, 15, 68, 68n. 124
populations of Roma 12
*Porrajmos*/Holocaust 4, 6, 8, 15, 101, 111–25

post-*Porrajmos*/Holocaust
  treatment of victims 125–9
  *see also* restitution
  trauma from 134, 138–43
post-colonial, post-colonialism, 3,
  36–9, 49
*Pro Juventute* 5–6, 15–16, 103,
  174–5, 218, 239, 240
prostitution 121–2, 154–8n. 16,
  197n. 95
purity and pollution taboos *see*
  taboos; "*mahrime*"

race, racial, racism 31, 35–6, 41,
  101–2
  ethnicity and 44–7, 49n. 32
  laws related to 62, 76, 112n. 4,
  114–16, 173–4
  Roma attitudes towards 131, 217
racialization 3, 46–7
*Radgenossenschaft der Landstrasse:*
  *Dachorganisation der*
  *Jenischen der Schweiz* 7, 16,
  21–2, 240
rape, *Porrajmos* meaning 8
  in concentration camps 11, 121–3
  in literature by Roma 181, 183,
  234
*Rassenhygienischen und*
  *Bevölkerungsbiologischen*
  *Forschungsstelle* (Research
  Unit for Racial Hygiene and
  Population Biology) 112n. 4
Ravensbrück concentration camp
  123, 127, 136, 237, 240, 243,
  244
Reinhard, Lolo 9
Reinhardt, Dotschy, biography 241
  *Everybody's Gypsy: Popkultur*
  *zwischen Ausgrenzung und*
  *Respekt* 241
  *Gypsy: Die Geschichte einer großen*
  *Sinti-Familie* 7, 201, 204–9,
  241

relativism, cultural versus moral
  105–6
religion, religious 44, 47, 103, 120,
  145, 165 *see also* Christian,
  Christianity
restitution, post-*Porrajmos*/
  Holocaust; denial of 4,
  16–17, 22–3, 34, 111n. 1,
  115–16, 126–9, 239, 240
Ritter, Robert 27, 28, 112n. 4,
  118–19, 173, 217
Romani Library Project 235n. 14
*Romano Centro* 9, 21
Romantic period, literary mages of
  "Gypsies" in *Rombase* 13, 52,
  55, 75–6, 82, 87, 103
Romany language 4, 6, 8, 15,
  17–18, 26–7, 66–70, 71, 75,
  91, 111, 131, 141, 144, 156n.
  10, 160, 175, 205–6, 227–8,
  232, 235, 241, 243, 244
Rose, David 206–8, 241
Rose, Romani 112–13n. 6, 127
Rosenbach, Franz 60–1, 120
Rosenberg, Marianne 82n. 47,
  145–6, 242
Rosenberg, Otto, biography 241–2
  *Das Brennglas* 25, 27, 79,
  91–2, 93, 94, 100, 113, 116n.
  18, 119, 121, 124, 241–2
*Rroma Foundation, Rromani*
  *Fundacija* 21

Sachsenhausen, concentration
  camp 123, 238, 242, 244
sadomasochism 180–1, 192
Said, Edward 49n. 30
*Samudaripen* (Roma Holocaust)
  8 *see also Porrajmos*/
  Holocaust
sanitation 117–18, 143
Scarry, Elaine 178, 182, 184–6, 199
Schacter, Daniel 140–1
Schönett, Simone; biography 242

*Im Moos* 201, 209–14, 216, 218–19, 228, 242
*re:mondo* 168n. 48, 201, 214–22, 232, 242
schooling, policies and laws restricting Roma 57, 58–9, 70, 112, 117, 139, 212
Roma encouragement of 59, 70–1, 82, 106n. 164, 147
Serb, Serbia, Serbian 8n. 16, 71, 241
sexuality, gender and 54, 73–4, 78, 84, 103–4, 121, 140
  in Romani literature 164–5, 168, 185, 187
  taboos against talking about 15, 73–4, 101, 207, 221
  theories about 35
shaving of hair in concentration campus 4, 113, 118–21, 143
Siegfried, Alfred 196–7
Silverman, Carol 13–14, 24n. 55, 33n. 97, 38–9, 54, 98, 108
singing, song 8, 26, 37, 72, 97–9, 131, 138, 144, 147, 147n. 60, 148, 155, 209, 234, 241, 242
Sinti, Sinto, Sintiza, Sintizza, Sintitsa, Sinteza, Sintezza, terms 7
  culture, customs, and history 11–12, 13n. 11, 57, 58–60, 66, 67, 73, 75–6, 77–8, 81–2, 83, 84–8, 91n. 86, 92, 95, 105, 116, 124, 127, 128, 131, 133, 145–6
  in literature by Sinti 155, 159–61, 204–9, 229, 232
  populations 12
*Sinti Allianz Deutschland* 21
skin color 32, 49–53, 53n. 53, 56, 62, 227
skirt tossing pollution 78, 80, 103
slavery/slave trade 56–7, 225
sexual *see* prostitution

Smith, Anthony 24, 28, 47, 111n. 2
solidarity, in literature by Roma 215, 218, 220, 229
  among Romani men 123–4, 147–50
  among Romani women 78–80, 122–4, 147–50
  of Roma 1, 24, 35, 39, 42, 46, 48, 60, 66, 113–14, 130, 143
spheres, public and private 98–9, 108
spies, spying, Roma perceived as 61
Spivak, Gayatri C. 23–4, 37–8, 46, 130, 215
statistics of Roma *see* populations
stealing 7, 48, 51, 51n. 39, 76, 96, 124, 147–8, 155, 157, 157nn. 15, 16, 226
Steinbach, Bernhard, biography 239
  writing in *"Da wollten wir frei sein!": Eine Sinti Familie erzählt* 43, 91n. 86, 232
stereotypes of Roma 3–4, 6, 19–20, 35, 39, 44–5, 50–1
sterilization 4, 22, 73, 112–13, 114–17, 127–8, 129, 143, 182, 197, 218–19, 221
Stewart, Michael 13n. 11, 45, 97, 99, 146
Stippinger, Christa 241
Stojka, Ceija, biography 242–3
  "Amenca ketane" 1
  "'Du darfst keine Andere sein.' Ceija Stojka im Gespräch mit Karin Berger," 1, 100, 102–3, 137, 143–4
  "Ich lebe mit meinen Verstorbenen," 133, 145–6
  *Meine Wahl zu schreiben—ich kann es nicht: Gedichte (Romanes, deutsch) und Bilder* 243

*Reisende auf dieser Welt* 25, 60, 243
"Sie waren Rom vom Stamm der Lowara" 31, 81, 107
*Träume ich, dass ich lebe?: Befreit aus Bergen-Belsen* 134n. 3
"Unsere Seele war krank" 21, 27
*Wir leben im Verborgenen: Erinnerungen einer Rom-Zigeunerin* 1, 25, 42, 70, 100, 117, 123, 124, 135, 139–52, 243
Stojka, Harri 130n. 77, 244
Stojka, Johann Mongo, biography 243–4
*Papierene Kinder: Glück, Zerstörung und Neubeginn einer Roma-Familie in Österreich* 91, 95, 138–9, 141, 148–9, 243
"Unsere alte Welt" 65, 76, 78, 81, 84–5, 86, 88, 91, 93, 99, 102, 108
Stojka, Karl, biography 243–4
*Auf der ganzen Welt zu Hause: Das Leben und Wandern des Zigeuners Karl Stojka* 25, 42, 48, 65, 78, 81, 86, 93–6, 102, 130, 141, 148, 243
*Nach der Kindheit im KZ kamen die Bilder* 25, 43, 64–5, 67, 70, 93, 126, 131, 139, 157, 243
*Wo sind sie geblieben? Geschunden, gequält, getötet—Gesichter und Geschichten von Roma, Sinti und Juden aus Konzentrationslagern des Dritten Reiches* 139
Stolperstein (Stumbling Stone) 83, 83n. 55, 85
storytelling, storytellers 4–5, 6, 14, 37, 74, 97–108, 132, 137, 144, 155–6, 161–5, 171, 201, 205–6, 209–10, 211, 213, 219, 222, 223, 228–31, 235, 244
subaltern 23–4, 28, 37–8
Switzerland, Roma in 11, 12, 49, 53
  removal of "neglected children" from families in 197n. 95
  *Verdingkinder* (children used as cheap labor) in 201n. 1
  *see also* Jenisch history; Mariella Mehr
taboos, against naming the dea, 83–4
  breaking 105, 181
  purity and pollution 74–6, 221, 233 see also *"mahrime"*
Romani cultural 4, 221
  sexuality and the body 15, 73–4, 117, 119–20, 145–6, 162–4, 166 *see also* sexuality
Sinti 207–8,
Tauber, Elisabeth 13n. 11, 95, 133
Tebbutt, Susan 33n. 97, 144
terminology for Roma, "Gypsy," "Zigeuner," Sinti, *Porrajmos*/Holocaust, minority 6–8
*Todesmarsch* (death march) 136, 238, 240, 242, 243
Toninato, Paola 8n. 16, 26n. 62, 57
trauma, traumatic, gender and 4, 143–52
  in narratives by Roma 5–6, 105, 134, 139–41
  psychological effects of 115–16, 120–1, 124–9
  writing and 30
travellers, Roma as 63–9, 210–20, 231–5
Trollmann, Johann "Rukeli" 83n. 55, 85, 125
Trumpener, Katie 69
Tschawo, Latscho, biography 244

*Die Befreitung des Latscho Tschawo: Ein Sinto Leben in Deutschland* 76–7, 244
vagrancy, vagrants, stereotypes of Roma 51n. 42, 54, 55, 56, 57, 61, 112n. 4, 126, 189, 196–7, 218
Vermeersch, Peter, conceptualizations of Romani ethnic identity 43–5
Vienna 2, 21, 25, 28, 67, 135, 136, 139, 147, 151n. 76, 210, 238, 241, 242, 243, 244
violence
against children 175, 181, 188–9
against Roma 17, 116–17, 122n. 45, 182, 195
against women 35, 122n. 45
gender and 150, 196–8
in Mariella Mehr's works 5–6, 173–99
physical 178–9, 189
power of 198–9
racism and 33
resistance against 117, 122–3
ritualized 179–80
self-perpetuating 195–6
state-sanctioned 176
"strategic" 199
terms for 176–7, 188
textual 190–1
*see also Gewalt*; masochism; sadomasochism
virginity 13, 84–7, 101–2, 104, 228
in literature by Roma 168, 208, 221
Vlach Roma 12, 75, 76, 99
voice, voices, importance of Romani 1, 14, 19, 21, 22, 26, 33, 62–3, 69, 106, 113, 132, 158–9, 210, 229, 231–3, 235
body and 178–9

"coming to voice," "giving voice" 31–2, 37–8
lack of in scholarship and public market 23, 41, 127, 205
in literature by Roma 189, 192, 194, 198–9, 210
subaltern 23

wagons 55, 58, 59, 77, 92, 94, 97, 133, 136, 217
and purity laws 76, 79, 81–2, 145–6,
in stories by Roma 153–4, 159–60, 164
and travelling 63–6, 176
*Wehrmacht*/German army 90
Weimar Republic 126 *see also* interwar period
*Wiedergutmachung* 127
Willems, Wim 45
Winter, Walter, biography 244
*Winterzeit: Erinnerungen eines deutschen Sinto, der Auschwitz überlebt hat* 244
Z 3105 25, 27, 42, 60, 64, 66, 67, 68, 70, 71, 81, 82, 90, 92, 96, 98, 105, 107, 118, 120, 125, 130, 244
Wittenberge an der Elbe 123, 125, 238
Wittig, Monique 6, 190
Wolf, Naomi 233–4
women, Romani, division of labor and 13, 47, 93, 106, 142
power and influence 4, 13–14, 73–5, 78–80, 84, 92, 94–5, 98–9, 103–4, 108, 123–4, 161–2, 164
responsibilities 13, 87, 101–2, 206
separation between men and 13, 74–6
*see also* gender; patriarchy; work

Index 275

work practices, workers, gender norms and 81, 91, 98–9, 104–6, 108, 144–5, 233
 in literature by Roma 201, 211, 213–14, 216, 218–22, 226, 227, 228, 229
 men's and women's 91, 92–7, 206, 233
 Roma and 4, 13, 57, 58, 60, 62, 70, 74, 108–9, 231
 service work and restrictions under the Nazis 90n. 84, 112
 "work-shy" (*arbeitsscheu*) categorization of Roma as 61, 128, 227, 240
World Romani Congress (WRC) 127
World War I 61–2, 90, 90n. 86

Zantop, Susanne 49n. 30, 32
*Zentralrat deutscher Sinti und Roma* (Central Council of German Sinti and Roma) 21, 229n. 57, 238
"Zigeuner," negative connotations 8–9, 35, 45, 50n. 35, 58, 59, 61, 204n. 2, 234
 origin of the word 8–9
*Zigeuner-Grunderlaß* (Circular on the Fight Against the Gypsy Nuisance) 112n. 4
"Zigeunerlager" *see* "Gypsy Camp"
Zimmermann, Michael 112n. 6, 114n. 10
Zipes, Jack 5nn. 6, 7, 155
Zürich 21, 175, 239, 240

www.ingramcontent.com/pod-product-compliance
Lightning Source LLC
Chambersburg PA
CBHW071808300426
44116CB00009B/1237